SPORT AND POSTMODERN TIMES

SUNY Series on Sport, Culture, and Social Relations

Cheryl L. Cole and Michael A. Messner, Editors

Sport and Postmodern Times

Edited by
Geneviève Rail

State University of New York Press

GV
706.5
.S6943
1998

Published by
State University of New York Press, Albany

© 1998 State University of New York

For information, address State University of New York Press,
State University Plaza, Albany, N.Y. 12246

Production by M. R. Mulholland
Marketing by Patrick Durocher

Library of Congress Cataloging-in-Publication Data

Sport and postmodern times / edited by Geneviève Rail.
    p.   cm. — (SUNY series on sport, culture, and social relations)
    Includes bibliographical references and index.
    ISBN 0-7914-3925-9 (HC : alk. paper). — ISBN 0-7914-3926-7 (PB : alk. paper)
    1. Sports—Sociological aspects.   2. Physical education and training—Social aspects.   I. Rail, Geneviève, 1958–   .
II. Series.
GV706.5.S6943   1998
306.4′83—dc21   97-50231
                                                                          CIP

10 9 8 7 6 5 4 3 2 1

CONTENTS

INTRODUCTION

In the last few decades, the nature of Western societies has changed radically. Social theorists have imagined these changes through the development of concepts such as media society, society of spectacle, consumer society, post-industrial society, and post-Fordist society. Social and cultural critics have described the Western world as one dominated by capitalism, consumption, media, and new technologies of communication and computerization. Also noted has been the blurring of the traditional distinctions between "high" and "mass" culture, and the resulting *penchant* for fragmentation and recombination through *pastiche* and *collage*. Evidence of the fragmentary has been detected in the theorization of language, time, the human subject, and society itself. Indeed, observers have commented on the fragmentation of monolithic political structures and the emergence of political initiatives made manifest through struggles over the body, gender, sexuality, ethnicity, race, peace and the environment.

Either at the local or the global level, the terrain of these new discourses and struggles is somewhat removed from the traditional Marxist one of class conflict. In fact, it has become increasingly apparent that the plurality of autonomous discourses and disperse power relations cannot be simply unified by grand explanations of reality such as those proposed by Marxist or liberal theory. The social and cultural interpreters' critique of grand theories of the past has thus become more virulent and expanded to include an interrogation of their indebtedness to "modern" assumptions, particularly the belief that "Reason" and technological innovation can guarantee progress, enlightenment, and universal emancipation. The various challenges to classical theories now have in common a dismissal of universal principles, totalizing theories and the search for one "Truth," as well as a new celebration of difference and diversity. They also share a conviction that "post-modern" times are marked by a different cultural logic and require new social theories, epistemologies, and ontologies.

While exploring such innovative theoretical approaches, this book examines "sport" and its significance in the construction and diffusion of dominant cultural meanings and values. *Sport and Postmodern Times* brings together various works from a number of North American and European specialists currently researching these issues related to sport, the body and the broader "physical culture" that have become central in the emergent and interdisciplinary field of Sport Studies. Using the new concepts and methods of postmodernism, poststructuralism, radical feminism and cultural studies, these contributors not only offer their understanding of sport and the cultural space it re/produces in our postmodern societies, they also focus attention on political relations of power, domination, oppression, resistance, and struggle, particularly as these intersect with issues of race, ethnicity, class, gender, sexuality, and locality.

Conceptualizing the contemporary as postmodern suggests a break with or shift away from the definitive features of modernity, involving the emergence of a new social totality. However, this makes "postmodernity" a relatively ill-defined term as we are only on the threshold of the shift, and not in a position to regard the postmodern as a fully fledged positivity that can be defined in a comprehensive manner. Bearing this in mind, the confusion that surrounds the terms derived from "the postmodern" is such that it may be useful to work toward some preliminary understandings of this concept.

Postmodern/isms

Many attribute the origin of the term postmodernism to Federico de Onis, who, in the 1930s, used it to suggest a reaction to modernism. The term became popular in the 1960s in New York when it was used by young artists and writers to refer to a movement contra the institutionalized high modernism of the museum and the academy. It gained wider usage in architecture and the arts in the 1970s and 1980s. Thereafter, European and North American debates multiplied as the search for theoretical explanations of artistic postmodernism widened to include discussions of postmodernity. Postmodernism, then, is not easily encapsulated in one phrase since it has been used in various fields (e.g., music, art, fiction, film, drama, architecture, photography, literary criticism, philosophy, sociology, anthropology, geography) to convey very different meanings. Furthermore, it is an amalgam of often purposely ambiguous and fluid ideas. It is nevertheless crucial to specify the boundaries of the postmodern at the outset because a critique of the tyranny of grand social theory is not well served by the prevailing tendency (among pro-PoMos as well as among no- or post-PoMos) to deploy "postmodernism" as a totalizing device that obscures the basic differences between the various postmodernisms. Although many variants are already in existence and being constantly altered, and despite the fact that other variants may emerge, we can tentatively distinguish between the following five.

Postmodernism is at times used to describe a *style* qualifying the transformations in artistic representation inside architecture and generally including phenomena observed in the whole aesthetic field. The term makes evident the departure from the modern style and its elitism and authoritarianism. The postmodern style is rather inspired by aesthetic populism or the collapse of the hierarchical distinction between high and popular culture, eclecticism, and the mixing of codes; parody, playfulness, paradox, and irony.

Postmodernism as *artistic practice* refers to something quite different, that is, a structure of experience, a mode of sensibility. It often refers to the diverse contributions of literature, theatre, dance, and other "performance" arts. If this mode of sensibility implies a radical break in the artistic modes, there is no unity within or between postmodern artistic practices and, as the term acquires common currency, it takes new connotations.

Another variant is often associated with the claim that postmodernism represents an epochal transition, a radical break with the past. Fredric Jameson is the foremost supporter of postmodernism as *epoch* as he believes in the emergence of a new cultural logic corresponding with a new type of social life, both being associated with a transition from a national system of state/ monopoly capitalism to a multinational corporate capitalism. The notion of an epochal break from modernity can also be detected in the writings of Jean Baudrillard and Jean-François Lyotard. Baudrillard argues that new forms of technology and information are central to a shift from a productive to a reproductive social order in which the distinction between simulations and the real disappears. Lyotard is interested in the effects of society's computerization on knowledge and stresses that, in postmodernity, the loss of meaning needs not be mourned when it points to the replacement of narrative knowledge by a plurality of language games, the substitution of localism for universalism.

Postmodernism as a *method* comes from literary theory and can be seen as a revolt against modernism and structuralism. Postmodernism, phenomenology and ethnomethodology emerged from similar sources, notably the philosophies of Friedrich Nietzsche and Martin Heidegger that rejected the Enlightenment's attempt to create a universal knowledge. Challenging the grand narratives of modernism, postmodernism as method favors a deconstruction of linguistic structures and systems (as in the work of Jacques Derrida). The focus on language and text explains why the term "poststructuralism" has often been preferred, although recent writing in the social and cultural domain has emphasized the transgression of boundaries between writing genres and the term postmodernism has emerged to refer to a method which, not unlike that of radical feminism and feminist cultural studies, challenges the traditional ways of "doing" social science. Norman Denzin, for example, has noted the importance of overtly recognizing the "fictional" aspect of all social "science" writing, including the ways in which researchers write reality and people's understanding of it.

In the last sense of the term, postmodernism means a theoretically inclined reflection on all the previous areas. It most often refers to a "discipline"

that escapes disciplinary boundaries and that is variously thought of as pragma-
tist (e.g., New Times theorists and other pragmatic "truth-seekers") or anarchist
(e.g., Arthur Kroker and other "postmodern story-tellers"), from the Left (e.g.,
some neo-Marxists and critical theorists) or the Right (e.g., neo-conservative
Jean Baudrillard), and leaning toward economic reduction (e.g., Fredric Jameson)
or semiotic dissolution (e.g., Jacques Lacan). Postmodernism as *theoretical
reflection* represents a new kind of scientific knowledge as it legitimates otherwise disparaged discourses to give them the same epistemological status as
the dominant discourse.

The Postmodernism as theoretical reflection and as method of sociopolitical
analysis and cultural critique is one of the principal concerns of this book.
But this is highly paradoxical since any work that sets out to represent and
discuss the postmodern in a structured and unambiguous fashion is by definition
modern rather than postmodern in orientation. Whether or not the modern
bias of this book can be avoided, it should be stressed that the various texts
offered by the contributors are intended as (although few take the form of)
postmodern narratives that encourage diverse interpretations rather than as
accounts that seek to structure and limit the reader's interpretation. To
summarize a number of basic ideas related to postmodernist thought, the
following discussion is similarly (and problematically) presented in what
postmodernists would characterize as a linear and decidedly modernist form.

Postmodernist Thought

There are two important tendencies in postmodernist thought. The first
emphasizes the idea that the world is fragmented into many isolated worlds;
it is a collage, a pastiche of elements randomly grouped in a plurality of local,
autonomous discourses that cannot be unified by any grand theory. The second tendency emphasizes a poststructuralist element; preoccupied with the
problem of meaning, it results in a position presenting meaning as fundamentally slippery and elusive. The main exponent of such view is Jacques Derrida,
along with other French theorists such as Roland Barthes, Julia Kristeva,
Jacques Lacan, Gilles Deleuze and Félix Guattari.

The two main tendencies of postmodernist thought were interwoven
early on by Jean-François Lyotard in his book *La condition post-moderne*
(1979), in which he summarized postmodernism as above all maintaining an
incredulity toward "*les grands récits*" (grand theories or metanarratives).
Postmodernists, he argued, question the assumptions of the modern age, notably
the conviction that scientific progress is possible and desirable, and that rational thought and technology will bring advancement and enlightenment to
humanity. They thus refute the existence of a reality characterized by structure, patterns, and causal relationships; a reality that can be studied objec-

tively and usefully represented by theories. They dismiss grand theories as products of an era wherein Europeans and North Americans mistakenly believed in their own invincibility, and no longer see metanarratives of such thought as truth, but as privileged discourses that deny and silence competing and dissident voices.

Michel Foucault, one of the leading poststructuralist/postmodernist thinkers, has also emphasized the inadequacies of metanarratives. In his work, he dismisses reason as a fiction and sees truth as simply a partial, localized version of reality. He argues that discourse is the site where meanings are contested and power relations determined. He also points to the false power of hegemonic knowledge and suggests that it can be challenged by counterhegemonic discourses that offer alternative explanations of reality.

Foucault's writings have drawn attention to the power of language and discourse, as well as to their impact on the way people understand and assign meaning to their lives. This has led to a call for the dismantling or "deconstruction" of language/discourse in order to discover the way meaning is constructed and used. Jacques Derrida in particular emphasizes the crucial role played by binary opposites (e.g., truth/falsity, unity/diversity, man/woman, culture/nature), whereby the nature of the first term is superior to, and depends on the definition of the second. He and other postmodernists have called for the critical deconstruction of written and oral texts and greater attention to the way differences (particularly those embedded in binary thinking) are constructed and maintained.

For postmodernists such as Jean-François Lyotard, Michel Foucault, Jacques Derrida and Jean Baudrillard, all of reality is based on language and can be thought of as text. All aspects of the text are "intertextual" and any attempt to represent anything will necessarily be incomplete, inaccurate, and biased. Truth is so relative as to be nonexistent in any general sense. It follows that these postmodernists consider science domineering and dangerous when it is treated as privileged discourse because of its truth claims. Instead of building theories, then, they suggest the deconstruction of texts to reveal their contradictions and assumptions, and the construction of mininarratives that make no truth claims and within which difference, uniqueness, irrationality, and paradox can surface.

Epistemologically oriented postmodernists characterize the postmodern mostly in terms of the breakdown of belief in scientific truth and objectivity. Other postmodernists (such as myself) see the global ravage of consumer capitalism as central. For them, the ceaseless proliferation of products and images strongly figures in their "story" of the postmodern. Thanks to Fredric Jameson and David Harvey, the term postmodern has even been equated with the late-capitalist or "post-Fordist" historical period and its putatively hegemonic regime of flexible accumulation. These ways of reading the postmodern are important precisely because they render contemporary cultural and political changes intelligible within a structural Marxist framework. However, they also tend to ignore a growing body of cultural and ethnographic studies that describe how people's everyday practices, feelings, and understandings of their conditions of existence often modify those very conditions and thereby shape rather than merely reflect new modes of culture. It seems also that efforts to subordinate cultural processes to the master discourse of Marxist political economy downplay the ontological and epistemological challenges that postmodernism poses for all forms of essentialism and modernist assumption. In this regard, postmodernism and some types of feminist theorizing share a common critique of the modernist épistémé.

Postmodernism/Feminism

The encounter between feminism and postmodernism has always been ongoing and has led to many alliances and numerous debates. Feminists have both contributed and responded to postmodern thought in a number of ways. Some feminists believe that feminist theory has always dealt with postmodern issues and feel comfortable with the label "postmodernist." Others recognize the problem associated with a division between many postmodernists and other theorists; a division continually reinforced by the obscure power language that has become increasingly present in academe and elsewhere. Yet other feminists respond to postmodernism by concluding that feminist theory has more to offer women than male-centric poststructuralist/postmodernist writers.

Not surprisingly, feminists working in the liberal (modern) or Marxist traditions (both of which are embedded in Enlightenment thinking) are strongly opposed to postmodernism. The postmodern conceptualization of subjectivity as permanently discontinuous, displaced and destabilized has also been problematic for many feminists. For instance, standpoint feminists (e.g., Sandra Harding) who focus on women's lived experiences as the basis for feminist knowledge reject the postmodern "assault" on the subject since their critique of male hegemony is based on the authority of women's subjectivity as it is grounded in their daily lives. Feminists of various persuasions have also expressed concern about the political implications of a postmodernist feminist perspective (e.g., the writings of Linda Hutcheon). Other feminists (e.g., Susan Bordo) have worried about the overemphasis on difference leading to further political fragmentation within the feminist movement.

While agreeing that postmodernism taken to its extreme linguistic impermeability and as practiced by a number of white middle-class male-centered proponents does nothing to further the feminists' search for a more egalitarian world, a growing number of feminists believe postmodernist thought has much to offer feminist theorizing and action. Indeed, many feminists have come to realize that attempts to challenge male hegemony from within essentialist and male-centric Enlightenment thoughts are doomed to failure. They have come to appreciate the alternative ontology, epistemology and methodology inherent in postmodernism, as well as the anti-authoritarian and anti-dogmatic components. Of course, one of the most appealing aspects of postmodernism to many feminists has been its focus on difference and its legitimization of the search for the voice of displaced, marginalized, exploited and oppressed people.

More recently, an important number of feminists (e.g., bell hooks, Audre Lorde) have argued for a reconceptualization of the subject as shifting and multiply organized across variable axes of difference (class, race, ethnicity, age, gender, sexuality, etc.). They have stressed how such mobile subjectivities are embedded in the historical, spatial and institutional contexts of daily life and how they must be understood in this context. This approach has successfully integrated the position of standpoint feminists and the postmodernist perspective as heterogeneity, discontinuity and displacement have been shown to point to real elements of contemporary experience.

While the above discussion provides one "account" of postmodernism, it remains that any attempt to represent this perspective is inexorably superficial, incomplete, inaccurate, and biased. Perhaps, then, the best way to speak of postmodernism and the postmodern is not to further develop this book as an argument but rather to think of *Sport and Postmodern Times* as a critical space for diverse narratives and as many stories of the everyday relations of power, domination, resistance and struggle in sport, as they are articulated through issues such as race, ethnicity, gender and sexuality.

Sport and Postmodern Times

The book is organized in five parts. The first part sets the tone by focusing on the issues of "Postmodern sports writing and the transgression of boundaries." Toni Bruce discusses the challenges of postmodernism to the traditional ways of doing research in social sciences. She suggests that scholars of sport experiment with new forms of writing (e.g., short stories, drama, poetry, performed dialogue) that violate prescribed conventions, but offer possibilities for new insight and understanding. Bruce also offers three experimental stories about women sports writers and problematic locker room encounters to show, in practical and vivid fashion, some of the writing possibilities offered by postmodernism.

Boundaries of the traditional social science writing genres are further transgressed with Nate Kohn and Synthia Sydnor's (Slowikowski's) dialogue. The highly personal, ironic and reactionary account of their daily encounters with the "hegemony of sport" is a concrete example of a text which emotion grips the reader and which brings understanding to the postmodern sport culture of mid-America. Evident signs of postmodern writing are found in the authors' inconsistent positions and moving identities, as well as the text's uncertainty, fragmentation, multivalence and lack of closure. Kohn and Sydnor not only speak of varsity football, golf carts, Native sport mascots, Nike, Michael Jordan, Stairmasters, baseball cards, Olympic pins, and rock-climbing on simulated rock cliffs in New York City, they also move us to reflect on what it means to be a scholar of sport. More importantly, their dialogue offers seduction, melancholy, impatience, indifference and other original strategies for resistance to, and subversion of those hegemonic forces so cavalierly found in everyday life.

Robert Rinehart presents a third postmodern text within which issues of ideology and resistance are also central. Rinehart examines the world of private swimming lessons and uses this experience as a starting point for his discussion of the place of the researcher in "vital" stories. This discussion leads him to focus on ethics, particularly as they relate to the complex dynamics between him and the evangelical swim school clientele. Throughout his lived experience of the swimming school and throughout his writing, Rinehart's location moves from outsider to observer as participant, to participant as observer, to complete participant. These epistemological shifts allow for a poignant postmodern "story" in which Michel Foucault's ideas of disciplinary practices are brought, in order to shed light and understanding on the teaching of swimming and on the use of sport as an evangelical tool. Ultimately, by writing about the swim school's panopticism and the coaches' gaze, surveillance and discipline, Rinehart allows us to see the swimming lanes as as many theaters of punishment, and sport, as an unquestioned but ethically problematic ideology.

In Part II, the book enters the arena of "Sport and the postmodern (de)construction of gender." Indeed, the four chapters deconstruct gender and bring understanding to the resulting gender "fragments" by contextualizing them in our patriarchal, heterosexist and racist postmodern society. Cheryl Cole and Samantha King discuss the popularly acclaimed, low-budget, independent documentary *Hoop Dreams*. Focussing on the lives of two inner-city male youths who aspire to play professional basketball, the documentary was declared an American "epic" that offered an atypically brutal and honest portrayal of black masculinity and the realities of urban life. Cole and King rather suggest that the endorsement of *Hoop Dreams* as an official representation of urban America cannot be separated from America's collective desire to imagine itself as a democratic, caring, and compassionate nation in a period dominated by heightened poverty, uncertainty, resentment, and acts of revenge directed at the residents of America's poor inner cities. Cole and

King show how familiar dynamics that govern knowledges of black masculinity and inner city poverty relate to particular narrative strategies surrounding the film. They further show how these knowledges actively discourage
critical thinking about middle-class implications in the conditions of the inner
city as they facilitate the audience's sense of self as ethically and morally
superior.

Caroline Fusco is interested in expanding the repertoire of gendered
identities. She deconstructs the idea of a gender binary by giving lesbian
athletes the opportunity to tell stories about their experiences in sport. The
result is a thick pastiche that produces meaning and makes visible the silencing of lesbian existence in the sport community, the systemic intolerance for
differing sexualities, the overt and covert discriminatory practices, and the
lesbian athletes' struggle to resist and reject the "heteronormative" ideology
affecting their lives. In the end, Fusco's piece shows that there is room on and
off the sports field for resistance to patriarchal and restrictive notions of
gender and sexuality.

Mélisse Lafrance argues that Nike's corporate colonization of the female
body has both articulated and accompanied the postfeminist, neo-conservative
and nostalgically liberal ideological moments in the "American" imaginary.
Through her discussion of these phenomena, she illustrates how Nike came to
dominate both the "American" postmodern's semiotic and social, while critically assessing the contextual implication of such domination. Lafrance proceeds to deconstruct two important 1997 Nike advertisements; one profiling the
"If you let me play" social philosophy, and the other promoting the Nike
P.L.A.Y. initiative. She then links these ads to Nike's global strategies and
proposes that any hypothetical benefits derived by upper-class American women
from Nike products are inevitably obtained at the expense of Third World
women, thus defeating and attesting to the paradoxical nature of Nike's social
concern. In the end, Lafrance's piece explains how the neo-conservative American imaginary has enabled Nike to position itself as a producer of not only
shoes, but also discourses of truth, deviance and normalization.

In the third part of the book, the authors confront the new reality of
sport, namely, that of "Virtual sport, representation, and the postmodern
mediascape." In my own chapter, I present three theses of implosion and
catastrophe which, in my view, well reflect the postmodern condition affecting late capitalist society. First, I argue that postmodern art has developed to
become fragmentary, ironic, cynic, as well as inclusive of popular culture. It
now envelops mass mediated images and the various symbols of consumer
capitalism, including sport and its commodities-signs. At the same time, sport
appropriates and reproduces postmodern aesthetic forms in order to better
constitute itself as an object of hyperconsumption. Second, I present epistemological, ideological, technological, and semiological arguments to show

the subordination of the sporting body to the postmodern power system. Third, I contend that the contemporary model used to mediate sport contributes to an "excremental" culture by being anti-mediatory and by fostering aesthetic populism, fragmentation, depthlessness, stagnation and non-action. The theses I offer (the implosion of art/body/image) are meant as discursive devices to deconstruct sport in order to better understand its functions of re/ producer of the postmodern social and expose its links with the issues of power, ideology, resistance and transformation.

The next chapter is by Margaret MacNeill who presents a critical analysis of recent blockbuster workout videos (Jane Fonda, Cher, Cindy Crawford) to consider how the act of constructing the "fit body" and consuming images of celebrities via home videos has become a postmodern locus of social control. MacNeill argues that the political and cultural North American economies are intimately related with the production and consumption of these videos. She uses interviews and a social-semiotic text analysis to explore the slippery levels of representational and ideological codes of the celebrity expert. Her research reveals that the relationship constructed with the video audience allows for the possibility of cultural "reperfussion," that is, the reattachment of the celebrity icon into a mediated reality of everyday life. It also reveals one extremely powerful way in which gendered female bodies are contained within narrow cultural boundaries.

Also deconstructing postmodern representations, David Andrews intends to contribute to the resistance against the superficiality and meaninglessness of today's promotional culture by offering an interpretive survival strategy. In his essay, he develops a progressive understanding of the hyperreal world of mediated sport as a key element of the popular promotional culture. He then shows how televisual politics of the American New Right locates itself within the affectively-charged sphere of mediated popular culture, and how Michael Jordan constitutes an affectively-oriented post-Reaganite commodity-sign. Andrews' essay disrupts the affective euphoria that has dominated the consumption of Michael Jordan's image, and excavates meanings and political implications of wanting "to be like Mike." His critical pedagogy is emancipatory in that it offers ways of resisting postmodern forms of domination and, ultimately, empowering citizens to engage in processes of progressive social transformation.

The third part of the book ends with Steve Redhead's essay on the media representation of USA '94, the soccer World Cup held in Los Angeles. In it, Redhead critically appraises Jean Baudrillard's *Amérique*, and assesses its implications for the study of the hosting of the World Cup by a country engulfed in a mediascape, a country sometimes said to live "in perpetual simulation, in a perpetual present of signs" (Baudrillard, 1988). Redhead writes about a fictional journey in which Baudrillard meets Jack Kerouac,

Bob Dylan, R.E.M., and others who have provided great insights into the American "dream." The end result is something of a postmodern "travelogue," which constitutes an interesting alternative to the conventional framework for the analysis of the production, media representation, consumption and regulation of a globalized TV event like the World Cup.

"Sport and postmodern body invaders" are the topic of the book's Part IV. Here, the reader can feel the direct influence of Michel Foucault's work as the four chapters focus on issues of discipline, normalization, rationalization, surveillance, panopticism and other forms of power that are used to "invest" postmodern sporting bodies. The first chapter is by Jacques Gleyse who uses the Foucauldian "archeological approach" to delve into the process of instrumental rationalization of the body. Gleyze's exploration leads him to speak of three major metamorphoses of discourse on the body. The first one comes about in the 16th century and emulates the "appeals to order" characteristic of the Renaissance. Bodies must also be in order. This marks the birth of biomechanics and the use of a discursive model which speaks to the manufacturization of bodies. The second one develops primarily from the end of the 18th century. The goal is also to rationalize bodies and movements, but this time, the discursive model is based on the idea of the steam engine and the theory of thermodynamics. The third one comes about in postmodern times. Discourse is now dominated by the codes of language and information, and the model is that of semiotic bodies, hyperreal bodies, bodies rationalized through computers and advanced computer languages. While breaking away from the traditional history of games and sport, Gleyze's remarkable strategy allows him to unveil the premises of the discourse on these physical activities.

The next chapter is set in a context in which national and bodily borders are inextricably bound. Drawing on genealogical and deconstructive strategies, Cheryl Cole interrogates the production of the "exercise addict" by examining the ensemble of historical, political, economic, and cultural forces through which this new type of person has been forged. Cole builds on the literature that examines the relation between "scientific truths" and the production of difference, threat, and deviance through the body. More specifically, she examines addiction discourse and its articulation with exercise as a "technology of the body" that produces and classifies bodies as normal or as pathological/deviant/excessive. She also argues that in the context of the postmodern epidemic of addiction attribution, drugs/addiction and exercise/sport can be seen as networks and strategies of power that constitute "normalizing" practices. Ultimately, Cole's project is an exploration into the "general logic" of the emergence of exercise addiction, as it is intertwined with Reagan's America, the logic of the hard (masculine) body, the logic of biological self-betterment (Just do it), the rise of the fitness industry, the "war on drugs" (Just say no), and AIDS.

Like Cheryl Cole, Brian Pronger focuses on a number of modern boundaries and binaries: man/woman, nature/culture, heterosexual/homosexual, white/"other," normal/pathological, legitimate play/illicit sex, order/chaos. He argues that as a result of the modernizing process, the natural/primordial body is erased by culture. In this process, the primordial body becomes a cultured body, a body which is defined by the inscriptions upon it of cultural discourses such as the oppositional boundaries mentioned above. Pronger further argues that modern sport contributes to this process, and his critical essay can be conceived as an attempt to make the realities of cultured bodies a little freer. He introduces the idea of a postmodern body that would be both a cultured body (gendered, raced, cyborged, etc.) and a wild body (primordial, erotic, etc.). And so, whereas modern sport is a project of differentiation and socio-cultural boundary maintenance, Pronger sees postmodern sport as a wild, transgressive event of "boundary pollution," "dedifferentiation" and celebration of the erotic ecstasy of the primordially moving body. At the end, Pronger's essay opens a number of doors for scholarly investigations as well as political actions in sport and the larger physical culture.

Finally, in the last part of the book, authors discuss the issues of "Physical culture, consumer culture, and postmodern geography." Lawrence Wenner uses the method of critical geography to assess the cultural space of the modern and postmodern sports bars. His chapter deals with conceptions of public drinking places and gender; with the cultural place and public spaces of sport and their relation to the gender order; and with gendered cultural histories of alcohol and sport. Wenner argues that the cultural logic of sports bars functions at the nexus of a holy trinity of alcohol, sport, and hegemonic masculinity. He distinguishes the modern sports bar, a traditionally gendered place, from the postmodern sports bar, a place where gender relations are rearranged as a commoditized bricolage. Through the transparency of these constructions, Wenner finally shows how the "rupture" of the postmodern sports bar appropriates traditional meanings of masculinity in the context of a world where "real men" no longer exist.

Nancy Midol's subcultural analysis also brings us to the heart of postmodern cities, but this time, to explore a different element of physical culture. She looks at the Hip-Hop movement, a popular American street and black movement. Midol suggests that this movement—which includes break dance, rap music and tag—presents itself as "total art" in the sense that it is also politically active. She discusses how and why, in a 1980s environment marked by despair and hate, wars between gangs sometimes gave place to artistic works that became acknowledged and copied worldwide. Midol then takes us to France, where the Hip-Hop movement quickly made inroads, and contrasts the American policy of repression to the French policy of supervision. She explains how the French government officially recognized the movement as an artistic one worthy of integration in the network of subsidized artistic groups, but how this also represented a means of socio-political control of those youths whose dissidence and violence were feared. Midol concludes that Hip-Hop losts its ground when it suffered artistic, intellectual, political and commercial appropriations, but that the latter have also made it a major postmodern art form.

William Morgan's chapter further delves into the issue of how the cultural leaves its imprints on the physical, and vice-versa. Morgan's empirical example is that of Hassiba Boulmerka, an Algerian whose remarkable athletic achievements (women's 1500m World Champion and Olympic Gold Medal Winner) at first earned her the accolades of all Algerians despite her violation of the Muslim decree that women be covered from head to toe, but later earned her the scorn of certain militant Muslims. In tracing Boulmerka's athletic struggle to define a new place for women in Islamic culture, Morgan shows the many parallels that connect her story to that of Salmon Rushdie. Furthermore, Morgan inquires as to how stories like Boulmerka's should be normatively evaluated using the postmodern writings of Jean-François Lyotard and Michel Foucault. He concludes that despite all their strengths, these writings fail to do justice to conflicting stories like Boulmerka's because they do not sufficiently consider the conflicting backgrounds out of which such stories emerge.

In the last chapter of the book, Rob VanWynsberghe and Ian Ritchie's chapter center on the symbolic consumption of the Olympic logo in postmodern media culture. Specifically, these authors investigate the five-ring insignia (which the International Olympic Committee claims as a representation of the universal ideals of sport), and its malleable image and specious origins. VanWynsberghe and Ritchie argue that the Olympic ideals have been originally fabricated to bring the world together through sport, and that they have been ironically successful in that the Games now lure billions of viewers to their television sets. However, they also argue that the Olympic rings do not represent ideals inherent to the Games, but are the product of carefully crafted media endeavors. Their analysis points to the logo as an advertizing tool for the IOC and for the multinational corporations attempting to link themselves to the Games. In the global marketplace, the Olympic logo serves the needs of consumerism. This explains the transformation of the quadrennial festival into an event like the McDonald's Olympics (1984) or the Coca-Cola Games (1996). VanWynsberghe and Ritchie conclude that the rings operate as an open-ended signifier that enables their continued symbolic consumption as both an affective cultural icon and a linguistic item whose meaning emerges out of the link between "Olympic" consumer goods and people's everyday lives.

PART I

POSTMODERN SPORTS WRITING AND THE TRANSGRESSION OF BOUNDARIES

1

Postmodernism and the Possibilities for Writing "Vital" Sports Texts

Toni Bruce

The challenges of postmodernism to traditional ways of "doing" research have been felt throughout the social sciences and humanities. In combination with feminism, cultural studies, constructivism, and other interpretive approaches, postmodernism has changed the way many researchers look at their work. However, it is only recently that researchers have begun to consider the implications of postmodernism for how they "write" their research. A number of scholars are, however, experimenting with new forms of writing that violate prescribed conventions and "transgress the boundaries" of traditional social science writing genres (Richardson, 1994, p. 520). Transgressions involve, among others, writing drama, poetry, performed dialogue, and short stories. Recognizing that all forms of writing constrain the kinds of knowledge that can be gained, postmodern writers see the possibilities for new insights in new ways of writing. This chapter discusses the theoretical issues that impact on new forms of writing, and outlines some of the work in sociology of sport that puts it into practice (e.g., Denison, 1994, 1996; Kohn & Slowikowski, 1993, 1994, 1998; Markula, 1993; Rinehart, 1992, 1993). In addition, it "shows" in practical fashion (through three experimental "stories") some of the writing possibilities offered by postmodernism.

First Things First
My Story: A Woman Sports Writer in the Locker Room

The first time I entered a men's locker room, I was 22, and terrified. My mother, a high school English teacher, had attended Catholic high school and Catholic college. My father, raised in the Netherlands, had no notion of what a sportswriter was. The idea that I would willingly walk into a room full of naked men appalled them beyond belief. I remember having a near anxiety attack the first time I had to enter their sacred enclosure. I tried to memorize all the questions I needed to ask, lest I be in the position of glancing around while trying to collect my thoughts. I kept the notebook poised a myopic four inches from my face. And I stared straight into every player's eyes: never below them.[1]

I acted as if I belonged, because I did, but nothing could prepare me for how I felt once I stepped inside. I felt very uncomfortable when I was in the locker room or near the shower.[2] The nakedness was just so thick. They were everywhere. My natural instinct was to look down but that's where you don't want to look! So I'm looking around at the top of the lockers.[3] You know, with very few exceptions, nobody has to be naked in front of everybody if they don't want to be. I really think it's a choice they make and we have no choice. We have to go in as long as everybody else does.[4] I've been in on a regular basis and I hate it every time. I take a deep breath and go in there—knowing, when I do go in, that there is the potential for anything to happen.[5] I've heard the other stories. Will someone throw something? They'll throw their dirty socks around, throw wads of tape, whistle or make a comment or something that would distract me. I can let some of that ride off my shoulders but I don't want to be accosted, I don't want to be harassed in any real overt form.[6]

I mean, we're talking about professional sports, a field that unfortunately is still dominated by males who think a woman's place is to be a cheerleader, a wife or a mistress.[7] I mean, the players and their wives both seem to think you're some kind of groupie who's been clever enough to get her hands on a press pass.[8] I remember Donahue had one show where they had the wives of some of the players and they were saying, "Well, you know, we don't want women in there because they're looking at our husbands, trying to get our husbands," and stuff like that.[9] And many think we go into locker rooms just to look at naked men.[10] I guess they still feel we're the voyeurs.[11] But that's because men are doing the projecting. They know if they were sports writers in a woman's locker room, they would be looking at the naked women.[12] They're already looking at you as a woman, a sex object, which is all most football players think of women anyway.[13] If you walk in in a sundress, you're gonna get ten "hey baby, pick you up at 10."[14] So I need clothes that are attractive but not seductive; clothes that say, "I may be a girl but I ain't meat."[15]

One time, I went in and a normally loud locker room screeched to a halt and it became very quiet and you could hear a pin drop. You could hear people breathe. Then it started: they called me names, "Get the blank out of here," "What's that blank doing here? She doesn't have any right,"

"She's in the way," just one after the other and it built and it built. And I was sort of frozen. I didn't know what to do because I've been given permission. I didn't think I was in there against anybody's rules. So finally, an assistant coach came up and grabbed me by the arm and he said, "Get outta here." And I am still frozen and I said, "I'm just doing my job. I'm just doing my job," and he said, "Well you can do it outside." I said, "Well I can't really do it outside because everybody's inside." He said, "You'll do it outside," and he grabbed me and he yanked me out of the locker room. So I'm standing outside all by myself and I could feel my cheeks flush and my stomach turning. I was an adult—I'd been through this before—yet I felt like a teenager again, out of control and really didn't know what to do. Then a couple of minutes later the coach came out and let me interview him and then I told him, "I need to talk to this particular player. He's my story," and he said, "We'll send him right out. Don't worry about it." Twenty-five minutes later and he had not come out. I was on deadline. So finally I decided I'd just open up the door. I open up the door and there were, like, two guys in there combing their hair. There was a back door and they all had left by the back door. By this time I was angry that they had done this to me so I went to the team bus and got on the team bus and found him and interviewed him, again to the derision of those around me but I had got the story and got out of there.[16]

That's something I never told anybody about because I figured that it happened to everybody else too[17] and, on top of that, I have always been afraid of being labeled a complainer, a whiner, an oversensitive woman. That's why I kept my mouth shut eight years ago when a football lineman gyrated naked behind my back while a locker room full of people laughed. That's why I kept my mouth shut when another player told me during an interview that I'd look better with my blouse unbuttoned. That's why I kept quiet when an NFL coach told me to wear skirts to practice.[18] I think you'll find with most people that they will tolerate quite a bit before they're actually going to stand up and say something because it puts you in a very bad position. I want to be able to walk into those places without it being like, "Oh there she goes. That's the one that caused the problem."[19]

I remember when that Lisa Olson incident happened, she was very public, she went on TV, she went on Entertainment Tonight, she was interviewed all over the place and I had a very visceral negative reaction to that.[20] I thought, "Nothing happened to her that hasn't happened to me and that hasn't happened to virtually every woman that I know in sports writing. Why is she talking? Why is she making such a big deal out of this?" I think that a lot of us, our knee-jerk reaction was, "Oh shut up. We've all been through this." And it wasn't until I heard her talk and listened to what had happened to her that I honestly felt bad about my reaction and I thought, "you know, just because you never made a stink doesn't mean that maybe you shouldn't have."[21]

Later, when I was covering the Anita Hill thing here in Washington and doing a story about what sexual harassment is and what is allowed and what isn't, I said: "Oh God, you know I've been putting up with this for years when I really could've cried foul and never did."[22] But at the time, the only thing that any of us found incredible about the Anita Hill accusations was that there was such heated debate gripping the entire country over such trifling comments. That's the way the Anita Hill stories seemed to those of us who have worked in sports for any length of time. Trifling.[23] We listened to Hill and then told ourselves, "Aw, that's nothing!" and, "Listen to what happened to me!" and, "I guess I've been sexually harassed every ten minutes for the last ten years!"[24]

I think society has sort of allowed us to [start seeing this] because there's been an evolution in what is the ground-floor sort of things that women have to put up with. In 1982 there was no such thing in law—and even when Anita Hill was harassed, there was no such thing in law—and so to say that you're gonna do the right thing and make the bold stand and confront people is fine but even within the small space of the locker room, you're very aware that you are in a place where you cannot count on anybody to support you.[25]

> [In] the postmodern moment . . . calls for new forms of ethnography, polyvocal texts, multigenre narratives, impressionistic tales, cinematic reconstructions, lyrical sociology, and poetic anthropology are prominent. (Rose, 1990, p. 5)

The "story" above draws upon postmodern forms of textuality demonstrated by Denison (1994, 1996), Kohn and Slowikowski (1993, 1994, 1998), Krieger (1991), Mulkay (1985), Rinehart (1992, 1993) and Rose (1990), and argued for by Atkinson (1992), Denzin (1992), Lather (1991), and Richardson (1994). (Re)presented as a monologue, the story melds the voices of 22 women sports writers to illustrate some of the key features of locker room life for women who interview male professional or college athletes. The story is (re)constructed from personal interviews with women sports writers, newspaper and magazine articles, keynote speeches, a conference discussion session, and a novel.

In this chapter, I attempt to "show" and talk about some of the possibilities of postmodernism in terms of writing social science research, particularly in sociology of sport.[26] In the 1990s, questions of writing and representation are most prominent in forms of research that are often categorized as "qualitative" or "interpretive" such as those influenced by hermeneutics, constructivism, critical theory, feminism, and cultural studies (Denzin, 1994).

The challenge to traditional writing styles reflects the broader postmodernism questioning and undermining of the fundamental assumptions upon which social science is based (Lather, 1990). It should be noted that postmodernism is not the only historically subordinate approach raising such challenges to the ontology, epistemology, and methods of social science. Others such as feminism, hermeneutics, and cultural studies form part of the growing challenge to traditional ways of "doing" social science, especially in the sociology of sport realm (Bruce & Greendorfer, 1994). For Lather, "those choosing to encourage rather than resist this movement are using it to stretch the boundaries that currently define what we do in the name of science" (p. 315).

Particularly under the influence of postmodernism, critiques of traditional qualitative social science writing have seen a growing trend towards "experimental representations" (Richardson, 1994, p. 520) or "radical experimentations" (Denzin, 1991, p. 27) which blur and jumble different writing genres. For Richardson (1994), "one practice these experiments have in common . . . is the violation of prescribed conventions; they transgress the boundaries of social science writing genres" (p. 520). Transgressions involve researchers writing drama (Mulkay, 1985), poetry, (Richardson, 1992), multiple takes on the same experience (Rinehart, 1992, 1993), performed dialogue (Kohn & Slowikowski, 1993, 1994, 1998), and short stories (Denison, 1994, 1996) as alternative ways of theorizing about, interpreting or representing their work. For Atkinson (1992), this means that:

> the taken-for-granted distinction between "serious" and "playful" writing is dissolved. . . . The fragmentation of the textual surface is achieved by a mixing of styles and genres within the same text, or within the same corpus. There is a deliberate transgression of literary boundaries; a promiscuous mingling of modes. (pp. 44–45)

Recognizing that all forms of writing constrain the kinds of knowledge that can be gained (Atkinson, 1992; Cole, 1991), researchers influenced by postmodernism consider that writing in different ways offers the possibility of new insights (Cole, 1991; Rabinow, 1986; Richardson, 1994). In addition, rather than merely being seen as a "mopping-up activity" taking place at the end of a research project, writing is now conceptualized as a way of "knowing," a way of discovering and analyzing work in new ways (Richardson, 1994, p. 516).

In the past, a belief in the transparency of language and representation meant that writing was "reduced to method: keeping good field notes . . . 'writing up' results" (Clifford, 1986, p. 2). As researchers/writers worked through the questions raised by poststructuralism and then postmodernism about language, however, the door opened to more overtly recognizing the "fictional" aspects of all social science writing, including the ways in which researchers write reality, and people's understandings of it (Clifford, 1986; Clough, 1992; Krieger, 1991; Rabinow, 1986).

Fiction, in this sense, is not opposed to truth; rather, it means fabricated or fashioned (Clifford, 1986; Rabinow, 1986). It suggests that reality is always partial and constructed (Clifford, 1986) and that there is no reality outside of human understanding to which researchers can refer for final validation (Carey, 1989). Rather, different and competing explanations, understandings, and interpretations of reality exist, none of which comprise the one-and-only "Truth" (Cole, 1991; Stanley & Wise, 1983). Geertz (1973) captured the essence of this issue: "What we call our data are really our own constructions of other people's constructions of what they and their compatriots are up to" (p. 9). Thus, as "writers" of research, we are always constructing partial truths; truths that inherently reflect our location and our subjects' locations in specific discourses of gender, race, ethnicity, class, sexuality, and culture (Denzin, 1994).

In addition, researchers from all paradigms draw heavily upon narrative forms to understand reality and (re)present it in their writing (Richardson, 1990). People understand the world narratively, through the stories they tell themselves and others about their experiences, and the cultural stories that are told about them (Atkinson, 1992; Denzin, 1994; Hall, 1984; Richardson, 1990). Recognizing the power and importance of narrative, and drawing upon literary rather than scientific models, newer forms of writing tend to emphasize narratives and storytelling. This move may, in part, be a response to growing critiques of traditional social science writing as "boring" (Denzin, 1994, p. 504; Richardson, 1994, p. 517), "tedious," and "losing its power to convince" (Rose, 1989, p. 5). From the field of sociology, Richardson (1994) claims that:

> For 30 years, I have yawned my way through numerous supposedly exemplary qualitative studies. Countless numbers of texts have I abandoned, half-read, half-scanned. I'll order a new book with great anticipation . . . only to find the text boring. . . . Undergraduates are disappointed that sociology is not more interesting; graduate students

confess that they do not finish reading what's been assigned because it's boring. (pp. 516–517)

Researchers stimulated by this problem have sought ways to present vital texts that are "good reads" (Richardson, 1994, p. 517). For Denzin (1994), a vital text is the opposite of boring. "It grips the reader (and the writer). A vital text invites readers to engage with the author's subject matter" (Denzin, 1994, p. 504). Vital texts are (re)presented in the "voices" of those whose experience is being written. Such texts attempt to stay close to the everyday language of the world rather than relying upon more abstract concepts or theories (Denzin, 1989).

The "story" which opened this chapter is one such attempt. It stays close to the voices of women sports writers and avoids changing their experiences into abstract concepts. Theoretical explanation is absent. Instead you—the reader—are left to engage with a narrative that takes a different form from "normal" science writing. Based on hundreds of pages of interview transcripts, newspaper and magazine articles, and three novels, the story is one "take" on how women sports writers experience the locker room. However, the influence of feminism, cultural studies, poststructuralism and postmodernism forces a recognition that the "truth" told in the story is ultimately an author's truth. While the voices in the story are those of women writers, the vision or narrative is mine. The "self" of the writer is never absent from writing (see Krieger, 1991; Richardson, 1994). For Krieger (1991):

I think it is important to try to grasp experiences that are not one's own. However, such attempts should not be masqueraded as other than what they are: they are attempts, they grasp only small pieces of experience, and they are impositions of an authorial perspective. (p. 54)

The author's perspective is inherently partial and subjective. Accepting that what we write is always influenced by who we are, means that we cannot help but tell our own story in some way through other people's stories (Krieger, 1991). For example, Myra (in Krieger, 1991) suggests:

I am not telling other people's stories, I am telling my take on their stories. I am not changing their stories actively. . . . However, I fully believe that the stories that people tell me, and that I seek out and gather, are absolutely dependent on my own sets of issues and interests . . . (p. 193)

However, this does not mean that no truth can be told. Such stories succeed if they create verisimilitude (Denzin, 1989), that is, the conditions for "deep emotional understanding" where readers live their way into the experiences, emotions, and interpretations represented (Denzin, 1994, p. 506). Postmodernism has, however, forced a more self-conscious approach to constructing the experiences of others. Thus, in the opening story, the superscript numbers work against the presentation of a seamless monologue by emphasizing the constructed nature of the text. In addition, the first note at the end of the chapter states that "Some tenses, subjects (e.g., I or you), and transitions have been changed for consistency and flow" and this reinforces the understanding that transcriptions are always created (Atkinson, 1992). Direct quotations are always selected, edited and represented in ways to make them more comprehensible and readable (Atkinson, 1992). It is impossible to capture exactly what people say (Atkinson, 1992; Higgins, 1990) and, even if it were possible, the results would be virtually unreadable. Higgins (1990) elaborates:

> Transcripts make excruciating reading. . . . Whether the speakers talk in relaxed but misguided belief that their words are not being overheard, or deliver their utterances in the uncomfortable awareness that everything they say is not only being taken down but may be used in evidence against them, they stammer, elide words, leave out prepositions, omit transition sentences, dangle participles, leave infinitives not only split but drawn and quartered on the highway, and generally trample upon all the rules of syntax. (p. 110)

One influence of the recent focus on writing and representation is the exploration of what possibilities are opened up by the recognition that transcriptions are already reconstructions. Some researchers have more consciously experimented with the constructed nature of dialogue and speech. For example, Mulkay (1985) works primary materials such as interviews into different formats such as a one-act play and fictional speeches. While more radically experimenting with the creative use of interview transcripts than many researchers, Mulkay's inventions are not arbitrary. Rather, as Atkinson (1992) points out:

> The fictional versions are put together out of fragments of "real" utterances and exchanges. As with all "analyses," the texts are arranged and constructed by the author out of shards of evidence. The difference between conventional ethnographic accounts and Mulkay's literary inventions is not a hard-and-fast separation between the factual and the fictional. Mulkay's are notable because the analyst explicitly claims the right to fashion the materials into new arrangements and to mould them into a range of different formats. (p. 46)

In the sociology of sport field, Denison (1994) wrote a his-story or "a narrative of the self" (Richardson, 1994, p. 521) about retirement from elite athletics. Presented in short story form, Denison integrated his own experiences with "stories" gathered from other athletes during intensive field research and from cultural texts such as movies and novels. More recently, Denison (1996) presented the experiences of retired elite New Zealand athletes in the form of three short stories. By drawing upon the techniques of fiction, Denison's texts are based upon criteria unlike those of traditional science:

> Accuracy is not the issue; rather, narratives of the self seek to meet literary criteria of coherence, verisimilitude, and interest. Because narratives of the self are staged as imaginative renderings, they allow the field worker to exaggerate, swagger, entertain, make a point without tedious documentation, relive the experience and say what might be unsayable in other circumstances. (Richardson, 1994, p. 521)

Kohn and Slowikowski's (1993) "performance" demonstrated a postmodern vital text that engaged audiences' emotions. Accepting the postmodern contention that knowledge and writing are always partial and local, Kohn and Slowikowski based their two-way dialogue upon personal stories. The theoretical arguments and support for their personal dialogue were contained in written footnotes and were not part of the performed/presented work. Kohn and Slowikowski (1994, p. 1) further developed this approach in the form of a one-hour e-mail exchange "about, around, through and with Norman K. Denzin." As Kohn and Slowikowski explore "Denzin," the reader/listener gains a perspective or understanding of Denzin that "feels" markedly different from, say, a biography.

Markula (1993) interweaves four personal vignettes with scholarly writing to bring alive the theoretical debates around nostalgia. Markula's writing embeds the theoretical discourse in concrete events which embody the experiences of postmodern subjects seeking authenticity in dance.

Rinehart's (1992) multivocal text presents a series of "takes" on the same experience: Super Bowl XXVI. His multiple interpretations of Super Bowl XXVI engaged with and came at the event in different ways from each other. Each successive chapter of Rinehart's (1993) dissertation demonstrated his transition from traditional social scientific writing towards more personal, radical, postmodern forms.

The works of Rinehart, Kohn and Slowikowski, Markula, and Mulkay, explore experiences from a variety of perspectives. Incompatible and inconsistent positions are juxtaposed and there is a distinct lack of closure and certainty, all of which reflect elements of postmodern writing (Rosenau, 1992). Rather than striving for coherent narratives, "contradictions, inconsistencies, and disruptions" (Cole, 1991, p. 41) are sought out and represented. Presenting such inconsistencies can create texts whose surfaces are more faithful "to the presumed complexity and fragmentation of the social world" (Rose, 1990, p. 15). In addition, new forms of writing are premised upon the assumption that there is no correct story to be told (Denzin, 1994). Rather, "there are only always different versions of different, not the same, stories, even when the same site is studied" (p. 506). Meanings must then be "constructed by the reader, rather than being constructed for the reader" (Atkinson, 1992, p. 44).

In this chapter, the introductory "story" may be seen as a hesitant first step in the direction of postmodern experimental representations. While violating prescribed social science writing by combining and "changing" quotes to create one woman's narrative, the story still reflects elements of modernism. For example, it is a linear monologue in which contradictions and alternate viewpoints are avoided in the interests of a coherent text.

However, the postmodern world is fragmented and contradictory. Therefore, the "story" fragments that follow offer other forms of (re)presenting women sports writers' experiences which attempt to more closely reflect contradictions and incoherencies. Atkinson (1992) suggests:

> If culture itself is seen as fragmentary and incoherent, then the texts of its representation may appropriately be likewise. The [researcher] can no longer subordinate all of his or her "data" to unifying themes and models. The work of the texts is more overtly recognized as an act of bricolage: the fragments of "data" (which are themselves crafted rather than found) are thus juxtaposed. The textual arrangement therefore becomes a kind of "collage." (p. 41)

Rather than attempting to construct a coherent, linear narrative, the form of the following story fragments reflect the contradictions and inconsistencies in women sports writers' explanations for problematic locker room encounters. Again, the dialogue is (re)constructed from the voices of 12 women writers recorded in various formats (see notes). Yet, unlike the opening story, quotes stand isolated and without context. They jostle with and against each other, challenging the reader to make sense of them. The partial subjectivity of "truth" is uncomfortably overt. As they clash, coincide, or move, the women's explanations for problematic locker room encounters offer up multiple world views or takes on reality.

In the first fragment (below) the physical placement on the page and juxtaposition of conflicting interpretations create a different response for readers: in Hulme's (1983) words, "a tiny, subconscious, unacknowledged but definite response" (Preface).[27] Following Kohn and Slowikowski (1993, p. 2), the hope is that in "collision," clarity may result.

Colliding Interpretations[28]: Women Sports Writers' Struggles to Understand Problematic Locker Room Encounters

Voice 6: By and large, we're all going about our business just fine. At the professional level, I'd say the vast majority, even up to 90 per cent of the guys are professional and fine to deal with.

Voice 1: Well, there's one thing I know it's NOT about and that's nudity. Men certainly have a right to be modest and they are entitled to their privacy but it's the very people who claim, "You're just trying to see me naked," who drop their towels when women come in— so there's a little bit of a contradiction there.

Voice 6: It's funny. It's the organizations that are usually well run in other ways—the teams that win, the teams that are in Super Bowls are also the teams that have never really had a problem with the locker room. Don Shula in 1981 had equal access, has never had a problem, and I think he's seen a few Super Bowls. The Chicago Bears, never a problem—they're maniacs in other ways—they've been to Super Bowls.

Voice 11: It's critical journalism now. It's not friendly journalism. I think that's really the problem and it's not women. I think women are being used as the excuse but basically they want the locker room doors closed.

Voice 2: When you go into a strange locker room, it's kind of tense and they'll kind of play with you and test you. They're just trying to figure out what you're all about.

Voice 12: I don't think the problem is women. I think it's more about the growing adversarial relationship between writers and athletes and coaches.

Voice 1: I think what you usually find is that if there's a problem, it's always because of our gender. The men get very aggressive actions towards them because of something they wrote but not because they are men. And with us, in my experience, it's always, "Well, you're a woman and I have a problem with that," as opposed to something professionally about my business.

Voice 9: It's not about women. It's about power. There's a power play going on there that has nothing to do with us. It's about a coach declaring this is his territory and "not even Pete Rozelle and Paul Tagliabue is going to tell me what to do, damn it." It's not about anything other than that. And it's so obvious to us.

Voice 7: I think there's some correlation with losing teams and angry, petulant owners who won't let you do your job.

Voice 8: The whole thing is like the way men and women view each other. Like men (laughing) couldn't go into a place with naked women and not just go crazy, you know. And so, therefore, they can't relate to the fact that we could go into a situation like that and do our job. They can't relate to it because we look at each others' bodies differently, you know.

Voice 8: I've been in the business nine years, always in sports and I really don't have a locker room tale. I've covered a lot of college football and a few NFL games and I've had no problems there. It's been very easy for me.

Voice 10: Its just some players but you are always going to get those. They are jerks in general life too, not just in the locker room.

The second fragment (below) takes the form of a conversation between three writers. As the conversation flows and moves, various interpretations engage with each other on the way to potentially new understandings.

Voice 3: I always thought NBA players treated women the best and I always thought baseball players, generally speaking, treated women the worst, and football players were somewhere in between. And I decided it was college education—sort of the socialization process—because most baseball players go from high school straight to the minor leagues, never go to college.

Voice 4: Except hockey's the same way and I don't hear horror stories about hockey the way I do about baseball and football. And hockey players, very few of them have much of an education. Maybe it's because they're Canadian. Now we'll make a generalization that all Canadians are great (laughs).

Voice 3: There were probably women covering hockey before women covered anything else, certainly before baseball. I mean, baseball was also sort of the last thing for women to start covering at the major league level.

Voice 4: And the NBA as a league is ahead of every other league: on drugs, AIDS awareness, women in the locker room, all kinds of issues.

Voice 5: The other thing too though. It's 80 per cent black and I really think the guys are sensitized more to issues like discrimination.

Voice 3: I remember one convention we had some players come to talk to us and some of the black players were all saying that too. They said they felt that black players treated women sports writers better than white players and they felt was because, as one player said, "I know what it feels like to walk into a room and know that I'm not wanted or know that I'm an outsider and I know when women walk in, that they feel the way I—as a black man—have had to feel sometimes in my life." We all talked about it at the convention—sort of took a vote—and 90 per cent of the women said athletes in this country who are black generally treat them better than athletes who are white.

Voice 5: But when you look at the incidents that happen, the big ones that have gotten the most publicity, they've all been black players.

Voice 3: Then how much of that is because it's a black player and a white woman?

The examples of "writing" used in this text could have come in many other forms. In a postmodern world, no form of narrative has a lock on representing truth/s. There is no one right way to "write" postmodern texts, only myriad ways which may be explored. These explorations should, however, take place from a position informed by postmodern theorizing. I leave the final words to Richardson (1994) who suggests:

> The greater freedom to experiment with textual form, however, does not guarantee a better product. The opportunity for writing worthy texts— books and articles that are "good reads"—are multiple, exciting, and demanding. But the work is harder. The guarantees are fewer. There is a lot more to think about. (p. 523)

Notes

My thanks to Stephen Hardy, Bob Rinehart, and Heather Barber whose discussions helped clarify my thinking and presentation.

1. Source of quote for "Story 1": Lesley Visser (1991), p. 117. Note that for all quotes, some tenses, subjects (e.g., I or you), and transitions have been changed for consistency and flow.

2. Source of quote for "Story 1": Joy Spencer (1994), p. 5.

3. Source of quote for "Story 1": informal conversation at Association for Women in Sports Media (AWSM) convention in Minneapolis, MN (1993).

4. Source of quote for "Story 1": Johnette Howard (1993), group interview in Washington, D.C.

5. Source of quote for "Story 1": locker room discussion at AWSM convention in San Francisco, CA (1994).

6. Source of quote for "Story 1": Michele Himmelberg (1993), individual interview in Minneapolis, MN.

7. Source of quote for "Story 1": Lisa Olson (1990), p. 74.

8. Source of quote for "Story 1": Diane Shah, in Angell (1979), p. 68.

9. Source of quote for "Story 1": Valerie Lister (1993), group interview in Alexandria, VA.

10. Source of quote for "Story 1": Joan Ryan (1985), p. 8.

11. Source of quote for "Story 1": Rachel Shuster, in McManamon (1985), p. 20.

12. Source of quote for "Story 1": locker room discussion at AWSM (1994).

13. Source of quote for "Story 1": locker room discussion at AWSM (1994).

14. Source of quote for "Story 1": Johnette Howard (1993), group interview in Washington, D.C.

15. Source of quote for "Story 1": A.B. Berkowitz, fictional writer (1990), p. 94.

16. Source of quote for "Story 1": Cathy Henkel (1993), individual interview in Minneapolis, MN.

17. Source of quote for "Story 1": Julie Ward (1993), group interview in Alexandria, VA.

18. Source of quote for "Story 1": Michelle Kaufman (1994), p. 4.

19. Source of quote for "Story 1": locker room discussion at AWSM (1994).

20. Source of quote for "Story 1": Kristen Huckshorn (1993), group interview in Washington, D.C.

21. Source of quote for "Story 1": Tracee Hamilton (1993), group interview in Washington, D.C.

22. Source of quote for "Story 1": Kristen Huckshorn (1993), group interview in Washington, D.C.

23. Source of quote for "Story 1": Tracy Dodds (1991), p. 2.

24. Source of quote for "Story 1": Susan Fornoff (1991), p. 3.

25. Source of quote for "Story 1": Johnette Howard (1993), group interview in Washington, D.C.

26. In-depth theoretical discussions of the contributions of postmodernism to social science are presented elsewhere in this book.

27. Although Hulme was talking about the "shape of words," I believe the response is similar to the form of presentation.

28. Sources of quotes for "Story 2" and "Story 3":

Voice 1. Julie Cart (1993), group interview in Minneapolis, MN.

Voice 2. Tracy Dodds (1993), individual interview in Minneapolis, MN.

Voice 3. Kristen Huckshorn (1993), group interview in Washington, D.C.

Voice 4. Tracee Hamilton (1993), group interview in Washington, D.C.

Voice 5. Johnette Howard (1993), group interview in Washington, D.C.

Voice 6. Christine Brennan (1993), individual interview in Minneapolis, MN.

Voice 7. Michelle Himmelberg (1993), individual interview in Minneapolis, MN.

Voice 8. Valerie Lister (1993), group interview in Alexandria, VA.

Voice 9. Claire Smith (1993), group interview in Minneapolis, MN.

Voice 10. Informal conversation at AWSM (1993).

Voice 11. Cathy Henkel (1993), individual interview in Minneapolis, MN.

Voice 12. Mary Garber (1993), keynote speech at AWSM.

References

Angell, R. (1979). "Sharing the beat: Women sportswriters in locker rooms." *New Yorker*, pp. 46–96.

Atkinson, P. (1992). *Understanding ethnographic texts* (Qualitative Research Methods Series, 25). Newbury Park, CA: Sage.

Bruce, T., & Greendorfer, S.L. (1994). "Postmodern challenges: Recognizing multiple standards for social science research." *Journal of Sport and Social Issues*, 18(2), 258–268.

Carey, J.W. (1989). *Communication as culture: Essays on media and society.* Boston: Unwin Hyman.

Clifford, J. (1986). "Introduction: Partial truths." In J. Clifford & G.E. Marcus, *Writing culture: The poetics and politics of ethnography* (pp. 1–26). Berkeley, CA: University of California Press.

Clough, P.T. (1992). *The end(s) of ethnography: From realism to social criticism.* Newbury Park, CA: Sage.

Cole, C.L. (1991). "The politics of cultural representation: Visions of fields/fields of visions." *International Review for the Sociology of Sport,* 26(1), 36–51.

Denison, J.M. (1994). "Sport retirement: Personal troubles, public faces." Unpublished dissertation, University of Illinois at Urbana-Champaign.

———— (1996). Sport narratives. *Qualitative Inquiry,* 2(3), 351–362.

Denzin, N.K. (1989). *Interpretive interactionism.* Newbury Park, CA: Sage.

———— (1991). *Images of postmodern society: Social theory and contemporary cinema.* Newbury Park, CA: Sage.

———— (1992). "Lectures in Sociology 380: Field research methods." Unpublished manuscript, University of Illinois at Urbana-Champaign.

———— (1994). "The art and politics of interpretation." In N.K. Denzin & Y.S. Lincoln (Eds.), *Handbook of qualitative research* (pp. 500–515). Thousand Oaks, CA: Sage.

Dodds, T. (1991, Fall). "It's time to act on harassment." *Association for Women in Sports Media Newsletter,* p. 2.

Fornoff, S. (1991, Fall). "Because we've conformed before." *Association for Women in Sports Media Newsletter*, p. 3.

Geertz, C. (1973). *The interpretation of cultures: Selected essays.* New York: Basic Books.

Hall, S. (1984). "The narrative construction of reality." *Southern Review*, 17, 3–17.

Higgins, G.V. (1990). *On writing.* New York: Henry Holt & Co.

Hulme, K. (1983). *The bone people.* Toronto: Spiral.

Kaufman, M. (1994, February). "No sounds of silence this time." *Association for Women in Sports Media Newsletter*, p. 4.

Kohn, N., & Slowikowski, S.S. (1993, November). "'How do you warm up for a stretch class?' Sub/in/di/verting hegemonic shoves toward sport." Paper presented at the annual conference for the North American Society for the Sociology of Sport, Ottawa, Canada.

———— (1994, May). "'Lovely': Dialoguing about, around, through and with Norman K. Denzin." Paper presented at the Stone Spring Symposium "Taking stock methodologically: Validity, truth and method in contemporary interactionist thought," University of Illinois at Urbana-Champaign, Illinois.

———— (1998). "'How do you warm up for a stretch class?' Sub/in/di/verting hegemonic shoves toward sport." In G. Rail (Ed.), *Sport in postmodern times.* Albany, NY: State University of New York Press.

Krieger, S. (1991). *Social science and the self: Personal essays on an art form.* New Brunswick, NJ: Rutgers University Press.

Lather, P. (1990). "Reinscribing otherwise: The play of values in the practices of the human sciences." In E.G. Guba (Ed.), *The paradigm dialog* (pp. 315–332). Newbury Park, CA: Sage.

———— (1991). *Getting smart: Feminist research and pedagogy with/in the postmodern.* New York: Routledge.

Leavy, J. (1990). *Squeeze play.* New York: Doubleday.

Markula, P.H. (1993, November). When did they dance La Bamba?: Nostalgia in dance. Paper presented at the annual conference of the North American Society for the Sociology of Sport, Ottawa, Canada.

McManamon, P. (1985, February). "The media guide: When men are men and women are reporters." *Sport*, pp. 19–20.

Mulkay, M.J. (1985). *The word and the world: Explorations in the form of sociological analysis.* London: Allen & Unwin.

Olson, L. (1990). "A lesson from 'the chick.'" *Boston Herald*, September 24, p. 74.

Rabinow, P. (1986). "Representations are social facts: Modernity and post-modernity in anthropology." In J. Clifford & G.E. Marcus (Eds.), *Writing culture: The poetics and politics of ethnography* (pp. 234–261). Berkeley, CA: University of California Press.

Richardson, L. (1990). *Writing strategies: Reaching diverse audiences* (Qualitative Research Methods Series 21). Newbury Park, CA: Sage.

———— (1992). "The consequences of poetic representation: Writing the other, rewriting the self." In C. Ellis & M.G. Flaherty (Eds.), *Investigating subjectivity: Research on lived experience* (pp. 125–140). Newbury Park, CA: Sage.

———— (1994). "Writing: A method of inquiry." In N.K. Denzin & Y.S. Lincoln (Eds.), *Handbook of qualitative research* (pp. 516–529). Thousand Oaks, CA: Sage.

Rinehart, R.E. (1992, November). "Sport as epiphanic marker: The case of Super Bowl XXVI." Paper presented at the annual conference of the North American Society for the Sociology of Sport, Toledo, Ohio.

———— (1993). "'Been there, did that': Contemporary sport performances." Unpublished dissertation, University of Illinois at Urbana-Champaign, Illinois.

Rose, D. (1990). *Living the ethnographic life* (Qualitative Research Methods Series 23). Newbury Park, CA: Sage.

Rosenau, P.M. (1992). *Post-modernism and the social sciences: Insights, inroads, and intrusions.* Princeton, NJ: Princeton University Press.

Ryan, J. (1985). "Women in the locker room." *Editor & Publisher*, March 23, pp. 8–9.

Spencer, J. (1994). "A young writer shares her experience." *Association for Women in Sports Media Newsletter*, p. 5.

Stanley, L., & Wise, S. (1983). *Breaking out.* London: Routledge & Kegan Paul.

Visser, I. (1991). "A locker room with a view." *Mademoiselle*, January, pp. 116–117, 130.

2

"How Do You Warm-Up for a Stretch Class?": Sub/In/Di/verting Hegemonic Shoves Toward Sport

Nate Kohn and Synthia Sydnor

Like Victor Turner, who strives to move from lived experience to theory and back again, and in the spirit of Richard Schechner who believes theory to be performance of real life, we have attempted to produce a dialogic narrative about what it means to sport, to live in a sport-culture, to be a scholar of sport in mid-America. Our narrative is a highly personal-theoretical-ironic-reactionary account of our daily encounters with the hegemony of sport as seen through the refracted light of the postmodern. This work, among other things, is an examination of the thrust of sport into the practice of everyday life, a rendering of lived experiences at large in a sea of conflicted and collapsing hierarchies, and an attempted end run around the assault of cultural studies sensibilities as they travel to attach themselves to our interpretations of sport. It climaxes in our unenlightened idiosyncratic attempts to understand, subvert, invert, and divert those mattering-altering hegemonic forces that we find so cavalierly at play in the fields of our everyday life.

* * *

These words from Bakhtin are our template:

> The unique nature of dialogic relations. The problem of the inner dialogism. The seams of the boundaries between utterances. The problem of the double-voiced word. Understanding as dialogue. (1986, p. 119)

In this dialogic process, we find ourselves behaving in ways similar to Walter Benjamin's allegoricist who:

reaches now here, now there, into chaotic depths that his knowledge
places at his disposal, grabs an item out, holds it next to another, and
sees whether they fit: that meaning to this image, or this image to that
meaning. The result never lets itself be predicted; for there is no natural
mediation between the two. (quoted in Buck-Morss, 1989, p. 241)

Welcome to our exploratory process.

* * *

A few years ago, in several presentations (Slowikowski, 1991, 1992a,
1992b, 1992c), I made a call[1] for scholars in kinesiology to move with the
postmodern turn; to be self-reflexive, to open up their title and text pages to
their "subjects/informants"; to wonder more about the collecting and travel
that occurs within the bounds of sport. I pointed out that living in the sport
world has become too easy for us as scholars, that it is too easy for us to
explain away the riddle of sport with our rote critiques and ethnographies of
gender, race, class and so on, as we sit among the "Other"[2] in stadia, gym-
nasia and sport sociology classes.[3]

Where is the intentionality and transformation of cultural studies that
scholars were to take to the streets? Where is work—in Stuart Hall's (1990)
words—"that matters?" Can a new space, one such as Deleuze's that poses
"questions of echoes and resonances" (1985, p. 283), re-negotiate sport for
victims such as me? Nate and I cojoined, sensing that in dialogue we might
be able to map these contradictions onto sport.[4] We approach this text from
opposite directions and we collide in it,[5] hoping that any explosion we might
trigger will be in the cause of clarity, commonality, community.[6]

* * *

An innocent adrift in a productive world of conflicting and conflicted
signals, I open my mouth and say things that don't seem to be of me. As I
listen to myself speak, I hear the words of a primitive, as if of a child. "How
do you," I say to my wife, "warm up for a stretch class?" It is like a Steven
Wright joke, a verbal version of a cubist taunt, and at the same time a serious
inquiry, something I think I need to know in order not to injure myself in a
new enterprise urged upon me by doctor, family, Richard Simmons and the
Nike Shoe Company. "I can't," I say in reply to the suggestion that I buy a
treadmill, "work out at home. I know; I tried some pushups and jumping
jacks. I need the gaze of Others, the fear of being laughed at, in order to
generate sweat." I look around me and wonder: what is this world I am now
living in? How did I get here? The question is not what dream have I awak-

ened from, but what dream have I awakened into. "You wanna feel alive," beat the tom-toms of our times, "you gotta move."

* * *

In my own work, I now try to journey from consecrating theories that illuminate the "what and how" of studying sport (e.g., Harris, 1989), of documenting the postmodern moment of sport (e.g., Andrews, 1993), to playing with theory and confronting the seduction of a thick sport culture whose temptations and whose tensions I feel in the fundamentally different worlds that I transverse daily—the worlds of mother-wife, scholar, and resident of a small community. I yearn for a discourse that moves betwixt and between these worlds,[7] that answers my neighbors' interrogations: "You must get tickets to all of the games?" "Can you help me with my golf swing?" and challenges colleagues' assertions that National Endowment for the Humanities Grants do not matter in kinesiology. Travelling between these theories and communities[8] I hope, is a grammatology[9] of sport.

* * *

On CBS This Morning, a reporter is describing the sudden popularity of the sport of rock climbing among city dwellers, how New York stock brokers and advertising executives scale simulated rocky cliffs, purpose-built facsimiles of the face of Everest located indoors only a block from the office. From the stairmaster in the Fitness Center I watch a geared-up girl explain, as if to a child: "Rock-climbing is a sport that really matters. I mean," she says directly to me, "you can actually get hurt or die. It's not like hitting some golf ball around. Here, something actually matters." A less-than-hyperreal urban wall of simulated knob-holes and plastic finger-holds and toe-rests as a "mattering map," I think to myself, using Lawrence Grossberg's phrase,[10] trying to get a grip myself, looking for a little purchase on the suicide ledge of life. A map of what matters. A sport where a little slippage will kill you. I pump up the volume on the stairmaster, deciding to stay longer and even miss the start of the day's Wimbledon match, so that I, too, can do something that truly matters. I feel the sweat coming. I feel alive.

* * *

I breast-fed my child while reading Lyotard's *Pacific Wall* (1990). While teaching a "corruption, academics and athletics" section of my sport issues course, I agreed to act as "Honorary Football Coach" at my university, a position I imagined hinged on my passing the 30 football players in the class, a status that gave me one of the greatest rushes of my life: running onto the field of 50,000 fans, my name on the billboard, dreams of more graft—like a BMW—directed my way. I screamed, "You idiot!" from the bleachers at my six-year-old son as I watched him play his first soccer match, having just introduced the American Coaching Effectiveness Program to my Anthropology of Play class. And I wrote about the alienated, how things like baseball card collections[11] empower them with a cultural currency that lulls them into believing that they can dissolve the panopticon, that they matter, while I wallowed in my authentic Olympic pin collection, visiting it weekly at a bank-safe deposit box.

* * *

My cousin catches fish he won't eat, shoots birds others will pluck and devour, watches with a lustful eye as women leap for volley balls, plays golf from an electric cart, wears orange-and-blue to Friday lunches with the coach and tailgates as an honored guest of the radio station pre and post game. He gave up exercise in favor of diet and gets to park his Corvette within 20 yards of the stadium gate. He says to me, "How about them Bulls?" And I hear myself saying back, "How about them Bulls!" I find myself beginning to envy his evident pleasures in the fullness of his world, this chronic euphoria born of being a sporting man in a sporting culture. Give me what he has, I think, along with a stairmaster and the thrill of a climbing wall, and I will die a complete, satisfied, fulfilled human.

* * *

I was born an athlete, I cradled balls and ran races,[12] I exercised and vomited my way to an athlete's body. I married an athlete; we told ourselves that our children would be Olympians . . . Then I grew soft, sitting, writing on the tenure track.

Now I have a creeping realization that living as a scholar of sport has in far-reaching ways numbed me to the joys of spectating and living in sport terrain, a source of exhilaration for so many of my community members. I have sapped this sport-spirit too from my children, who are finding it difficult to negotiate in their universes without it. In school my daughter had to name her favorite baseball player and was embarrassed when she couldn't name any; my son, asked to draw a cap with his team's logo and colors, drew one bright yellow blob that was questioned by his teacher; and I, the author of "Cultural Performance and Sport Mascots" (Slowikowski, 1993) that focuses on the racism of Native American images, ran around my house in a panic to find costumes for my children when a Chief Illiniwek (University of Illinois sport mascot) apparel day was proclaimed for the first through third grades. How can I relay the "critique" of representation to my young children, who have to explain their blank sweatshirts and un-war-painted faces to their peers?

* * *

"Dustin," says my cousin, "wants to be Michael Jordan when he grows up."[13] Dustin is his nine-year-old son. "I told him that this is America: you can be anything you want to be." In my mind I see a short, Jewish Michael Jordan. I see Spike Lee. I say, "I shot some hoops the other day, first time in thirty-something years . . ." "You did?" says my cousin. He continues: "I never play basketball. But watching it, now that's another story!" Later, doing laps in the pool in the presence of a supremely supine cat, I ask myself: "Do those who move vicariously[14] still move?" Then I ask myself, "If all sports were ripped from the fabric of my cousin's life would there still be a cousin alternately to envy and hate?" Then I think: "Would there be an America?" "Would there be a me?" Then I stop thinking. I swim over to the cat stretched out at the pool's edge. I am breathing heavily. The muscles in my arms and chest feel pumped up, alive. I touch them and am surprised at how hard they feel, how resilient. The cat slowly opens her eyes. She winks at me, lazily. Maybe the sporting life isn't a bad substitute for the real thing. Maybe it is the real thing. There is a sudden, brief flash in my mind's eye of a possibility, of me on the 10m board executing a well-applauded dive. Co-opted, subverted, commodified, addictive, essentialized, reduced and reified, this sporting life beckons like the arms of Morpheus. Hey, I think as I stroke the cat, as I strategically abandon myself into the seduction, maybe it isn't so bad after all.

* * *

The paradox of "how is sport radically liberating and also constraining" can be posed from our dialogue (and has been posed by many others, such as Brohm and Hoberman). Yet, a rejoinder to this paradox also exists within our dialogue: the way we read sport, how we are self-conscious of living in sport and how we make ourselves both comedians and intellectual critics of sport, offers up residual and emergent counters to navigate the hegemony of sport in late 20th century America. Through such strategies as "seduction," "melancholy," "impatience" and "indifference," passions that Abbas, in his reading of Baudrillard, identifies and praises as new strategies of resistance, we can find, as Abbas writes, "a space for the critical to criticise itself, for the intellect to empty itself of pre-empted ideas, for the body to empty itself of pre-empted desires" (Abbas, 1990, p. 90). In these seductions, melancholies, indifferences, impatiences, we might even find an employable irony guided by, in Baudrillard's words, a "mendacious and deceptive clear-sightedness"[15] (Baudrillard, 1989, p. 45).

* * *

Exposed and basking, I glide happily and lost along the road marked "detour through theory."[16] I barely glimpse the walls of fluorescent billboards that obscure all possible remnants of reality. Mine is now the sporting life, a life for all to see and know, a shameless and guiltless celebration, infinitely repeating, of "the thrill of victory, the agony of defeat."[17] I am one of them now; I have crossed over.[18] As I move on down the road to nowhere,[19] one dulled and rusty billboard beckons to me, as if with a curled arthritic finger. Indifferently, impatiently, and with a hint of melancholy, I scan the words. They tease: with a contrary last gasp and with apologies to Ray Charles, let us posit that humankind is "born to move,"[20] and that, after Sansone (1988), all such movement is an essential, ritualistic sacrifice[21] of energy.[22] This inexorable, lifelong lunge toward death, this need to move that we can neither deny nor escape, turns suicide ontological and makes sport the weapon of that sacrifice, of that self-destruction.

* * *

So, I run in cold weather fast enough that I feel as if my brains are flooding out of my nostrils, and I am suddenly clearsighted . . . I covertly capture on video a Pee-Wee football coach extolling his young players, "This isn't any ordinary game. We're not called the Animals for nothing," an impeccable moment that I will use over and over again in class lectures. I read Susan Sontag's words and they free me. She writes: "Pity the uniquely valuable objects whose destiny is to be made available, in toy form, to everyone" (1993, p. 137). Or more precisely, her words free my Olympic pins from the safety deposit box, for I dispose of the pins in a paper sack along with tattered clothes at the Salvation Army drop-off bin.[23] I am satiated; I have purged myself with and of the equipment[24] of sport. Empty, I am strangely full.

* * *

I am eager to get started. But where to begin? Skydiving, bobsledding, skiing, boxing, bull fighting, alligator wrestling?[25] My mind boggles at the choices. I tingle with expectation, with an intensity of feeling never before imagined as I survey the seductive mattering map before me. Perhaps, I think, I can find some hint of direction in Michel de Certeau's *The Practice of*

Everyday Life (1984), a little blue book that I picked up in the self-help section of Brentanos. It falls open in my hands and a poem by Boris Vian reads itself to me:

> I don't want to kick off
> No sir, no way,
> before I've tasted
> the taste that tortures me
> the strongest taste of all.
> I don't want to kick off
> before I've tasted
> the savor of death. (de Certeau, 1984, p. 193)

On a pale Pink Post-It note, in my own suddenly highly legible hand, I write what will become the first in an increasingly reckless series of suicide notes. As I walk out the door, I stick it to the mirror in the hall for all to see. It reads: "Gone bungee-jumping. Back in time for supper."

Notes

1. In 1991, Cole claimed that sport sociologists had failed to consider the implications of recent interdisciplinary dialogues on critical ethnography. In one of the few (if not only) pieces in sport sociology to overview the philosophies of postmodern/critical/experimental ethnography, Cole calls for the building of "textual constructions" that require "ongoing critical dialogues among local voices, theory and the ethnographer in which what counts as knowledge remains contestable and is contested" (1991, p. 37).

2. The "Other" has been much considered in cultural studies discourses that contemplate sexuality, travel, colonialism, etc. (e.g., Said, Clifford, Crick, Borsboom, White). Here we try to challenge the ways that the "Other" is subverted, empowered, dominated within the bounds of sport; these sport "bounds" referring to any aspect of sport, play, games, contests, coaching, athletic festivals, physical education, the discipline of kinesiology, and all peripheral, metaphoric, ideological or symbolic representations of these.

3. Sport studies' "ceaseless flow" of research makes sport seem "controllable," but it clearly isn't. Instead, as Denzin (1991, p. 54) says, "This world, out there and in here, is out of control."

4. Perhaps to the dismay of sport purists, we self-consciously call attention to the process of being aesthetically and theoretically saturated in sport.

5. Perhaps we have engaged in what Cole describes as "experimental ethnography . . . a form of political graffiti . . . in which there are no guarantees" (1992, p. 172).

6. This "community" is our attempt to lash Agamben's (1993) "theory out of bounds" to the bounds of sport. As Agamben says, "if humans could . . . not be-thus in this or that particular biography, but be only the thus, their singular exteriority and their face, then they would for the first time enter into a community without presuppositions and without subjects, into a communication without the incommunicable" (pp. 64–65).

7. Making sense of one destination is the traditional quest of the anthropologist; we attempt to bounce between discourses suggesting that this strategy is the only means of survival in theoretical/real sport culture.

8. Within his "travelling others, travelling selves" conjuncture, Clifford (1992, p. 97) might call our work a "'work in progress,' work entering a very large domain of comparative cultural studies." Our work in progress is museum-like (Boon, 1992, pp. 261, 267) too: we pillage and pastiche sport as we visit, select, edit, boil down and curate our sport experiences within our text, and we travel in multiple voices/bodies in order to create that text (e.g., Denzin, 1992). Our text, then, is a hyperreal (Eco, 1973) souvenir of our travels, a souvenir that may have the power to transform, transcend, change culture (Bruner, 1989).

9. With apologies to Derrida (1976). Following Denzin's project, we "unhinge" speech from "original" sources, creating a montage of multiple texts that potentially becomes an agent for the articulation of an emancipatory project.

10. "Mattering maps" according to Grossberg in his book *We Gotta Get Out of This Place*, "are the places at which people can anchor themselves into the world, the location of the things that matter" (1992, p. 82).

11. — or sport figurines and other "authentic" sport memorabilia. Susan Stewart theorizes miniaturization like this to be a dialogue between inside and outside, between partiality and transcendence with regard to authority and authorial knowledge. The sport miniature presents a diminutive and thereby manipulatable version of experience that is domesticated and protected from contamination (Stewart, 1984).

12. These words culled from a favorite childhood poem, "So Run Your Race," by Patsy Neal.

13. By wanting to "be" Michael Jordan, not merely "be like" Michael Jordan, Dustin enacts Baudrillard's preference for the model (perhaps, in this case, role model) over metaphor. As Abbas says (1990, pp. 70–71), "models do not follow the real or await the establishment of a symbolic order . . . the superficiality of the model (like the changeability of fashion) is a strategy for keeping pace with disappearance. In this connection, we might note the effect of speed in Baudrillard's own . . . style of discourse, in his quite deliberate use of generalizations not weighed down by qualifications. Why write a book when you can write an essay? Why write an essay when you can produce an aphorism? Why even bother with an aphorism when you can come up with a pun?" Why put forth the time and effort to "be like" if, somehow, you can instantaneously "be"?

14. Olalquiaga points out (1992, p. 39) "Vicariousness—to live through another's experience—is a fundamental trait of postmodern culture." Further, she says (1992, p. 42) "the postmodern broadening of the notion of reality, whereby vicariousness is no longer felt as false or secondhand but rather as an autonomous, however incredible, dimension of the real, facilitates the current circulation and revalorization of this aesthetics . . . the logic of organization is anything but homogeneous, visual saturation is obligatory, and the personal is lived as a pastiche of fragmented images from popular culture."

15. To live, perform and theoretize sport culture means living, as we said earlier, betwixt and between these discourses, of being at a threshold, a liminality. Seductions, melancholies, indifferences, impatiences, ironies are found at thresholds. Postmodern sport culture may itself be a threshold. Schechner's work is important here: "This inbetweenness, thresholdness, has something to do with performance, with the flow and evanescence of human life" (Schechner, 1985, p. 296).

16. This detour is a crowded highway, it being a necessary side trip for all students of cultural studies who desire to do work that matters.

17. With no apologies to ABC Sports, who have promoted this cliche into a way of life.

18. In the Baudrillardian sense, we can read "the sporting life" for "culture." As Featherstone (1991, p. 99) says: "For Baudrillard, culture [the sporting life] has effectively become free-floating to the extent that culture [the sporting life] is every-where, actively mediating and aestheticizing the social fabric and social relationships. A move beyond the discursive reflexive primacy of language towards figural cultural forms which emphasize the immediacy and intensity of aural and visual sensations which provide inchoate and dispersed pleasures for decentered subjects." Decentered subjects include those who have crossed over.

19. See (or listen to) the Talking Heads' song, "The Road to Nowhere."

20. Our concept "born to move" and Ray Charles' lament "born to lose" can be articulated such that movement becomes loss. The knowledge that each move we make marks the loss of a bit of life can inspire a chronic melancholy, the pain/pleasure of which is perfectly captured in our affective reading of Ray Charles' lovely song. Celeste Olalquiaga (1992, p. 58): "More than a lamentation for what is lost, this melancholic sensibility is deeply embedded in the intensity of the loss—not seeking to reconstitute what is gone, but to rejoice in its impossibility. The melancholic spirit lives contemporary culture as a splendorous and baroque memento mori, whose different layers must be uncovered like those of Pompeii."

21. See also Kroker, Kroker and Cook (1989, p. 172): "It is the age of sacrificial sports now: that point where the Olympics, under the pressure of the mass-media, re-enter the dark domain of mythology. No longer sports as about athletic competition, but postmodern sports now fascinating only because the athlete's body is a blank

screen for playing out the darker passions of triumph and scapegoatism." Girard's (1972) ideas about scapegoatism implode, too, on the idea of sport as ritual sacrifice.

22. Sansone defines sport as "the ritual sacrifice of human physical energy" (1988, p. 142). He hypothesizes that for thousands of years through neolithic times early human communities invested their energy on the hunt, its rituals and motifs. With the advent of complex agricultural and technological based societies, hunting was no longer the focus of human community. For Sansone, the energy (including the motifs, ideologies, rituals and actual physicalities) used in hunting continued to be ritually and/or symbolically expanded in human communities in the form of sport. Participating in sport, spectating, reading about sport, even adorning one's self in sport related attire for Sansone constitutes a ritual, symbolic sacrifice. Sansone believes that this ritual sacrifice of energy is a bio-cultural imperative pursued by modern humanity in the form of sport, with the athletic him/herself being the ultimate sacrificial victim, a blurred representative of both the hunter and the victim of the hunt.

23. Sontag on the destruction of collections (1993, p. 187): "Perhaps every collector has dreamed of a holocaust that will relieve him of his collection . . . destruction is only the strongest form of divestment."

24. "Equipment of sport" being the actual physical sacrifice of energy (Sansone, 1988); as well as travelling-creating-reading theory onto sport.

25. Rinehart (1993) reconsiders such sport in various ways: as *kitsch*; as *avant-garde*; as epiphanic marker; in contrast, many sport researchers decline to open up their definitions of sport to activities like bungee-jumping. For instance, Sage (1990, p. 126) in a popular sport textbook: "One of the most disturbing influences of televised sport for those who cherish traditional sport forms has been the creation of various pseudo-sport events, popularly and appropriately called trash sports."

References

Abbas, A. (1990). "Disappearance and fascination: The Baudrillardian obscenario." In A. Abbas (Ed.), *The provocation of Jean Baudrillard* (pp. 68–93). Hong Kong: Twighlight.

Agamben, G. (1991). *Theory out of bounds: The coming community* (M. Hardt, trans.). Minneapolis, MN: The University of Minnesota Press.

Andrews, D. (1993). "Deconstructing Michael Jordan: Popular culture, power and everyday life in postmodern America." Unpublished doctoral dissertation, University of Illinois at Urbana-Champaign, Illinois.

Bakhtin, M.M. (1986). "The problem of the text in linguistics, philology, and the human sciences: An experiment in philosophical analysis" (V.W. McGee, trans.). In C. Emerson & M. Holquist (Eds.), *Speech genres and other late essays* (pp. 103–131). Austin, TX: University of Texas Press.

Baudrillard, J. (1989). "The anorexic ruins" (D. Antal, trans.). In D. Kampfer & C. Wulf (Eds.), *Looking back on the end of the world* (pp. 29–45). New York: Semiotext(e).

———— (1983). *Simulations*. New York: Semiotext(e).

Boon, J. (1991). "Why museums make me sad." In I. Karp & S. Levine (Eds.), *Exhibiting cultures: The poetics and politics of museum display* (pp. 255–278). Washington and London: Smithsonian Institute.

Borsboom, A. (1988). "The savage in European social thought: A prelude to the conceptualization of the divergent peoples and cultures of Australia and Oceania." *Bijdragen*, 144, 419–432.

Brohm, J.M. (1972). *Sport: A prison of measured time*. Paris: Maspero.

Bruner, E.M. (1989). "Tourism, creativity, and authenticity." *Studies in Symbolic Interaction*, 10, 109–114.

Clifford, J. (1992). "Traveling cultures." In L. Grossberg, C. Nelson & P. Treichler (Eds.), *Cultural Studies* (pp. 96–116). New York and London: Routledge.

Cole, C.L. (1991). "The politics of cultural representation: visions of fields/fields of visions." *International Review for Sociology of Sport*, 26, 37–51.

———— (1992). "Ethnographic sub/versions: culture-identity-politics." Unpublished doctoral dissertation, University of Iowa.

de Certeau, M. (1984). *The practice of everyday life*, Berkeley: University of California Press.

Deleuze, G. (1985). "Mediators." In J. Cray & S. Kwinter (Eds.), *Zone 6. Incorporations* (pp. 268–280). New York: Urzone.

Denzin, N.K. (1991). *Images of postmodern society: Social theory and contemporary cinema*. London: Sage.

———— (1992). *Symbolic interactionism and cultural studies: The politics of interpretation*. Oxford and Cambridge: Blackwell.

Derrida, J. (1976). *Of grammatology* (G. Spivak, trans.). Baltimore: Johns Hopkins University Press.

Eco, U. (1973). *Travels in hyperreality*. San Diego: Harcourt Brace Jovanovich.

Featherstone, M. (1991). *Consumer culture and postmodernism*. London: Sage.

Girard, R. (1972). *Violence and the sacred* (P. Gregory, trans.). Baltimore and London: Johns Hopkins University Press.

Grossberg, L. (1992). *We gotta get out of this place*. New York and London: Routledge.

Hall, S. (1990). "The emergence of cultural studies and the crisis of the humanities." *October*, 53, 11–90.

Harris, J.L. (1989). "Suited up and stripped down: Perspectives for sociocultural sport studies." *Sociology of Sport Journal*, 6, 335–347.

Hoberman, J. (1992). *Mortal engines: The science of performance and the dehumanization of sport*. New York: Free Press.

Kroker, A., Kroker, M., & Cook, D. (1989). *Panic encyclopedia. The definitive guide to the postmodern scene*. New York: St. Martin's Press.

Lyotard J.F. (1990). *Pacific wall* (B. Boone, trans.). Venice, CA: Lapis Press.

Olalquiaga, C. (1992). *Megalopolis*. Minneapolis and Oxford: University of Minnesota Press.

Rinehart, R.E. (1993). "'Been there, did that.' Contemporary sport performances." Unpublished doctoral dissertation, University of Illinois at Urbana-Champaign.

Sage, G.H. (1990). *Power and ideology in American sport: A critical perspective*. Champaign, IL: Human Kinetics.

Sansone, D. (1988). *Greek athletics and the genesis of sport*. Berkeley, CA: University of California Press.

Schechner, R. (1985). *Between theater and anthropology*. Philadelphia: University of Pennsylvania Press.

Slowikowski, S.S. (1991). "Travelling and collecting: A consideration in light of the ancient and postmodern Olympic festivals." Paper presented at the annual conference of the Association for the Study of Play, Charleston, South Carolina.

——— (1992a, November). "Postmodern turns in history and anthropology, with applications to the study of physical culture." Paper presented at the annual meeting of the North American Society for the Sociology of Sport, Toledo, Ohio.

——— (1992b). "On primitive physical culture in civilized places." Paper presented at the annual meeting of the International Society for the History of Physical Education and Sport, Turku, Finland.

——— (1992c). "The postmodern turn in historical and anthropological scholarship, with application to kinesiology." Paper presented at the Big Ten kinesiology capstone of knowledge Symposium, Ann Arbor, Michigan.

——— (1993). "Cultural performance and sport mascots." *Journal of Sport and Social Issues*, 17, 22–43.

Sontag, S. (1993). *The volcano lover*. New York: Farrar Straus Giroux.

Stewart, S. (1984). *On longing: Narratives of the miniature, the gigantic, the souvenir, the collection*. Baltimore, MD: Johns Hopkins University Press.

3

Born-Again Sport: Ethics in Biographical Research

Robert Rinehart

. . . paradoxically, the more the individual is concerned with the reality that is not available to perception, the more must he concentrate his attention on appearances.

(Goffman, 1973, p. 249)

The purpose of this chapter, initially, was to examine the world of private swim lessons as epitomized by my experience as a teacher for a privately-run, Christian-oriented, swim school. However, I intend to use that experience as a starting point for a discussion of the place of the researcher in personal stories, and more specifically, in the domain of lived experience. I mean this as one sense in which the issue of "ethics," in quotes, comes up in research—though the use of such a term itself is problematic.[1]

As Howard Becker quotes Everett Hughes: "Introductions are supposed to introduce. How can you introduce something you haven't written yet? You don't know what it is. Get it written and then you can introduce it" (1986, p. 50). A short explanation of my use of the word "ethics" might be appropriate. I do not mean the term as an entry into a formal philosophical discussion; rather, I see ethics as an underpinning for dialogue regarding the place of researcher vis-à-vis researched; for discussion of the space between religion and sport; for development of the subtle yet insidious conflation of sport, religion and zealousness; and for an enactment of stories that we all know versions of, that demonstrate, probably more tellingly, such dynamics.[2]

My own biography dovetails into this [written] discussion, as I spent 16 years as a competitive swimmer and 22 years coaching swimmers. I have coached summer league teams, high school and collegiate teams, and a year-round, United States Swimming club; I've coached eight collegiate All-Americans, and one U. S. high-school record-holder. I have also taught for the American Red Cross since 1968, and have been an instructor-trainer for Water Safety programs since 1981. All of this is merely to say that I have an extensive background in the field of swimming.

This past summer, my skills and knowledge helped me to become employed[3] with a private swim school. I found myself feeling as if I were prostituting myself, especially when the owner of the school (I will call him Winston[4]) insisted that I learn "the Winston Method" of teaching swimming. Winston was a former basketball coach, who had never been a competitive swimmer. We met at a hotel swimming pool, and Winston proceeded, over the course of four days and nearly 12 hours, to explain in minute detail breath-holding, exhalation, various drills: in short, he labored over the most basic skills, even though he knew my background in swimming. He was, to parallel Red Cross discourse, attempting to standardize my training. In fact, several times he said, "Forget all that you know, so you can learn my method. I've worked on developing this for nearly 20 years."[5] Yet I found myself marveling at how much the act of swimming remained the same, despite his attempts to "package" his program as unique.

My attempts to purge myself of all I had done and known were, of course, ludicrous. I found myself putting on a stolid look of interest, exclaiming, "I see!" as enthusiastically as I could muster, and hoping that I could learn some of the slightly different procedures and terminologies he had designed. I told myself that he was in business, that he had to somehow demonstrate that his method was both unique and successful. He also made several allusions to the fact that he knew I was a "good Christian." I initially thought these comments rather bizarre, and remained silent, puzzling over whether being a good Christian had anything to do with teaching swimming. I wondered how adamant he would be in pushing this aspect of himself onto the teaching endeavor, and onto me.

In disguising critical parts of me to him, was I deceiving my employer? Certainly, to an extent. Was I any different from any other evaluating employee who swallows her protests and tries to learn how her employer wishes her to act? No. In fact, I felt I was taking on the role of "Active-Member Researcher" suggested by Adler and Adler (1987).

Becoming a researcher through this process often changed my exasperation with Winston to a more thoughtful consideration of his motives. It freed me, in a sense, of intimate involvement, so that I could become more dispassionate. Thus, the very act of consciously being a researcher changed my attitude toward the task, and certainly colored my impressions and view of the process and behaviors. Though I did not make my researcher role overt or explicit, I felt my expertise made me a ready member of the aquatic world of which I was researching. By remaining silent, a strategy I often use when I am thrust in the midst of deeply dogmatic verbiage and situations, I felt I could best allow the most natural course of things to transpire. I neither enthusiastically joined in, nor obviously showed distaste. In this sense, my role as researcher was compromised. I was both an active-member researcher, albeit somewhat skeptical, while teaching swimming; and I was a passive, peripheral member in relation to Winston's religious zeal. [6] I was becoming an amalgam of nuances for my employer. I felt grounded, however, in my knowledge of swimming—thus, I could use my expertise in the one to influence the other.

In writing himself into his text, Hamabata (1986) created a new presence, a role which accomplished several things. It affected his relationships with his so-called informants: it may have affected their responses, his questions, the delicate space that is social intercourse. And at any point in the inclusion process, where, to use the Adlers' (1987) terms, Hamabata ran from peripheral to active to, in some instances, complete (albeit infantilized) membership, this new evolution of identity affected his research. As Homan (1980, p. 57) implies, one of the major concerns of the covert researcher should be "with the effects of such methods upon those who practise them."

Similarly, I found myself in conflict: the evangelistic zeal with which my employer approached swimming (and his business) mirrored, to me, his zest for his particularly proselytizing religion. The parallels between these two types of fervor struck me as odd, and I became hesitant to discuss either one with him, for fear of [re]opening up a critique of my own life. Had my relationships with young swimmers been similarly symbiotic or predatory? Did my zeal for the sport of swimming force choices upon children who admired me, and funnel them into something which, with a less-benign coach, might become obsessive? It was as if I had come upon a taboo (and obviously fascinating) topic, this confluence of religion, zeal, and swimming.

One of the issues which Richard Mitchell (1993) discusses in his book *Secrecy and Fieldwork* is the backstage/frontstage persona of the fieldworker. Though it is somewhat a tautology, it is this developed persona that mightily influences the relationships the fieldworker has with those researched. The lightly filigreed network that establishes trust, cooperation, and, in some cases and to some degrees, collaboration, is a tenuous network at best and one that is endlessly worked at, reconstituted, and renegotiated. The type of research that delves into these renegotiations is typically filled with depth, with false steps (which themselves are enlightening), and with the (often unsaid) understanding that, between researcher and researched, there forms a new entity, that of the "text" they together write.

Mitchell (1993) locates the researcher's role in a schema that accounts for cognition (from low to high), affect (from unsympathetic to sympathetic), and the perception (including novices, outsiders, allies, and spies) of the researcher. The intricate relationship of researcher to researched in each of the hypothesized research roles forms a dynamic relationship that impinges upon that which is allowed to be studied, that which is freely given, that which is given at a cost.

The researcher's perceptions correspond somewhat to Norman Denzin's researcher role categorizations. Thus, Mitchell's "novice" category coincides with Denzin's "complete participant"; the "outsider" loosely corresponds to "observer as participant"; "allies" somewhat relate to "participant as observer"; and the term "spies" aligns with the category of "complete participant" (Denzin, 1989, pp. 162–165). My location within my research moved among and between the categories, so that, from Winston, the clientele of the swim school, and me, emerged dynamic, complex relationships, irreducible to such discrete categorizations. In a further elaboration and refinement of his previous work, Denzin states that:

> twentieth-century qualitative, interpretive sociology [has been haunted by] the myth of the fully present subject who could reveal the innerworkings of his or her mind to another [and by] the myth of an observer with a method who could somehow prevail upon this subject to reveal her inner world of experience to the kindly knowing scientist. (1991, pp. 67–68)

The success of an effort between subject and observer to produce a text that reveals the subject's actual experience is likewise a myth. Text is simply not the same as the original experience. Text-reading, or text-listening, or text-writing—these can be experiences, but, as Denzin writes:

> Perhaps we can not produce a writing method that realistically captures the world out there. Our focus must become smaller. Like the filmmaker, we can tell tiny stories about the human condition, showing how these histories we live are constrained by larger cultural narratives that work their interpretive ways behind our backs. (1991, p. 68)

In the remainder of this piece, then, knowing full well that this ethnography is filled with constraints as regards its explication of lived experience, I will tell some of the patchwork of experience I know from working with an evangelical private swim club owner, and explore the relationship of affect to sport. Then I will discuss Foucault's ideas of disciplinary practice as they relate to the teaching of swimming, and relate that back to religious/sport evangelicals. If some of this begins to sound like a story, and some seems imbricated with fictional elements, that is because it is a story: it is my story, my view of "what happened."

I contracted to work four days a week, ten hours a day (from 9am to 8pm). I spent my time teaching private swim lessons to children and some adults. I even instructed a parent-tot class, where the parents, who were all mothers, held their children in a variety of positions (which I taught), including the Red-Cross-named face-to-face shoulder support, chin support, and armpit support positions and cheek-to-cheek support positions. I had no rules given me on how I should teach this particular class; these classes were what is termed "water adjustment," designed to instill confidence and a sense of enjoyment in the children. Thus, Winston, during the training period, never discussed or prescribed how to teach both the children and the parents.[7]

The owner of the swim school and I were the only two full-time employees, and we worked with two students each half hour (with a five-minute break between classes), for ten hours a day. Sometimes it rained, but most of the time, the Indiana sun and humidity sapped us so that we were both exhausted by the evening. It was honest, outdoors work, and the cadre of part-time teachers who worked half-days could never totally empathize with either one of us. Thus, Winston and I developed a sense of oneness, a shared sense of mutual suffering.[8] To a degree, we "bonded." Though I initially went into the job for the pay, and later, as an opportunity to observe critically a private-sector sport setting; though I felt a deepening sense of cynicism; and though I never felt totally comfortable with Winston's strange behavior of reaching out and holding my hand in prayer over our lunch, I thought I could retain my stance of criticality, my critical edge. I may have been mistaken.

In creating an image for the swim school, the establishment of face work, for the owner, was an ongoing process. I heard him slip only once during the whole summer, when the pump for a pool broke. Instead of a hearty "Gosh darn it," or some such, he swore. In a way, I admired his normal consistency, yet I was usually looking for dents in the seam he had developed. One of the most innocuous rips may have been the eerie feeling that his was a carefully established, consistent and ordered world. There were *Guidepost* magazines in his home, he used as his motto "Technique, technique, technique," he would generally preface a criticism of a patron with some phrase like, "Bless her heart, she's trying, but . . ." By repetition (over, I imagine, a 20-year period), he had established his program—and variance from it, I was told, was reason for dismissal. A former employee was a former employee because he, it was hinted, had not lived up to the standards that were Christian in their derivation. Yet there existed paradoxes—largely unexamined and taken-for-granted—within this carefully constructed Christian workaday world.

I was astounded, for example, when, during a swim-team mini-camp (held a week before the actual swim lesson program began), the owner insisted that all the youth swimmers circle, hold hands, to "thank Jesus for the bounty He has given us." During this prayer, as I lifted my head, I noticed one girl, who I later found out was Jewish, looking around as well. Her face was neutral, betraying no distaste for this Christian rite, or for any insensitivity to difference. Apparently, she felt the tradeoff—getting the instruction in stroke work and technique—was worth this seemingly innocuous ritual.

On Swimming: Two Stories

When the shot sounded, she flexed her arms, springing from the starting block in a smooth motion to the plane of water. She'd practiced this so many times, this racing start, that she could predict success eight or nine times out of ten attempts.

"How'd that feel?" I said.

"Good. Pretty good," she said. "I piked a little, and I think my feet were sloppy on entry."

"Yeah. You've got to tighten your legs as soon as you drive off."

She'd seen herself on videotape, in slow motion and stop motion, seen the correct angle of entry repetitively. The scienticity was reassuring; the ability to control, within human reason, reassured her as well. But she was wrong. When she looked back on her swimming career, she realized that she'd fooled herself. She'd focused so much on winning, or on practices to ensure winning, she'd forgotten the joy of swimming. She'd understood why interval or lactic acid or tethered swimming training worked for a sprinter; she'd followed the nutrition regimen, so that her glycogen stores would be high for glycolysis, her body fat would remain optimum; her stroke had been analyzed so that buoyancy, strength, endurance, body shape, and breathing ratio would maximize efficiency. She became like an automaton, predictable and steady. But the process that got her there in the first place, her love of the water, was ignored.

She'd bought into the science of swimming, and she felt hollow. The magic she'd once felt, the unrefined joy, was lost. For the first time, she'd felt a sense of control, but it wasn't real. Her coaches dictated practices, her teammates voted for team suits. At away meets, she couldn't even eat at a restaurant she chose: the team would vote. Her voice was drowned in a sea of triumphant voices, all vying for some semblance of control. Even during races, when she should have been able to ad-lib, to rely on herself for changing strategy—even then, she could hear her coach's—or her teacher's—voice whispering, "We've planned for this. Remember the visualization drills we

did? You saw her taking it out fast—you've already done this, visually."
There were no surprises left. No joy. So she quit the team, and began working
for her college's television station, editing film collages for lead-ins, eating
pita bread sandwiches. It made no sense whatsoever, and she was happy.
Soon, many of the swim team began working with her, so she quit and found
something else to do with her life. She wrote a book entitled *Multiple Personalities I Have Known*. She made a different kind of bread every day. She
prayed at a different church every week. She wrote poetry, disregarding meter
and rhyme and rhythm.

There was another swimmer, who attended all the best swim camps,
took private lessons, ate and breathed and lived swimming, at first because
the water felt so startlingly cool against her body, then later because swimming became a comfort zone, a setting in which she could excel, a haven
from school and boys and competitions that seemed to really matter. Her
father encouraged her to swim competitively. He and his wife felt that her
swimming was a phase she would pass through; but when she turned out to
be so good, the father, who had no other children, wanted to share in his
daughter's enthusiasm.
He volunteered to be a timer at a few meets. Then he became the head
timer for home meets. After a year of this, he began attending stroke and turn
clinics for officials. He became certified as a judge. His daughter, only eight
at this time, welcomed her father's involvement. They would travel to meets
as a family, she and her father and her mother, but she and her father had a
special knowledge, a sure knowledge of the justness of swimming. Times
were objective measures of excellence. You simply couldn't cheat an electronic clock. This her mother did not seem to know.
By the time she was 12, she was ranked in the top five in the 200-,
500-, and 1650-yard freestyle events in her zone. Her father had become the
representative for the Local Swim Club for United States Swimming. As
well, his business was flourishing. Life was good. He decided to build a pool
in the backyard. After some thought, he settled on a surprise configuration for
his daughter: he installed a 25-yard, one-lane pool, running diagonally across
the back lot. "It's for lap swimming," he announced proudly. "We can have
some extra workouts." His daughter agreed: extra workouts would only make
her better. Only they didn't. After a month-long layoff in September, puberty
began to change the girl. Her breasts began developing, her hips widened
slightly. "I knew you shouldn't have dropped off your yardage," said her
father as he stood above her. "I'm sorry, Daddy," she said, adjusting her
goggles. "Maybe I can push these 100s a little harder."
By the time I taught her, she was a young woman, returned from college for the summer. She had changed events, and now claimed her specialty

as backstroke. She and her father had decided that those bothersome breasts wouldn't be such a burden if carried out of the water. But she had a more sinister burden that hampered her from swimming to her fullest. Before every meet, before every event in which she was to swim, this young woman, apprehensive about failing in the one thing in which she had ever excelled, would spontaneously (yet on demand) vomit her full stomach contents. Weakened from each bout, she would swim poorly. So we worked not on technique, technique, technique, but rather on life, life, life. For whom did she swim? I asked. What did she get out of swimming competitively? How could she regain some control over her life?

Contemporary swimming has [d]evolved into a highly technical, disciplined practice. But it wasn't always so: "the [water] element that to the Greeks seemed so mysterious and fugitive, the Romans attempted to regulate and control" (Sprawson, 1992, p. 59). Linked with this regulation and control is the idea of the disease-free—indeed, sexual and youthful—body: "In the wake of Hollywood, swimming [in the United States] has become symptomatic of the search for physical perfection, the desperate effort to remain forever young" (1992, p. 269). Linked with the impulse toward seeking eternal youth is a thrust to impose upon the body an ironically abnegating yet self-absorbed discipline: the swim school/camp thus becomes a viable arena for playing out both the elixir of youth and the subjugation of self.

The swimming body has discipline imposed from both outside and inside: it is inscribed by others, including coaches and parents, and it is inscribed by itself. In competitive swimming, "time is paramount. Even winners are disappointed if they don't better their times"[9] (Kottak, 1989, p. 127). The root of this time-concern may lie in "a way of ordering earthly time for the conquest of salvation" (Foucault, 1977, p. 162), yet its persistence is pervasive and obvious. The use of technological advances such as electronic timing devices, "attentive parents with stopwatches" (Kottak, 1989, p. 129), even pace clocks fastened to a wall, create both implicit and explicit time-tables that "establish rhythms, impose particular occupations, [and] regulate the cycles of repetition"[10] (Foucault, 1977, p. 149). At the swim school, for the competitive swimmers, such regimes of control were constantly reinforced: every stroke change, every change in starts and turns, broken down to minute parts, carried the implicit (and often explicit) objective of lowering time in a race.

Though the self is implicated in disciplinary procedures, the very "temporal elaboration of the act" (Foucault, 1977, p. 151) of swimming itself is largely controlled by others. In swimming, gaining clear knowledge of processual results is quite difficult. Thus, early on in her career, the swimmer learns to trust the evaluation of someone outside the self—a kind of being coached by faith. As well, the breaking down of movement patterns—usually, and most efficiently, those patterns performed by others—begins at the most basic level of learning. For example, the American Red Cross aquatics program has built upon both the part-whole and the progressive-part method.[11] Within the progressive-part approach, "Sub-grouping of students may become necessary," and in the part-whole method, "The advantage . . . to instructors, especially those with little experience, is that they find it easier to control the group" (American Red Cross, 1981, p. 15). Skills are broken down from gross to fine, from complex to simple, for the sake of efficiency.

As Foucault writes, "Exercise is that technique by which one imposes on the body tasks that are both repetitive and different, but always graduated" (1977, p. 161). At the swim school, we refined this imposition upon the body to such a degree that I found repetition to be my greatest ally. For example, I repeated set phrases, such as "elbow high," "slide on entry," and "lift the hand—loose, not steel—with the shoulder." All well and goo . . . The rote was only bothersome because I had my own particular brand of rote which I felt worked for me. Part of the experience—feeling like an automaton—was due to the fact that we saw two individuals every half-hour for ten hours a day. The sheer number of individuals we worked with produced a glazed feel of sameness in my teaching. Behind my dark sunglasses, under the hot sun, I discovered myself droning on about head position in the breathing phase while closing my eyes for a quick rest. If someone performed "incorrectly," it was a simple thing to return to a more basic unit of instruction. In competitive swimming, stroke analysis, the minute setting of cadence and pace, establishment of rhythmic breathing patterns (e.g., crawl or butterfly 3:1, 2:1, 1:1) all contribute to:

> a web . . . of anatomo-chronological schema of behavior . . . [in which] the act is broken down into its elements; the position of the body, limbs, articulations is defined; to each movement is assigned a direction, an aptitude, a duration; their order of succession is prescribed. (Foucault, 1977, p. 152)

Thus the most infinitesimal gestures are controlled, with efficiency of movement being the ultimate goal. This imposed control mechanism for discipline works within a complex of systems that form a "coercive link with the apparatus of production" (Foucault, 1977, p. 153). Though coaches often seek those swimmers with a "feel for the water,"[12] the feedback they give their athletes is often ambivalent and confusing. Thus, a swimmer works to produce the ideal movement—not necessarily ideal for his or her buoyancy, flexibility, body type, but an idealized movement as seen on film, as portrayed by some [usually] Olympian bodies. To this end, swimmers may even view themselves in a large reflecting mirror placed on the bottom of the pool. As well, an integral part of a serious swimmer's program—and of the swim camp's program—is "film work," wherein the swimmer and coach analyze stroke mechanics and body movement of the swimmer and of other swimmers.

The swim school came to resemble Foucault's "punitive city": in this setting was born the controlled, economical lesson. The swimming pool, divided into areas for lessons (or lanes for the swim practice), became symbolic of "hundreds of tiny theatres of punishment," where there occurred:

> a visible punishment, a punishment that tells all, that explains, justifies itself, convicts: placards, different-coloured caps bearing inscriptions, posters, symbols, texts read or printed, tirelessly repeat the code. . . . the essential point, in all these real or magnified severities, is that they should all, according to a strict economy, teach a lesson: that each punishment should be a fable. (Foucault, 1977, p. 113)

In this manner, the pedagogical, zealous mission of swimming (and its relationship to Christianity) may be, and is, justified. The surveillance procedures in competitive swimming—which carried over into our little swim school agency—inscribe a regime of the body which resonates with Foucault's concept of the "use [of] procedures of individualization to mark exclusion" (Foucault, 1977, p. 199). Coaches typically assign swimmers to events, thus overtly or covertly labelling them as, for example, sprinters or IMers (individual medley swimmers). For the most part, Winston assigned me the novice swimmers; of over 50 students I worked with, only five were competitive swimmers. But Winston's lessons consisted of 90 percent competitive swimmers, and he told me that one of his practices was to further refine specialization. Keith Bell, a noted sport psychologist writing of swimming for age-group swimmers, entitled one of his motivational books, *Winning Isn't Normal*, in which he detailed and attempted to problem-solve the fact of the exclusiveness (or differentness) of the outstanding swimmer. The markers between swimmers signify an exclusive club that further fragments and disciplines the swimmers.

Of course, at the swim school, we treated water adjustment, learn-to-swim, and competitive patrons differently. We broke movements down to component parts—usually breathing, pulling, kicking. We sold T-shirts advertising the lessons, and gave away other T-shirts to the swim camp attendees on which were inscribed the words "Technique, Technique, Technique" as the rungs of a ladder to success. We, and I include myself in this indictment, believed that swimming was one of the best possible outlets for these youngsters.

But the relative freedoms of swimming—the long-ago practice of nudity, for example, in outdoor bathing, which "draws one back through earlier stages of evolution, as a resistance against the indifference and vulgarities of contemporary life" (Sprawson, 1992, p. 176)—have gradually eroded, to be replaced by a disciplinary system both insidious and tenacious. Frivolity, for the most part, was discouraged. The "compact model of the disciplinary mechanism" (Foucault, 1977, p. 197), the existence of a form of panopticism within swimming, is evidenced in such practices as taking attendance, checking off sets and goals accomplished, and setting and re-evaluating (and seeking approval from the coach for) daily, weekly, seasonal, and yearly goals. This form of panopticism is built into the coach- (or teacher-) centered team (class) concept; it is reinforced in the hierarchical structure of lane- (lesson) assignments; and it is recollected in the lane-timing squad, whose decision supercedes the experience of the individual swimmers. And in swim schools and camps, the panopticism remains uncontested; a sort of faith-learning that reproduces itself.

Today, competitive swimmers manipulate the hand-paddles of an isokinetic "Swim-Bench" to learn the stroke more efficiently and to dry-land weight train. At the swim school, if a child was not progressing well, we insisted that she was not practicing enough in front of mirrors at home. This was for children taking lessons! I was told to tell mothers, "Now Mother, Susie needs to practice 20 times on her right hand, 20 times on her left hand, at least four times a day in front of the mirror." Of course, discipline devours spontaneity,

Whether a student practiced or not became a test for moral fortitude. If the child/adult was working on his or her swimming outside of our lessons, he or she was praised in front of others who had not performed such efforts. While there were turnarounds and improvements, there were just as many who worked at it and remained exactly the same as when they began lessons. I felt as if I were at a revival meeting, watching a lame believer miraculously shed a crutch and walk, when Winston would yell, "Bob! Will you look at Joclyn's right arm? She's been practicing! See what practice will do?" All this, a performance for the watching parents, the kids in my lessons, Joclyn's young partner, and a living, self-promoting, advertisement for the swim school. And my response was supposed to be something like, "Gosh! With a little effort, Stan might get there too." It was transparent, I thought; but, since we were the experts, our "act" was never questioned.

I term this type of fervency "sport evangelism." Because "we all know" swimming is a valuable skill, devoutly to be wished for, this type of sport evangelism is, I believe, unethical behavior. Touted exclusively as unquestioned ideology (just as much of evangelical religion may tend to be[13]), sport, already a powerful tool for control (viz. Greendorfer, 1987), becomes increasingly effective. The promotion of sports, as a tool for a modern-day panopticon, becomes, finally, a series of questions of ethical behaviors. As Charles Prebish asks:

How has modern evangelism utilized sport in furthering its own endeavor? Equally, how has sport utilized religion? Who are the so-called 'jock evangelists,' and what do they preach? What groups have arisen to further the pursuit of the Christian athlete, and how have they emphasized a missionary endeavor? (1993, p. xvii)

How, indeed?

Notes

I wish to thank Jim Denison, Jana Garrity, Gina Lay, Pirrko Markula, and Tim Winter for their helpful comments regarding this chapter.

1. See, for confirmation of the positivist stance, Nicholas Von Hoffmann and Sally W. Cassidy's article. Note the use of deeply connotative terms in the following excerpts: "we resembled . . . a detective or a spy"; "we were invading other people's private domain"; "Participant-observation has been described as the business of being a professional fifth wheel" (1956, p. 195). In contrast, see Richard G. Mitchell's book (1993) for a discussion of both "liberal opposition to covert research" and "humanist advocacy for covert research" (pp. 23–35).

2. See Karen McCarthy Brown (1991) for a lucid explanation of the use of stories as evocative of emotional outlays.

3. A traditional ethnography might use the phrase "to gain entry into the world of private swim lessons": the us/them, researcher/researched dichotomy that these words imply is antithetical to the purpose of this research project.

4. This name and other names and places are pseudonyms to help ensure privacy for "the researched."

5. This process, always in the public [sub]consciousness, has been explored by many, but see especially Victor Turner (1974) or Arnold van Gennep (1960).

6. Of course, the best research intentions may go astray. Witness, for example, Matthews Masayuki Hamabata's (1986) efforts where he was mistaken for a knowledgeable insider in Japan until the degree of his Americanization gave him away and redefined the questions he could ask as well as the answers he might receive. Hamabata found, in the end, that "I may have wanted the 'other me' to die when I left the field, but he simply refused to stop existing. He haunts me still" (p. 368).

7. But the Red Cross has begun to prescribe this: there is now a program, which definitively directs the teaching of infants. This, by the Red Cross, follows several attempts by other privately-owned groups to gain the market for "water adjustment" classes.

8. I imagine his day-to-day suffering was ameliorated by two facts: (a) he was taking in a decently large amount of money from the swim lessons, and (b) the success or failure of the swim school intimately affected both he and his family. Also, he seemed to feel that he was performing an altruistic function for the local community. For my part, the investment was similar to the investment in any terminal job: I worked, got paid, and tried to forget about the work when I left.

9. A recent example is the press' criticism of Rick Carey, who had won the 200-meter backstroke in the 1984 Los Angeles Olympics, yet was visibly disappointed because he had not bettered his time.

10. Interestingly, a recent brochure put out by the International Swimming Hall of Fame advertises a "time window," which is described as a "miniature stop watch [that] fits on the lens of your favorite goggle. (Suction cup allows for easy installation)."

11. Only recently has the whole method been utilized. See *The American National Red Cross, Swimming and Aquatics Safety* (1981).

12. Or try to "teach" such a feel for the water. See, for instance, Cecil Colwin (1987/1988).

13. See Homan (1980, pp. 48–49) who notes that "[pentecostal] old-timers hold a generalized view of sociology as 'communist inspired' or 'atheistic.' . . . [They said] that pentecost was something in the heart, in implicit contradistinction to sociological research which belonged to the head." Also see David Briggs (1993, p. B1) who wrote that "[Former New York Jet Dennis] Byrd was left paralyzed from the neck down, beginning a painful spiritual odyssey in which the religious athlete alternated between focusing his hopes on the biblical passages that tell of miraculous healings and those that admonish believers to accept God's will, what ever the consequences. . . . 'I believed it was Satan that moved against me,' he says" or see Von Hoffmann and Cassidy's (1956) article on "Interviewing Negro Pentecostals."

References

Adler, P.A., & Adler, P. (1987). *Membership roles in field research*. Newbury Park, CA: Sage.

Becker, H. (1986). *Writing for social scientists: How to start and finish your thesis, book, or article*. Chicago: University of Chicago Press.

Bell, K. (1982). *Winning isn't normal*. Austin, TX: Keel Publications.

Briggs, D. (1993). "Football player keeps faith after debilitating injury." *The Idaho Star Journal*, September 24, p. B1.

Colwin, C. (1987/1988). "That magic touch." *Swimming Technique*, 24, 10–14.

Denzin, N.K. (1989). *The research act: A theoretical introduction to sociological methods*, 3rd ed. Englewood Cliffs, NJ: Prentice-Hall.

———— (1991). "Representing Lived Experiences in Ethnographic Texts," *Studies in Symbolic Interaction*, 12, 59–70.

Foucault, M. (1977). Discipline and punish: The birth of the prison. New York: Pantheon.

Goffman, E. (1973). *The presentation of self in everyday life*. Woodstock, NY: Overlook Press.

Greendorfer, S.L. (1987). "Psycho-social correlates of physical activity." *Journal of Physical Education, Recreation and Dance*, 58(7), 59–64.

Hamabata, M.M. (1986). "Ethnographic boundaries: Culture, class and sexuality in Tokyo." *Qualitative Sociology*, 9(4), 354–371.

Homan R. (1980). "The ethics of covert methods." *British Journal of Sociology*, 31(1), 46–65.

Kottak, C.P. (1989). "Swimming in cross-cultural currents." In A. Podolefsky & P.J. Brown (Eds.), *Applying anthropology: An introductory reader* (pp. 126–131). Mountain View, CA: Mayfield Publishing Company.

McCarthy Brown, K. (1991). *Mama Lola: A Vodou priestess in Brooklyn*. Berkeley, CA: University of California Press.

Mitchell, R.G. (1993). *Secrecy and fieldwork*. Newbury Park, CA: Sage.

Prebish, C.S. (1993). *Religion and sport: The meeting of the sacred and profane*. Westport, CT: Greenwood Press.

Sprawson, C. (1992). *Haunts of the Black masseur: The swimmer as hero*. New York: Pantheon.

The American National Red Cross, Swimming and Aquatics Safety (1981). Washington, DC: The American National Red Cross.

Turner, V. (1974). *Dramas, fields, and metaphors: Symbolic action in human society*. Ithaca, NY: Cornell University Press.

van Gennep, A. (1960). *The rites of passage*. Chicago: University of Chicago Press.

Von Hoffmann, N. & Cassidy, S.W. (1956). "Interviewing Negro Pentecostals." *American Journal of Sociology*, 62, 195–197.

PART II

SPORT AND THE POSTMODERN (DE)CONSTRUCTION OF GENDER

4

Representing Black Masculinity and Urban Possibilities: Racism, Realism, and *Hoop Dreams*

Cheryl L. Cole and Samantha King

Introduction: Heaven Is a Playground

At first glance, the new journalistic take on poverty seems liberal, but conservatives will find a lot to like.

—Michael Massing

Over two decades ago, Rick Telander, now a well-known, popular sports journalist, wrote *Heaven is a Playground*. The ethnojournalistic narrative, based on "research" Telander conducted during the summer of 1974, chronicles the ways in which basketball shapes the lives of a group of African American youths who spend their time at Brooklyn's Foster Park. Foster Park borders a four city block housing project, the Vandeverr Homes, which shelters over 10,000 people.[1] The values and themes organizing *Heaven is a Playground* are condensed in what Telander, late in the book, depicts as an epiphanic moment during a game that occurs between the Subway Stars (a team constituted by second tier and undisciplined Foster Park players who have recruited Telander to serve as their coach) and a team from Bedford-Stuyvesant. Telander describes the scene in Bedford-Stuyvesant that sets the stage for his clarifying moment:

At the park itself decay is manifest. Three of six rims are missing, the fences are bowed, garbage litters the area like leaves in a forest. The main court is so coated with glass fragments that it sparkles in the sun like a beach. Everyone [the locals] at the park seems angry, it appears to me, with sneers and frowns and evil looks creasing their dark faces. What they are angry at, I can't tell. (1976, p. 159)

By Telander's view, the Subway Stars play a disorganized, self-centered, flashy playground game while the Bedford-Stuyvesant Restoration League team plays highly disciplined, fundamentally sound, team-oriented basketball. As he watches the game, Telander keys in on the Bedford-Stuyvesant coach, George Murden. He witnesses (what he understands to be) Murden's respect for his players and the threat of violence in Murden's eyes as he insists on player silence and obedience. Moreover, as Telander watches Murden and the action on the court, he narrates what he imagines to be causal links between disciplined coaching and disciplined play, success, transformation, and transcendence. As the Bedford-Stuyvesant players "work and sweat and succeed they fill up with pride, the angry furrows disappear. I watch as he [Murden] scolds them during a break, see the respect that comes from being important enough to be scolded, and while I'm watching the game ends" (1976, pp. 161–162). Despite Telander's bewildered response to the anger he noted upon his arrival, he confidently identifies the cause of its dissipation: a style of play cultivated by exercising discipline over players; the instillation of the work ethic and self-restraint; the effectivity and affectivity of the surrogate father-coach who performs his role properly. Given his newfound wisdom, Telander is uncharacteristically scolding and authoritative with the Subway Stars as they travel back to Foster Park.

Rick Telander's depiction is unwittingly revealing. While visualizing discipline through a particular style of play apparently responsible for the transformation of facial features and anger, Telander evaluates that discipline in terms of a therapeutic function that apparently abstracts, at least temporarily, the players from their historical and structural conditions. Additionally, Telander's valuation of "discipline" imagined in the space of basketball is inseparable from its ability to relieve his bewilderment, anxiety, and discomfort. Given the events and transformations he witnessed in Bedford-Stuyvesant, Telander now views his implication in the practices governing and shaping the lives of these inner-city youths in terms of his ability and willingness to properly perform as the surrogate father-coach. The necessity for discipline, the sanctioned surrogate father-coach, and transcendence (the continual elision of context) appear in various incarnations throughout the book. Discipline's worth, ultimately, is affirmed narratively and settled in Telander's conclusion that characterizes the Subway Stars, in various ways, as successful.

Written at least five years before the National Basketball Association (NBA) began its advance as a primary site of global sports-entertainment and well over a decade before Michael Jordan's achievement of unprecedented celebrity, *Heaven is a Playground* prefigures the position that urban basketball would eventually occupy as a national symbolic space of relief, reassurance, and transcendence. Moreover, Telander's book also suggests that the racially coded dichotomy of sport and gangs (which accrued psychic and social force as the NBA and Michael Jordan gained visibility during the mid to late 1980s America) had been set in motion:

> It is common saying in the ghettos of Brooklyn that if a boy is bad he joins a gang; if he is good he plays basketball. Indeed, outright crime or idleness aside, there is not much else a boy can do. To ask any sampling of young men from Brownsville, Williamsburg, Bedford-Stuyvesant, or East New York about their formative years, is to get variations on only two answers: "I ran with the wrong dudes," or "I played basketball" . . . . Of course, the two roles are not mutually exclusive. Ultimately . . . the paths of behavior—call it the good and the bad—must split and a choice must be made. (1976, pp. 12–13)

Although consistent with the contemporary popular codification of inner city life and its correlate masculinities, *Heaven is a Playground* never attained the wide audience achieved by Darcy Frey's (1994) *The Last Shot: City Streets, Basketball Dreams* or the documentary film *Hoop Dreams*.[2] Indeed, the popular receptions of *Hoop Dreams* and *The Last Shot* are intricately bound within an historical context that has shaped and has been shaped by America's fascination with and acquired literacy of "urban problems," particularly as those problems were rendered visible through coming of age narratives of African American male youth. Stated differently, *Hoop Dreams* and *The Last Shot* appear in an historical moment in which black bodies and masculinity have become highly commodified and marketable. Michael Massing (1995) underscores America's fascination with the racially codified sector of the post-industrial inner city by drawing attention to the now familiar journalistic translations of ghetto poverty into public consumer spectacle: "The inner city, a subject long neglected by journalists, is suddenly in vogue. So many writers, photographers, and documentary filmmakers are heading out to housing projects and street corners that it's a wonder they don't trip over one another. Their output from the last year alone would fill a small depository" (p. 32).

The 1980s and 1990s have seen a proliferation of popular books about the inner city, including Alex Kotolowitz's (1992) *There are No Children Here*; Daniel Coyle's (1995) *Hardball: A Season in the Projects*; Greg Donaldson's (1994) *The Ville: Cops and Kids in Urban America*; and Darcy Frey's (1994) *The Last Shot: City Streets, Basketball Dreams*. All of these narratives privilege "inner-city youth" and are organized as coming-of-age struggles that take shape in the post-Fordist—what Neil Smith (1996) has called the "revanchist"—city. While these journalistic portrayals of urban life potentially enter and intervene in America's public debate over federal assistance and urban problems, the analyses of urban youths' conditions and struggles are, according to Massing (1995), typically moved forward at the expense of their parents: an older generation of African Americans are held responsible for the obstacles and struggles that condition the youths' everyday lived experiences.[3] While "real" racially coded coming of age stories have increased in popularity, they have failed to introduce alternative or oppositional knowledges into public debates.

Moreover, racially coded coming-of-age narratives have accrued political purchase as they have been transmitted to consumers through figures such as Magic Johnson, Isiah Thomas, and Michael Jordan, whose increasing visibility in the public domain remains bound (enabled and limited) to the NBA's economic development and success. Both the NBA's increased economic viability and the array of African American celebrities who figure America's "favorite themes" have been, on the whole, resolutely shaped by late modern America's reordering of economic and cultural priorities. NBA superstars were created through and provided fertile ground for narratives of limited scope that emphasized recovery, transformation, transcendence, and utopic social visions. Racially codified versions of celebratory entrepreneurial tales associated with Lee Iacoca and Peter Ueberroth traverse multiple NBA bodies (e.g., Magic Johnson, Michael Jordan, David Robinson, Shaquille O'Neal, Grant Hill, and Penny Hardaway) and appear in various incarnations such as "I have a dream" ("A Penny from heaven"—Penny Hardaway); "savior" ("A Grant from God"—Grant Hill); "hero" ("Would I still be your hero?"—Michael Jordan).[4] Indeed, the complex marketing network that territorialized the NBA's celebrity zone privileged seemingly incontrovertible evidence of self-improvement, self-reliance, self-determination, and "choice" as it simultaneously produced an apparently endless supply of morality and cautionary tales. Although narrated through "personal qualities," NBA celebrities appear as objects of public consumption that embody the promise of commodities. Morality tales of promise and possibility for individuals, families, and nation (the consumption problematic) circulated through the NBA celebrity zone accrued purchase through the often invisible, but nonetheless affective, rhetorical figure of the gang member. Black urban masculinity was visualized (enacted and encoded) through a fundamental distinction between the athlete (primarily figured in the urban basketball player) and the criminal (typically figured through the gang member): the tension generated between the two categories served as the ground for well-rehearsed and familiar 1980s' stories continually circulated and fed by the mass media industry for public consumption and spectatorship. The appeal of the tension grounding those relationships (both the racially coded athlete and criminal and their consumption) is manifest in the popularity and fiscal success of the second wave of black filmmaking. The second wave included films such as Spike Lee's (1989) *Do the Right Thing*, Matty Rich's (1991) *Straight Out of Brooklyn*, and John Singleton's (1991) *Boyz N the Hood*.[5] Moreover, that tension has served as the impetus and basis for episodes of prime time "law-and-order" television shows like *New York Undercover* and *NYPD Blue*.

In this chapter, we discuss the popularly acclaimed, three-hour, low-budget, independent documentary *Hoop Dreams*. Perhaps no other media event demonstrates more forcefully than *Hoop Dreams* America's fascination with the particularity of the urban coming-of-age struggles as they are figured through urban basketball players. Although documentaries are typically relegated to the margins of the American film industry and popular media, *Hoop Dreams* drew a phenomenal amount of support and more popular attention than any other documentary this decade. Described as "beautifully made" and "one of the best and most deeply moving American films of 1994," *Hoop Dreams* quickly became a mega-hit in the United States. Popular critics have deployed "achievement" as the key term to indicate that the film intervened in, by offering a powerful contrast to, previous and more familiar documentations of the inner city, urban problems, and African American inner-city youth.

Given the weight of the racist order that the documentary would need to overcome to even simply disturb historically conditioned "ways of seeing" so-called "urban problems," "racism," "whiteness," and "America" (which we deploy as a signifier for an identity fabricated through imagined origins, community, and character), we examine the national celebratory reception of *Hoop Dreams*. Rather than offering a powerful contrast to previous and more familiar documentations of the inner city, urban problems, and African American inner-city youth, we think that the film encodes and enacts a series of now familiar themes, events, and figures whose terms actively limit how we imagine violence, power, and our selves in late modern America. We see the film and its popular representations as consistent with a national spirit and imagination inseparable from the prominence accrued by African American basketball players over the last decade. Moreover, we suggest that this prominence needs to be understood within wider global transformations that have devastated, reordered, and revitalized urban areas in ways that are indissolubly linked to the perverse profitability of the transnational corporations (in this case, we draw particular attention to those associated with the NBA and athletic apparel). We consider the "urban basketball player," who is implicated in these networks, to be a subject and object of late modern forms of discipline and consumption. In Lauren Berlant's (1993) terms,

> these stars [are] transformed into trademarks and corporate logos, prosthetic bodies that ideally replace the body of pain with the projected image of safety and satisfaction that commodities represent. (p. 178)

As such, these stars (NBA celebrities) are key figures in a reconfigured racism that allows American (middle-class) audiences to recognize themselves as compassionate and ethical subjects in 1990s America. Our primary concern in this paper is to examine the production of this self-recognition and its implication in the NBA body as a late modern form of discipline and object of public consumption. Investigating "the problematic" of this psychic and social consumption requires that we recognize race as not simply possessive or performative but always contingent and relational.

We contend that America's celebratory reception of *Hoop Dreams* is a celebration of a production whose truth-effect is the self-recognized ethical and compassionate subject.[6] As such, the celebratory reception is intimately bound to a series of exclusions and displacements that inform America's dominant reading of the film. To a great extent, these exclusions and displacements are embodied in the "origin stories" promoted by the mainstream media. By our view, these origin stories are indicative of both America's historical amnesia and its correlate conception of history shaping dominant readings. Moreover, we contend that the film's primary figure of exploitation and social wrongs, "Gene Pingatore," functions as a figure for displacements that allow American middle-class audiences to derive identification and pleasures from the film. In other words, guilt and the audience's implication in exploitative spectatorship and consumption practices are displaced onto Pingatore. We argue that such figures of exploitation and social wrongs work to protect particular understandings of America as they repress the banal violences and monstrosities that shape the everyday lives of already-vulnerable populations in urban areas. Stated differently, we read *Hoop Dreams* as an expression of a national imagination and spirit that represses and displaces violence under the guise of care, compassion, social cause, and ethical superiority.

The Urban Basketball Player: The Literal and the Figural[7]

What if there were no sports . . . would I still be your hero?

—Michael Jordan

In this section we draw from and build on Cole's (1996a, 1996b) previous work in which she discussed how, during the 1980s, knowledges of urban problems were, to a great extent, produced and rendered visible through the categories of "sport" and "gangs." Sport and gangs, visualized in terms established through their dyadic relation, were positioned as the two most important influences in the lives of African American youth. They were also recognized as not only external pressures but expressions of internal forces, which is to say, sport and gangs rendered intelligible the individual character. While gang members were seen as the embodiment of alien values, athletes were viewed as the embodiment of dominant values. These dominant values were displayed most prominently in assimilationist repetitions of "desires to exit," to "find a way out" of the ghetto. Sport and gangs appeared in the realm of public culture, mediating and representing African American male youth. As public consumer spectacle, the sport/gang dyad governed and organized a way of looking, seeing, and recognizing urban America, its problems, and their causes.

Although not immediately apparent, the figures of sport and gangs were "joined" by a third factor—the failed black family (perhaps the most familiar means of conceptualizing inner city poverty and dependency in 1980s America).[8] Represented not only as channels for what are understood to be the corporeal predispositions of African American youth, sport and gangs were represented as the available substitutes for the "failed black family" (figured through the welfare mother and the absent inseminating black male). That is, the "failed black family" (an historical mechanism for displacing the social, economic, and political forces shaping the lives of the urban poor) never simply lurked in the background lending plausibility to the significance of sport and gangs in the lives of urban youth. Instead, the racially coded pathological family, urban sport, and gangs occupied the same symbolic space: violations of the nuclear family form were a subtext in coming of age narratives. The racially coded pathological family, the most powerful defining feature of the dyad, braced and intensified the psychic power of the racially coded sport/gang relation in the national imagination.

It was in the context of 1980s post-industrial America that urban sport, most explicitly basketball, was narrated as indispensable to racially coded urban community production, independence, and well-being. As the figure of the coach came to represent the sanctioned surrogate father, sport was depicted as not only the individual's, but the inner city's means for realizing America's utopic promise. Gang members, whose alien values were represented through the breach of the work ethic, failed discipline, pathological greed, compulsion, and incomprehensible violence, were depicted as responsible for urban breakdown, disorder, and impoverishment. As gangs accrued their popular meanings in relation to sport, the structural conditions and social practices shaping America's inner cities were territorialized through the somatic corresponding to these two practices. This somatic territorialization works to displace the violences of late modern economy while reducing participation in sport and gangs to an expression of truth of being and individual choice—thereby organizing and directing cultural anxieties, deepening contempt, and exacerbating desires for revenge. Intensified policing and excessive punishment directed at urban black youth are clear expressions of the desire for revenge which, by William Connolly's (1995) view, underlie the contemporary will to punish.[9]

We assume that the sport/gang dyad tells us more about the national imagination than it does about African American youth. We take African American novelist James Baldwin's declaration that: "The country's image of the Negro which hasn't much to do with the Negro has never failed to reflect with a frightening kind of accuracy the *state of mind of the country*" (cited in Riggs, 1991, emphasis added), as our necessary point of departure. Baldwin's declaration suspends the modernist separation of subject and object as it contests the common sense (and scientific) epistemology of representation. Realist codes, in this case the documentary codes of *Hoop Dreams*, create an illusory separation between subject (the filmmakers) and object (that produced under observation) as they appeal to a scientific/realist epistemology of representation. That is, the documentary effectively and affectively recodes subjectivity, of which it is an expression, into objectivity.

Moreover, by following Baldwin's suggestion that images of blackness (in this case, two extremely different but intertwined representations of African American urban youth) are indicative of the nation's state of mind rather than the expression of an object's ontological status, we draw attention to the complicated links among the territorialization of space, political and moral orders, sight, and corporeal identity that constitute white normative culture. The visual domain is more complicated than it seems: processes of objectivity and subjectivity are intertwined and bound within the history of "nation." In other words, the sport/gang dyad never simply names what and who urban youth are, but is a mechanism for understanding what and who "we" (America and Americans) are. The figural expression produced through the dyad serves as a means of orienting our selves in terms of a nation and ethics.

It is in the context through which this racially coded dyad is forged and gains political, social, and psychic force, that the NBA, Nike, and Hollywood's second black film wave flourish economically and as sites of knowledge production. It is also in this context that other forms of black popular culture, like Hip-Hop, become controversial and threatening. It is against this background that NBA celebrities are embraced and Michael Jordan appears as an affective figure in the national symbolic (i.e., Jordan appears as a representative figure implicated in national fantasies of origin, organization, and character—what Cole has discussed as the making of "American Jordan"). It is also against and within these pressures that "the sneaker" gains an unprecedented semiotic position in the national imagination, particularly as it is recruited into a media hyped crime wave that feeds on the shocking and incomprehensible.[10] It is in this context that the "prison-industrial complex" becomes one of America's largest growth industries.[11] Finally, it is in this context that transnational corporations define themselves as socially responsible by aligning themselves with so-called inner-city sport programs like Nike's P.L.A.Y. Campaign—ostensibly designed to address urban problems. Such campaigns are not only embedded in the sport/gang dyad, but reposition the perverse profitability of transnational corporations like Nike as part of the solution rather than part of the problem.

Hoop Dreams: The Film

No movie has ever done more to deflate the hot air out of racial stereotyping without making a big deal out of it.

—Mike Clark

Contrary to the rave reviews it has received, there is nothing spectacular or technically outstanding about the film. It is not an inventive piece of work. Indeed, it must take its place within the continuum of traditional anthropological and/or ethnographic documentary works that show us the "dark other" from the standpoint of whiteness. Inner-city, poor, black communities, seen as "jungles" by many Americans, become in this film a zone white filmmakers have crossed boundaries to enter, to document . . . their subjects.

—bell hooks

Hoop Dreams is a three-hour documentary filmed between 1986 and 1991. The film focuses on the experiences of two African-American teenagers growing up in racially segregated Chicago neighborhoods. Although only 14, William Gates and Arthur Agee already demonstrate the sort of basketball skills that suggest that they will be recruited to play at the college level and possibly employed to play in the NBA. The film, which begins as they prepare to enter high school and concludes as they begin their career college careers, is organized around their high school years. Viewer position and context are immediately established through the opening juxtaposed images: the viewer travels the expressway north toward the Chicago skyline. As the elevated train running parallel to the expressway moves into the frame, a group of young men playing basketball on the court below come into view. The camera follows a player (who we will later recognize as William Gates), as he approaches the basket to shoot; the graffiti-laden concrete wall surrounding the court comes into focus. The camera moves around a concrete high rise, the sign of urban housing projects, to reveal the "Chicago Stadium" as fans enter to attend the 38th annual NBA All-Star game. A picture-perfect steal and dunk by the East's #23, Michael Jordan, is met by overwhelmingly white, exuberant spectators as they celebrate the physical achievement they have just witnessed.

As the All-Star Game (apparently) continues inside Chicago Stadium, the elevated train moves us to the Cabrini Green Housing Project, where William lives with his mother, Emma, and brother, Curtis. Although housing projects signify danger, the alien, and the anti-normative in the national imagination, Cabrini Green is introduced not through signs of decay nor danger, but signs of community. Signs of "typical" (normal) summertime neighborhood activity surround Cabrini Green: youngsters play in the high spray of an open fire hydrant as a local means of dealing with the heat; men, who lean against parked cars, and women, who mingle on the sidewalk and sit on their front stoops, engage in neighborly exchanges; two young boys play basketball on a make shift court in the corner of the building.[12] As the camera lingers outside the door to someone's home, the sounds of the NBA All-Star game inside suggest that despite their geographical dispersion, the images are temporally bound. Inside, we see William intensely watching the closing moments of the All-Star game. He steps outside his apartment, and onto the playground court, where we watch him, in slow motion, dunk on a netless rim.

> Right now [close up of William, expressing his aspirations through a wide smile], I want, you know, to play in the NBA like anybody else would want to be. That's who, tha's, tha's somethin I dream-think about all the time, you know, playin in the NBA. [Cut to another slow motion image of William dunking on the netless rim, now accompanied by the cheers we heard earlier in Chicago stadium. Then, to an extreme close up of William's mother:] He's just doin somethin' that he love so much. He jus love it so much, you know, I'm just happy for him. [Extreme close up of Curtis, William's older brother:] If someone can understan the way William play that will make me feel a lot better. I say they, well, they, they should've understood the way I play.

The camera takes us to the West Garfield Park Neighborhood where Arthur lives with his mother, father, sister, and brother. Again, in the intimacy of a home where the NBA All-Star game plays on television (we hear the announcer introducing Isiah Thomas), a smiling Arthur describes his desires and imagined NBA life:

> When I get in the NBA, I'm . . . ah, the first thing I'm gonna do is I gonna see my momma, I'm gonna buy her a house. I'm gonna make sure my sista and brotha's okay [met by shouts of approval from brother and sister]. Probably get my dad . . . a Cadillac, Oldsmobile, so he can

cruise in the game. [Over the image of an in trance-like state Arthur apparently gazing at the television screen, Arthur's mother describes her son's dream of fame and economic success in terms of his commodity identification.] He dreams about it . . . He look at those basketball commercials when . . . they be advertising like these Nike shoes and he'll tell, he'll tell his little small brother Joe: "Joe, that's me." [Cut to Arthur as he does a 360 on the way to the basket, ostensibly emulating Isiah Thomas. This effect is created by the images of Isiah Thomas (apparently taken from the televised All-Star Game) performing a similar move, and then of Arthur, repeating the move. This is then followed by a close up of Arthur's father, Bo:] I don't even think about it . . . You know, if he don't make it, I'm so, so focused on him making it, I just know he'll make it.

We watch as Arthur is "discovered" by Earl Smith on one of his "expeditions" to a park near Central and Congress Parkway. Smith, an insurance executive and "unofficial scout" for area high schools, instantly recognizes Arthur's talent and arranges for him to attend St. Joseph's summer basketball camp. St. Joseph High School, which remains the featured education-basketball structure in the film, is a predominantly white, private, Roman Catholic school in Westchester, a western suburb of Chicago. It maintains its position as one of Chicago's high school basketball powerhouses by recruiting players from across the city. As Earl Smith drives Arthur to St. Joseph's summer camp, the visual contrast of suburban houses, manicured lawns, and widespread serenity indicates that the distance Arthur and William will eventually negotiate daily exceeds the geographical.

Based on his basketball skills and performance at the camp, Arthur is recruited to play for St. Joseph High School by Gene Pingatore, the head basketball coach. In a conversation with Arthur and his family, Pingatore not too cautiously promises that Arthur's chances of securing a college scholarship will be enhanced by attending St. Joseph:

Basketball has to be second to your academics, if you don't get your grades, you're not going to play. But if you work hard at your grades, and if you work hard at basketball, then I'll be able to help you as far as going to college. And I guarantee this ["Gene Pingatore, Head Basketball Coach" appears on the screen]. I can't promise you where you're going to go and if you're going to be a star, but I guaran-*tee* that I will help you get into the school that will be best for you [cut to a photograph of Isiah Thomas, Arthur's idol, the embodiment of his hopes and dreams, in his Indiana uniform]. I'm making this commitment to you, if you make a commitment to be part of this kind of program.

Pingatore admits (apparently in conversation with the filmmakers who remain off camera) uncertainty about Arthur's potential given the "playground" (which he defines as talent without confidence) he sees in him. However, Pingatore sees it all, which he defines as a "combination of personality, confidence, talent, intelligence," in another new recruit, William Gates. Both Arthur and William are given partial scholarships from St. Joseph and, like Isiah Thomas, will commute three hours daily by train to attend the school. Their first year, William "starts" on the varsity squad while Arthur wins the freshman team starting point guard position. While both entered reading at a fourth-grade level, we routinely see William, whose academic skills improve dramatically his first year, in the classroom. Arthur's academic work does not advance at the same rate: he appears less interested in his high school education and seems to view it as a required detour on his way to the NBA. Gene Pingatore verbalizes his hesitations about Arthur's ability to adapt to the new environment:

> When Arthur first started at St. Joseph's, he was a good kid from what we saw, but he was very immature. He might have been a little more disruptive, speaking out, getting into childish things. He wasn't used to the discipline and control. He reverted back to, maybe, his environment, where he came from.

In contrast to Pingatore's reservations, we see signs of Arthur's desires to negotiate the distance between the inner city and suburban environment: a clip of Arthur in preppy attire is followed by a clip of his mother who says that she saw immediate changes in her son, particularly in terms of his maturity. Meanwhile, through a series of up-beat, last-minute, high-drama game-day scenes, we learn that William is also excelling on the basketball court and drawing attention from Division I schools and sports writers who appear on a television talk show and have identified him as the next Isiah Thomas.

A tuition increase at the beginning of their sophomore year creates potential problems for both students. Patricia Wier, President of Encyclopedia Britannica, makes a contribution to a scholarship fund that, in combination with other sources including "Cycle" (a Cabrini Green organization), covers William's tuition. In an interview, she tells the audience that she is also pleased to have given William a summer job with the company. By mid-semester, Arthur is forced to leave St. Joseph's because his parents have been unable to make the required tuition payments and now owe St. Joseph $1,500. This is due, in part, to the cycle of hiring and lay-offs that Bo Agee is caught up in throughout the film. Sheila Agee, Arthur, and the coach at Arthur's new school, Marshall High, believe that Arthur's expulsion was due to his failure to live up to coach Gene Pingatore's expectations. As Arthur enters the local public school, the visual narrative paints a stark contrast between the well-maintained, ordered, suburban private school with its conventionally polite and attentive students, and the dilapidated, overcrowded, and chaotic inner-city school that Arthur now attends. Shortly after Arthur has started at Marshall High School and against a backdrop of family photographs and a melancholic saxophone, the narrator tells us that after 20 years of marriage, Arthur's father, Bo, has left the family. When we next see Bo, he has apparently come to visit Arthur at the local playground. But, the narrator's voice-over identifies the playground court as a site that has "increasingly . . . become a place to buy and sell drugs," as we see Bo gesture with bills to a group of young men as he is leaving. The camera cuts to Arthur who appears visibly disturbed as he watches the interaction.

Forced to quit her job due to chronic back pain prior to Bo leaving the family, Sheila Agee eventually receives welfare. She expresses her discomfort with receiving public assistance (apparently aware of, as she implicitly responds to, dominant understanding of "welfare generations") by contrasting her situation to that of her parents who always worked for a living. Sheila Agree's economic vulnerability is made apparent when, within a year of receiving welfare, she is denied three months of payments for missing an appointment. Unable to pay utility bills, the electricity and gas are cut off in their apartment, and we see Sheila carrying a lamp which she has plugged in at a neighbor's house. The impoverishment cycle continues when Arthur turns 18 (a birthday of particular significance for his mother since, as she explains, many young black men don't live to 18) and is no longer eligible to receive public aid. In frustration Sheila Agee turns to the camera and asks: "Do you all wonder sometime how I'm livin? Or how my children survive? It's enough to make people really want to go out, lash out, and hurt somebody."

Soon after, Arthur's best friend and teammate Shannon moves into the Agee household to escape problems at his home. In an interview, Shannon talks about the importance of his friendship with Arthur, and Bo's drug use, violent behavior, and time in jail. As Sheila explains that she has taken out a protection order against Bo, her words fade to music, and the camera sweeps over a collection of legal papers. The camera lingers on black type that allows us to read documentation of Bo's criminal record:

GUILTY—BATTERY
GUILTY—BURGLARY
SENTENCED TO IMPRISONMENT—JAIL 37 DAYS
SENTENCED TO PROBATION 2 YEARS
[A hazy and darkened mug shot of Bo follows and the camera zooms in on this image until the mug shot fills the screen.]

William's freshman and sophomore challenges were narrated around and confined to trying to lead his team to the state tournament; however, during his junior year, William injures his knee and then reinjures it in an exhausting and intense practice session. Under doctor's instructions, he reluctantly sits out the rest of the season. Indeed, it is under the stress of his knee surgery and when his basketball career is in jeopardy that Emma Gates reveals her desire and investment in William's professional basketball career: "I really thought Curtis was gonna make it, but he didn't make it, so I just wanted this one to make it." Curtis, a high school stand out, and player of the decade at Colby Junior College (clips of Curtis' performances from 1985 while at Colby demonstrate his astonishing and exceptional basketball talent), developed a reputation for being difficult. Although awarded a scholarship to the University of Central Florida, he dropped out of school because of a conflict with the coach. The clips from Colby do far more than demonstrate Curtis' exceptional talent, they make inexplicable his refusal to abide by the rules. Both Curtis and his mother provide testimony confirming that the promises made in the name of sport were not realized because of the individual choices made by Curtis. Now working for a security firm, Curtis describes his life in term of his disappointment in being just another guy. When he loses his job, he identifies himself as a complete failure: "I ain't amounted to nothin'." He, too, expressed his investment in William making it: "All those basketball dreams I had is gone. All my dreams is in him now. I want him to make it so bad, I don't know what to do." Once injured, the instability of his knee most explicitly organizes William's narrative of uncertainty.

Arthur's narration remains governed by the unpredictability of his basketball and academic skills along with the unpredictability and potential reversibility of events in his family. While at Marshall High School, Arthur grows taller, his game improves dramatically, and he becomes a star in Chicago's public school league and the local media. While Arthur succeeds on the basketball court, he continues to struggle with his academic work. During visits to Marshall High, teachers, counselors, and Arthur's coach express concern at his mediocre grades and attitude toward his classroom work. We also see Arthur in Spanish class, in which he clowns around for the camera, and in summer school for students who have failed English. In the meantime, one year after he left, Bo has rejoined the family. Accompanying scenes of the reunited Agee family on their way to church, the narrator tells us that Bo has spent one year in jail and overcome an addiction to crack cocaine. Once inside the church, Sheila and Bo are blessed by the minister and Bo sings a song asking for God's forgiveness. Arthur watches with apparent skepticism, impatience, and even irritation. Immediately following the redemption scene, Arthur is shown describing his feelings toward his father:

When I was little, he had let me down. All these people use to come up sayin your father's a drug addict, your father's on drugs and stuff. And I'd be like, yeah, o.k., you know, I jus take so much, you know. Dat, you know, he has to start realizin dat, you know, that, you know, what he is doin, you know, cos I know sometime dat he used to try to go to church sometimes, you know, why he still on drugs, why he was still tryin to go to church.

Following the reunion of the Agee family, Arthur's mother graduates as a nurse's assistant. Arthur's high school team eventually makes it to the State championships in Champaign, Illinois, where Arthur leads his team to third place position, the team's best performance since 1960. Since St. Joseph's has yet again failed to make it to the state tournament, Gene Pingatore watches as a spectator. Arthur is on track for a scholarship to a major university but cannot meet the S.A.T. requirements. He receives an athletic scholarship from Mineral Area Junior College in Missouri where he lives in "Basketball House"—a dormitory located in the middle of a field, far removed from the rest of the campus—along with six of the seven black students at this predominantly white college.

In the meantime, William and his girlfriend Catherine have had a child, Alicia. In two scenes in which the three of them appear together, William and Catherine discuss the anxiety they suffered on learning of her pregnancy and the arguments caused by William being unable to attend the birth. He had an important game that day and Pingatore, William recalls later, was unsympathetic to his family commitments. At this stage in the film, William visits his father, who, according to the narrator, has not lived with the family since William was a baby. His father gives him a tour of his auto-repair yard and invites him to attend a performance by his band. In a postmortem of the visit, William expresses distaste for his father's behavior and claims that his father is only now showing interest because he hopes to profit from William's basketball career. William describes his disappointment with his father's absence from the family and declares his intention to be a good, loyal father.

Despite his recurring knee injury and struggles to attain the minimum S.A.T. score, William performed well at the Nike summer basketball camp and has received an athletic scholarship offer from Marquette University, Milwaukee. The movie ends with William on his way to Marquette, but uncertain of his desire to pursue a basketball career. In a written postscript, the filmmakers tell us that Arthur graduated from Mineral Area with a C average and went on to study at Arkansas State University, a Division I school, where he played starting point guard: "a national basketball magazine judged the team's success to be largely dependent on Arthur's success. In his first start, Arthur hit a 30-foot jump shot at the buzzer to win the game."[13] William, we are told, married Catherine, who moved to Marquette with their daughter. In his junior year, William became increasingly disillusioned with basketball and decided to drop out of school. His family persuaded him otherwise and the University agreed to let him continue studying, without playing basketball.

America Responds to Hoop Dreams

Hoop Dreams is the most powerful movie about sports ever made. . . . This extraordinary documentary about two teenagers who dream of becoming NBA stars is so absorbing and comprehensive and generally profound that it transcends the narrow parameters of the genre. . . . Certainly no other movie—documentary or dramatic feature—in recent memory provides such a vivid account of inner-city culture.

—Hal Hinson

Since its premier at the 1994 Sundance Film Festival in Park City, Utah (the premiere show case for independent films), *Hoop Dreams* has received widespread and enthusiastic endorsement. *Hoop Dreams* won Sundance's "Audience Award" over 16 other documentaries ranging in subject matter from insanity, AIDS, and apartheid to gangs, the L.A. riots, and Cuban youth (Seigel, 1994). Madonna even attempted to buy the story rights to the film. *Hoop Dreams*, also an audience favorite at the Toronto Festival, was the first documentary awarded the New York Film Festival's distinguished closing position. That showing was met with a 10-minute standing ovation which filmmaker Steve James portrayed:

The people at the festival said nothing like this had ever happened before. The audience was just standing there, clapping for the connection they felt for those families. It was the most amazing experience of my life . . . (quoted in Howe, 1994, p. G-4)

The filmmakers signed a contract with Turner Broadcasting. Turner who own Fine Line Features, the distributer of the documentary, hired Spike Lee as executive producer and director of its made-for-television counterpart. Additionally, Turner had the capacity to cross-promote the film during its airing of NBA games. Thus, the cycle of takeovers and mergers that resulted from Reagan's deregulation policies begin to come into focus. Various teams in the NBA, including the Altanta Hawks and Golden State Warriors, supported the film by showing trailers and conducting give-away contests during their games. Moreover, Fine Line Features announced that it had "taken the film as a personal cause"—a cause it advanced with an advertising budget of only $500,000. In the words of its president, Ira Deutchman, Fine Line formulated "the most complex marketing scheme we've ever pulled off" (Collins, 1994, p. B21). The company sought to target a broad audience which included art-house patrons, sports-film fans, teenagers and inner-city children and their parents. Nike was recruited to endorse television, radio, and billboard advertisements for the movie and subsidize promotional events (the Nike logo appears on print and movie ads). Nike also helped to establish the 800 number for local community group tickets and was also credited with persuading *Sports Illustrated* to pay for the publication and mailing costs of a student/teacher study guide which accompanied the release of the film. Nike also solicited the assistance of Gannett Outdoor, a signage company, who subsidized promotional posters and billboards. Nike, having never before endorsed a film, explained that they ". . . really believed in the message of the film," a message they identified as about hope, spirit, sport, and family (Collins, 1994, p. B21).

Despite Nike's portrayal of the film, mainstream reviews endlessly applauded *Hoop Dreams* for eluding and exceeding the boundaries of seductive sport cliches. Washington Post film critic Hal Hinson suggested that, "*Hoop Dreams* provides more emotion and human drama than 10 Hollywood movies" (1994, p. F7). Popular critics proclaimed the film "an American epic" as they identified the two youths on whom the film is based in terms of instant celebrity and its filmmakers as heroes and filmic pioneers. *Hoop Dreams*, we are repeatedly told, is about something of vastly greater significance than sport: *Hoop Dreams* is about the real urban America. In the words of Michael Wilmington, "We get the true, raw emotion usually buried under the glitz and hoke of the average Hollywood-ized sports movie . . . . It isn't a slice of life-but a huge chunk of it" (1994a, pp. 13–15). *Hoop Dreams*, touted as a film that all Americans should see, was recognized as a timely, "warts and all" account of urban life and, by extension, was deemed a potent educational tool.

Indeed, reviews intimated that the youths' dreams to play professional basketball set the stage for a larger diagnostics of the inner city. The complex, realistic, and positive portrait of black inner-city life represented in *Hoop Dreams* was not, according to most mainstream reviews, typically available to middle-class America. Mainstream media accounts repeatedly implied that America was prepared for—apparently even sought—an objective account of the inner city that would challenge the dominant versions on offer. In a telling comment that punctuates the affective purchase of the documentary drama, Steve James told the *Chicago Tribune*, "White people have told us that the only contact they have with inner-city neighborhoods is what they see from their high rise. . . . But seeing a film like this, they really felt connection" (Wilmington, 1994a, pp. 13, 20). Despite the stereotypical racially-coded mythical figures that saturate America's popular culture, "white high-rise America" saw and was apparently able to recognize and embrace the "real thing." Stated differently, mainstream media accounts produced (in collaboration with *Hoop Dreams* the film) and then represented an American consensus that designated *Hoop Dreams* the official version of real life in urban America. *Boston Globe* film critic Jay Carr summarized the image:

> Very seldom does anyone seem to be playing to the camera, or even aware of it, as they undergo some wrenching family upheavals, such as one kid's being forced to leave St. Joseph's when he can't afford the tuition—not to mention face the departure of his addict father, back on drugs, and his family's subsequent humiliation at being forced to accept welfare . . . . But he and his family rally. (1994, p. 55)

Claims to film's social consciousness are repeated in reviews. Most obviously such claims are substantiated through declarations of distinctions between the treatment of the inner city and its residents in *Hoop Dreams* and other Hollywood films. While Patrick McGavin contends that "the film does not demonize inner-city life" (1994, p. 26), academic critic Lee Jones claims that the film "decenters long held stereotypes about residents who happen to live in the inner ghetto" (1996, p. 8). Jones expressed the film's broader diagnostics in terms of its intervention in routine representations of inner city residents as less than human and improperly social:

> Within it [the film] lie simple stories about the strength of the often fragmented families, the importance of the extended family in the African American community, the love shared at family celebrations and gatherings, the tremendous resilience in the face of too frequent setbacks, and the role that black women play in maintaining the family unit under the conditions of near Third World poverty. These themes take us on a journey to the other United States, capturing real human stories that remain ignored within popular debates about inner city pathology. (p. 8)

Such pronouncements and conclusions reinforced and were consistent with that identified by director Peter Gilbert as one of the filmmakers' primary concerns: "One of the things that was very important to us is that the people in the film are human beings. That they don't fit the stereotypes of inner city life" (quoted in McGavin, 1994, p. 26). The *Chicago Tribune* captured that contrast and the film's excellence in terms of its "big-picture" effect:

Hoop Dreams has the movie-equivalent of all-court vision. It picks up everything happening in the gym, in the stands and even outside. It gives us the thrill of the game, but it doesn't cheat on the vibrant social context of a deep human interest story. We understand the problems— racial, social, and economic—Arthur, William, and their families have to fight. And, because *Hoop Dreams* is real, happening right now in front of us, it involves our emotions on an exceptionally intense level. (Wilmington, 1994b, p. C7)

Through numerous media reviews, *Hoop Dreams* has come to be understood as an exemplar of realism, social advocacy, and media activism. As we have discussed, some reviewers identified *Hoop Dreams'* achievement in terms of its documentation of the real story of inner city life. Others identified the film's contribution in terms of its humane representations of poor, urban African Americans. Mainstream reviews lauded the film for its affective dimensions which were routinely attributed to its realness. Moreover, the filmmakers were commended for providing a much needed critique of certain aspects of the sport-entertainment system in the United States. Overall, *Hoop Dreams* was revered and imbued with the status of a vanguard film that furnished America with an unique educational opportunity. While such knowledge claims are most obviously made possible by the realist pretensions of documentary filmmaking, that aesthetic dimension was complemented with a narrative of integrity culled through a network of recurring themes that drew attention to the good intentions and personal virtues of its three white filmmakers: Steve James, Fred Marx, and Peter Gilbert.

Origin Stories of History and Character

Most documentary filmmakers load their cameras, track and shoot their subjects, then move on to the next quarry. But when—as with *"Hoop Dreams"*— they spend years with their subject, something richer and more elusive than their initial purpose breaks through. Then the movie isn't about catching people in the viewfinder anymore. It's about connecting with them forever.

—Desson Howe

Filmic history and context are established through an origin story (the popular constructed history of the film) in which the film is represented as an unplanned and unforeseen social accomplishment. *Hoop Dreams*, we are repeatedly told, developed out of a modest project. Initially, the filmmakers undertook a six-month project to produce a 30-minute, non-profit educational film-short about Chicago's street-basketball culture. Their intent was to compare the lives of a former NBA player who had successfully made it through the system (apparently they had Isiah Thomas in mind), a "washed-up" player whose dreams had not materialized, and a talented high-school star who aspired to join the professional ranks. The original short film project was funded by Kartemquin Educational Films, noted for "its noble poverty" (Aufderheide, 1994, p. 32).

Kartemquin Educational Films is a Chicago-based production company founded in the 1960s by three University of Chicago alumni. Kartemquin survives by making for-profit films for industry in order to fund the production of its own documentaries. A $2,000 state arts council grant provided a base from which to begin filming the newly conceived project, while Kartemquin continued to sustain the production process by providing donations and office space. That Peter Gilbert owned his own camera equipment provided further financial relief. In the end, the film cost $600,000 to make and received funding along the way from the Corporation of Public Broadcasting (which provided the first substantial grant), PBS (with whom agreements were renegotiated three times because of the filmmakers' needs), and the MacArthur Foundation. According to James, it was not until the Sundance Film Festival that film distributors began to show any interest in the film.[14] Dominant accounts that imagine the film being plucked from a sea of independent films doomed for limited release maintain the film's commercial success as purely accidental (thereby maintaining the film and filmmakers' purity) by distancing the film from the capitalist imperatives of mainstream Hollywood production and consumer driven individualism.

Media collaboration in the production of truth-effects, narrative integrity, and valorized identities is most easily observed in the disproportionate commentary devoted to the "actual making" of the film rather than the narrative of the film itself. We are repeatedly reminded that the filmmakers shot 250 hours of film over a period of four-and-one-half years, that the film was made on an extremely low budget, and that all three men accumulated huge debts in the process. As Michael Wilmington of the *Chicago Tribune* remarked, "The odds are so stacked against their [Arthur and William's] success. There's an obvious analogy with the long shot world of independent filmmaking itself" (1994a, p. 5). Along a related theme, Steve James told *The Washington Post* that the fact that him and his colleagues drove "rust bucket cars" was an important factor in gaining their subjects' trust (Howe, 1994). These unifying thematics rely on and generate easy slippages between the socio-economic conditions of the filmmakers and the Agee and Gates families. These slippages trivialize the economic and social devastation defining the conditions of the concentration of poverty in the post-Fordist inner city and the everyday lives of those who inhabit such spaces. That reviewers felt able to draw parallels between the socio-economic situation of two African

American youths from Chicago's poor inner city and the economic hardship that defines independent filmmaking is testament to the filmic and popular erasures of the historical forces shaping the lives of the urban poor. Such erasures allow for the recontextualization and the production of the film's history which contribute to filmic truth-effects.

More telling are the repetitions that portray filmmakers James, Marx, and Gilbert as acutely loyal to Arthur, William, and their families, which are inseparable from those lauding them for the financial and personal sacrifices made in order to complete the film. In what we think are symptomatic repetitions, the filmmakers appear repeatedly through the categories of loyalty and ethical superiority. We are told, that unlike others before them, these filmmakers were persistently loyal despite the difficulties Arthur and William confronted. That which the filmmakers take to be, by definition, the subject matter of the film, the predicaments encountered by Arthur and William, are narrated as "tests" of the filmmakers' character. Numerous interviews recount Steve James' depiction of Arthur's astonishment that the filmmakers continued filming him after he was expelled from St. Joseph. Similarly, several reviews draw attention to Emma Gates' initial ambivalence about the film and filmmakers and her subsequent conversion experience: it was only after the filmmakers made clear that they would not abandon William's story when a knee injury threatened his career, the she came to trust them. For example, the *Washington Post* offered the following as evidence of the filmmakers' loyalty:

> Initially, William's mother, Emma Gates—who felt she had been badly represented in a television program about the Cabrini Green housing project—didn't even want to appear on the film. But things changed after William faced a career set-back—a lingering knee injury—and the filmmakers did not desert him: Emma finally agreed to be interviewed. "She realized," says Gilbert. "We weren't going to run away because things didn't fit the storybook ideal." When a different kind of trouble threatened Arthur's basketball future, "he was literally surprised when we showed up to film him," Gilbert says. "He told us, 'Why would you want to help me now?' We said, 'It's because we care about you.' " (Howe, 1994, p. G4)

At first glance, such anecdotes may simply appear to be true, real-life, "behind-the-scene" stories or background information; yet, such anecdotes reveal America's "political unconscious" (to use Fredrick Jameson's term) as they reshape America's historical consciousness and the public's reception of *Hoop Dreams*. Such repetitions suggest that the narrative is not simply about "trust"; instead, the narrative, which is most often and most explicitly organized around the unexpected material and financial success of the film and by extension the filmmakers, appears to be motivated by anxieties about guilt. The origin narrative repeatedly relieves anxieties about guilt by drawing attention to the innocence, good will, personal virtues, and highly principled and ethical behaviors of the filmmakers. Moreover, the concentrated attention to the philanthropy of the filmmakers reverses the critique that might have ensued through a different and more historical contextualization. For example, *Hoop Dreams'* origin story fails to account for the relationship between the rise of the NBA and its role in revitalizing America's post-Fordist cities. It neglects the correspondence between the making of the African-American NBA celebrity and America's war on inner-city youth. Not coincidently, *Hoop Dreams* was initiated the same year that both Michael Jordan and crack became national preoccupations. Although elided by the origin story, the conditions of possibility of *Hoop Dreams* (by which we mean the *Hoop Dreams* portfolio, the comprehensive *Hoop Dreams* phenomenon) are embedded in a complex of transnational corporate interests including the media, the NBA, and manufacturers of sports apparel that motivate the film and its popularity. The exclusions that govern the promotional *Hoop Dreams'* origin story effectively designate, establish, and stabilize the narrative integrity of the film.

Additionally, stories of the "honorable filmmakers" allow the film to be read as a celebration of the promise of political action, social change, and racial harmony based on humanism, individual intervention, and personal interactions. Lauren Berlant (1996) helps us understand the American response that positions the filmmakers as the real heroes of *Hoop Dreams*:

> If individual practice in and around the family becomes one nodal point of postmodern national identity, another intimate sphere of public citizenship has been created as sentimental nationality's technological mirror and complement: the mass-mediated national public sphere. . . . While at other moments in U.S. history the mediations of mass culture have been seen as dangers to securing an ethical national life, the collective experiences of national mass culture now constitute a form of intimacy, like the family, whose national value is measured in its subjugation of embodied forms of public life. (p. 400)

In the public response to *Hoop Dreams*, the filmmakers' friendship with the Agees and the Gates comes to represent (for the presumed white suburban audience invited to identify with the filmmakers) a real solution to America's racial and class tensions; a fantasy that elides questions about deep-seated systematic violence of racism and economic deprivation. The aesthetic and narrative work by which the film is endowed with integrity and social advocacy, both relies on, and is productive of, a notion of sameness in which race (and, by extension, racism) no longer matters. The appeal to sameness, which displaces racism, allows white middle-class America to view itself as democratic and compassionate even at a time of increased resentment and revenge directed at already vulnerable inner-city populations. But America's ability to derive pleasure from the film, to celebrate its ethical audience position, relies on the film's criticism of sport and more specifically, the easily identifiable figure of exploitation and wrong-doing, "Gene Pingatore."

Visualizing Social Critiques: Individuals and Moral Messages

Gene Pingatore, the head coach, who never lets the boys forget he launched Isiah Thomas, is the distillation of all the white coaches and recruiters in the film. He talks a good game about caring for the boys' future, but over and over again the film captures his hideously callous behavior. The strongest proof is what happens to Arthur.

—Caryn James

There are a number of ways in which *Hoop Dreams* indicts and fails to indict the economies of sport. We contend that while *Hoop Dreams* gestures toward criticizing the exploitative treatment and commodification of William, Arthur, and other urban African-American youths (an exploitation that we view as endemic to the contemporary sport-entertainment complex), criticism is ultimately directed to and displaced on to the bodies of particular social agents who are visualized as virtuous or vicious. An indictment of the sport-entertainment complex would require examining the economic, political, and cultural forces governing that system (the forces defining the post-Fordist city); a critical examination of the sport-entertainment complex which is an unlikely filmic possibility since the film's original story and narrative integrity are maintained through these exclusions. Rather than interrogating the sport system, the film displaces and explains racism, greed, and exploitation through individual character. By our view, such displacements work to position viewers ("white high-rise America") as apparently "discriminating" and "socially conscious" cultural critics who not only easily recognize but are distanced from the everyday violences that shape the lives of the poor in the inner city. Moreover, this dynamic aligns the viewers with "the socially conscious filmmakers": both the filmmakers and audience accrue identity and meaning as they are defined over and against figures of exploitation; defined as those who have been or are involved in exploitative relations with Arthur and William. Such narrative mechanisms relieve the audience of the responsibility of critical reflection about their implication in exploitative spectator and consumption practices as well as the everyday conditions that structure the lives of the urban poor. The responsibility of critical reflection is relieved in the sense that it is actively discouraged.

One of the film's more obviously critical moments of the sport system occurs during William's stay at the Nike All-American Camp at Princeton, New Jersey. Also known as the ABCD (Academic Betterment and Career Development), the camp brings together 120 of the nations's top high-school players for a week-long, all-expenses-paid program each summer. The camp, ostensibly designed as an introduction to student-athlete life, reserves mornings for academics and guest lectures and afternoons for games. But the camp is not, as claimed by William DuBois, the camp athletic director, solely an introduction to student-athlete life. Instead, it provides a convenient, centralized location at which university coaches and scouts can assess potential recruits at Nike's expense. The Nike Camp segment is presented through a collage of sound-bites from coaches, scouts, guest speakers, and William; on-court action; and highly stylized shots of tall, muscular, African-American, Nike-clad youth.

The viewers' arrival at the camp is signaled by an army of white Nike sneakers marching along the clean swept paths of the Princeton University campus. The camera cuts to an old, grand, red-brick building and then to a large lecture theater filled with young, predominantly African-American men decked out in bright red and blue Nike polo shirts. In the front room, Dick Vitale, a well-known sports commentator, performs an energetic, "inspirational" speech, in which he tells his audience: "This is America. You can make something of your life." From here, the film moves to a gymnasium with several basketball games in progress. With the court action as background, the viewer is offered a series of sound bites from various coaches including Kevin O'Neill, William's future coach at Marquette, and the infamous Bobby Knight of Indiana. According to Knight: "there aren't very many kids at any level, including the NBA, that really understand what basketball is all about." As a voice-over tells us that William needs to prove himself among the nation's best, the camera moves to a makeshift photography studio where players, wearing tank-tops with "ABCD Camp" emblazoned on the front, line up to have their picture taken. In a shift back to Chicago (temporality is implied), we see Arthur and Shannon who are working (at what is announced to be a summertime job) at Pizza Hut earning $3.35 per hour, and an informal game on a run down concrete inner-city basketball court, before the quick-edit back to the state-of-the-art Princeton stadium and William in action. William expresses his frustration with his teammates—who want to impress the coaches who are watching—for not passing the ball.

In the classroom, the young men appear bored as the Camp athletic director William DuBois claims: "We provide them with an experience they can't get anywhere else, in that we simulate what it's going to be like to be a student-athlete. The stats on Division I players graduating from college are really frightening." As we see a close-up of William's face, we hear Spike Lee: "Nobody cares about you. [The camera cuts to Spike Lee pacing around a lecture theater podium.] You're black, you're male, all you're supposed to do is deal drugs and mug women. [We see William, looking pensive.] The only reason why you're here, you can make their team win. If their team wins, these schools get a lot of money. This whole thing is revolving around money."

Back at the gymnasium, William is excelling on the court. Kevin O'Neill tells us that "recruiting is like any other sales business, we've got to win to keep our jobs." Bo Ellis, the assistant coach at Marquette, claims that "you look at some of these young boys' bodies . . . and they've got NBA bodies already." Bob Gibbons, an independent talent scout, announces, "It's already become a meat market, but I try to do my job, and, you know, serve professional meat." In the next frame, we see Gibbons with another scout discussing the various schools (DePaul, Marquette, Indiana, Michigan) that are interested in William. The camera cuts to William's dormitory as he and his roommates share pizza and jokes. A smiling William tells the filmmakers: "Right now, I'm just feelin good about myself. I really feel like since I've been down here that I was all-American. When I go back home I'm gonna feel unstoppable." Just after his optimistic prediction and over upbeat music, William sustains a muscle injury. Interspersed with shots of an athletic trainer examining his leg, we see coaches, including O'Neill and Knight, who "look," apparently concerned about the implications of his injury. The coaches' looks are not innocent, instead, the moment is symptomatic of the sort of "looking relations" through which William and the other African American youths are positioned and defined. As a result of a muscle injury, William is unable to compete for the final two days of the camp.

The progression of the scenes leading up to William's trip to Princeton establish the context that confirms the relevance and worth of the Camp experience: two scenes undermine the critical potential of the Nike Camp sequence. The first scene takes the form of a "tour" of the neighborhood in which Bo Agee used to buy drugs. As we go by decaying buildings and garbage-strewn patches of wasteland, Bo, our guide, identifies the street corners where he purchased drugs. In combined confession and testimony, he expresses regret for this period in his life and takes responsibility for Arthur's expulsion from St. Joseph's:

I think about it, had I not been on drugs when Arthur went to St. Joseph's just how good it would have been for him. He wouldn't ha' had to leave. Here one of the corners, right here, these four corners, here's were I cop, where I used to come up here and cop all the time.

They weigh a lot of money on these corner, boy. I almost did my life right along with it. He can just look at my life and say here's a good example of what not to do. If he had my ways, I'd be, I would be shakin [laughter] in my shoes right now.

Images of Arthur, Shannon, and a friend on a shopping trip punctuate Bo's comments. Jackets embroidered with team logos, a wall lined with sneakers, the Air Jordan silhouette on red shirts and shorts, and other signs of Nike fill the screen, as all three youths admire the display, try on various pairs of shoes, and make purchases. The camera closes in first on Arthur, as he hands $70 over the counter to pay for his goods, and then the dollars as they are placed in the register. As Arthur reveals that drug dealers in the neighborhood give promising ball players money to buy athletic gear and "to keep our careers going," we see a series of close-ups: sneaker after sneaker displaying the Nike swoosh in various colors; a shirt decorated with an image of a primitivized and monsterized Michael Jordan; and, finally, the brand name Nike and its signature swoosh emblazoned on shirts. A cut to the army of white Nike sneakers marching on the Princeton path follows the close-up images of Nike consumer goods.

The two scenes condense an array of issues immediately recognizable as "urban problems": drugs, gangs, drug money, family breakdown, sneakers, "sneaker crimes," and insatiable consumer desires. No explanation of the issues is needed nor is it invited by film: extensive attention directed at these problems in both the scientific and popular realms render them distinct, obvious, and easily intelligible. Although edited to make "Nike" the link between the camp and the sneakers purchased with drug money, Nike escapes interrogation. The camp, and by extension Nike, accrue their value and meaning in relation to what are presented in the film as alternatives. Despite the offensive attitudes displayed by some of the coaches and the meat market environment at the Nike camp, real possibility, control, and comfort are forged over and against first the menial labor that possibly awaits Arthur and, more forcefully, the despair, disillusion, and dystopic possibility that Arthur might go the way of his father and environment (a prediction made by Arthur's Marshall coach earlier in the film).

Familiar narratives of social problems also overdetermine identities through which characters function, regardless of whether they appear in newspaper reports or documentary films, function. In other words, because Bo Agee's identity is already overdetermined by these narratives, his admissions of failure and lack of moral worth, articulated through his claim of responsibility for Arthur's expulsion from St. Joseph's, are immediately understandable. The force of contrast and meaning in this filmic composition is established through the sport/gang dyad that governs the national imagination in general.

Combined with critical attention directed to the personalities of individual coaches, audiences are discouraged from thinking about urban violence, drug use, and the late capitalist economy and consumerism in all their complexity. Corporate investments and disinvestments are never broached as potentially crucial issues.[15]

Gene Pingatore is, as argued by Caryn James (1994), the distillation of the exploitative relationships we witness, but that distillation, which individuates and distances, is not simply revealed, nor is it easily achieved. Pingatore is positioned throughout the film as the embodiment of social wrongs and exploitation through the considerable time devoted to visual narratives of long, intense practice sessions in which he appears ruthless, impatient, aggressive, and loud. Moreover, Pingatore's unemotional and frank interview style supports this characterization and is particularly jarring when, in a matter-of-fact manner, he (the label "Director of Development" identifies him in this scene) explains Arthur's expulsion from St. Joseph's as an unfortunate but unavoidable financial necessity. His opening conversation with the Agees (here, Pingatore was labeled "Head Basketball Coach"), coupled with Arthur's dismissal, suggest that Gene Pingatore has feigned care and concern, which makes him an especially despicable character. Interviews with a depressed Arthur ("I thought Pingatore and them would help me out"; "He thought I wasn't going to be a big ball player"), Arthur's mother who expresses her anger at the school for expelling him mid-semester, and the Marshall High coach who argues that had Arthur fulfilled his potential St. Joseph's would not have been so swift to force him out, heighten the impact of Pingatore's words. Pingatore appears as uncaring and parasitic in what remains a legitimate and potentially even beneficial sport system. The figure of the coach who only sees young players as tools for victory works to eclipse the broader conditions and policies that deny Arthur as well as other inner city youths access to a solid public school education.

Pingatore's "obvious" questionable character is defined over and against other individuals in the system who appear caring, well-intentioned, and loyal. For example, Kevin O'Neill, the Marquette coach with whom William eventually signs, is represented as personable, committed to higher principles, concerned with William as a person, not simply a player. While recruiting William, O'Neil displays an unconditional commitment to William when he offers William a four-year scholarship to Marquette that will continue to pay for his education despite prohibitive injuries. In a repetition of the sort of concern and loyalty attributed to the filmmakers, O'Neil displays the sort of loyalty and ethical superiority that both constructs white identity and demonstrates the possibilities and promises of the sporting system.

Pingatore's position as the visible and locatable embodiment of guilt and wrong-doing is evident in what for the audience are two of the most satisfying scenes in the film. Since Gene Pingatore's parasitic and exploitative tendencies were apparently motivated by his endless desire to "go down state"—that is, to coach his team in the state high school championships—Arthur's trip to Champaign is experienced as particularly pleasurable. Audience satisfaction and pleasure can not be reduced to Arthur's outstanding play during the championships. Instead, since editing effects have established the sense that we can clearly see where guilt lies, we also sense that we can clearly perceive that justice has been achieved, within allowable bounds, when it is Arthur, whom Pingatore has most betrayed, who has the honor of delivering a stinging moral message to him. Pingatore watches as Arthur realizes his (Pingatore's) dream, leading his team to victory and a third place finish in the state championship in Champaign's Assembly Hall. While Pingatore did not betray William, at least not to the same degree that he betrayed Arthur, justice, within proper limits, is again served when William delivers *his* moral message to Pingatore. As Pingatore says goodbye to William, William tells Pingatore that he has decided to major in communications, so "when you start asking for donations, I'll know the right way to turn you down." Indeed, the affect of these moments suggest that the film has been edited in such a way that one of the biggest challenges presented to William and Arthur is defined in terms of Pingatore. These moments confirm Pingatore's central position in the production and stabilization of audience identity.

Conclusion

How and why have other relations of power and sociality—those, for example, traversing local, national, and global economic institutions—become less central to adjudicating ethical citizenship in the United States?

—Lauren Berlant

As we have suggested above, mainstream media identify the achievement of *Hoop Dreams* in terms of its brutally real and honest portrayal of the political realities of urban America. Popular narrations of *Hoop Dreams* also suggest that those representations differ markedly from those typically available in the national popular. Moreover, its representations were celebrated for their "big picture" effect in which the camera appears to have no limits. Steve James explains his understanding of the *Hoop Dreams* aesthetic:

I admire some filmmakers who have carved out a distinctive aesthetic style, but their aesthetic style is about who they are. I'm always interested in capturing something about the world out there. And I plead guilty to being interested in films that are accessible. (quoted in Auferheide, 1994, p. 34)

The conventions of documentary filmmaking (clearly adhered to by the makers of *Hoop Dreams*) deny the limits of the visual register and the significance of location and perspective by rendering them invisible. While *Hoop Dreams'* appeal is routinely cast in terms of its realness, we see that "realness" as symptomatic of a point of view whose limits and exclusion have been naturalized and are therefore not easily recognizable—an effect of familiar and undisturbing knowledges. As a formulaic hybrid, part NBA, part *Cops*, part *American Dream*, *Hoop Dreams* relies on stereotypes drawn from the national archive of the present. While the truth-effect of documentary aesthetics erases context and location, a familiar visual economy solicits a national appeal and pleasure. This dynamic is integral to the understanding of urban, consumer, racial, and national politics. In an effort to understand the stakes in the "reality effect" of *Hoop Dreams*, we want to revisit Steve James' depiction of the 10-minute ovation that met the film's New York Film Festival debut. James characterized the moment:

> The people at the festival said nothing like this had ever happened before. The audience was just standing there, clapping for the connection they felt for those families. It was the most amazing experience of my life . . . (quoted in Howe, 1994, p. G4)

Steve James also described the audience desire for connection in the *Chicago Tribune*:

> White people have told us that the only contact they have with neighborhoods is what they see from their high rise. . . But seeing a film like this, they really felt connection. They saw these families all wanted the same things that they wanted for their own children. That they have a lot more in common in terms of hope and desire, than they have not in common. (quoted in Wilmington, 1994a, p. 5:20)

We agree with Steve James who assesses the New York ovation as an expression of the connection that the audience felt for those families: the applause, at least on one level, is for the recognition of sameness, shared values and desires. Easy slippages between the conditions of poor, primarily African-American, inner-city residents who face inhuman conditions of poverty, public assistance, and employment possibilities and "white, high-rise America"—slippages routinely facilitated through the category of "family"— are not necessarily something to be celebrated; instead, by our view, they are indicative of the "knowledges" that govern the audience's understanding of the crisis of the inner city in ways that demonize single parents, welfare, welfare recipients, the under and unemployed, and African-American youths in general. Moreover, these slippages, particularly as they are aligned with and as they call for a reconstitution of the family, work in concert with the neo-conservative agenda of "empowerment"—will, self-sufficiency, independence. The affective dimension of the audience's desire to recognize itself in the lives of the urban poor and to celebrate that recognition is deeply problematic. It is also symptomatic of the position from which identity is forged and judgements made, of America's quest for sameness, and of America's inability to think adequately about difference and inequality.[16] Repeated visual codes and the narrative work not only to displace guilt and implication onto easily identifiable agents such as Pingatore but to reinforce a conservative, normalizing agenda in which the virtuous and vicious are easily distinguished. We do not mean to suggest that these easily identifiable agents are not implicated in exploitative relations; instead, our intent is to direct attention to how such figures of displacement operate in the national popular to relieve guilt and to produce ethically superior subjects. In *Hoop Dreams*, "Gene Pingatore" helps mainstream audiences reconcile the conflict between inner-city poverty and the sense of themselves as compassionate, virtuous, and morally superior. Moreover, the figure of the basketball player, defined over and against the criminal (the gang member that governs America's representation of African-American men in the mid-1980s to the mid-1990s), also functions as a means of displacement that reconciles middle-class America's sense of itself as compassionate as it calls for and endorses increasingly vengeful punitive programs.[17] Making a related argument, bell hooks (1995) draws attention to the treatment of Bo and Curtis in the film. By her view:

> *Hoop Dreams* merely shows the failure of black male parents to sustain meaningful ties with their children. It does not critically interrogate the complex circumstances and conditions of that failure. . . . Without any critical examination, these father-and-son dynamics simply confirm negative stereotypes, then compound them by suggesting that even when black fathers are present in their children's lives they are such losers that they have no positive impact. In this way, a cinematic portrait is created that in no way illuminates the emotional complexity of black male life. (p. 23)

hooks' point, and we agree, is aligned with Michael Manning's (1995) assessment of the recent journalistic writing on real life in the inner city in which urban youth are embraced at the expense of their parents. In *Hoop*

Dreams, Bo, who most clearly figures the failed black parent, appears responsible for his family's economic vulnerability.[18] This dynamic (child/parent) also figures, albeit less obviously, William, who is defined over and against Curtis (whose basketball talents suggest that his failures are a sign of his own characterological inadequacies) and his father, the quintessential absent inseminating black male. As we have discussed throughout this chapter, the racially coded pathologized family is a grounding subtext that provides the sport/gang dyad with its social and psychic power. Both the racially codified family and the sport/gang dyad (as one of its most compelling manifestations) help firm up boundaries that function to exclude the economic and political forces shaping the lives of the inner-city poor.

Hoop Dreams refuses to trouble the familiar categories that govern knowledges of the inner city; therefore, the exclusions that lend stability to those categories remain invisible and uninterrogated in the documentary. For example, the discursive distance between William and elements typically located in the formation of deviant black masculinity can only be maintained through exclusions. The introduction of Catherine (William's girlfriend) only after Alisa is born, is an editing strategy that "reassures" viewers by making clear that William will take on the nationally sanctioned familial responsibility. The filmmakers may have been attempting to (wittingly or not) intervene in myths of the hyper-sexual black male, but rather than challenging cultural fears of black sexuality, such exclusions corroborate attributions of deviant sexuality to black men. Indeed, William, who is distanced from the formation of racially coded deviant masculinity, functions to maintain familiar distinctions—the sharp differentiation between the inside and the outside, the human and nonhuman—that govern and organize the national imagination. In other words, while William figures the "human" (a stated authorial intention), the sport/gang dyad remains stable, marking what and who are less than human. Compassion and connection felt towards Arthur, William, and their families suggest that revenge directed at African American youth through excessive punitive measures is somehow legitimate since what calls for punishment is obvious, justified, and requires no interrogation.

Finally, Lauren Berlant's (1996) work underscores how attention on youth functions to allow American audiences' self-recognition in terms of compassion, care, and ethical superiority. Berlant argues that the celebration of the pre-political child and other incipient citizens are vital to the American public sphere because the image of the future, a future they convey, works to draw attention away from the more troubling issues of violence and equality in the present. In this sense, her argument is aligned with Massing's (1995) criticisms of journalistic preoccupations that marginalize inner-city adults "in their rush to embrace inner city youth" (p. 33). Berlant's argument takes us beyond Massing's point. She argues that the fantasy of the American Dream, a quintessential fantasy of futurity so absolutely central to the narrative of *Hoop Dreams* and its commercial success, is a central force in the mobilization of violence in the present. For Berlant, the American Dream is a public form of private history that promises public social and economic stability and support for those who work and make families. This promise, she argues, which "connects personal lives to capitalist subjectivity and the cultural forms of national life" (p. 431), allows America to imagine a national people unmarked by public history. Arthur Agee and William Gates, fine characters and promising basketball players, embody the kind of future that (white) America lives for and through.[19] Again, as a means of translating subjectivity into objectivity, the images of African-American youths and African-American families in *Hoop Dreams* tell us more about the state of mind of the country than it does about real urban life and conditions. The politics of *Hoop Dreams* are, to borrow Berlant's words, "vicious, symbolic, optimistic, and banal," embedded in a future that circumvents the terror of the present.

Notes

The authors would like to express their appreciation to Geneviève Rail and David Andrews for helpful comments and Melissa Orlie for her generous sharing of ideas.

1. As part of the early narrative context, Telander (1976) sketches what were then the fairly recent visible and systematic changes that reshaped the local environment and made basketball a compelling force in the lives of some of the local youth. White flight had shifted the demographics of the immigrant neighborhoods—predominately Jewish, Irish, and Italian—to predominantly black and poor. He also depicts the shifts in the signs of community from "tidy shops, taverns, and flower beds" (p. 7) to "broken glass, graffiti, garbage, and battered buildings" (p. 10). See Cole (forthcoming), for a detailed discussion of *Heaven is a Playground*.

2. Twenty years after *Heaven is a Playground* was published, Darcy Frey's *The Last Shot* became a nationwide best seller. Frey spent 12 months following the lives of four talented African-American basketball players from Lincoln High School in Coney Island, New York (including Stephon Marbury). Frey's book chronicles the teenagers' efforts to gain a college scholarship which, he argues, is their only possibility of escape from urban crime and poverty. While Frey's book was heralded as a timely portrait of all that is wrong in America and while he devotes considerable space to criticizing coaches, recruiters, and athletic companies, ultimately the identities through which the narrative is organized remain bound by the sport/gang dyad which we critique in this essay. In the midst of excitement over basketball, *Heaven is a Playground* was reprinted in an attempt to find the audience that it never had.

3. For an insightful discussion of how the category of dependency was articulated in post-industrial America and the complexity of intervening in public debates over federal assistance, see Fraser and Gordon (1994).

4. For a discussion of the entrepreneurial stories and how they operate, see Andrews (1996) and Cole and Andrews (1996). Reeves and Campbell (1994) provide a brief but useful discussion on the celebratory entrepreneurial tale as "one of the ideological hallmarks" that authorized individualism and Reagan's economic policies during the 1980s. Recognizing the racial specificity of the entrepreneurial narratives would have furthered their argument about the central position of basketball player Len Bias' cocaine-induced death just after being drafted to play for the Boston Celtics in advancing Reagan's war on drugs. Moreover, we suggest that there were three racially specific entrepreneurial tales on offer during the 1980s: athlete as entrepreneur; the gang member as entrepreneur; and the welfare mother as entrepreneur. Of course, the athlete as entrepreneur was nationally sanctioned, while the gang member and welfare mother were highly demonized.

5. For an excellent discussion on the second wave of black filmmaking, see Guerrero (1993).

6. For an extremely useful discussion on modern power, the see-able, the say-able, and the possibility of living ethically and acting politically, see Orlie (in press).

7. This section of our chapter is a slightly revised version of an argument that appeared in Cole (1996).

8. Coontz (1992) and Reid (1995) provide thought-provoking discussions on racism and the family.

9. Connolly (1995) argues that the desire for revenge underlying contemporary calls for punishment is linked to America's investment in what are basically unstable foundational political categories. As a result of highly racialized patterns of arrest, conviction, and sentencing associated with inner-city poverty and the war on drugs, at least one-third of the African American males between the age of 18 and 34 who live in a major urban area are under some form of control by the criminal justice system (U.S. Department of Justice, 1995). The overall incarceration rate of young African-Americans (age 18–34) is an astounding six times that of young white males.

10. By "media hyped crime wave," we refer to the media's excessive reportage that focuses on inner city crime and, more specifically, the media's fascination with the incomprehensible and shocking crime. For a discussion of how that shock and incomprehensibility function, see Connolly (1995). For a discussion of the media hyped crime wave and incomprehensible sneaker crimes, see Cole (1996).

11. Since 1980, 600 new prisons have been built in the United States and the prison population has increased from 500,000 to 1.5 million (Donzinger, 1996).

12. Under Reagan, Bush, and Clinton, publicly subsidized housing has become highly stigmatized space associated with racially-coded family breakdown, breach in the work ethic, and the source of America's crisis: it has become a prominent sign of highly charged debates around dependency and "welfare as we know it." Housing projects have also become highly stigmatized through drugs and gangs. The image of the housing project provided in *Hoop Dreams* suggests that this summertime carnival atmosphere, with no sense of danger or trouble, is a general feature of everyday life. While the image presented in *Hoop Dreams* apparently seeks to disrupt the visual associations that contribute to the highly stigmatized space (and may provide a more accurate representation that suggests that danger is sporadic rather than continual), we understand this intervention to be symptomatic of the liberal politics of positive images that informs the film.

13. In the cinema version of the movie, the postscript also tells us that Arthur has fathered two children. This announcement does not appear in the video release.

14. A public relations and film distributer team convinced Roger Ebert and Gene Siskel to review the film prior to its showing at Sundance. In their rave review, Siskel and Ebert identified the film as an "unforgettable portrait of American urban reality" (quoted in Aufderheide, 1994, p. 33). As a result of the Siskel and Ebert review, *Hoop Dreams* tickets were among the hottest at Sundance.

15. High rates of unemployment among the urban poor are largely due to the deindustrialization of American cities. According to Wilson (1996), between 1967 and 1987, Chicago lost 60 percent of its manufacturing jobs, while Philadelphia lost 64 percent and New York 58 percent. Since more than 70 percent of African-American men working in metropolitan areas held blue-collar jobs up until the late 1960s, they have been disproportionately effected by these shifts (Kasadara, 1993). As the number of African-American men working in manufacturing industries fell dramatically between 1973 and 1987 (for men between the ages of 20 and 29, the figure fell from 3 in 8 to 1 in 5) and the number working in lower retail and service jobs increased sharply, the average annual income for this group fell by 25–30 percent (Wilson, 1996). During the same period, the percentage of African Americans with income below 50 percent of the amount designated as the poverty line increased from 9.3 percent of the total African-American population to 16.7 percent.

16. Wilson (1996) argues that while Jim Crow' arguments in support of racial segregation have largely disappeared, this movement has not been mirrored by increasing support for government programs that work to aggressively combat discrimination. Indeed, whites overwhelmingly oppose government interventions targeted to African-Americans. For example, in 1991 only 1 in 5 whites believed that the federal government has a particular obligation to improve the living standards of African Americans. In 1975, this figure stood at over 1 in 4. Similarly in 1990, 69.1 percent of whites opposed quotas for the admittance of black students into institutions of higher education and 82.5 percent objected to the idea of preferential hiring and promotion of blacks.

17. Both Arthur and William are familiar figures in the national imagination. Their achievement on the basketball court, their rejection of the gang and street options, their motivation to leave their situation and to have a better life are familiar terms. Although gang members and drug dealers are given limited visibility in the film, they are the "Other" over and against whom William and Arthur are defined in the national imagination. When gang members and drug dealers appear, they appear in the dark or are shot from a distance, for instance, once Shannon is dismissed from Marshall's basketball team, he joins a gang, and becomes peripheral to the narrative.

18. According to Wilson (1996), in 1990 in the twelve Chicago community areas with ghetto poverty rates (all these areas are predominantly African-American), only 1 in 3 adults over the age of sixteen held a job in a typical week of the year, compared with the citywide employment figure of 57 percent. Wilson has also looked at a 1960 study of Bronzeville (an area comprising three African-American neighborhoods in Chicago) that showed that 64 percent of men worked in a typical week, and compared this figure with his own finding that in 1990, 37 percent of men worked in a typical week: Wilson has concluded that such high rates of joblessness among poor African-Americans living in the inner city are a recent, historically specific phenomena.

19. The centrality of the image of the future to the success of *Hoop Dreams* is particularly apparent in the public's continued interest in the lives of Arthur and William, three years after the release of the film. Magazines, newspapers, and popular television shows frequently produce features or segments on "what William and Arthur are doing now." These follow-ups, which most recently have focuses in William's work as an announcer on Chicago radio station WMAQ-AM and Arthur's move into a minor professional basketball league (the United States Basketball League), are presented as further evidence of the possibility and plausibility of the American Dream.

References

Andrews, D. (1996). "The fact of Michael Jordan's blackness: Excavating a floating racial signifier." *Sociology of Sport Journal*, 13(2), 125–128.

Aufderheide, P. (1994). "The dream team." *The Independent*, October, pp. 32–34.

Berkow, I. (1994). "Dreaming hoop dreams." *The New York Times*, October 9, pp. 1–2, 26–27.

Berlant, L. (1993). "National brands/national bodies: Imitation of life." In B. Robbins (Ed.), *The phantom public sphere*. Minneapolis: University of Minnesota Press.

——— (1996). "The face of America and the state of emergency." In C. Nelson & D.P. Gaonkar (Eds.), *Disciplinarity and dissent in cultural studies* (pp. 367–440). New York: Routledge.

Carby, H. (1993). "Encoding white resentment: Grand Canyon—A narrative of our time." In C. McCarthy & W. Crichlow (Eds.), *Race, identity, and representation in education* (pp. 236–250). New York: Routledge.

Carr, J. (1994). "Hoop Dreams: A real-life slam-dunk." *The Boston Globe*, October 24, pp. 47, 55.

Clark, M. (1994). "Hoop Dreams reaches for the rafters and soars." *USA Today*, October 13, p. D1.

Cole, C.L. (1996). "American Jordan: P.L.A.Y., consensus, and punishment." *Sociology of Sport Journal*, 13(4), 366–397.

——— (forthcoming). "Heaven is a Playground." *TASP Newsletter*.

Cole, C.L., & Andrews, D. (1996). "'Look—it's NBA ShowTime!': Visions of race in the popular imaginary." *Cultural Studies: A Research Annual*, 1(1), 141–181.

Collins, G. (1994). "Advertising." *The New York Times*, November 7, p. B21.

Connolly, W. (1995). *The ethos of pluralization*. Minneapolis: University of Minnesota Press.

Coontz, S. (1992). *The way we never were: American families and the nostalgia trap*. New York: Basic.

Coyle, D. (1995). *Hardball: A season in the projects*. New York: Harper Paperbacks.

Davis, M. (1990). *City of quartz: Excavating the future in Los Angeles*. London: Verso.

Donaldson, G. (1994). *The ville: Cops and kids in urban America*. New York: Anchor Books.

Donzinger, S.R. (Ed.) (1996). *The real war on crime: The report of the National Criminal Justice Commission*. New York: HarperCollins.

Dyson, M.E. (1996). *Race rules: Navigating the color line*. Reading, MA: Addison Wesley.

Feurer, J. (1995). *Seeing through the eighties*. Durham: Duke University Press.

Fraser, N., & Gordan, L. (1994). "A genealogy of dependency: Tracing a keyword of the U.S. welfare state." *Signs: Journal of Women in Culture and Society*, 19(2), 309–327.

Frey, D. (1994). *The last shot: City streets, basketball dreams*. Boston: Houghton Miflin Co.

Gray, H. (1995). *Watching race, television and the struggle for blackness*. Minneapolis: University of Minnesota Press.

Guerrero, E. (1993). *Framing blackness*. Philadelphia: Temple University Press.

Hinson, H. (1994). "'*Hoop Dreams*': A slam-dunk shot of truth." *The Washington Post*, November 4, pp. F1, F7.

hooks, b. (1995). "Dreams of conquest." *Sight and Sound*, April, pp. 22–23.

Howe, D. (1994). "'*Hoop Dreams*': An overtime victory." *The Washington Post*, November 13, p. G4.

James, C. (1994). "Dreaming the dreams, realizing the realities." *The New York Times*, October 7, pp. C1, C8.

Jones, L. (1996). "Hoop realities." *Jump Cut*, 40, 8–14.

Kasarda, J.D. (1993). "Inner-city concentrated poverty and neighborhood distress: 1970–1990." *Housing Policy Debate*, 4(3), 253–302.

Kotlowitz, A. (1992). *There are no children here*. New York: Anchor Books.

Kornheiser, T. (1994). "Dreams; bring us back to reality." *The Washington Post*, November 3, pp. B1, B6.

Massing, M. (1995). "Ghetto blasting." *The New Yorker*, January 16, pp. 32–37.

McGavin, P.Z. (1994). "From the street and the gyms to the courtroom and beyond." *The New York Times*, October 9, p. 26.

Miller, T. (1993). *The well-tempered self*. Baltimore, MD: Johns Hopkins University Press.

Orlie, M. (in press). *Living ethically, acting politically*. Ithaca, NY: Cornell University Press.

Reeves, J., & Campbell, R. (1994). *Cracked coverage: Television news, the anticocaine crusade, and the Reagan legacy*. Durham, NC: Duke University Press.

Reid, R. (1995). "Death of the family or keeping human beings human." In J. Halberstam & I. Livingstone (Eds.), *Posthuman bodies* (pp. 177–199). Bloomington, IN: University of Indiana Press.

Riggs, M. (1991). *Color adjustment*. San Francisco: California Newsreel.

Sandell, J. (1995). "Out of the ghetto and into the marketplace." *Socialist Review*, 95(2), 57–82.

Seigel, J. (1994). "Chicagoans' '*Hoop Dreams*' rises to the top at Sundance." *The Chicago Tribune*, January 31, p. 16.

Sherman, B. (1994). "The stuff of dreams." *The Boston Sunday Globe*, October 16, pp. B11, B14.

Smith, C. (1997). "Sneaker wars." *New York*, March 3, pp. 40–47.

Smith, N. (1996). *The new urban frontier*. New York: Routledge.

Sperber, M. (1996). "Hollywood dreams." *Jump Cut*, 40, 3–7.

Telander, R. (1976). *Heaven is a playground*. New York: St. Martin's Press.

U.S. Department of Justice (1995). *Prisoners in 1994* (NCJ-151654). Washington, DC: U.S. Government Printing Office.

Wilmington, M. (1994a). "When film dreams come true." *The Chicago Tribune*, October 2, pp. 13:5, 20.

——— (1994b). "Full court pressure: *Hoop Dreams* details the hope born of desperation." *The Chicago Tribune*, October 21, pp. 7:C, M.

Wilson, W.J. (1996). *When work disappears: The new world of the urban poor*. New York: Random House.

5

LESBIANS AND LOCKER ROOMS: THE SUBJECTIVE EXPERIENCES OF LESBIANS IN SPORT

CAROLINE FUSCO

> Lesbians are woman-seers. When one is suspected of seeing women, one is summarily spat out of reality, through the cognitive gap and into the negative semantic space. If you ask what became of such a woman, you may be told she became a lesbian, and if you try to find out what a lesbian Is, you will be told there is no such thing. But there is. (Frye, 1983, p. 173)

This quote by Marilyn Frye appears in her essay entitled "To be and be seen: The politics of reality." In this essay, she describes the erasure of lesbians from history and present day social life through the manipulation of our attention and reality by the dominant heterosexual culture. The maintenance of a patriarchal and heterosexual culture requires that women's attention be focused on men, and re-orienting one's attention to woman-loving is antagonistic to the maintenance of a heterosexual reality. In the decade since this essay was published, there have been many challenges to what Hennessy (1993) describes as "heteronormativity." There has been a movement away from analyzing sexuality as a personal or civil rights issue; discourses in recent years now critique the "normative" status of heterosexuality as a status that has been socially constructed. In North America, lesbian and gay activists have lobbied for equal rights in all aspects of life. Feminist and more recently, postmodern lesbian and gay theorists have not only demanded individual sexual freedom but continually challenge the regulation and organization of heteronormativity. We must ask ourselves how is the institution of sport affected by these challenges to heteronormativity? Is the world of sport and active living post-inequities and post-discrimination?

In women's sport the issues of heterosexism and homophobia have been addressed publicly in the last decade. Previously, individuals had written about women's sport but had skirted around the lesbian issue (Woods & Harbeck, 1992). Bennett (cited in Nelson, 1991) labeled this avoidance of addressing lesbianism in women's sport "a silence so loud it screams" (p. 139). Although lesbians have not been overtly denied access to participation in sports or active living, the heterosexual image of women in sports persists and is encouraged. The lesbian label is still used to intimidate lesbians and undermine attempts by all women to challenge constructed gender relations in sport. Griffin (cited in Nelson, 1991, p. 142) states:

> Women's athletics is, in fact, held hostage to fear of the "L-word." As long as women's athletics continues to deny that there are lesbians in sport . . . we will never control our sporting lives and will be forced to waste energy defending a counterfeit heterosexual-only image that we all know is a lie.

An article in *USA Today* (Brady, 1993) entitled "Gays in sport: Still in the shadows," suggests that sexuality issues are still a "hot topic" within sports. But the attitude in sports remains, like the United States military, "don't ask, don't tell" (p. 1B). The message constantly made apparent is that it is frowned upon to be gay in sports and this is manifested by the use of language and behaviour in sports that is both homophobic and heterosexist (Brady, 1993). We know that lesbians participate in sport but professionally, only Martina Navratilova, in women's tennis, has "come out." In the magazine *Out* (1994), she acknowledged that she has not "emboldened" other athletes to come out. She remarks that she has been "out" since 1980 and has "never noticed a line forming behind me" (p. 94). It can, therefore, be suggested that homophobia and heterosexism operate in sport to silence lesbians. This silence contributes to the divisions among women in sport, perpetuates lies about the meaning of being lesbian and functions to keep women's attention on heterosexual reality. More recently concern has been voiced about the lack of inquiry that specifically addresses the subjective experiences of these lesbian athletes who are constrained to remain invisible (Brown, 1991; Griffin, 1989a; Nelson, 1991).

With this in mind, the purpose of my research was to give a small sample of lesbian athletes the opportunity to tell their stories about their experiences in sport, and how the challenge to reject and resist "heteronormativity" has affected their lives. The athletes' accounts provide insight into the issues and concerns which they confront in the heterosexist institution of sport. I suspect that lesbians in sport attempt to pass and/or are actively encouraged to pass as heterosexual and this serves to perpetuate the silence and invisibility of their existence thus maintaining heterosexist norms. I believe that lesbians in sport have developed strategies to cope with heterosexism, homophobia and internalized homophobia; and that this process is on-going in all aspects of their lives and can affect their self-identity and self-image. In this chapter, I provide an overview of the background and rationale for the research, and present preliminary analysis of interview data with reference to the following themes; (a) how do lesbians experience heterosexism, homophobia and internalized homophobia in sports; (b) do lesbians develop strategies to cope with heterosexism, homophobia and internalized homophobia; and (c) what are the consequences of existing in a heterosexist institution? To contextualize my project, I would like to point out that my research focus is on a radical feminist understanding of lesbian sexuality; a sexuality that has been defined as being outside the norm of heterosexuality, a norm maintained by heterosexism.

In the following section I illustrate and describe the phenomena of heterosexism and homophobia, and how these phenomena have been theorized as social constructions. These constructions represent the cultural norms of what is considered appropriate sexuality and sexual expression in our society. Lesbians are categorized as sexual deviants and along with others who are classified as sexual deviants, for example, gay men and bisexuals, lesbians confront discrimination and are ostracized in mainstream society. The implication for lesbians in sport is that their existence is covered up and their direct experience is rarely addressed. I illustrate that the institution of sport is definitely not post-oppression.

Theoretical Perspective on the Social Construction of Hegemonic Heterosexuality

Cultural norms legitimized in our society are constantly reinforced until the values are experienced as reality. This inculcation of dominant values is pervasive and results in a "hegemonic order" which Whitson (1984) identifies as an "official system of meanings and values operating at the level of feeling as well as thought, in terms of which existing ways of doing things are experienced as sensible and right" (p. 68). Heterosexuality, as the only acceptable form of expression of emotional and sexual commitment, is legitimized and regulated in our society by the dominant patriarchal and heterosexual culture (Frye, 1983; Rich, 1986). Heterosexuality is assumed to be natural and right. It is understood to "be sexuality" (Frye, 1992, p. 55). It is not perceived as a choice. Pressure to be heterosexual is reflected in the idealization of heterosexual romance in art, literature, media and advertising (Rich, 1986). This pressure is systemic yet its "compulsory" nature is completely denied by the dominant heterosexual culture. However, those who do not conform to the norm of heterosexuality are pressured to remain invisible and are excluded from sharing the conformists' privileges. Pharr (1988) describes the "defined norm" as "a standard of rightness and often righteousness wherein all other are judged in relation to it" (p. 53). There is an attempt then by our patriarchal culture to limit, control and invalidate those who are outside the "norm" of heterosexuality.

A radical feminist framework critiques heterosexuality as a category that is socially constructed to maintain the exploitation of women as a class (Frye, 1983). The "heterosystem" (Durocher, 1991) has defined, limited and conditioned the expression of sexuality in our society and has resulted in what Rich (1986) identified as "the institution of compulsory heterosexuality" (p. 24). This has been imposed on women and has established the appropriation, the access and the attention of women for men. This analysis of "compulsory heterosexuality" and the "heterosystem" which describes the organization and regulation of sexuality in society, is being pushed further by postmodern queer theorists. They are exploring and deconstructing the meanings of heterosexualized gender relations and the multiple positioned lesbian and gay sexual identities. With both radical feminists and postmodern theorists, there is a tacit knowledge that the oppressive structures of "compulsory heterosexuality," the "heterosystem" and "heteronormativity" are maintained by the concepts of sexism, heterosexism and homophobia.

In our patriarchal society, women are subjected to sexist oppression. Although all women are affected by this oppression, lesbians are different from heterosexual women. Lesbians are subjected to specific oppressions and they are further marginalized (Kitzinger, 1987), as are many other women who face multiple oppressions because of systemic racism, ageism, and ableism. To be lesbian then is to be doubly oppressed in a sexist and heterosexist society. Lesbian existence is denigrated in our society because it is a rejection of compulsory norms and, directly or indirectly, it denies male access to women's sexuality. To reject this accessibility threatens the maintenance of patriarchal control in our society (MacKinnon, 1987; Rich, 1986). As a result, lesbians are excluded from sharing the privileges that are controlled by the dominant heterosexual culture:

> To be lesbian is to be *perceived* as someone who has stepped out of line, who has moved out of sexual/economic dependence on a male, who is woman-identified. A lesbian is perceived as someone who can live without a man, and who is therefore (however illogically) against men. A lesbian is perceived as being outside the acceptable, routinized order of things. A lesbian is perceived as a threat to the nuclear family, to male dominance, to the very heart of sexism. (Pharr, 1988, p. 18; italics in original text)

Lorde defines heterosexism as "the belief in the inherent superiority of one pattern of loving and thereby its right to dominance," and homophobia as "the fear of feelings of love for member's of one's own sex and therefore the hatred of those feeling in others" (1984, p. 45). Heterosexism is institutionalized to ensure its predominance. It is acceptable for heterosexuals to be open about their sexuality but if lesbians do, then the usual response is to say "we are flaunting it" (Pharr, 1988). This maintains lesbian invisibility and excludes lesbians from being equal members of our society. Lesbians are denied the rights and privileges afforded to heterosexuals. Exclusion based on sexual orientation still remains one of the most acceptable forms of discrimination in our society, and as yet the rights of lesbians and gays have not been explicitly stated in the *Canadian Human Rights Charter*. The defeat of Bill 167 in the Ontario Legislature demonstrates that homophobia prevails in our highest institutions. Despite advocacy efforts to ensure rights, lesbian and gay people continually experience a lack of affirmation of themselves, their culture and their relationships within societal institutions.

Despite the mainstream assumption, lesbianism is not just about sex but can be an option to resist patriarchy (Phelan, 1993); its existence signals to other women the possibility of resisting constructed sex categories (Frye, 1983). Choosing a lesbian existence can signal that the "appropriation of women results from a social relationship and not a biological fact, that the category 'woman' is a social construct and not a 'natural group'" (Durocher, p. 16). It is precisely because, stereotypically, lesbians are not committed to the maintenance of a heterosexual culture that they confront discrimination in societal institutions (Arnup, 1984; Crumpacker & Haegan, 1984; Hall, 1986; Khayatt, 1990; Levine & Leonard, 1984; Wine, 1990).

Heterosexism, Lesbians, and Sport: Relevant Research

The institution of sport is a microcosm of society and contributes to the perpetuation of values that sustain "heteronormativity." Sport is "a dynamic social space where dominant ideologies are perpetuated" (Messner, 1988, p. 198), and lesbians in sport do not escape the overt or covert discrimination that reflects the systemic intolerance of differing sexuality in our patriarchal culture. Heterosexism and homophobia are pervasive within sport and this is demonstrated by the persistent lack of tolerance for sexual diversity within its community. Sports associations and governing bodies rarely address or acknowledge the existence of lesbian athletes, resulting in the invisibility of lesbians. There seems to be an unwritten yet understood agreement among associations, governing bodies and athletes to avoid direct discussion on lesbian issues (Peper, 1994). If lesbianism in sport is mentioned, it is rarely valorized. As stated previously, the issues of heterosexism and homophobia in women's sports have only been addressed publicly in the last decade (Lenskyj, 1991). The effects on the lesbian athletes have been documented. This literature has highlighted the consequences of homophobic harassment and behaviour for the lesbian athletes. The athletes have confronted invisibility, silencing, and rejection (Baxter, 1983; Griffin, 1989b; Griffin & Genasci, 1990; Lenskyj, 1987, 1990, 1991). The "institution of compulsory heterosexuality" has been identified as the cause of discrimination which leaves lesbian athletes isolated, denying their emotional lives and retreating into sameness (Baxter, 1983; Kidd, 1983; Lenskyj, 1990).

In addition, lesbians lack economic power in sports (Nelson, 1991; Rounds, 1991). In professional women's athletics, corporate sponsors often threaten to withdraw financial support from sports events and conferences if there is any acknowledgment of lesbianism. Lesbian athletes remain silent to protect their earnings and many of the contracts with sports agents and corporate sponsors "include a 'moral clause' forbidding 'conduct unbecoming a professional' or any behaviour bringing disrepute or bad publicity" (Nelson, 1991, p. 139). These clauses are used against lesbians. Martina Navratilova acknowledges that her sexuality has been the reason why companies thought her too controversial for sponsorship. The repercussion of being an out lesbian for her has been the financial loss of millions of dollars in endorsements. Financial concerns will undoubtedly influence both professional and amateur national, provincial and varsity athletes' openness about their sexuality. The limited opportunity for women at this level and the emphasis on success interrelated with scholarships and funding fosters an environment for sexual and homophobic harassment of lesbian athletes (Lenskyj, 1992).

Men have considered sports their private domain and as women challenge inequities, gain power and some control of economic resources, homophobia flourishes. Subsequently, the oppression of lesbians is actively reproduced in order that the dominant group, predominantly male, white and heterosexual, can enjoy its privilege and power (Griffin, 1989b). Scare tactics are used to silence women into submission. Sabo (cited in Nelson, 1991) suggests that homophobia is not so much about sexuality but that "homophobia in sports perpetuates male dominance and the male monopoly of existing resources" (p. 145). For a woman, to be both athletic and lesbian is the antithesis of the constructed traditionally passive feminine role. The lesbian athlete, therefore, who is interested in pursuing a sports career through an organized national, provincial or varsity programme does so within a sports system that is generally homophobic.

Considering the hurtful effects of heterosexism and homophobia documented in the literature, it is difficult to comprehend why lesbians continue to play within the sports institution. The number of lesbians participating in sports has never been calculated; this would be an arduous task as so many lesbians are terrified of "coming out" (Brown, 1991). Nevertheless, it has been suggested that the number of lesbians involved in sport and physical education is significant (Bennett, Whitaker, Woolley-Smith & Sablove, 1987;

Palzkill, 1990; Reed, 1994). In addition, lesbians have also expressed anxiety that they might not meet any other lesbians once they stopped participating in sports (Pronger, 1990). It seems ironic then, that despite the insidious discrimination that exists against lesbians in sports, that they continue to enter the sports world. Related to this, Griffin states:

> Lesbians are not stupid. They know to go where there are other lesbians. Sports arenas have been the place where there are women who are striving to be strong and independent. (cited in Nelson, 1991, p. 146)

Through sport, lesbians can develop knowledge and an intimate awareness of their own bodies. Sport can promote competence, empowerment and assertiveness, and allows lesbians (and women in general) to maintain some control over their own bodies, so often denied to them by our patriarchal culture. Sport may constitute an environment in which lesbians can celebrate their physicality and for certain athletes, it becomes a refuge from society. Given what Griffin stated above, some women may gravitate towards sport because they believe they might find support there for their lesbian identity (Baxter, 1983; Palzkill, 1990; Peper, 1994; Reed, 1994). Rather than reflecting and reproducing heterosexist relations, sport may provide an avenue to resist patriarchal and heterosexual notions of reality. Despite this, it is generally acknowledged that lesbians are still silenced, sanctioned, denigrated and made invisible. There is a systematic harassment of lesbian athletes throughout the sports institution (Baxter, 1983; Griffin, 1989b; Lenskyj, 1986, 1987, 1991) that is indicative of systemic patriarchal and heterosexual oppression (Frye, 1983; Lenskyj, 1991; Rich, 1986).

Acknowledging the existence of lesbians in sport has encouraged the development of a discourse that has begun to illuminate issues of concern for lesbians. Lenskyj (1987, 1991) documented the attitudes of academic sporting organizations towards lesbians in sport. For the most part, the responses have been positive. In 1988, the Canadian Association for Health, Physical Education and Recreation (CAHPER) resolved that "homophobia be recognized as an equity issue in physical education," and that "opportunities to discuss the ramifications of homophobia in physical education be promoted" (p. 67). In addition, there have been sessions organized at many academic conferences in which the heterosexist and homophobic nature of sports has been discussed. Despite this, Lenskyj (1991) suggests that the issue of homophobia remains a pervasive concern and that the institution of sport creates a negative environment within which lesbian athletes participate.

Studies addressing lesbian issues in sport have been mainly theoretical. Some have challenged the inadequacies of the sports literature and critiqued the institution of sport from a feminist perspective, identifying patriarchal and heterosexual hegemony as a powerful constraint on women's lives and sexuality (Bennett *et al.*, 1987; Lenskyj, 1987, 1990, 1991). Other studies have used anecdotal information and collective vignettes to highlight lesbian experiences (Baxter, 1983; Kidd, 1983; Griffin, 1989b). It is essential to note that these studies have provided a pioneering step towards giving lesbian athletes a voice and making their existence in sports visible. In conclusion, the experiences of lesbians in sport are concurrent with lesbians' experiences in other institutions. Discrimination has resulted in the silencing and the exclusion of lesbian reality from all aspects of life. The underlying assumption that society is inherently heterosexual denies and erases lesbian existence.

A "Methodology from the Margins"

This research is informed by a feminist methodology that identifies women's experiences as the centre of the research focus, and that strives to achieve approaches that can be used to understand women's world (Harding, 1987; Kirby, 1991). Historically, women have been systematically denied the possibility of producing knowledge (Harding, 1987) and because lesbians are marginalized in society, the language of science, rooted in male definitions, has contributed further to exclude the lesbian experience. Frye (1991) states that having "no linguistic community, no language and, therefore, in one important sense, no knowledge . . . keeps our [lesbian] experience from being fully formed and articulate" (p. 6). In this research, each lesbian participant had the opportunity to articulate her understanding of her life, and to give meaning to her social situation using her language, therefore, becoming an agent of knowledge (Frye, 1983; Harding, 1987; Kirby, 1991). Women-centered research in sport is needed; its goal is to empower women through acknowledging their location in the broader social context. With this is mind, I have attempted to make the research process both egalitarian and collaborative. The objective was to record and report descriptions of a way of life, to discover how the lesbian participants construct their realities in sport and how they describe their social context. This type of methodology has been identified as one that stems from the margins:

> The methodology from the margins is based on the commitment to advancing knowledge through research grounded in the experience of living on the margins . . . In particular, methods from the margins must focus on describing reality from the perspective of those who have been excluded as producers of research. (Kirby & McKenna, 1989, p. 64)

To meet the research objectives and obtain a rich description of the multiple realities of the athletes, I conducted a series of semi-structured, in-depth interviews. Interviews have been described as "a strategy for documenting women's own accounts of their lives" and as "a tool for making possible the articulated and recorded commentary of women" (Oakley, 1981, p. 48). The goal of the interviews was to have the participants reconstruct and reflect upon their experiences as lesbian athletes and reflect upon the meanings of such experiences. The interview schedule was designed to establish a picture of their lives and questions explored: their early influences in sport; sport as an activity; being lesbian in sport and society; and their lesbian identity. All participants signed a letter of consent that outlined the purpose of the research and the rights and obligations of both the participant and the researcher. The interviews ranged from one to two hours in length and each interview was tape recorded upon the consent of the participant. Following the interview, the tape-recording was transcribed verbatim for subsequent data analysis.

I had established criteria for the participants' involvement in the study. First, all participants had to identify themselves as lesbian. Only two of the participants acknowledged that they were totally "out" in their sports and other environments; yet all had disclosed their sexual orientation at some point in their lives as students, teachers and workers to at least one other team member, colleague, family member or friend.

The study was limited to lesbian athletes who had participated in team sports at an inter-varsity or elite level of competition and who had participated on teams that are not all lesbian. Participants were invited to join in the study by "snowball" or "friendship network" sampling and were selected for participation based on the following criteria: (a) an interest in the research; (b) an ability to articulate their personal experiences; (c) a willingness to participate in the research within the conditions I had set for confidentiality/privacy; (d) a willingness to be part of the on-going process of the research; and (e) the local availability.

I have conducted in-depth interviews with seven lesbian athletes in the following team sports: basketball, field hockey, ice hockey, lacrosse, and water-polo. All these participants are white and between 18 to 35 years of age.

As I reviewed each transcript, I made content notes, coding and identifying key phrases and words that assisted in determining and developing categories. These categories identified themes that provide a description of the lives of the lesbian athletes and explain how these lesbians construct their experience within the institution of sport. More generally, data analysis proceeded in accordance with the principles of grounded theory methodology set forth by Glaser and Strauss (1967) and described by Kirby and McKenna (1989).

Through the systematic review of the interview transcripts, I identified several emergent themes or categories. The emergent themes from the athletes' accounts that I have chosen to describe here identify conditions, strategies and consequences affecting the inter-relations between the participants' sporting life and lesbian sexuality. These themes are particularly relevant to the current discussions on sexuality and sport. All seven participants spoke about the importance of sport in their lives, however, despite the attractions that sport has had for these women, heterosexism has denied and continues to deny them an accepting environment in which to pursue active living.

Experiencing the Conditions of Heterosexism: The Element of Risk

One common element in the participants' stories is the assumption that there is a definite risk involved in being "out" (openly identifying as lesbian) in their sports. The concept of risk is raised consistently by the participants. It varies in its significance to each lesbian, but all athletes emphasize at least one aspect of this concept. Risk describes the perceived consequences each participant either anticipates or actually faces upon disclosing her sexual identity. The athletes have feared (and still fear) that once their lesbian identity is known, they may lose the status which they occupy within teams, in their jobs or in their social groups. This status is not necessarily one in which they have much power, instead it is the status of being respected by others. The greatest feeling of risk was the perception of losing this respect. Risk has also been identified as a cause for concern for lesbians in other areas of sport and physical education (Griffin, 1992; Woods & Harbeck, 1992).

The athletes' feelings of risk are first precipitated by the knowledge that society rarely validates women's physical ability or achievements without some conditional labeling (Lenskyj, 1986). They are aware that society, in general, tends to question a woman's ability especially if she is playing in a sport that is defined as "non-traditional" for women. For example, one athlete mentioned:

if you play a sport like hockey, they're going to think "there's a good chance that the woman's going to be gay." Like you think of a figure skater, you're not going to see any gay figure skaters but you're probably going to see a lot of gay hockey players. Depending on the sport you play you're probably going to have that much more of a chance as being recognized as being a gay athlete.

The athletes, who are all involved in team sports, are therefore in a position that is stigmatized and realize that disclosing their sexuality would confirm the assumptions that people have about women playing particular sports. Confirming and being open about one's lesbianism in sport leads some athletes to believe that this will only cause a further rise in negativity. One athlete noted:

Even now, I'm thinking that there are more women in sport who are out, you know? Or it can be talked about more openly. With that I think there's a more negative view. There's greater exposure to lesbians in sport, maybe more are coming out of the closet, that kind of thing, but I think there is a rise in negativity.

Despite the increase in the number of women coming out as lesbians, for instance, in the entertainment industry (e.g., kd lang, Melissa Etheridge, Janis Ian) the participants in this research still perceive that it is not completely safe to be "out" in sports. Martina Navratilova is perhaps the most famous professional sports person who is openly gay. In a recent interview, she remarks that, in sport, no one is coming out and she views herself as the "Lone Ranger out there" in the sports world (Kort, 1993, p. 51). Greater visibility, however, inevitably provokes a backlash as heterosexism works constantly to silence and make lesbianism invisible (Durocher, 1991). This is illustrated in the account of one athlete:

two of the girls on the team were going out, they hung around a lot and comments were given and everything. And once she left the team, it seemed like those things slowed down. It wasn't as bad because they weren't seeing it. They weren't seeing them together. It's like when they see it, when they're around it or when they know it's there, then they're more nervous or more tense about it. But if it's not there it seems like, well, it's no big deal.

Feelings of risk are also provoked by observing the reaction of their coaches to the topic of sexuality. Some athletes describe their coaches as "homophobic" and the issue of lesbianism appears to be "frowned upon," "not understood" or "not addressed" by those who are in positions of power over the athletes. This, undoubtedly, leaves the athlete devoid of any validation. Some of their coaches go as far as making sure their players know they are not lesbian. One athlete tells the story of how she "came out" to her coach. The initial support and acceptance demonstrated by her coach switched dramatically to an incessant attack on her sexuality throughout the following season. She describes her coach's reaction to her wearing clothes that might associate the athlete with "a contingent of dykes":

I had a jean jacket on over top of a white t-shirt and my track pants, and I think I was wearing a baseball cap. And I came into my [coach's] vicinity and she said: "oh, you look like those women [lesbians] over there. Take your jacket off and your hat off and spruce yourself up a bit." And she said: "they look like hell and I don't want that type of woman reflected on our team."

The reactions of the participants' peers to the topic of lesbianism is ultimately one of the main conditions for the lesbian athletes to feel intense risk. As varsity and elite level athletes, they practice four to five times a week together and they spend hours with their teams on road trips. Given that the athletes think they would be rejected if their teammates knew they were lesbian, this is a lot of "time" to cover up one's sexuality. The athletes tell stories of how they have listened to numerous conversations during which the "topic of the day" was "who was and who wasn't [lesbian]." The issue seemed to cause, generally, a "rolling of eyes" and "groans of disgust." Some of the athletes are not and have not been identified as lesbian by their peers; they thus can gain access to conversations that denigrate their own sexuality. The athletes perceive that there is "definitely not a level of understanding" among players on some of their teams. Although it seems that the topic of homosexuality is frequently raised, one athlete describes this as "homo-curiousity." Nevertheless, comments are usually destructive, negative and anti-gay. Hearing others address your sexuality as "disgusting" or "sick" intensifies feelings of risk. One athlete tells of how her team always "showers up quickly and leaves if a couple of girls [are] in the shower," and "make little comments about dropping the soap." Not surprisingly, she does not want to expose her sexuality given these conditions as she feels she would be "thrown aside and ignored" by the main crowd. Some athletes, however, have been identified as lesbian and, consequently, suffer harassment from others. The women describe how they have been confronted and verbally abused by teammates and others. One woman recounts:

Last year a girl came up to me—like I just came out of the closet two years ago—and she said "oh, I hear there is a lot of rumors going on?" And I said "oh?" And she said "I hear you're gay." I said "oh really?" I handled it very calmly. I never really answered it. And she said "well, I just wanted to let you know that if you were I'd treat you differently. I wouldn't like you, you know?" And she left it at that. So that kind of really woke me up, like "wow," you know?

A second woman tells of how her ex-partner's boyfriend threatened her:

he came over and threatened me and that just hurt those feelings I had. He came over to my house and I was the only one there and he said what I was doing was "abnormal and unnatural."

When athletes do "come out" the risks they perceive can often become reality. The account of one athlete is particularly disturbing. Having "discovered" her lesbian sexuality, she disclosed to her closest friend in the hope of receiving some emotional support but she found only rejection and disgust:

> It was a really hard time for me and I thought she would be there for me and I said, "you know, I'm lesbian." And she said "what did you say?" I said, "I'm gay, I'm lesbian." And she said "oh? I'm shocked, I'm horrified. Oh my god I can't believe it." Her head was in her hands and she just kind of got up and walked away. She said "well, you can't justify yourself, you can't explain this, can you? It's all mental."

Given such reactions, it is not surprising that the athletes interviewed are "hyper-sensitive" and "paranoid" about disclosing their lesbianism. They are cognizant of the wrath of their social group and justifiably are scared to "come out." In order to reduce the amount of risk they feel, the athletes have developed strategies to cope with their situations. I have identified three themes: (a) silence and secrecy, (b) assimilation, and (c) risk-taking. These themes highlight the extent of the strategies the athletes actively pursue to cope with heterosexism and homophobia, and they describe the consequences that suppressing their sexual identity has had on the participants, namely, feelings of isolation, anger and of being de-energized.

Dealing with Heterosexism and Homophobia

Silence and Secrecy

All the participants have experienced having to be silent and secret about their sexuality. This has required not making comments to identify themselves. The athletes cope with heterosexism and homophobia by "stuffing in" their feelings, "making up stories," and "side stepping questions" about their sexuality. Even in a climate where one athlete's sexuality could be celebrated and affirmed, for instance when being involved in the Gay Games, it was still necessary for her to be secretive. This athlete was on the organizing committee for the Games but felt it was essential to conceal her identity:

> One of the stipulations that I gave was that my name not be used on any brochures or anything of that nature. There's tremendous stigma attached to it, unfortunately, with a lot of people I work with. So I was protective about my identity and I said, "on no pamphlets, no brochures, nothing." Well I ducked TV cameras all the time and I ducked reporters all the time at the Gay Games

Although athletes realize that being silent has not been particularly healthy or good for their self-esteem, they have felt pressured to keep things quiet because they have not felt safe enough to be out as a lesbian in sport or in other areas of their lives:

> At that time everybody was always talking about homosexuality because some of the coaches were sort of labeled as being lesbian. And I just sort of said "oh, this is taboo, this is not right."

Another athlete states:

> I'm not willing to be subjected to the wrath of my colleagues. They will make comments that are very anti-gay. They often refer to my "boyfriend" that I'm in a relationship with and me knowing it's "girlfriend"— I just have to be aware of the one word, boy or girl. And it's just convenient for me to carry it on. I don't have to speak specifically about gender. I can say what "we" did, gender doesn't really become necessary to refer to. And it appeases them and keeps it easier for me.

"Shutting off" emotions helped one athlete cope. One woman suggests that if she had not "managed to keep [her] feelings under lock and key, [she'd] be a basket case." Another used alcohol as a medium for dealing with the secrecy in the hope that it would "go away if we [partner and herself] drink one more." Despite wanting to say "this is who I am, this is who I'm with" these athletes have felt compelled to guard their private life. When the negative comments begin, the self-silencing is imposed. The secrecy becomes more difficult and heightened when other lesbian athletes are involved. This is the point where divisiveness occurs between lesbians, increasing the control of the heterosexual group. One athlete explains:

> In front of the other players, I don't really say anything at all. I don't. I'm not negative to the gay athletes. I definitely don't try to be negative at all to them. Like I want to stay neutral, make it seem as if I'm neutral about the whole situation. Cause I don't want to be throwing digs about them, like the gay athletes, just to make others think that I'm not. I just like to stay as neutral as possible.

Being silent and secretive has caused the athletes to put up a facade and to suppress their desire to respond to heterosexist and homophobic comments. In their lives as lesbian athletes, they have felt constrained to neutralize their sexual identity and to "give the impression that they feel the same way as the predominantly heterosexual crowd." The combination of feeling compelled to be silent and secretive diminishes the athletes' potency in challenging assumptions about lesbian sexuality.

Assimilation

It has been suggested that lesbians "pass" as heterosexuals and "cover up" their lesbianism to cope with the risk they perceive in being identified (Griffin, 1992; Woods & Harbeck, 1992). This premise of assimilating into heterosexual culture (or retreating into sameness) has been articulated in the radical feminist literature. Due to heterosexual prejudice, lesbian safety in our societal institutions can depend on her ability to pass as a heterosexual woman for fear of harassment and discrimination (Durocher, 1991; Kitzinger, 1987; Rich, 1986). The sports literature indicates that lesbians in sport, generally, live closeted double lives for fear of being identified (Baxter, 1983; Griffin, 1989; Lenskyj, 1991). Assimilation describes, in this research, the process by which the lesbian athletes feel pressured to assimilate into "normal" society as defined by heterosexist assumptions. Lesbians have been forced to push aside their feelings and acquiesce to heterosexism. In this instance, I believe that assimilation is coercive and definitely not a positive result. There is no room for lesbians to celebrate and be affirmed for their sexual diversity when they assimilate with heterosexual culture. Identities, communities, cultures and diversities may be subverted and both individual and group differences can be standardized and appropriated as they are co-opted into mainstream culture. The two elements of assimilation that I will describe are: (a) retreating into sameness and (b) de-politicizing lesbian identity.

When athletes "retreat into sameness," they actively suppress expression of their sexual identity because "they feel pressure to conform" and "want to appear like one of the crowd." At some stage, the participants have or still actively attempt to cover-up their lesbianism and pass as heterosexuals. Given the risks they identified in being "out" in sports, it is not surprising that they work to conceal their sexuality:

In my third year, I was pretty much trying not to raise eyebrows. I wanted to get somewhere with hockey and I wanted to get somewhere with my team. I wanted to be accepted in this team. Field hockey was my only really personal space. And I really wanted to feel very comfy and accepting and everything. So I didn't bring any of my lesbianism into field hockey.

The conditions that cause the participants to "retreat into sameness" are either self-motivated, where the athlete makes a conscious decision to deflect suspicion from herself, or she is responding to explicit anti-lesbian comments or feelings expressed by her social group or team. Comments like "we'll have none of those [lesbians] on our team" influence and pressurize the athlete into hiding her lesbian identity for fear of being ostracized. Many of the athletes perceive that they have to follow "some socially prescribed way of acting and behaving." This elicits emotions which the athletes describe as "tense," nervous," and "uncomfortable" as they anticipate the risks of being outside the "defined norm":

> I see how they dig at the other players [gay players] and how they're kind of excluded from a lot of things. And I've always been part of the crowd, the main crowd and I didn't know if I'd get thrown into that other group. Cause I still wanted to be part of everything that went on.

The extent to which assimilation occurs is dependent on the amount of pressure the athletes feel, at any given time, to remain invisible. Assimilation involves "putting on an act" or a "facade":

> Jokes and things, I can even remember telling them in first year. Amazing actually. But I do remember making comments and that kind of thing. I remember taking part in conversations speculating and not being really positive about it [lesbianism].

Avoiding lesbian and gay issues, silence, laughing at gay jokes, mentioning straight bars, not speaking specifically about gender, and denying being in a relationship are some of the techniques used by the athletes to assimilate into a heterosexual culture that can disassociate them from the lesbian label. In addition, some athletes have done "the dating guys thing" to cover up their lesbianism. This accessibility of women for men fulfills the requirements of both our sexist and heterosexist culture. One athlete describes how some friends had heard rumors that she was lesbian because she was living with two lesbians so when she talked about a male friend, "they got all excited, happy and they just thought it was great." The athletes have changed their behaviour and conversation in order to deflect suspicion. They have also compromised and taken drastic measures to ensure their credibility with their heterosexual peers:

> I didn't fit in with all those girls, that's big time. I didn't fit in because they all had boyfriends and I wasn't seeing anyone. And in my first year of university, I was so pressured about everyone having boyfriends, everyone had sex, that I went and had sex with this guy, just to get that pressure off my back and what a stupid thing to do, you know?

Concurrent with the process of "retreating into sameness," I have observed that some of the athletes assimilate by "normalizing" their lesbian identity. This involves equating their lesbianism with heterosexuality and/or making their lesbianism a "non-issue." This constitutes the de-politicizing of lesbian identity as described by Kitzinger (1987). The element of de-politicizing the lesbian identity is demonstrated firstly in the language participants use to self-define themselves. Four women identify as "lesbian" but prefer to use the label "gay" because of the "negative connotation of lesbian," and that "sometimes it just seems a little bit too strong." The other three participants are comfortable with "lesbian," "dyke" or "queer." It is interesting to note too that some of the athletes often describe "lesbianism" or "being lesbian" as "it," "that way," or "that situation." Again the language for self-identifying appears to be too strong. The dominant heterosexual culture, generally, controls naming and defining: the label given to things can determine how we think or feel about it (Frye, 1983). The message the athletes receive from society is that lesbianism is vilified. Overwhelmingly, these athletes desire to "be treated like any other normal person". Some feel that they are "the same but different" and speak of their "lifestyle" as not being "all that different from a heterosexual relationship," making a conscious effort to align themselves with a "defined norm." In that regard, one woman states: "I mean we do everything just like heterosexual couples." Another athlete adds:

I think the thing for all of the athletes is to treat you, first as an athlete not as a lesbian, you know? Treat you as any other normal player. That's right, you're there to play sport, you're not there to shower with the girls after. You're there to go out and play. And you shouldn't be treated differently just because of what you do in your bedroom. Like that's your own business, that's no-one else's.

Normalizing and privatizing one's lesbian identity are strategies that de-politicize the meaning of "lesbianism." The athletes can feel compelled to take this action as this can facilitate assimilation into the heterosexual culture (Kitzinger, 1987). Another strategy is to "make it [being lesbian] seem like it's no big deal." One participant describes her experience on a team that was more tolerant:

you weren't either straight or gay at polar opposite of the spectrum— you were sort of enmeshing, enmeshed all the time. Sexual identity second or third, which was really wonderful because it became a more normal quality about someone, or trait or identity. Almost became a non-issue.

Suppressing the political meaning that lesbianism may have by making their sexuality a non-issue was/and is a strategy which some athletes believe will lead to greater acceptance. Many talk about having qualities which they saw as being as much an integral part of themselves as their sexuality. They do not always want to be labeled or judged solely because of their sexuality, which one athlete describes as being such a "minute" part of herself. De-politicizing their lesbianism can make some athletes feel "like it's not so bad," "less isolated" and "more comfortable" about being lesbian. The struggle, however, that some are often faced with is the way in which they must disclose their sexual identity and educate about diversity while at the same time make lesbianism seem a "normal existence":

> it's a hard thing to do and I haven't figured out how to like, come out. It's a hard thing. It's not as if you go, "well team, I'm queer, OK? Now go run a couple of laps around the gym." Do you know what I mean? I don't know how to incorporate being "out"—to make it so it's not a big deal without making it some big production. I haven't figured out a way of just doing it—and it's hard to educate without making it a big production in a way.

All the participants have assimilated into heterosexual culture at some point in their sports lives, however, assimilation removes the potential threat that these lesbian athletes may pose to the status quo because differences are subverted and invisibility prevails (Durocher, 1991; Kitzinger, 1987). Team-mates, friends, family and colleagues, consciously or unconsciously, through covert or overt discrimination, have actively discouraged these athletes' identification as lesbian. From their stories, it is apparent that a degree of acceptance and tolerance is granted if privacy and invisibility is maintained. Presently, given the risks that remain in being "out" in the sports, many of these athletes have no other choice but to assimilate and maintain silent about their sexuality.

Risk-Taking

Some participants have, at times, chosen to ignore the risks involved in being "out." Some do not always remain silent or secret about their sexuality, and definitely do not assimilate into the status quo. The decision to take risks is often premeditated. One athlete describes how she brings her "homopho-bia" coffee mug to work. Another tells of how she will often put her hand on her partner when they are shopping, kisses her in the car and then realizes "oops, we'll get caught!" In sport it seems difficult to confront homophobia by taking risks, however, some athletes take risks to address issues of dis-crimination. Although there is an initial hesitation to confront people directly on lesbianism, some athletes have become the "language police" on their teams and at their work. They are able to address the issue indirectly speaking out against all stereotypical comments about minority and marginalized peoples. In this way they are able to educate about diversity and confront comments about lesbians without feeling too vulnerable.

Although athletes have felt pressured to lead "double lives" they do not always isolate themselves from the lesbian community. They all have socialized at lesbian bars and have participated in all-lesbian or gay events. One athlete has competed at the 1990 Gay Games in Vancouver and two more at the 1994 Gay Games in New York. Although these events do not gain extensive exposure outside the lesbian and gay community, it is sometimes difficult for the lesbian athletes to conceal what they are doing. As one woman notes about the sport milieu: "everybody knows every intimate detail of what you're doing and if they're not asking, they're too afraid to ask." Each time an athlete chooses to disclose her sexuality to someone or approaches another "presumed" lesbian, this constitutes a risk-taking behaviour:

> You don't want to approach someone on another team and be wrong, right? Cause you would look really stupid and you're putting yourself at risk. I think that risk is a big thing, you might be comfortable with yourself but you don't want to put that person in jeopardy because you know how much you've put yourself out.

The youngest participant who still struggles with how and when to fully "come out," has carefully selected a group of people and taken the risk to "come out" to them. She has gained support and this satisfies her need for acceptance and reduces her feelings of isolation. In contrast, one athlete has developed an "in-you-face" attitude and takes risks by shocking and confronting her heterosexual peers with stereotypical lesbian behaviour:

> I think I really shock the field hockey players sometimes, like if I'm wearing my cowboy boots with silver buckles on them and my labrace, they're not used to seeing me like that. Sometimes I come in looking pretty "dykey!" Oh, I've got quite the swagger and I just love it. I'll just wear whatever I want and they can deal with it. I love it, I can't get enough of it!

Consequences of Heterosexism and Homophobia

Isolation

The risks and actions taken by the lesbian athletes can result in them feeling disconnected from the very community that can affirm their sexuality. The segregation from the lesbian community may be self-imposed, however, since some athletes may be unaware of the presence of a community "out there." Heterosexism sanctions the invisibility of lesbians and, therefore, the participants have at times perceived themselves to be isolated and alone. While they were "coming out," all the athletes were actively involved in their sports. Despite the assumption that sportswomen, especially in the so-called "gender inappropriate" sports, are lesbian, some of the participants figured that they "were the only ones [lesbians] around" on their sports teams. In fact, one woman felt that she had never come "in contact with real live lesbians." These assumptions were most intense when the athletes were discovering or coming to terms with their lesbian sexuality:

> I was kind of left having had this major awakening and there was no place to go. I didn't know who to turn to and I didn't know anybody in the community. I didn't know where to go. I didn't have any resources. I didn't have anyone.

Isolation seems to occur at the very point when athletes need affirmation and are looking for a safe place, a "home" where they might be themselves or feel comfortable talking about their sexuality. When they struggled with self-acceptance, a time they describe as "confusing," "difficult," and "scary and personal," they perceived the world into which they came out as "incredibly oppressive," "not healthy," and "pretty poisonous sometimes."

The feelings of isolation were also intense when the athletes were not dating or were not in an intimate relationship with another woman. Nevertheless, having a partner, although fulfilling certain needs, did not always diminish feelings of being disconnected. Despite "finally feeling free within a love relationship" one woman recounts:

> The problem was that we thought we had to stay within our own environment. Because I didn't know what support was out there in the world beyond our private space. I didn't know who was out there.

Several women describe the experience of being involved intimately with someone on their team. The benefits of having frequent contact at team practices were, for the most part, outweighed by the fact that no one else on their teams knew about their relationship so they did not have the "feeling like there was anyone to talk to or share [their lives] with." Two women also describe the isolation they felt when they were involved with their physical education teachers or coaches. The ethical implications and precariousness of the teacher/pupil and coach/athlete relationships elicited, for these women, increased feelings of being disconnected:

She still wanted to sleep with me and with this other person at the same time when I was in high school. And I had no-one to talk to. And I was forbidden to say anything. She's a teacher, she can get into big trouble. So I didn't tell anybody. I didn't tell anybody until I got to [the city], and that was two years.

Isolation is further accentuated when the athletes are away on road trips or training with a national, provincial or varsity team. One athlete explained how she felt while comforting a heterosexual teammate, who missed her fiancé:

I felt really caught up in that emotion, thinking, "god, how incredible for you, under all the stress that we're under here, to be able to release to somebody about your personal life. And how a gay individual within the context of a straight world, the expectations of a straight world, has a hesitation about doing that or feels she can't." I noticed it, just full force at that time. How I wished I could tell somebody about how much I missed my partner back home. Because it was really hard, really, really hard.

The athletes' feelings of isolation were also caused by the lack of positive and open discussion about sexuality among teammates, friends and family. However, they were at all times conscious of what people might know about them and some of the athletes assumed that things were said that they never heard. This contributed to feelings of being under scrutiny. One woman describes the insidious discrimination that took place when, on road trips, "people were reluctant to be in the same room alone with me" even though she had not told them she was lesbian. Another woman tells of how she felt "under the microscope" when she was questioned by heterosexual teammates about where she slept in her own home. The isolation felt in this situation was further compounded by the fact that she felt another lesbian player was using her as a "scapegoat" to avoid questions about her sexuality. When lesbians are pitted against each other, the isolation of each is magnified.

It is apparent from the stories so far that the issue of sexuality is actively avoided and suppressed in sports teams. The "everybody knows but nobody says anything" syndrome (Griffin, 1992) works to isolate the athletes through invisibility and silence. One athlete describes how this made her feel "like you're in a bit of a fish bowl." This feeling of isolation and vulnerability is illustrated by one participants' account of her experience during a discussion that her team was having after a major earthquake in San Francisco:

this player turned and said, "You know what I wish? I really wish there was a whole bunch of fags underneath that bridge and it came crashing down and killed them all." And I just stood there, turned around and looked at everybody. And nobody blinked an eye or anything. They didn't say anything or acknowledge what she said. They just kept on doing what they were doing. That was the time I was "oh, what am I doing with life?" Sort of coming out . . . I felt powerless.

In addition, the superficial nature of their interactions with some people have left the athletes with the realization that "they don't know the real me." The impact of isolation is summarized by one participant who often feels like she does not know "what myself is":

I almost feel right now that I'm almost two different people. Like I have a night life and I have a day life. I go to school, I'm this person, when I come home I'm different and I can say the things that I might have wanted to say during the day—so in that way I feel like I'm two different people.

To deal with the isolation they experience, these athletes have used various coping strategies. All seven women describe that remaining silent and secret about their sexuality has kept them from being ostracized by their social group. Other strategies such as avoidance and passing are also enacted to lessen feelings of isolation. Ironically, one woman withdrew from her team and another left her province as a strategy to deal with her own isolation: self-imposed separation became a means to control the isolation they felt within their group.

Anger

Many of the athletes have felt and continue to feel "isolated" and "ostracized" from their social group. This has evoked feelings of anger towards the individuals in those groups who openly vilify the participants' sexuality. After hearing a teammate's wish that "a bunch of fags" were killed, one athlete describes the intensity of her emotions:

To wish that upon people that you don't even know, thousands of miles away—I was just flabbergasted that something so hateful would come out of somebody's mouth? I just left, I was so mad. I was fuming. I was ready to explode and I'll never forget her saying that. I never said anything to her about it, I don't know what I was going to say. Like I was just so mad, I was enraged. I had to leave. I don't know where I went. I just sat for awhile and came back later and did whatever I had to finish doing.

The ignorance, hatefulness and contempt demonstrated by those around them have fueled the anger some athletes have experienced. One athlete who has felt betrayed by her coach wants her coach to know just how much she has been hurt. She anticipates a confrontation that will "start calm and get angry" and she plans to "totally devastate her!" Another woman describes her emotions as she came to terms with the overt harassment she experienced from a teammate:

I think I get worked up about her. She's taken a lot out of me, like it's very strained—a lot of energy. Like sometimes I just feel like, you know, taking her against a wall and really wringing her neck, you know? But then [my partner] says "she's not worth it." And she's right but I mean when is it worth it? When is it time to explode, you know?

Anger has also be manifested in the athletes' personal relationships, especially if the athlete and her partner play on the same team:

[it] made it difficult, you know, in terms of seeing that person everyday at practice and competing against each other for spots. I think we spent a lot of time being mad at each other, being mad at not being able to express your feelings or talk to people about this.

Even though these athletes perceive a risk in being identified as lesbian, they still, at times, appear to be surprised by the intensity of homophobia. They question both the lack of understanding and open-mindedness that their university educated peers (coaches, students and colleagues) have demonstrated about lesbian sexuality. They feel that people have judgmental attitudes because they do not understand lesbianism nor have they experienced the situation. To overcome anger, some athletes have reversed the non-tolerance attitude:

People have the most hilarious perceptions, they say, "oh, we accept you," and that's wonderful, but I say "we'll too bad I don't accept you!"

Anger may be demonstrated by this strategy, however, it also causes a release of tension as the athletes can take control over their own affirmation by asserting that their sexuality is "part of me, if you don't accept it that's your choice but it has nothing to do with me."

De-energizing

Many of the athletes state that they have felt "frustrated," "drained" and "insulted" with the reaction of those that surround them to lesbian issues. This hurt has caused the athletes to feel "betrayed" by those who have constantly demonstrated contempt for their lesbianism:

> there's been lots of little incidences: "oh, my goodness, we can't have any of that [lesbianism] on this team." It's the little comments like that. I'm just not prepared for them, and immediately, it's just the next order of business. It's hard to be objective about it—I am very insulted.

Despite being "pretty good at the facade," acting and assimilating can cause frustration. All the athletes mention that the pressure they feel to conform to the heterosexual image is "de-energizing" and that they are often tired of appeasing the heterosexuals:

> It can be so de-energizing when you have to change your behaviour and the things you say, almost a mind set, depending on the circle of people you're exposed to. How do I protect my sexual identity from the wrath of my family? Well, at some point you either take the risk and you expose yourself hoping that you are going to get support or you cower or you compromise constantly. It's very de-energizing. It's incredibly oppressive.

For some athletes it can even be difficult to play the "language police" and call people on discrimination issues because "sometimes you're just too tired, sometimes there's just too many of them." One athlete realizes that it took so much energy to maintain the facade that "it makes her tired even thinking about it now!" They demonstrate a sense of frustration at the "double life" or "dancing routine" that they feel they have had to lead:

> It does make me feel like I'm lying. It makes me feel like they don't know the real me. They think they know things about me but in actual truth they don't know half of me. That's the one thing that bothers me the most, that people think they know what I'm like and what I'm like to be around. In actual truth they don't know me at all.

All the participants express frustration, anxiety, and exhaustion as they have had to come to terms with keeping their emotions hidden. This has compounded their feelings of being disconnected from other lesbians and from those who might have affirmed their sexuality. In their lives in sport, they have frequently felt and continue to feel limited by the oppressiveness of heterosexism. The restrictions that they have placed on themselves, and which have been imposed upon them by a homophobic society have, at times, led to diminished self-worth as their lives, loves, friends and politics are rarely validated:

> the negative side and the limiting side was the oppressiveness that I felt that other people put upon me. I couldn't be open with them and have them validate such an important component of my life. And yet they could tell me endless numbers of stories about their boyfriends, gain all sorts of support during emotionally troubled times, during euphoric times. It was just really, really tough.

The themes described above identify some of the experiences of the lesbian athletes participating within the institution of sport. Many categories overlap but the overwhelming theme emerging from their stories is that the pressure to remain closeted has served to maintain the invisibility of these athletes and to limit the possibility of their empowerment and validation through sport. This preliminary analysis of interview data illustrates the issues that concern these athletes and highlights the fact that homophobia and heterosexism have greatly affected their lives in sport.

Conclusion

The sporting environment in which these lesbian athletes participate is not free from heterosexism and homophobia. These lesbians have been silenced and discredited on their teams while heterosexuality has been vehemently acknowledged as the norm. The athletes have survived by employing strategies to guard against harassment and discrimination. As a decade of studies have demonstrated, there remains a price, in terms of emotional energy and self-esteem, for having to be silent about one's lesbian sexuality (Woods & Harbeck, 1992). However, despite the systemic harassment that these athletes have experienced, their love of sport is evident. The participants have succeeded in their sports and some have achieved honours at the highest level possible. There is room, therefore, for these athletes to resist patriarchal and heterosexual gender relations in sport and use sport as a means of empowerment.

Hopefully, this study and needed others will demonstrate how some athletes are struggling but striving to create their vision of an open, safe and empowering sports life where diversity can be celebrated. Sports associations, governing bodies, coaches and athletes need to affirm diversity and educate against the heterosexism and homophobia that is perpetuated in the

lives of athletes. More open communication is required to initiate the elimi-
nation of discrimination and promote acceptance and accessibility for lesbians, and for all minority peoples in sport (Griffin, 1989b; Griffin & Genasci,
1990; Lenskyj, 1992; Rotella & Murray, 1991). It is hoped that this research
will be a catalyst for dialogue and change.

However, the heterosystem resists change (Durocher, 1991). The current hierarchy of power and subordination is maintained by both institutions
and individuals, and campaigns to promote lesbian visibility and challenge
inequities are often obstructed. More ominously, the heterosystems' resistance has the capacity to "absorb and transform critical and dissenting positions and discourses to fit its own image and, in doing so, defuses any threat
to its own existence" (Durocher, 1991, p. 14). The subversion and appropriation of lesbian "chic" into the heterosexual mainstream reflects this transformation. Lesbian "chic" has entered our consciousness through media
representations (especially in magazines such as *Vogue* and *Newsweek*) of the
"new" post-modern, post-feminist, post-butch, post-granola lesbian. The lesbian or "lipstick-lesbian" may be tolerated in heterosexual culture when is
reinforced the notion that "she is just like a heterosexual woman except for
who she sleeps with." In addition, the heterosystem has co-opted the term
"homophobia" by categorizing individuals who cannot accept lesbians, as
homophobic. Personalizing the discrimination is myopic and ignores institutionalized systemic oppression which feminists have theorized as not personal or incidental, but the consequence of challenges to heterosexual
hegemony (Kitzinger, 1987).

Theoretically, it is essential that our emphasis remains on de-constructing
"heteronormativity." We must continue to ask why there is so little tolerance for
diversity and why heterosexism and homophobia are so central to our society
(Phelan, 1993). A commitment to a radical feminist discourse provides a conceptual framework to analyze the challenge lesbianism poses to the heterosystem
and how this is manifested in the inter-relations between sport and sexuality.
Furthermore, radical feminism critiques masculinist and positivist methodological
frameworks, legitimates the articulation of women's stories, and interprets and
re-interprets them in ways that may link multiple positioned experiences.
Postmodern politics similarly de-constructs the categories that serve to oppress
groups and challenges the legitimized knowledge of dominant discourses. From
this point of view, the theoretical claims of both radical feminism and
postmodernism are not incompatible. However, it is important to acknowledge
that the exploitation and oppression of lesbians occurs also because of their
gender; the category of being both woman and lesbian has social and political
significance in our sexist society (Durocher, 1991; Frye, 1983).

The lesbian athletes' experiences articulated here are subjective, not
representative or generic, and this research acknowledges that we are all

differently positioned and privileged, therefore, conclusions cannot be generalized. However, the lesbian stories of their experiences are placed in a context of a sports world that is dominated and defined by white, heterosexual males. The research recognizes that lesbians are "knowers" and that their experiences are "legitimate knowledge." This chapter provides a vital commentary on our understanding of the sports world as a heterosexist institution and challenges our assumptions about the "rightness and righteousness" (Pharr, 1988) of heterosexuality. In conclusion, this research is committed to a vision of a more equitable and affirming sports world and recognizes that all individuals are entitled to the privileges so far reserved to the "defined norm." We do not have the right to deny lesbians or indeed other marginalized peoples the access to active living or the possibility of their empowerment through sport.

References

Arnup, K. (1984). "Lesbian mothers and child custody." *Review of Canadian Studies*, 1(2), 35–40.

Baxter, B. (1983). "Lesbians in sport: The dilemma of coming out." *Kinesis*, Summer, 19–20.

Bennett, R.S., Whitaker, K.G., Woolley-Smith, N.J., & Sablove, A. (1987). "Changing the rules of the game: Reflections toward a feminist analysis of sport." *Women's Studies International Forum*, 10, 369–379.

Brady, E. (1993). "Gays in sport. Still in the shadows." *USA Today*, June 25, pp. 1B–2B.

Brown, K. (1991). "Homophobia in women's sports." *Deneuve Lesbian Magazine*, 1(2), 4–7, 29.

Crumpacker, L., & Haegan, E.M. (1984). *Integrating the curriculum: Teaching about lesbians and homophobia*. Wellesely, MA.

Durocher, C. (1991). "Heterosexuality: Sexuality or social system?" *Resources for Feminist Research*, 19(3/4), 13–17.

Frye, M. (1983). *The politics of reality: Essays in feminist theory*. Freedom, CA: The Crossing Press.

Frye, M. (1991). "Lesbian sex." In J. Barrington (Ed.), *An intimate wilderness: Lesbian writers on sexuality* (pp. 1–8). Portland, OR: Eighth Mountain Press.

———— (1992). *Willful virgin. Essays in feminism 1976–1992*. Freedom, CA: The Crossing Press.

Glaser, B.G., & Strauss, A. (1967). *The discovery of grounded theory: Strategies for qualitative research*. Chicago: Aldine.

Griffin, P. (1989a). "Gender as a socializing agent in physical education." In T. Templin & P. Schempp (Eds.), *Socialization in physical education: Learning to teach* (pp. 219–233). Champaign, IL: Human Kinetics.

———— (1989b). "Homophobia in physical education." *CAHPER Journal*, 55(2), 27–31.

———— (1992). "From hiding out to coming out: Empowering lesbian and gay educators." In K. Harbeck (Ed.), *Coming out of the classroom closet. Gay and lesbian students, teachers and curricula* (pp. 167–196). New York: Harrington Park Press.

Griffin, P., & Genasci, J. (1990). "Addressing homophobia in physical education: Responsibilities for teachers and researchers." In M.A. Messner & D.F. Sabo (Eds.), *Sport, men and the gender order: Critical feminist perspectives* (pp. 211–221). Champaign, IL: Human Kinetics Books.

Hall, M. (1986). "The lesbian corporate experience." *Journal of Homosexuality*, 12(3/4), 58–74.

Harding, S. (1987). "Introduction: Is there a feminist method?" In S. Harding (Ed.), *Feminism and methodology: Social science issues* (pp. 1–13). Bloomington, IN: Indiana University Press.

Hennessy, R. (1993). "Queer theory: A review of the differences special issue and Wittig's the straight mind." *Signs: Journal of Women in Culture and Society*, 18, 964–973.

Khayatt, D. (1990). "Lesbian teachers. Coping at school." In S. Stone (Ed.), *Lesbians in Canada* (pp. 81–93). Toronto: Between the Lines Press.

Kidd, D. (1983). "Getting physical: Compulsory heterosexuality and sport." *Canadian Women's Studies*, 4(3), 62–65.

Kirby, S.L. (1991). "What do feminist methods have to do with ethics?" In S. Kirby, D. Daniels, K. McKenna, M. Pujol & M. Valiquette (Eds.), *Women changing academe: The proceedings of the 1990 Canadian women's studies conference* (pp. 167–179). Winnipeg, Manitoba: Soroal.

Kirby, S.L., & McKenna, K. (1989). *Experience, research, social change: Methods from the margins*. Toronto: Garmond Press.

Kitzinger, C. (1987). *The social construction of lesbianism*. London: Sage.

Kort, M. (1993). "Net results: The Advocate interview Martina Navratilova." *The Advocate*, October 5, pp. 46–53.

Lenskyj, H. (1986). *Out of bounds: Women, sport and sexuality*. Toronto: The Women's Press.

——— (1987). "Female sexuality and women's sport." *Women's Studies International Forum*, 10, 381–386.

——— (1990). "Power and play: Gender and sexuality issues in sport and physical activity." *International Review for Sociology of Sport*, 25, 235–243.

——— (1991). "Combating homophobia in sport and physical education." *Sociology of Sport Journal*, 8, 61–69.

——— (1992). "Sexual harassment: Female athletes' experiences and coaches' responsibilities." *Science Periodical on Research and Technology in Sport*, 12(6), 1–6.

Levine, M.P., & Leonard, R. (1984). "Discrimination against lesbians in the workforce." *Signs: Journal of Women in Culture and Society*, 9, 700–710.

Lorde, A. (1984). *Sister outsider*. Trumansbury, NY: Crossing Press.

MacKinnon, C.A. (1982). "Feminism, marxism, method, and state: An agenda for theory." *Signs: Journal of Women in Culture and Society*, 8, 515–544.

——— (1987). "Women, self possession and sport." In *Feminism unmodified. Discourses on life and law* (pp. 117–124). Cambridge, MA: Harvard University Press.

Messner, M.A. (1988). "Sports and male domination: The female athlete as contested ideological terrain." *Sociology of Sport Journal*, 5, 197–211.

Messner, M.A., & Sabo, D.F. (1990). "Toward a critical feminist reappraisal of sport, men and the gender order." In M.A. Messner & D.F. Sabo (Eds.), *Sport, men and the gender order: Critical feminist perspectives* (pp. 1–15). Champaign, IL: Human Kinetics.

Nelson, M.B. (1991). "A silence so loud it screams." In M.B. Nelson (Ed.), *Are we winning yet? How women are changing sports and sports are changing women* (pp. 132–154). New York: Random House.

Oakley, A. (1981). "Interviewing women: A contradiction in terms." In H. Roberts (Ed.), *Doing feminist research* (pp. 30–61). Boston: Routledge & Kegan Paul.

Palzkill, B. (1990). "Between gymshoes and high-heels—The development of a lesbian identity and existence in top class sport." *International Review for Sociology of Sport*, 25, 221–233.

Peper, K. (1994). "Female athlete = lesbian: A myth constructed from gender role expectations and lesbiphobia." In R.J. Ringer (Ed.), *Queer words, queer images: Communication and the construction of homosexuality* (pp. 193–208). New York: New York University Press.

Pharr, S. (1988). *Homophobia: A weapon of sexism.* Little Rock, AR: Chardon Press.

Phelan, S. (1993). "(Be)coming out: Lesbian identity and politics." *Signs: Journal of Women and Culture in Society,* 18, 765–790.

Pronger, B. (1990). *The arena of masculinity: Homosexuality, sport and the meaning of sex.* Toronto: Summerhill.

Reed, S. (1994). "Unlevel playing fields." *Out,* June, pp. 92–96.

Rich, A. (1986). "Compulsory heterosexuality and lesbian existence." In A. Rich (Ed.), *Blood, bread and poetry. Selected prose 1979–1985* (pp. 23–75). New York: W.W. Norton & Co.

Rotella, R.J., & Murray, M.M. (1991). "Homophobia, the world of sport, and sport psychology consulting." *The Sports Psychologist,* 5, 355–364.

Rounds, K. (1991). "Why men fear women's teams." *Ms. The world of women,* 1(4), 43–45.

Whitson, D. (1984). "Sport and hegemony: On the construction of a dominant culture." *Sociology of Sport Journal,* 1, 64–78.

Wine, J.D. (1990). "Outsiders on the inside. Lesbians in Canadian academe." In S. Stone (Ed.), *Lesbians in Canada* (pp. 157–170). Toronto: Between the Lines Press.

Woods, S.E., & Harbeck, K.M. (1992). "Living in two worlds: The identity strategies used by lesbian physical educators." In K. Harbeck (Ed.), *Coming out of the classroom closet. Gay and lesbian students, teachers and curricula* (pp. 141–166). New York: Harrington Park Press.

6

COLONIZING THE FEMININE: NIKE'S INTERSECTIONS OF POSTFEMINISM AND HYPERCONSUMPTION

MÉLISSE R. LAFRANCE

In 1987, Nike made its first attempt to annex the women's fitness market. The first advertisement of the 1987 campaign was characterized by hard, sweaty female bodies enduring a seemingly Spartan workout; bodies moving religiously to the Nike catch-phrase voice-over "Just do it." As the ad draws to a close, the viewer becomes increasingly transfixed by the sense of female power and agency possessed by these women: they seem to have unearthed the perfect, authentic self from beneath their troublesome feminine body. As an afterthought, (saturated with sweat and meticulously disheveled hair,) triathlete Joanne Ernst sits on a locker-room bench, towel casually resting on her shoulders, and preaches: "It wouldn't hurt if you stopped eating like a pig" (Cole & Hribar, 1995, p. 360).[1]

Needless to say, women did not respond well to the ad. Goldman (1992) remarks: "Contemporary women have been so inundated by photographs of beautiful women that they often react to the images with feelings of anger" (p. 130). Nike's marketers should have known that playing on women's vulnerabilities and acute sense of bodily guilt is the oldest trick in the book! As Nike executives watched Reebok's profits in the women's market climb, they became increasingly determined to corner the "feminine" market. After the 1987 machismo advertisement disaster, Nike executives put their industrious heads together and decided that in order to successfully colonize the female body, they needed a bit of "feminine sensitivity."

In 1990, Nike hired two alleged feminists of the Wieden and Kennedy ad agency. By focusing on issues that "really matter to women," these business women revolutionized Nike's ad and marketing strategy. The way many advertisers in the postmodern media have done, Nike's marketers "pursued a wide range of superficial ideological grafts that spliced together signifiers of feminism with the consumer narrative of femininity as envy, desire and power"

(Goldman, 1992, p. 130). Suddenly, instead of appealing to women's bodily consciousness through guilt, they appealed to it through what has become renown as the "empathy/dialogue" campaign. Instead of telling a woman that she is acting like a pig straight out, Nike started to tell her that she is a pig through dissuading her from liposuction, face-lifts or diets, in favor of a nice pair of Nike shoes (see Cole & Hribar, 1995). Because remember, "Strong is sexy" and "Girls can do sport too"[2] (careful not to get stronger than your boyfriend though).[3]

Nike's profit continues to soar. Nike has indeed managed to corner the women's market. Yes, Nike has a winner on its hands: appeal to women's insipid sense of self, come off looking like an advocate of women's equality, and make money while you are at it. Perfect! Take the women-centered discourses of empowerment and corporeal liberation pioneered by feminists, turn them into conveniently commodified packages of postfeminist catharsis, and benefit all the while from the consolidation of masculine power, control and feminist backlash. Who could ask for anything more?

In the late 1990s, Nike's marketers have truly outdone themselves. In this post-Reaganist and post-Fordist epoch, marketers have conceded that it is not enough to simply empathize with women. Nike must instead transform its image from rabid business competitor to good public citizen (Cole, 1996; Cole & Hribar, 1995). It is time for Nike to give something back to the community, you know, do a little public service work. Nike's co-founder, Bill Knight, stipulates that he wants Nike to be thought of as a company with a "soul that recognizes the value of human beings" (quoted in Shalespeare, 1995, p. C1). The fact that these random acts of kindness just happen to secure present and future markets while further monopolizing the sport symbolic is, one might say, a wild coincidence. Hence, the birth of the "If you let me play" ad campaign and the P.L.A.Y. initiative.

Situating Nike in the Postmodern American[4] Imaginary

To understand Nike's success, its triumphant mass seduction of women and men, its hypnosis of both the culturally privileged and culturally marginalized, one must understand the social-political context out of which it grew. It is imperative to trace out the visible and invisible systems that work to sustain and propel the Nike philosophy, its inordinate appeal to women, and its unprecedented fiscal success. I identify three primordial and relational components—postfeminism, neo-conservatism and nostalgic liberalism—that function not only to maintain the Nike cultural aesthetic, but also to reinforce and consolidate Nike's monopoly over the social and, by extension, the semiotic.[5]

The first two concepts, postfeminism and neo-conservatism, must be viewed as mutually contingent categories that have emerged from the demonization of 1960s and 1970s feminism, and from the pathologization of the welfare state. By postfeminism, I understand three major ideas. First, a discursive field characterized by the belief that women have achieved full equality, and that consequently, the women's movement is no longer required (Goldman, 1992; Humm, 1995). Second, a cultural context wherein there is a presumed causal relationship between feminist activism and the decay of traditional moral values, the collapse of the nuclear family, and the obfuscation or "pollution"[6] of gender boundaries (Faludi, 1992; Harman, 1992; Press, 1991). As Cole and Hribar (1995) explain:

> Postfeminism can be characterized as the process through which movement feminism was reterritorialized through the normalizing logic . . . governing 1980s America. While movement feminism generated spaces and identities that interrogated distributional and relational inequalities, meanings, differences, and identities, the postfeminist moment includes spaces that work to homogenize, generate conformity, and mark Others, while discouraging questioning . . . Regardless of the limitations of the political spaces available in the postfeminist imaginary, in the postfeminist moment, the politics associated with movement feminism seem troubled, less compelling, and outdated. (p. 356)

Third, I understand the postfeminist experience as distinct from the antifeminist one. Although postfeminism is not a simple rejection of feminist ideas, but rather a recuperative and distorted vulgarization of them, it replaces activism and consciousness-raising with benefits and solutions attainable only through consumption. Where the very nature of feminism presupposes a hostility and discord with consumption, the postfeminist imperative reformulates social conflict and renders it negotiable only through consumption (Avenose, 1992; Cole & Hribar, 1995). As Goldman writes: "Mass media advertising to women represents an aesthetically depoliticized version of a potentially oppositional feminism. It is a feminism tailored to the demands of the commodity form" (1992, p. 130).

Neo-conservatism follows logically from postfeminism, although it is significantly more active in the process of demonization of the culturally marginal. As Erwin (1993) declares: "In the United States, the very emergence of a 'New Right' during the Carter and Reagan presidencies was predicated on the fusion of a cultural politics of family, sexuality and reproduction with a backlash against welfare and government spending" (p. 401). By neo-conservatism, I understand not only the demonization of movement feminism, queer activism, and Leftist organization, but the active bodily marking of those considered deviant and a corresponding political and economic order. Lewontin, Rose and Kamin explain the historical context in which neo-conservatism emerged:

The post-war period in Britain and America, especially in the last 25 years, has been marked by increasing militancy on the part of groups that had previously made few pressing demands. This militancy was in part a consequence of economic and social changes produced by the Second World War . . . In the United States large numbers of blacks and women had been incorporated into the industrial work force and armed forces. But the post-war economic boom was short-lived, and, by . . . the early 1960s in America, economic difficulties began . . . Black militancy in America grew even as the economy cooled . . . *There was a strong sense that an embattled majority was under constant siege from an unstable minority.* (1984, p. 21, italics added)[7]

Following the mass radicalization of blacks and women in the 60s and 70s (which coincided with the general decline of Western economies), both the Canadian and American polities became the locus of economic instability, eventually leading to debt and deficit hysteria and the decimation of public expenditures. This historical period can be seen as laying the groundwork for extended political hostility toward all that was apparently contributing to the devastation of the state/empire. Hence the demonization of bodies marked by relations of unproductivity: the drug-addicted body, the welfare body, the AIDS body, the queer body, the body out-of-wedlock, the cancer body.

Resources were becoming increasingly scarce, and the pernicious competition for such resources continues to be politically, economically and socially scapegoated by dominant class(es). To justify the central contradiction of North American capitalist societies—the antagonistically dialectical relationship between the concept of formal equality and the reality of widespread inequality (Lewontin, Rose & Kamin, 1984)—the proponents of dominant discourse have had to make us believe that everyone who deserves to be equal is indeed equal. If there are objects of inequality in society, it is because they are somehow exempt from the same standards of equality (Fleras & Elliott, 1996). Those who appear plagued by socioeconomic problems have sealed their own fate: they have contributed to the disintegration of the oh-so-productive family, they have had children out of wedlock, they have taken drugs, they have dropped out of school, they have had "unnatural" sexual relations, or they have quit their jobs just to go on welfare. Discursive scapegoating is a gendered and racialized process resulting from a cultural context that purports to declare war on drugs, when it is really declaring war on inner cities; that purports to declare war on welfare, when really it is declaring war on single mothers. In this neo-conservative, postfeminist context, the derivative economic processes must be seen as tools that seek to sort out the normal from the deviant in order to justify the starkly unequal state of affairs.

Cole's (1993) and Cole & Hribar's (1995) Foucauldian analysis of the modern production of deviance and pathology is important when considering the postmodern obsession with the body and, subsequently, the North American craze over Nike and its images of normal and deviant bodies. Cole and Hribar (1995) write:

> The normal and abnormal must be understood as both contingent and mutually implicated and dependent categories: The border that marks the self is continuously generated through a social process of producing and policing the other. Although the techniques and strategies of modern power are masked, the productivity of power is rendered visible in its effects: the deviant, the pathological, and delinquent. (p. 355)

Thus, the occidental postmodern imaginary is not only preoccupied with the hard, productive body, but also involved in the reinforcement of dominant normalcy achieved by the cultural saturation of images of unhealthy, addicted, soft bodies (Cole & Hribar, 1995; Morrison, 1993; Snead, 1994). Indeed, to feel normal, one must be faced with the abnormal; to feel free, one must be able to measure one's privilege against the unfree.

Morrison (1993) puts forth a similar explanation of dominant American culture, proposing that the Other assumes a critical part of the "American" consciousness. She contends that the Othering process intersects with the settling of the New World and the advent of liberal notions of freedom. Morrisson (1993) writes:

> The need to establish difference stemmed not only from the Old World but from a difference in the New. What was distinctive in the New was, first of all, its claim to freedom and, second, *the presence of the unfree within the heart of the democratic experiment*—the critical absence of democracy, its echo, shadow, and silent force in the political and intellectual activity of some not-Americans. The distinguishing features of the not-Americans were their slave status, their social status—and their colour. (p. 48, italics added)

And indeed Nike is especially worshipped for the effervescent feelings of choice (through consumption) and postfeminist empowerment it instills within us. Our liberal nostalgia and corresponding delusional notions of freedom and choice are further articulated through Nike's tag-line "Just do it," and the marketing that follows suit. Nike is seductive precisely because it allows us to disavow our material realities (Cole & Hribar, 1995) in favor of a cozier truth wherein structural relations of domination and subordination can be overcome by equipping oneself with a great looking pair of shoes, and wherein we can actively purge our own guilt for our direct or indirect role in the systems of oppression by adopting a more open-minded stance towards girls participating in sports, or perhaps by donating a few dollars to the P.L.A.Y. initiative (you know, to give those inner-city kids a chance). Nike's discourse can thus be mapped onto a ruling liberal ideology that allows us to believe (more comfortably) that we have the (buying) power and the choice to amend patriarchal capitalist "foibles."

"If You Let Me Play": Permission for Postfeminists

Nike advertisement A: A sweet, powerless, almost destitute little girl sits pensively on an outdoor swing. Her hair is blondish-brown, her eyes appear almost black against her otherwise depressed complexion. She has a freckle on her left cheek, adding to the generally infantilized aura of the *mise en page*. She is wearing a white corduroy top, complete with a pink and blue floral pattern. Her small, weak hands feebly clutch the only part of the swing visible on the page: a large, protruding black chain. Surperimposed is the Nike swoosh and the text "If you let me play." At the bottom of the page, in much smaller print, one can read the alleged benefits of "playing sports": "I will like myself more. I will have more self-confidence. I will suffer less depression. I will be 60% less likely to get breast cancer. I will be more likely to leave a man who beats me. I will be less likely to get pregnant before I want to. I will learn what it means to be strong."

For the critically inclined, one thing is for sure, the "If you let me play" ad campaign is dead on arrival. The blanket request for permission (presumably an appeal to white, bourgeois heterosexual males) is problematic, to the point where it would be theoretically impossible to propose a genuinely feminist reading of the ad. The visual effect of such gendered powerlessness juxtaposed with a plea for permission to "play sports" is stunning. Coupled with the phrases below, the semiotic consequence of the ad is one that reinforces dominant forms of masculine, racial and sexual privilege. Here is how this is so.

"I Will Suffer Less Depression"

To better tackle the implications of this narrative, one must first examine some of the primordial causes of women's depression: violence, poverty, and women's work (Evans, Barer & Marmor, 1994; Walters *et al.*, 1995). In examining these issues, some perspective can be gained on how Nike trivializes and distorts the gendered and structural nature of depression by suggesting that "If you let me play sports," "I will suffer less depression."

In Canada, recent studies (*Comité canadien*, 1993; Statistics Canada, 1995) show that violence against women is epidemically pervasive, and this is taking into account the fact that 62 percent of sexual assault victims do not report assaults to police. A recent Canadian study (*Comité canadien*, 1993) notes that: "taking all three kinds of sexual assault as defined in the Criminal Code into account ... two out of three women, well over half the female population, have experienced what is legally recognized as sexual assault" (p. 28).[8] The Canadian Committee on Violence Against Women stipulates: "The short and long term effects of sexual assault include depression, anxiety, trouble with interpersonal relationships, reduced job effectiveness, diminished sexual satisfaction, sexual dysfunction and sleep disorders, and increased use of sedatives and sleeping pills ... with that comes a profound loss of self-esteem and self-worth" (*Comité canadien*, 1993, p. 29).

In terms of poverty as a cause of depression, it is crucial to underline the fact that recent studies (e.g., Health Canada, 1996; National Council of Welfare, 1996; Walters *et al.*, 1995) have confirmed socioeconomic status as the major determinant of physical and mental health. In a country where the health system manages to provide almost equal access to care for everyone, inequalities in health status persist. The latest *Report on the Health of Canadians* could not be clearer: "The rich are healthier than the middle class, who are in turn healthier than the poor" (Health Canada, 1996, p. iii). At the same time, in North America, the feminization of poverty is intensifying. Harman (1992) explains the Canadian context:

> While female economic dependency is not new, some of the manifestations of what happens when women live in ways other than traditional dependency arrangements, are becoming gradually more visible ... As recent statistics reveal, women's poverty is most striking among those living without men. According to the National Council on Welfare, 75 percent of never-married female single parents, 52 percent of previously married female single parents, 44 percent of unattached women over the age of 65, and 33 percent of unattached women under 65, are living in poverty in this country. (p. 8)

Granted the feminization of poverty, it is understandable that "on measures of self-rated health, psychological well-being, stress, and depression, women do not score as well as men" (Health Canada, 1996, p. 27). As Harman (1992) has demonstrated, depression caused by poverty must be viewed as a gendered issue.

When one reviews the current findings on the Canadian work force, one finds that women dominate the lower ranks of all types of employment. Women are paid substantially less than their male counterparts, women's skills are devalued and there is seldom standardization or regulation (Armstrong & Armstrong, 1994; Clement & Myles, 1994; Ng, 1993). Women's work in both private and public spheres is more often than not characterized by monotony, repetition and poor working conditions. Indeed women's work in the paid labor force is often an extension of private duties and is thus devalued both in the public and private spheres. Li (1992) notes that gender groupings produce significantly unequal effects on earnings; white males make the most followed by non-white males, white females make considerably less than either of the latter, and non-white women make even less than all three of their counterparts. Hence, while there are many who say that the wage gap between women and men is slowly drawing to a close, the current literature on the political economy of gender indicates quite the opposite. As demonstrated by Armstrong and Armstrong (1994) there is no reason to believe that women will make any significant gains in wage equity, as their work becomes increasingly devalued and deregulated.

All this being said, it is clear that claiming that "playing sports," presumably with a shiny pair of Air Jordans, will contribute to solving the problem of feminine depression, denies, trivializes and renders invisible the very concrete and structurally articulated oppression of women and its contribution to depression.

"I Will Be 60 Percent Less Likely to Get Breast Cancer"

Is the statistic contained within this phrase supposed to assert the reliability of the claim? Where did this figure come from, from what research, and who commissioned it? Who is 60 percent less likely to get breast cancer if they do sport? White bourgeois women living in clean neighborhoods? Lesbian women who have higher rates of breast cancer infection (Martindale, 1994; Winnow, 1992)? Poor women who live in "inner-city" neighborhoods often characterized by industrial pollutants (Zambrana, 1987)? Recent medical studies show that heightened breast cancer rates are largely due to environmental pollutants as well as to drugs commonly prescribed to women (e.g., hormone replacement therapy), and not to individual predisposition (Castleman, 1994; Worcester & Whatley, 1992). Lewontin, Rose and Kamin (1984) provide a striking example of how Nike's logic can be seen in other neo-conservative social factions:

An extension has been made from disordered brain to defective body. It is now clear that certain work hazards—for example noxious chemicals, high noise levels, and electromagnetic radiation—are responsible for a great deal of chronic illness including permanent respiratory disorders, nervous disorders and cancer. While the first obvious response to this knowledge is to alter the conditions of work in favor of the worker, it is now being suggested seriously that workers be screened for susceptibility to pollutants before they are hired. (p. 21)

This argument can be mapped on to issues of quality of life and environmental spaces. Nike's contention de-responsibilizes those corporations systematically polluting the air and consequently the agricultural and natural elements. Nike's statement locates the breast cancer problem within women and their "susceptibility" to disease. Again, Nike's discourse not only trivializes but colludes with those inherently capitalistic forces making our natural lives unsafe, and makes it look as though the deviant female cancer body can be avoided if women would break with their lazy lifestyles.

"I Will Be More Likely to Leave a Man Who Beats Me"
"I Will Be Less Likely to Get Pregnant Before I Want to"

Right, women stay with men who abuse them because they have low self-esteem and somehow manage to get themselves pregnant! These sorts of statements intimate that women can freely and without difficulty leave the men who beat them, who rape them, who harass them in the workplace, and who coerce them into sex. Of course, they conveniently omit the economic realities of male domination, the psychological manipulation experienced by abused women, and the mixed messages directed at all women; does a real woman "Just do it" or "Just say no?"

Most importantly, these Nike narratives locate the source of crucial problems within the women themselves: after all, they are the ones who allow such male behaviours to take place! In this sense, the advertisement represents a textbook manifestation of the neo-conservative "blame-the-victim" philosophy. In contrast, a truly subversive ad[9] would subvert the presupposed acceptance (and indirect advocacy) of male violence and feminine subordination. It would profile a male swearing that he would stop abusing his wife or girlfriend, that he would stop harassing his employees, that he would stop pressuring his girlfriend into sex, and that he would take responsibility for condom-use and other measures of sexual safety. Instead, with Nike, the abused female body is marked as deviant while the abusive male body (and behaviour) is normalized.

"I Will Like Myself More"
"I Will Have More Self-Confidence"

There is a well-known correlation between physical activity and a positive self-concept. However, both sociologists and those responsible for equipping their children or themselves with sporting gear can attest to the increasingly exclusive and inaccessible nature of sports. Not only is the cost of equipping oneself with a pair of shoes, a T-shirt and a pair of shorts exponential, but with the general rape and destruction of natural outdoor space, individuals are increasingly led to having to participate in physical activity in some sort of organized context (especially women, for whom many outdoor facilities are unsafe). It does not suffice to throw on a pair of old running shoes, pick up a baseball bat and head to the park. Urban reality requires most to suit themselves up in Nike attire, pay for bus fair to the closest sport complex, pay an entry fee at the complex, and pay a fee for participating in a given sport league. For those women who have children, or who are balancing multiple jobs (read most women), the cost, time and energy associated with this excursion renders it an impossibility. This leads me to the question: who has the means to increase her self-esteem *à la* Nike? To whom is this ad really directed?

Nike claims that improved self-esteem and confidence will result from girls and women being permitted to play sports. What Nike does not say is that permission is the last thing girls and women need! Recent Canadian research (see Donnelly and Harvey, 1996) has shown that the foremost determinants of involvement in physical activity are class and gender. According to Harvey and Donnelly (1996, p. 4), what girls and women need is a way to first overcome a number of "systemic barriers" to access to sport and physical activity: "infrastructural barriers" (e.g., high cost, lack of transportation, lack of time, lack of facilities, lack of security, etc.), "superstructural barriers" (e.g., sexist policies, traditionally masculine nature of activities, lack of role models or pro-women facilitators, lack of cultural exposure to the activities, lack of information on the activities, prejudice, sexist language, etc.) and "procedural barriers" (e.g., lack of social support, lack of rights to services or opportunities, lack of decision-making power regarding the organization of the activities, lack of women in the organizational structure, top-down and hierarchical management style within the organization or the facilities, etc.).

Granted the existence of these systemic barriers and the fact that they are all deeply rooted in determinants such as class and gender, it is quite possible that adult women who do participate in physical activity and sports are a breed apart. In Canada, these women are most likely white, urban, educated, able-bodied, young, and middle and upper-class who are rich enough to have decent living and working conditions as well as leisure time. It should be understood then, that it is those characteristics (and not the fact that they get involved in sports during their leisure time, as Nike would have us believe) that may explain their levels of self-esteem, self-confidence, and mental and physical health.

General Problematization of Nike Narrative(s)

First off, I will dwell on a previous interrogation, for I think it is an important one: To whom are the Nike ads genuinely directed? To look at them, one would presume that the target audience consisted of young children, particularly young girls. Perhaps, if we really wanted to stretch things, we might say that the ad is directed at parents or even female parents of young girls (due to their buying power). This is the assumption of scholars Lucas (1996) and Poeppelman (1996) who have proposed empowering feminist readings of the advertisements. And yet, one finds these ads appearing in issues, for example, of *Men's Health* and the excessively macho *Inside Sports*.[10] What does this imply in a postfeminist, neo-conservative and nostalgically liberal American imaginary?

It implies that the target audience is composed, at least in part, of white middle-aged bourgeois males. In light of such understanding, we can begin to unearth the Nike discourse at work. What makes these images of pathetic, powerless girls draped in hyper-diluted postfeminist rhetoric so ideal for male consumption? These young destitute bodies are marked by their unfreeness, their sickness, their dependency; this marking serves to normalize the free and healthy (?) bodies consuming the ad. White male power and privilege are reinforced and sustained. The dominant body is normalized; the deviant body further pathologized.

Second, one must interrogate the ad's recuperation and subversion of class issues. Those most acutely affected by the issues delineated by Nike are those who live on the discursive margins of society. Yet, Nike proposes a solution (i.e., consumption) that is only accessible to those who make up the dominant class. This attests to the paradoxical if not bogus character of Nike's "concern."

Third, we see a blatant manifestation of the remaking of "women's" issues. What is ingenuous about Nike is how it has managed to position itself such that it can effectively rearticulate "women's problems," their cause, and their solution (Cole & Hribar, 1995). In each phrase, the gendered problem delineated is individualized, de-politicized and naturalized. Where movement feminism saw unwanted pregnancies, violence against women, and low self-esteem as assuming an inherently systemic and historical character (as well as occupying an epidemic social proportion), Nike renders these events issues of personal choice (America: The land of the free) that can be easily amended by the individual (Michael Jordan worked his way out of the ghetto). Pursuant to postfeminist discourse, feminist problematization is rearticulated into hyper-simplistic, conformist and ridiculously cautious and colloquial phrases such as: "I will like myself more." When compared to Nike's "celebrity" feminism, both the activist and theoretical feminist projects appear redundantly complex, uselessly stressful and borderline hysterical. Where movement feminism asked women to interrogate their own bodies, sexualities, and beliefs, where it required them to fight against the complex systems that oppress them, where it proposed that they boycott some of their favorite clothing lines, that they become vegetarian and that they denounce degrading male jokes, Nike proposes a far easier and more comfortable solution. Nike offers woman-centered emancipation and asks for very little in return; no discomfort in the class room, no clothing or food boycotts, no late-night strategic meetings, no stress when reading the newspaper. All Nike asks for is your bank card and a little home-style consumption.

Fourth, the "If you let me play" ad idealizes and naturalizes post-Reagan conservatism not by what it says, but by what it does not say. Discourses of compulsory heterosexuality, "natural" male aggression, the nuclear family, and family planning are presupposed; capitalist productive processes go unquestioned; liberal notions of freedom and choice are both imagined and secured. When the most fundamental values of the "American" imaginary seem threatened by feminists, blacks, immigrants, queers and social activists, Nike manages to rejuvenate them. Cole and Hribar write:

> We do not suggest that Nike simply co-opted feminist rhetoric and values; instead, we argue that Nike's financial success as well as Nike's position in the National imaginary must be understood within the dynamics of what has been called post-Fordism and its corresponding postfeminist imaginary and affective culture. We contend that Nike has become a celebrity feminist through its rearticulation of women's issues and the position of the bodily work and consumption in stabilizing identity in a historical moment marked by instability and insecurity. (1995, p. 350)

We see then, that the Nike "If you let me play" advertisement amounts to three things: (a) an exploitation of gender, racial and class subordination; (b) a remaking of "women's" issues; and (c) a consolidation of postfeminist, neo-conservative and liberal discursive domination.

P.L.A.Y.: The Mythologization and Marking of the Deviant Body

> Nike advertisement B: "A girl is being born in America; and someone will give her a chance" reads the text superimposed on a young African-American woman. This "girl" has well developed breasts. This "girl" is dressed in baseball attire. Prominently situated on her baseball jersey is the team logo: "Devils." All we see on her shirt is the particularly ominous image of a devil. The black and white nature of the ad makes the logo's contrast particularly strident. The young woman leans unassumingly against a formidable mesh-wire fence, the horizon is dark, there is no one around, the location is ambiguous; she could be in the diamond dug-out, or she could be in prison.

To analyze this second advertisement, I will use Snead's (1994) framework for understanding spectatorship. Inspired by Eco's theory of semiotics and Barthes' S/Z, Snead devised a framework that: (a) permits an analysis of narrative stereotypes; (b) elucidates how the codes they form become legible; and (c) reveals what such codes might conceal. To make sense of what is being expressed and/or concealed in the P.L.A.Y. advertisement, I will use two Sneadian concepts: "mythification" and "marking." Snead defines mythification as:

> the replacement of history with a surrogate-ideology of elevation or demotion along a scale of human value . . . . [It] also implies identification, and requires a pool of spectators ready to accept and identify themselves with film's tailor made versions of reality . . . . [By] mythification and repetition, white and black filmed images become large-scale models . . . [describing] structures, limits and an overall repertoire from which both white and black viewers in the real world select possibilities of action and thought. (1994, pp. 4–5)

Snead (1994) discusses the concept of marking in the following terms: "As if the blackness of black skin itself were not enough, we seem to find the colour black repeatedly over-determined, marked redundantly, almost as if to force the viewer to register the image's difference from white images. . . . Common markings include 'Negro dialect,' . . . elevation/lowness; motion/stasis; cleanliness/dirtiness; distinction/group-mass" (pp. 5–6).

The discursive forces working to create and sustain Nike's success can be seen as the "identification" component outlined by Snead; the postfeminist, neo-conservative imagination blatantly constitutes a spectator ready and able to apprehend Nike's narrative codes (albeit often unwittingly), to synthesize them, and to identify and accept them. This attests to the historical nature of Nike's success. Let us, then, interrogate those codes present in the P.L.A.Y. advertisement.

First of all, the black and white character of the ad, amidst a sports/fitness magazine overflowing with colour, makes the ad appear particularly maudlin. The fact that Nike's ad campaigns are often characterized by an effervescence of colour, attests to the sort of effect the ad is supposed to have. The young woman's blackness, within the context of this dual-tone ad, is marked; the spectator is forced to register the all-consuming nature of the young woman's racial identity.

Second, consider the fence. Even if she is genuinely standing beside the baseball diamond dug-out, the landscape is terribly reminiscent of a prison. With Nike's marking of the black body, the blatantly overt "Devils" logo, and the ambiguity of the setting, Nike successfully goads the interpreter to associate this "girl" with the failed inner-city. The fact that a spectator might associate the welfare mother, the drug addict, the armed robber with the ad's image, an image so far removed from any of these phenomena, speaks to the power of racial codes at work.

Third, in the same way the issue of unwanted pregnancy was discussed in the first ad, without broaching the issue of abortion or reproductive freedom, this ad negotiates a particularly tense issue of cultural identity. Note once again the text superimposed on the image: "A girl is being born in America." I contend that Nike wanted to ensure that there was no doubt about the young woman's country of origin; for had there been any question about her Americanness, the neo-conservative cultural context would have refused its sympathy (after all, she could be from Cuba, the Barbados, Africa, God knows where, and she might have been the one who stole my white uncle's job). Thus Nike succeeds at marking the "girl" as both American (as overtly stated in the ad) and not American enough—for she might have been covertly questioned had her country of origin not been specified.

Fourth, the claim that she is only now being born poses a question of historical significance. Does the young woman not have a history of her own, or can Nike determine it? Certainly the ad insinuates that she is ahistorical, that Nike has both the power and ability to attribute a past or signification to her. In making the young woman appear "newly born" not only does Nike position itself such that it can rewrite the young woman's history, as well as that of her entire culture, but it effectively marks her as a new American, a tolerated Other, an individual who will finally be taken into the arms of America because she is finally playing by white America's rules. As delineated in Snead's (1994) concept of marking, wherein history is replaced by surrogate-ideology, Nike's historical revisionism ostensibly erases the oppression and the multitudinous concrete and systemic violences committed against the African American, and replaces her struggle with a plea for help to the kindred dominant white American.

As with the first advertisement, Nike has imposed a discursive dependence on the culturally marginalized. The marking of the weak, unfree bodies in both cases serves to further naturalize the power of the dominant classes. What appears to many (at first glance) as a counter-mainstream message aimed at improving the lot of those disadvantaged by American society, turns out to be an instrument of boundary maintenance, where absolutely no relations of domination are destabilized.

Women, Nike, and the Global Order

Since the mid-1960s, socialist and Marxist feminists have argued that we cannot understand the organization of production without understanding the particularly gendered forces and relations of such production. In this particular case, not only must we grasp the gendered processes and sexual divisions of labour that go into sustaining Nike's fiscal empire, but Nike's newly forged "pro-woman" image demands that we unearth what really goes into making the product that promises to prevent and cure so many gynocentred social and physiological ailments. Once I have located and understood the gendered nature and impact of Nike's "Just-in-time" post-Fordist mode of production, I will be able to fully illustrate why the women who benefit from the consumption of Nike products inevitably do so at the expense of Third World women.

Nike's Corporate Organization

To start, Nike must be situated in a post-Fordist economic context. By post-Fordism, I understand an economic mode of production built on concepts of "flexible" accumulation (Cole & Hribar, 1995), "Just-in-time" marketing and production[11] (Armstrong & Armstrong, 1994), and what Harvey, Rail and Thibault have called "a new international division of labour . . . [wherein] a growing proportion of the population in developing countries is engaged in the production of goods for the reproduction of the lifestyles of those living in developed countries" (1996, p. 265). Nike's transnational corporate organization involves managing the design and promotion of its product domestically, but sub-contracting the actual production processes to foreign-owned, Third World factories (Cole & Hribar, 1995; Harvey, Rail & Thibault, 1996). Subcontracting is especially efficient among multinational corporations like Nike, for it theoretically "absolves" them of any responsibilities vis-à-vis the worker. Nike led the way when in 1980 it moved its production from the United States to Korea, Taiwan and China. The Third World's cheap labor and low standardization coupled with low-volume, niche production have contributed to Nike's fiscal success exponentially (Cole & Hribar, 1995; Harvey, Rail & Thibault, 1996; Stasser & Becklund, 1991).

Cole and Hribar (1995) contend that the impetus for the de-localization and global dispersion of production comes from the neo-conservative notions of productivity, efficiency and progress that haunt the American imaginary. Consequently, the Nike sneaker has come to represent massive financial market success not only for the American imaginary, but also for that of the Third World. The de-politicization of development ideology has been accompanied by the notion that Americans are doing the honorable thing on an international level, "giving" jobs to those who would otherwise have nothing. For instance, Dusty Kidd, Nike's head of communications, said: "We can't dictate to governments how they run their labour laws" (cited in Shalespeare, 1995, p. C1). Kidd proceeded to highlight the fact that "in a country where the population is increasing at the rate of 2.5 million per year; with 40 percent unemployment, it is better to work in a shoe factory than not to have a job at all" (cited in Shalespeare, 1995, p. C1). This old and tired co-opted version of white man's burden continues to serve as the justification for incessant human rights violations in the Third World—violence taking place at the hands of massive transnational American corporations. One Third World woman worker responds to Kidd's statement by declaring: "We need protection from our government. We don't need foreign companies to come to Indonesia to take advantage of Suharto's denial of human rights" (cited in Shalespeare, 1995, p. C1).

Situating the Exploitation of Third World Women

In an effort to stimulate foreign interest and investment, Third World governments attempt to maintain a "stable" workforce using any/all necessary means. These governments extend tax breaks, low rents, and deregulated wages and standards to multinational corporations wishing to set up shop in their country. More importantly, these governments also ensure that the workforce itself is "stabilized." Kirshenbaum (1996) comments on the Indonesian situation: "Among the most repressive in Asia, the regime has tried to guarantee a stable workforce through fear. Security forces monitor factories and break up strikes, and every now and then a particularly outspoken worker "mysteriously" winds up dead" (p. 23). Shalespeare also reports that "The Indonesian government admits that its minimum wage of 4,600 rupiahs ($2) a day is fixed below the poverty line to encourage foreign investment" (1995, p. C1). To guarantee a cheap and exploitable workforce, these foreign-owned factories employ 85 percent women (À propos de Nike, 1995; Shalespeare, 1995). Women are less likely to be organized, they are in a socially more desperate situation and they can be paid less. These women are repeatedly (if not constantly) exposed to toxic chemicals, dangerous, outdated machinery and poorly ventilated spaces (Kirshenbaum, 1996). Moreover, these women are often the objects of sexual and physical intimidation by their male "superiors" (Kirshenbaum, 1996; Shalespeare, 1995).[12] Cole and Hribar (1995) draw on the research of Annette Fuentes and Barbara Ehrenreich when explaining the plight of the woman worker:

> Factory provided housing is typically inadequate and unhealthy: For example, as many as three workers who work different shifts may share the same bed and up to 20 women may be crowded into one small room. Work conditions extend from monotonous and repetitive tasks and dangerous work with acids and other chemicals without safety equipment, to exposure to dangerous sources of light and hazardous lint fibers and chemical fumes. (p. 364)

After wide criticism of Nike's failure to ensure that the workers making the "all American shoe" are paid the minimum-wage salary to which they are entitled and that the working conditions are safe and sanitary, Nike responded by saying that they have a full time Nike employee on site to ensure adherence to the "Nike code of conduct." Unfortunately, what Nike neglected to say, was that this same person is in charge of surveying production performance (À propos de Nike, 1995). Minor detail . . .

Minimum wage for these women workers in Third World countries is fixed at approximately $1.30 per day. In 1992, Nike paid Michael Jordan $20 million for his efforts; this is roughly equivalent to the cumulative amount Nike paid 12,000 Indonesian women workers for their efforts (À propos de Nike, 1995; Shalespeare, 1995). When women workers have collectivized, organized and struck, they have most often been greeted with severe physical repression by State authorities, sexual assault, and the loss of a job. In some areas, where strikes and other forms of organization have been successful (e.g., South Korea and West Java, Indonesia), Nike has left the area in search of factories that are less organized and where labour is less expensive. Cole and Hribar write: "In the pursuit of profit and the lowest possible production costs, Nike has moved from Taiwan, Hong Kong, Singapore, and South Korea to Malaysia, the Philippines, Thailand, China, Indonesia, Vietnam and Burma, which share the ambition of conserving inexpensive labour forces in order to attract multinationals" (1995, p. 365).

The above information is quite telling in terms of the inevitably exploitative nature and impact of consuming Nike products. One can now appreciate the pernicious nature of hyperconsumption—the fact that it not only creates empty societies, empty cultures and empty people, but also that it is contingent on the brutal exploitation of Third World women.

One Woman's Freedom: Another Woman's Straitjacket

In this chapter, I have attempted to show, among other things, that no matter the benefits that some white, North American, bourgeois women might extract from Nike products, no matter how much more they like themselves after they work out, or how much self-esteem they muster up because someone "has let them play sports," they acquire these benefits inevitably at the expense of women workers in the Third World. No matter how empowering or disempowering Nike manages to be toward these North American women, they are doing so on the backs of Third World women.

I would liken the "invisible" relationship shared by the female North American consumer and the female Third World worker to that found in Canadian households where a bourgeois white woman works outside the home and, in turn, hires a foreign domestic worker to sustain the nuclear family. In a situation where the domestic will not obtain Canadian citizenship (and by extension, is under the constant threat of deportation), unless her employer writes official letters of endorsement, the white bourgeois woman has the same power and potential for exploitation as did/does her husband. As Macklin (1994) explains:

> Though female employer and domestic worker share gender as a common attribute, they are separated by race, class and citizenship. Each of these vectors exert their own force on the nature, trajectory, and distribution of power in society. They also permit one woman to objectify another in various ways that are influenced, but not precluded, by gender. (p. 35)

This example speaks to the relationship that accrues between the North American consumer and the Third World worker. The novel thing about this illustration is that it speaks to the power of racism as a tool for the justification of even the most obvious forms of female subordination. Indeed, Nike is capitalizing on the fact that white supremacist and patriarchal ideology has given white women the tools to use their various social and economic power and privilege to distance themselves from the "Other" women they either intentionally or inadvertently oppress (hooks, 1981; Macklin, 1994). Certainly those women who participate in Nike (sub)culture directly or indirectly align themselves with the white men whose power they seek to share. As hooks (1981) writes:

> white men have supported changes in the white woman's social standing only if there exists another female group to assume that role. Consequently, the white patriarch undergoes no radical change in his sexist assumption that woman is inherently inferior. He neither relinquishes his dominant position nor alters the patriarchal structure of society. He is however, able to convince many white women that fundamental changes in "woman's status" have occurred because he has successfully socialized her, via racism, to assume that no connection exists between her and black women. (p. 155)

Those women who continue to consume Nike products, while aware of the cruelly exploitative situation of Third World women, have somehow managed to convince themselves of at least one of three things: (a) women workers are better off with what little Nike pays them than nothing at all; (b) the pain and suffering of North American women is more important; and/or (c) it is their right and privilege, as members of the developed world, to hyperconsume and exploit in the process—it is within the natural economic order of things. Whatever complex racist processes go on in the minds of

North American women to justify the systematic subordination of non-white women (because, don't forget, Nike not only exploits the Third World women, but pathologizes non-white women right here at home), they must truly believe that there is, as hooks says, no relationship between themselves and the women who make their shoes.

When one sits down with the facts in front of her, Nike's "pro-woman, pro-self-esteem" image seems fraudulent and repulsive at best. The overwhelmingly seductive and hegemonic representation of Nike desires, however, is that which has at once allowed, assuaged and reinforced white women's distance from non-white women. Both domestically and internationally, it is the racist and socially constructed distance between black and white that allows Nike to continuously portray itself as "socially progressive." And it is this distance that allows white, bourgeois women to participate in Nike's inevitable exploitation of Third World women without guilt or reflection.

Conclusion

Having situated Nike in a neo-conservative, postfeminist and nostalgically liberal cultural imaginary, and having analyzed Nike's production and marketing processes, one comes to appreciate the extent to which Nike has become the creator of discursive modes of domination and subordination. From feminism and black activism to postfeminism and post-Fordist production, Nike has led the way in rearticulating the needs of the American people, re-writing the history of black struggle in America, vulgarizing and distorting the feminist cause, all the while systematically effacing the visible and invisible oppressive structures of both Third World production and dominant discourse that sustain and propel Nike's success.

Notes

1. For an exhaustive and highly insightful discussion of the politics of Nike, see Cheryl Cole and Amy Hribar's (1995) "Celebrity feminism: Nike style post-Fordism, transcendence, and consumer power."

2. Phrases appearing in quotation marks have been taken from popular Nike expressions; expressions that once appeared in advertisements, but that have now found their way into the popular vernacular.

3. Bordo (1991) and Bartky (1993) have observed the phenomenon of how when women are encouraged to go to the gym to workout, it is not to become "strong," but rather to sculpt their body. They comment on the social disapproval of those women who develop bodies that might challenge the feminine ideal while competing with the masculine one.

4. I find the term "American" problematic because of the way it denotes United States' imperialism. It should be noted that I use the term "American" loosely, primarily to refer to the United States experience, though I often liken the U.S. experience to that of the Canadian one when situating Nike in the cultural imaginary. I have used the term nevertheless, to capture the truly "imaginary" character of a national imagination that views the United States of America as the only America that matters.

5. Kristeva (1970) also argues that there is an important connection between the social and semiotic. She contends that all individuals have two subjective levels in common: the conscious, social or symbolic; and the pre-language or semiotic. The duality of this interpretational process not only moulds but creates the signification of all social phenomena.

6. Haraway (1985) coined the notion of the "pollution" of boundaries. For her discussion, see "A manifesto for cyborgs: Science, technology and socialist feminism in the 1980s."

7. For an excellent Marxist analysis of scientific practice, see Lewontin's (1984) *Not in Our Genes: Biology, Ideology and Human Nature.*

8. Sexual assault is only one of many forms of violence against women. I am focusing on this specific form of violence against women simply for the sake of illustration. For a recent and comprehensive analysis of the different types of violence against women, see Comité canadien sur la violence faite aux femmes (1993) *Changing the Landscape: Ending Violence—Achieving Equality.*

9. Of course, the subversive potential of most advertisements, given their relationship to consumption, is minimal at best.

10. I have not done an exhaustive media search of all periodicals. What I posit is based on a limited investigation. However, the fact that these advertisements appeared in such unequivocally male-oriented periodicals at all suffices to prove my point.

11. Armstrong and Armstrong (1994, p. 21) define the post-Fordist mode of production: "Rather than economies of scale they employ economies of scope, shifting nimbly from one product to another with the help of sub-contracting and programmable equipment. They have tried to replace buffer stocks with just-in-time production, and see themselves as both demand- or customer-driven and knowledge-intensive . . . This system is then organized through sub-contracting arrangements with a diversity of suppliers, to get the right clothes into the right stores very quickly. With an almost obsessive emphasis on advertising that blurs the distinction between private consumption and social concern, and indeed that between commerce and art, it is also selling an image."

12. Shalespeare (1995, p. C1) relays the words of Eni, a worker in an Indonesia shoe factory: "If we make a mistake, they call us dogs and prostitutes and some-

times they hit us." Shakespeare goes on to report: "Marsinah was murdered after leading a strike in the Patur Putra Surya watch factory to ask for a 23-cent pay rise. She was 25 years old and had been tortured, raped and stabbed. The Legal Aid Foundation believes this was the work of local military called in by the factory owners" (1995, p. C1).

References

"À propos de Nike" (1995). *La démocratisation: l'économie au service des personnes.* Ottawa: Les personnes d'abord!

Armstrong, P., & Armstrong, H. (1994). "Women's work in the labor force." In P. Armstrong & H. Armstrong (Eds.), *The double ghetto: Canadian women and their segregated work* (pp. 15–45). Toronto: McClelland and Steward Inc.

Avenose, K. (1992). "Forum." *Advertising Age*, November 23, p. 18.

Bartky, S.L. (1993). "Foucault, femininity, and the modernization of patriarchal power." In M. Pearsall (Ed.), *Women and values: Readings in recent feminist philosophy* (pp. 151–165). Belmont, CA: Wadsworth.

Bordo, S. (1991). " 'Material girl': The effacements of postmodern culture." In L. Goldstein (Ed.), *The female body: Figures, styles and speculations* (pp. 106 130). Ann Harbor, MI: University of Michigan Press.

Castleman, M. (1994). "Why? The answer is worth knowing because, in this case, knowledge could be power—the power to redirect the nation's research priorities toward discoveries that might save thousands of women." *Mother Jones*, May/June, pp. 34, 39–42.

Clement, W., & Myles, J. (1994). *Relations of ruling: Class and gender in postindustrial societies.* Kingston: McGill-Queen's University Press.

Cole, C.L. (1996). "American Jordan: P.L.A.Y., consensus, and punishment." *Sociology of Sport Journal*, 13(4), 366–397.

Cole, C.L., & Hribar, A. (1995). "Celebrity feminism: Nike style post-Fordism, transcendence, and consumer power." *Sociology of Sport Journal*, 12(4), 347–369.

Comité canadien sur la violence faite aux femmes (1993). *Changing the landscape: Ending violence—Achieving equality.* Ottawa: Supply and Services Canada.

Donnelly, P., & Harvey, J. (1996). "Overcoming systemic barriers to access in active living." Unpublished report submitted to Fitness Canada, Ottawa, Ontario, Canada.

Evans, R.G., Barer, M.L., & Marmor, T.R. (1994). *Why are some people healthy and others not? The determinants of health of populations.* New York: Aldine.

Faludi, S. (1992). *Backlash: The undeclared war against women.* London: Chatto and Windus.

Fleras, A., & Elliott, J.L. (1996). *Unequal relations: An introduction to race, ethnic and aboriginal dynamics in Canada* (2nd edition). Scarborough, Ontario: Prentice Hall Canada.

Goldman, R. (1992). "Commodity feminism." In *Reading ads socially* (pp. 130–154). New York: Routledge.

Haraway, D. (1985). "A manifesto for cyborgs: Science, technology, and socialist-feminism in the 1980s." *Socialist Review,* 80, 65–107.

Harman, L.D. (1992). "The feminization of poverty: An old problem with a new name." *Canadian Woman Studies,* 12(4), 6–9.

Harvey, J. & Donnelly, P. (1996, November). "Bringing class back in: The case of access to sport and physical activity." Paper presented at the annual conference of the North American Society for the Sociology of Sport, Birmingham, Alabama.

Harvey, J., Rail, G., & Thibault, L. (1996). "Globalization and sport: Sketching a theoretical model for empirical analyses." *Journal of Sport and Social Issues,* 20(3), 258–277.

Health Canada (1996). *Report on the health of Canadians.* Report prepared by the Federal, Provincial, and Territorial Advisory Committee on Population Health for the meeting of Ministers of Health. Ottawa: Supply and Services Canada.

hooks, b. (1981). *Ain't I a woman: Black women and feminism.* Boston, MA: South End Press.

Humm, M. (1995). *The dictionary of feminist theory* (2nd edition). New York: Prentice Hall.

Kirshenbaum, G. (1996). "Nike's nemesis." *Ms. Magazine,* November/December, p. 23.

Kristeva, J. (1970). *Le texte du roman : Approche sémiologique d'une structure discursive transformationnelle.* The Hague: Mouton.

Lewontin, R.C., Rose, S., & Kamin, L.J. (1984). "The politics of biological determinism." In R.C. Lewontin (Ed.), *Not in our genes: Biology, ideology and human nature* (pp. 17–36). New York: Pantheon Books.

Li, P.S. (1992). "Race and gender as base of class fractions and their effects on earnings." *Canadian Review of Sociology and Anthropology,* 29(4).

Lucas, S.M. (1996). "'If you let me play': Tools of resistance revealed in primetime." Paper presented at the annual conference of the North American Society for the Sociology of Sport, Birmingham, Alabama.

Macklin, A. (1994). "On the inside looking in: Foreign domestic workers in Canada" In W. Giles & S. Arat-Koc (Eds.), *Maid in the market: Women's paid domestic labour* (pp. 13–39). Halifax: Fernwood Publishing.

Martindale, K. (1994). "My (lesbian) breast cancer story: Can I get a witness?" In M. Oikawa, D. Falconer & A. Decter (Eds.), *Resist! Essays against a homophobic culture* (pp. 137–150). Toronto: Women's Press.

Morrison, T. (1990). *Playing in the dark: Whiteness and the literary imagination.* New York: Vintage Books.

Murray, J. (1991). "TV in the class room: News or Nikes?" *Extra!,* September/October.

Ng, R. (1993). "Sexism, racism, Canadian nationalism." In H. Bannerji (Ed.), *Returning the gaze: Essays on racism. Feminism and politics* (pp. 223–241). Toronto: Sister Vision, Black Women and Women of Colour Press.

Poeppelman, T.R. (1996). "Creating an 'advertising language' for and about the female athlete." Paper presented at the annual conference of the North American Society for the Sociology of Sport, Birmingham, Alabama.

Press, A.L. (1991). *Women watching television: Gender, class, and generation in the American television experience.* Philadelphia: University of Pennsylvania Press.

Shakespeare, J. (1995). " 'Just do it' for 25¢ an hour." *The Ottawa Citizen,* December 14, p. C1.

Snead, J. (1994). *White screens, black images.* New York: Routledge.

Statistics Canada (1995). *Women in Canada: A statistical report* (3rd ed.). Ottawa: Statistics Canada, Family and Social Statistics Division.

Strasser, J.B., & Becklund, L. (1991) *Swoosh: The unauthorized story of Nike and the men who played there.* Orlando: FL: Harcourt Brace.

Walters, V. et al. (1995). *La santé des femmes dans le contexte de la vie des femmes.* Ottawa: Supply and Services Canada.

Winnow, J. (1992). "Lesbians evolving health care: Cancer and AIDS." *Feminist Review,* 41, 68–76.

Worcester, N., & Whatley, M.H. (1992). "The selling of HRT: Playing on the fear factor." *Feminist Review,* 41, 1–26.

Zambrana, R.E. (1987). "A research agenda on issues affecting poor and minority women: A model for understanding their health needs." *Women and Health,* 12(3–4), 137–160.

PART III

VIRTUAL SPORT, REPRESENTATION, AND THE POSTMODERN MEDIASCAPE

7

SEISMOGRAPHY OF THE POSTMODERN CONDITION: THREE THESES ON THE IMPLOSION OF SPORT

GENEVIÈVE RAIL

Like a seismography of the postmodern condition, this essay presents three "theses" and links them to the phenomenon of sport: (a) the implosion of art and sport, (b) the implosion of the body and sport, and (c) the implosion of images and sport. Postmodern art, the "plastic" body and contemporary mass-mediated images are presented as the results of veritable implosions: they are without depth, fragmented, scattered and, to satisfy the needs of a late capitalist society, they are produced and dispersed with vertiginous speed. The nihilism inherent to these elements explains the theme of catastrophe underlying the theses that explore their intersection with sport in contemporary culture.

The theses suggest respectively: (a) sport's appropriation and reproduction of postmodern artistic and aesthetic forms, for the hyper-consumption of sporting goods and images; (b) sport's appropriation and transformation of the natural body into a "perfect" sporting body/machine under the control of postmodern social power; and (c) the media's production and reproduction of sporting images that are seductive, though empty and soporific for the already amorphous viewing masses. The three theses also suggest that far from being a simple descriptive and classificatory term positioned outside of history, language or science, sport is in fact a discursive and historical construct at the intersection of a multiplicity of domains (e.g., arts, politics, science, technology, medicine, media, etc.), all of which being part of, and marked by postmodern culture. The essay allows us to deconstruct sport, to better understand its forms and functions of producer and reproducer of the social, and to expose its links with the issues of social power, domination, ideology, resistance and transformation.

The Postmodern Moment

At the beginning of the 1980s, the debates concerning postmodern art, culture and society became quite intense in North America and in many West

European countries. It is in the arts that postmodernism first became the center of attention, as artists renounced modern forms in architecture, literature, cinema, dance, painting, sculpture and other domains (Burger, 1984). The purity and elitism associated to modernism were discarded in favor of a populist eclecticism and the "pastiche" of forms and styles from different periods.

In philosophy, the emergence of a postmodernist current was also observed; a current that was to replace the tradition of the Descartes-Locke-Kant trio (Baynes, Bohman & McCarthy, 1987). Some argued that modern philosophy had destroyed itself with its impossible dream of a philosophical foundation made of absolute truths (e.g., Rorty, 1979). Others underlined the problems associated to the metaphysical assumptions of Western philosophy. Derrida (1967), for example, mentioned that modern philosophy was defective because of its binary thought system and its bias for oral (as opposed to written) language. The precursors of the postmodern critique of philosophy were Nietzsche, Heidegger, Wittgenstein, Dewey, Bataille and Artaud, if we set aside, of course, the critical works done by those often considered within the post-structuralist current (e.g., Derrida, Foucault, the Tel Quel group, and Barthes, in his most recent writings).

Postmodern social theories also appeared. In Barthes' writings on mythologies and popular culture (1957) and those of Lefebvre on everyday life (1968), we could anticipate the postmodern social theories of writers such as Baudrillard, Lyotard, Deleuze and Guattari. Baudrillard (1980), for instance, described the postmodern society as one oriented toward the production of simulations and simulacra that create new types of subjectivity, experience and culture. Lyotard (1984) discussed how the postmodern "condition" marked the end of the great dreams of modernity, and suggested the dismissal of revolutionary politics of the past and totalizing social theories. Attempting to preserve what Lyotard called *"les grands écrits,"* Jameson (1984) reformulated the notion of postmodernism and argued that it should be interpreted as the "cultural logic of late capitalism." This gave new life to great Marxian theories. However, not long after, authors such as Kroker and Cook (1987) clearly explained why contemporary society is a scene escaping all social categories and theories of the past and, therefore, requires a new form of theorizing.

In fact, the postmodern moment had arrived. Perplexed, intellectuals, artists and those who could be labelled "cultural entrepreneurs" wondered whether they should join the carnival or sit on the side-lines until the fad disappeared into a whirl of cultural *nouveautés* (Cheal, 1990, Kellner, 1989). But postmodernism refused to go away. Still today, what was supposed to be a fad continues to have effects on a variety of academic disciplines and other domains within contemporary culture.

What is postmodernism? It is what we see on television, in theaters, in schools, in offices, and in the streets of our cities: not the beginning of something new nor the end of something old, but the catastrophic implosion of contemporary culture in a series of scenes that reflect excess, disaccumulation and panic (Kroker & Cook, 1987).

The Implosion of Art and Sport

It is from architecture, literature, painting, sculpture, cinema, photography and their connected domains that emerge the new forms of postmodern culture (Frampton, 1986; Paoletti, 1985). These forms include artifacts clearly detached from modern art practices. In fact, this "post-modern" art represents a fraction of the modern experience that modernism had always attempted to suppress: that which is decentered, contingent, unstable, fragmentary, and popular (while a few modernists appreciated the vitality of popular culture and incorporated some of its elements in their art, these elements were always subordinated, domesticated by their formal order: somehow modern art was opposed to popular culture at least as much as it was to bourgeois culture). In the 1960s, modernism became greatly impoverished, apparently victim of its own formalism (Jencks, 1987). Indeed, which direction to take after an absolute purity of styles? What next after Ad Reinhard's all-black paintings and Barnett Newman's straight lines?

Modernism had always marginalized and exercised its hegemony over other artistic models. However, toward the end of the 1960s occurred a range of art practices not subordinated to modernism (Crowther, 1990). Opposed to the seriousness of "high modernism," these postmodern practices exhibited a new carefreeness, a pure eclecticism, an element of play even, embodied in oeuvres such as those of Andy Warhol. Their new elements were paradox, ambiguity, contradiction, pluralism, double-coding, multivalence, anamnesis, nostalgia, pastiche, anastrophe, disharmony, and anthropomorphism (Jencks, 1987). Unlike the formally sophisticated and aesthetically exacting modern art, postmodern art developed to become both fragmentary and inclusive of elements found in high culture and pop culture.

Today, the contents of art are imprinted with the forms, categories and elements of the (late-capitalist) cultural industry, and new art "spaces" emerge. For example, magazines, billboards, T-shirts and other unconventional places have become privileged artistic premises. Artistic productions take shapes and adopt surfaces that connote promotional culture. Transcending the frontiers of aesthetics and of art itself, postmodern art envelops the advertisement images, the television mosaïc, and the various symbols of consumer capitalism. The "morality" of modernism is substituted with irony, cynicism, commercialization and, in some cases, explicit nihilism (Kellner, 1989; Kroker &

Cook, 1987). In brief, we are witnessing the implosion of art and the appearance of postmodern art.

While the political *avant-garde* of the modernist movement celebrated dissidence and advocated a revolution of art and contemporary life, postmodern art happily exists in a world that reflects the pluralism of aesthetic style and play (Huyssen, 1984; Jameson, 1984). Art seldom operates at a critical level: the political horizon becomes detached from contemporary art practices. Postmodern art comes to not only represent the consumer society in which we live, it becomes one of its privileged commodities.

In the 1970s, "committed" art had been one of the pillars of artistic postmodernism. Issues of gender, race and class had become central, particularly following the publications of Michel Foucault. Local, contingent, and institutional struggles as well as gender relations became principal concerns, as was notably the case for American artist Barbara Kruger. However, artists quickly realized that in a late capitalist society, commodification spares nothing and nobody. Hence, the work of postmodernist artists of the 1980s and 1990s implies an acknowledgment of the inescapable commodification, the inevitable assimilation of postmodern art by the market forces (Wood, Frascina, Harris & Harrison, 1993). Just as committed art had been underwritten by the theories of Foucault, the work of latter postmodernist artists owes much to the ideas of Jean Baudrillard (1973).

Baudrillard claims that the Marxist stress on work and production merely mirrors the work ethic of capitalism, and that the "leftover" area of aesthetic play is only the other side of this mirror: neither side can promise emancipation. Instead, Baudrillard proposes to focus on the political economy of the sign, that is, on the media, information, and the production of meanings. Baudrillard argues that reality is no longer a concrete world of work and production but rather a world of representations, signs and images. Commodities/signs are pre-eminent in this "hyper-reality" and it is on them that postmodernist artists fix. It is from this perspective that may be viewed the works of Jeff Koon and Haim Steinback, for example, where consumer items are selected, prised loose from their normal context, and displayed in ways usually reserved for precious objects (see Wood *et al.*, 1993). Alone or juxtaposed, commodities/signs found in popular culture (e.g., vacuum cleaners or designer sportswear) are elevated in the contexts of art. Postmodern art goes beyond ideological complicity in the reproduction of commodities and becomes the perfect site for the re-commodification process characteristic of late capitalism.

Postmodern art is made of the signs and consumer goods that flood the social space, hence its evident link with the body and sport so present in contemporary culture. Among other things, postmodern art includes fashion, television, cinema, and photography; domains that are more and more connected to the body in general, and sport in particular. The social space is traversed with sport, its merchandises, and its heroes (e.g., Michael Jordan) or anti-heroes (e.g., O.J. Simpson). All of these entities constitute commodities/signs at the center of the postmodern citizens' media space (Andrews, 1992). Postmodern art envelops popular culture and (re)produces sporting images, commodities and signs (Errais, 1991). On the one hand, the media's obsession with the body and sport and, on the other, the cybernetic reality of contemporary culture (Andrews, 1991), help us to understand the dynamics between sport and the commodification of postmodern art.

The dialectical relationship between art and sport is completed by the fact that sporting images and commodities are constructed in such a way as to reproduce postmodern aesthetics (or anti-aesthetics) and facilitate their hyper-consumption. Sport invests itself with postmodern elements in order to better constitute itself in an object of consumption designed for the citizens of postmodernity. Aesthetic production is integrated into the production of mass-mediated images of sport and sporting goods. In late capitalism, the economic necessity for the constant production of seemingly new commodities explains the essential structural role played by innovation and aesthetic experimentation.

The Implosion of the Body and Sport

The self that had been lost in the culture and structures of modernity (Huyssen, 1986) struggles to return in postmodernity, while the body is more and more engulfed in the field of social power (Rail, 1991b). Epistemology, ideology, technology and semiology reveal this subordination of the body to the postmodern apparatus of power; an apparatus of advanced capitalism designed to regulate the mass production and hyper-consumption of those commodities, images, messages and signs that come to structure daily life.

Epistemologically, the postmodern body moves to the center of subjectivity. The self in touch with the body, the self caring for the body, that is what sport is said to offer. Through sport, the self becomes conscious of the body, the self is embodied, exteriorized (Rail, 1992). Not only bodily practices, but the body itself become a sign of the self. Enhancement of the outside is undertaken in the service of the inside, and body image becomes not only a symbol of physical health, but of mental health as well (Glassner, 1989) By conveying the idea that spirit can shape matter, postmodernity tends to reduce surface and depth to a relative sameness (Brown & Clignet, 1988). The postmodern self is only skin deep.

Ideologically, the "body to excess" (Kroker & Kroker, 1987) becomes the perfect analogue to the general economy of excess structuring postmodern society (Bataille, 1976). The body is inscribed by the signs of the fashion industry and the arts. Skin itself becomes clothing for the body, and body parts become artistic creations. The body, especially the impossibly ideal athletic body, holds a signal position in the somatic culture as locus for billions of dollars of commercial exchange and site for moral action (Crawford, 1984; Harvey & St-Germain, 1995; Loret, 1990). In publicity and marketing, glorification of the perfect body means that the natural body is condemned to be shattered in parts that are bought, sold, exchanged, replaced, molded, trained, modified, tanned, photographed, filmed and reified. The orgy of body parts that flood our society reveals how media present the plastic-fantastic body as a reality, and the natural body, as a fraud of the second order (Featherstone, 1983; Kuhn, 1985). Sports media provide particularly compelling examples of how body parts (e.g., arms of tennis players, legs of runners, feet of soccer players, etc.) undergo alienation and commodification to excess.

Sport constitutes a particularly powerful ideological mechanism because it is dominated by the body, a site of ideological condensation which meaning is intimately linked to the biological (Cole, 1993). Biologizing knowledges (Foucault's *"effets de vérité"*) and their appeal to the natural tend to dissolve the traces of training and cultural work done on the body and its movements. The logic of the sport/body combination contributes to the illusion that sport and the body are transparent; outside of politics, culture and economics. But the reality is quite different. Postmodern citizens see the body through conceptual glasses; they apprehend it once interpreted by the arts (Klotz, 1984), the fashion industry (Faurschou, 1987), medicine (Becker 1986; Foucault, 1970) or sport sciences (Cole & Rail, 1994; Meier, 1988), and once compared to media-fabricated images (King, 1993; Kuhn, 1985). In the postmodern condition, the natural body disintegrates and what is apprehended as the body is only a simulacrum.

Technologically, the body is subordinated in many ways. The perfect (i.e., the plastic, cyborg) body and the operations necessary to produce it become elements essential to the functioning of society. Meanwhile, the natural body becomes a failure from the point of view of this society, a useless object when considering the late capitalist system. In abolishing the distinction between work and leisure, the human body comes to have a rhetorical existence not only in the world of work, but also in the world of sport and fitness. The natural body becomes an object superfluous to the operation of a postmodern sport system. The natural body is covered with aerodynamically-designed clothes; shaved for speed; locked into ankle, knee, arm, and neck braces; invaded by diuretics, growth hormones, high-calorie foods, vitamins, carbohydrates, "pure" blood and multiple drugs; divided in parts to be separately trained and shaped with computerized machines; and divided in pieces that are sometimes thrown away and replaced by artificial versions (e.g., Teflon articulations). The natural body disappears. In modern times, the image was modelled after the human body. In postmodernity, the reverse is true: the human body is modelled after the image.

In postmodern society, high performance sport is increasingly contingent upon computer-revealed genetic potentialities (e.g., physical and psychological), absorption of chemical substances, individualized diet and training, and publicity and marketing. The body becomes a means of production that can be sacrificed for the product. At risk for injury or death, the body-machine is often pushed to the limit: it must produce exploits, medals, records, and thrilling sensations for the spectators. The human machine is appropriated by the political-economical system, and the search for solutions to problems such as stress, violence or injuries in sport is granted not to educators (i.e., those susceptible of changing sport or the attitudes of its participants), but to the scientific and medical communities. In that perspective, when the athletic body is damaged, efforts are geared to quickly repair it and return it to its production function. Furthermore, when this human machine becomes obsolete, it is replaced by less-human, high-tech versions of the body made possible by postmodern technology. Technologically, the reality of the natural body becomes that of "ultra-refuse" (Kroker & Kroker, 1987).

Semiotically, the body constitutes a sign system that is processed through the imperatives of postmodern social power. Mediation of the body, advertisement of the skin and exteriorization of body organs match a social system that depends on the outering of body functions (we need only to think of Walkmans as ablated ears, *in vitro* fertilization as alienation of the womb, or computers as external memory). In our civilization of signs (Baudrillard, 1970), objects are consumed in their sign form and their meaning is derived from their position in a system of differentiation (De Wachter, 1988). In postmodern somatic culture, the body is seen as a sign of the self: it constitutes identity.

As natural objects, bodies are all more or less identical, all subject to the same laws: these are the bodies found in anatomy and physiology books. But in the process of sculpting and transforming these natural objects into cultural creations, men and women appropriate their own bodies. Sport practices thus allow for the establishment of identity. But the sporting body is not simply made to be seen: it is also designed for action. Sport thus implies another system of differentiation, one based on the performance of this sporting body. Hence, sport practices represent a mean of identification and double differentiation.

The body experiences its immersion in nature when it grows old or sick. Nature mercilessly contradicts the human dream of self-mastery, freedom or infinitude. If, as a sign, the athletic body fascinates, it is because it signifies this dream. The perfect body fabricated and glorified by the sport institution and the media (Meier, 1988) symbolizes infinitude and self-mastery:

a body that belongs not to nature but to the self. While sport should allow for the discovery of human limits, the glorification of the sporting body orchestrated by the postmodern power apparatus rather incites a refusal of human finitude. However paradoxical, it is in this vision of the "rational self" controlling bodily existence that enters the computerization, medicalization and pharmacologization of the athletic body. In such vision, the alienating power of nature is replaced by a power that is not only technical, but that requires the infrastructure of an entire social, economic and political system (Becker, 1986; De Wachter, 1988, Foucault, 1970).

The recent questioning of binaries that have long structured Western thought (e.g., nature/culture, body/mind, man/woman, etc.) as well as the debates present in postmodern society (e.g., those concerning drugs, violence, abortion, new reproductive technologies, AIDS, sexual orientation, bioethics, eugenics, etc.) bring to the fore the body/power relationship and the notion of the body as a political and ideological resource *par excellence* (see Cole, 1993). Interestingly enough, sport (as an ensemble of cultural practices) is traversed by the same political debates: drugs, AIDS, sexuality, genetic engineering, gender testing, violence (of athletes or ex-athletes), and so on. These debates suggest that in the era of "cyborgs" (Haraway, 1985), of "pure body" and "plastic body" politics (Cole, 1993) and of scientific and state panopticons (Cole, 1993; Rail & Harvey, 1995), it is crucial to reconsider how sport and fitness (including their knowledges, discourses and technologies) are spread out in everyday life and represent a veritable "body McCarthyism" (Bordo, 1989).

The Implosion of Images and Sport

The term "postmodern" has often been used to describe the culture of late-capitalist societies. The postmodern space is one of endless needs and over-consumption, a space that commodifies everything present in its hegemonic field, even knowledge (Baudrillard, 1970; 1988). Postmodernity features a commodification of information and a transcendence of the print era (Guiraud, 1975): it is based on and fed by signs, images, spectacles (Dator, 1989; Debord, 1983; Kuhn, 1985). Thanks to technology, mass media interpret, produce and distribute images and therefore revolutionize ways of knowing and apprehending reality (Carey, 1989). In fact, mass media are so present in societies of reproduction that they tend to become reality. The overproduction of images creates a world marked by a proliferation of information and a decrease in meaning. Meaning is literally imploded when the information is devoured and then reformulated by the media. This implosion is characterized by the obliteration of distinctions between fantasy and reality. The "real" is absorbed by televisual screens and the cybernetic images they produce become reality. Nature is dying and culture is taking over: representation, not direct experience, comes to determine all meaning.

These tendencies partly explain the growing importance of mediated sport in postmodern society. While interest, emotion and pleasure are more and more absent from the day to day routine, mediated sport allows for a "mimetic" type of excitement (Elias & Dunning, 1986) which resembles that produced in real life situations, but in a safe and pleasurable way (Goodger & Goodger, 1989). No longer based on an economy seeking to satisfy the needs of modernization, postmodern society corresponds to a surplus economy which is driven to perpetually create new desires (Bataille, 1976; Jameson, 1984; Kroker & Cook, 1987). In postmodernity, there is less of a desire for sport than there is of a sport of desire: a constant and growing desire for new products, sensations and emotions—a desire fed but never fulfilled by the media, by the images.

Sports media do not escape this logic. The postmodern era has witnessed a veritable explosion in media sport (Wenner, 1989b), and the need to reach larger audiences has fostered the appearance of new technologies allowing to create more attractive, dramatic and exciting sport spectacles (Coakley, 1990). It is suggested here that the contemporary "model" (see Rail, 1991a) used to broadcast sport events is one oriented toward the creation of more and more desires, while being anti-mediatory and contributing to the aesthetic populism, fragmentation, depthlessness, and effacing of history characteristic of the cultural space of late capitalist society (Jameson, 1984).

Anti-Mediation

The model used to mediate sport is anti-mediatory in that it does not allow communication. The viewer is always positioned as a passive observer or listener and has no freedom but to consume or reject the sport spectacle. In fact, to borrow Baudrillard's terms, we could say that sports media are:

> anti-mediatory and intransitive. They fabricate non-communication . . .
> if one agrees to define communication as an exchange, as a reciprocal
> space of a speech and a response. . . . [Media] are what always prevents
> response, what makes impossible any process of exchange. (1976, p.
> 208)

More recently, sports media have adopted a certain reversibility of circuits (e.g., via readers' mail, viewers' phone calls, surveys, "interactive" programs, etc.), however they have neither given space to an original response nor changed the existing discrimination between the roles of producer and spectator. In postmodern culture, when the audience can influence production or programming, it is only in the most reified fashion (see Eastman & Meyer, 1989).

The cultural impact of mediated sport and the postmodern technologies associated with it does not lie on the diffusion of images and messages as much as on the imposition of a "model" through which the meanings of sport events are framed, organized and interpreted according to the terms and needs of a patriarchal, racist, heterosexist and capitalist postmodern society (Baudrillard, 1980; Rader, 1984; Wenner, 1989a).

This model is such that viewers are lead to believe that what is presented to them constitutes the natural and universally accepted version of sport. In reality, however, the model underlies an ideology that transpires not only in the choice of programs and narratives, but in the choice of production techniques and technologies. For example, the model portrays male professional team sports as more important and more deserving of coverage than others, although they have little to do with reality. Furthermore, materials, camera locations and editing styles are used to transform sport into a dramatic event to which the audience is invited to attach itself (Cantelon & Gruneau, 1988; Whannel, 1984). Pre-game analyses, camera angles, close-ups, slow motion, focus on certain athletes, game summaries and highlights are as many pieces of a model oriented toward the production of emotion, drama and heroism, and centered on the meaning of the outcome for those present (Cantelon & Gruneau, 1988; Coakley, 1990; Gruneau, 1989).

The media model used to broadcast sport prevents real exchanges from taking place. The viewer does not participate. The viewer only consumes a sport spectacle already analyzed, interpreted, digested, regurgitated. Furthermore, with the help of postmodern technologies, sports media elicit a type of "fetishism" (Duncan & Brummett, 1989), or fascination directed toward a spectacle, which encourages sports consumption. Fetishes or objects of fascination are created when athletes and their actions are commodified—transformed into commodities to be examined, appraised and consumed (Duncan & Brummett, 1989). Commentators recite athletes' personal statistics and fill non-action time with performance evaluations. The game analyses and color commentaries invite the spectator to look intently at the screen. The rapid succession of images is unified through the technology of replays, slow motion, superimposed images and split screens. These devices enhance the fascination for the spectacle and keep the viewer from participating in its production.

Cultural Reproduction

The contemporary model of mediated sport implies both a real and a symbolic separation between the audience and the producer. It also implies a univocal type of communication. Broadcasted sport spectacles become ideology: they incite the negation of real life and maintain the impoverishment and servitude of consumers. The media recreate sport and transmit values that produce and reproduce culture (Cantelon & Gruneau, 1988). Values such as success, winning at all costs, progress, male superiority, individualism, conformity, nationalism, science, technology, quantification and specialization are all keys to decode mediated sport and apprehend its real meaning (Bryant, 1989; Duncan & Hasbrook, 1988). The current model of mediated sport also contributes to postmodern culture by fostering aesthetic populism, fragmentation, depthlessness and effacing of history.

Aesthetic populism. In postmodernity, the technological capacity to produce images favors a production of signs that are increasingly divorced from their epistemology. This loosening of signifiers from received signifieds leads to an aestheticization found in all types of media (Faurschou, 1987; Featherstone, 1990; Huyssen, 1986). This aestheticization translates into a mode of empty discourse in which the social becomes a "commodified object of contemplation, rather than a condition of praxis" (Lucaites & Charland, 1989, p. 32). The analytical and the critical are displaced with the pleasures of sign consumption, and media must appeal to aesthetic shock effects to mobilize or at least motivate the population (Kroker & Kroker, 1987). In these conditions, sports media have a distinct advantage, granted the importance of aesthetics in sport. However, sports media must still resort to the spectacular and create (sometimes out of nothing) aesthetic effects in order to satisfy their audiences. Music, amplification of noises on the sport field, collages, superimposed graphics, rapid cuts, computer simulations, color arrangements, shocking images: everything is made to capture and sustain the audience's gaze. Mediated sport is oriented toward the consumption of images, aesthetic forms, and brilliant but empty signs.

Fragmentation and depthlessness. Postmodernity can be distinguished by its fragmentation of time, space, the human subject, and society itself (Hardison, 1989; Hassan, 1987; Lyotard, 1984). The contemporary model of sports media contributes to this fragmentation in many ways. For example, the fundamental principle of mediated sport is to choose elements from one or several sport events, isolate them from their global context, and then juxtapose them to other isolated fragments. This principle called "montage" (Sarup, 1989) presupposes a fragmentation of reality, a loss of meaning, and a creation of new meaning. Fragmentation also occurs when televised sport events are interrupted by advertisements, special reports, replays, pre-recorded interviews and so on. In fact, for many sport spectacles, the percentage of live-play time represents less than 10% of the total broadcast time (Meier, 1984).

The fragmentation of mediated sport is inextricably linked to its characteristic depthlessness. The type of narrative that would produce knowledge is simply absent. Since observations are focussed on the personal rather than the social, and since social problems and political questions are not analyzed or discussed, we can speak of a veritable "anti-sociological bias" (Hilliard, 1994) on the part of the sports media. The superficial discourse of the commentators is harmonized with the manipulative speed of the images and the shrunk attention span of the viewers. For instance, play and players are constantly reified in the form of abstract statistics that break from the deep reality of the sport experience and that prevent any epistemological effort. Sports media are in *"l'ère du vide"* (the era of emptiness), to borrow an expression from Lipovetsky (1983).

Effacing of history. Postmodern society is characterized by an effacing of history, which Jameson (1984) links to the tendencies toward "pastiche" and "schizophrenia." The practice of pastiche, or the imitation of dead styles, indicates our incapacity to focus on the present. As for schizophrenia, it is associated with the experience of isolated, disconnected signifiers that fail to link up into a coherent sequence and therefore do not permit an experience of time.

The model used to mediate sport contributes to both tendencies. For example, pastiche work is realized when segments of "nostalgic" films featuring heroes of the past are cut and pasted everywhere in the television production of sport spectacles. The lost ability to locate ourselves in the present can be seen in the use of replays, slow motion or stop action. The successive play of isolated cameras, wide angles, close-ups and superimposed graphics also modifies the sport spectacle by shattering the natural rhythm of the event. Time is manipulated, lost, in order to dramatize the action. Split screens and screen windows concentrate events that are diffuse in space, while highlights concentrate events that are diffuse in time. In several ways, mediated sport defies localization and adds to the effacing of history.

Cultural Hegemony

Cultural hegemony, along with anti-mediation and cultural reproduction, is not only a result but also a part of the ideology of the sports-media model found in postmodern society. To the same degree that this mediated ideology becomes more widely known, revered and internalized, it catalyzes a type of uniformity that suggests cultural hegemony (Cantelon & Gruneau, 1988; Mosco & Wasko, 1988). For more than 40 years, "mass-culture" theorists of the Left such as Adorno and Marcuse have written about television as a mesmerizing conduit for the hegemonic orders of capitalists squeezing ever more consumption from the viewing masses. This perspective has remained strong although it has often been questioned by Right-wing theorists, and other perspectives and concepts have been used as counter-arguments (see Fiske 1986, 1987; Jensen, 1990; Peters, 1989). Fiske, for example, has introduced the concept of "polysemy" to refer to the audiences' ability to interpret and make their own sense out of media texts. This concept implies the possibility for audiences to move beyond what may have been the preferred reading, in order to construct a reading expressive of the opposition to the dominant forms of understanding implied by the media. Fiske's further suggestion is that audiences may be resistant to the mass-mediated constructions of reality and thus also to any ideological impact.

Following conservative arguments and the concept of polysemy, it could be suggested that the postmodern technology used to mediate sport is not *inherently* a structure of hegemonic power. However, the perspectives on which these arguments and concepts are based do not challenge the present media model, which is precisely what must be overturned if cultural hegemony is to be resisted. As suggested by Baudrillard (1976), any attempt to modify, subvert or control media contents is without hope if is not broken the monopoly of speech. Not that everyone must speak, but that we must allow speech to be received, given, exchanged. In the last instance, what must disappear is the notion of medium, of intermediary. As Baudrillard (1976) said: "we meet the neighbors at last when we watch, with them, our apartment building on fire."

Conclusions

In this essay were presented three theses of implosion and catastrophe; three theses relecting the postmodern condition affecting late capitalist society. (a) In "the implosion of art and sport," it was argued that postmodern art has developed to become fragmentary, ironic, cynic, as well as inclusive of both high culture and pop culture. Transcending the ever moving limits of aesthetics, it now envelops the kaleidoscopic mosaics of television, publicity images, and the various symbols of consumer capitalism. Sport and all its signs and symbols are thus recuperated by pop culture. At the same time, sport appropriates and reproduces postmodern artistic and aesthetic forms in order to better constitute itself as an object of hyper-consumption made for postmodern citizens. (b) In "the implosion of the body and sport," it was contended that the self, which had been lost in the culture and structures of the modern era, fights to resurface in postmodernity, while the body disappears under the weight of social power. Epistemological, ideological, technological and semiological arguments were presented to show the subordination of the (sporting) body to the postmodern power system. (c) Finally, in "the implosion of images and sport," it was shown how the contemporary model used to mediate sport contributes to a culture sometimes characterized as "excremental" (Kroker & Cook, 1987) by being anti-mediatory, by eliciting fetishism, and by fostering the aesthetic populism, fragmentation, depthlessness, and effacing of history found in postmodern culture. It was further shown that the production and reproduction of sporting images is seductive for the viewing masses, but that it also works as an opium and guarantees stagnation and non-action.

These theses bring to the fore the idea that sport (re)produces the culture present in postmodern society and, at the same time, becomes a privileged object of over-consumption. These theses also allow to draw a conclusion that may seem paradoxical, but that is, in fact, a perfect mirror of the contradictions present in postmodernity: we are witnessing the implosion of culture and, simultaneously, the triumph of this culture and of postmodern sport. It is this imploded sport which, at the same time, reflects and contributes to the postmodern social condition.

A more global conclusion is also in order: postmodern sport implies multiple practices (e.g., art, science, medicine, technology, politics, media, etc.) that produce and reproduce multiple bodies (e.g., marked by race, gender, class, sexuality, etc.) fixed in consumer culture (Cole, 1993). Images, knowledges and practices produced by sport are not contained in institutional spaces: they are rather dispersed and expressed in the daily social practices of identity production and reproduction. In postmodernity, it is thus crucial to leave behind understandings that limit sport to its modern institutional forms, and to think anew of the division of intellectual labour and identities invested (or not invested) in sport as an object of study (Cole & Rail, 1994). In a postmodern and post-disciplinary era, research must be oriented toward a destabilizing of the category "sport" for a new understanding of the categories that are associated to it: body, gender, sexuality, race, class, science, power, representation and subjectivity.

References

Andrews, D. (1991, November). "All consumed bodies: Baudrillard, hyperreality and the cybernetic construction of the postmodern body." Paper presented at the annual conference of the North American Society for the Sociology of Sport, Milwaukee, Wisconsin.

———— (1992, November). "Desiring to be like Mike: The implosive seduction of the American masses." Paper presented at the annual conference of the North American Society for the Sociology of Sport, Toledo, Ohio.

Barthes, R. (1957). *Mythologies*. Paris: Seuil.

Bataille, G. (1976). *Oeuvres complètes: Volume VII*. Paris: Gallimard.

Baudrillard, J. (1970). *La société de consommation*. Paris: Gallimard.

————— (1973). *Le miroir de la production.* Tournail, France. Castorman

————— (1976). *Pour une critique de l'économie politique du signe.* Paris: Gallimard.

————— (1980). "The implosion of meaning in the media and the information of the social in the masses." In *The myth of information: Technology and post-industrial culture* (pp. 137–148). Madison, WI: Coda Press.

————— (1988). *America.* New York: Verso.

Baynes, K., Bohman, J., & McCarthy, T. (1987). *After philosophy—End or transformation?* Cambridge, MA: MIT Press.

Becker, M.H. (1986). "The tyranny of health promotion." *Public Health Reviews,* 14, 15–25.

Bordo, S. (1989). "Reading the slender body." In M. Jacobus, E. Fox Keller & S. Shuttleworth (Eds.), *Women, science, and the body politic: Discourses and representations* (83–112). New York: Methuen.

Brown, R., & Clignet, R. (1988). "The emergence of post modernism." Paper presented at the annual congress of the Eastern Sociological Society, Philadelphia, Pennsylvania.

Bryant, J. (1989). "Viewers' enjoyment of televised sports violence." In L.A. Wenner (Ed.), *Media, sports, and society* (pp. 270–289). Newbury Park, CA: Sage.

Burger, P. (1984). *The theory of the avant-garde.* Minneapolis: University of Minnesota Press.

Cantelon, H., & Gruneau, R. (1988). "The production of sport for television." In J. Harvey & H. Cantelon (Eds.), *Not just a game* (pp. 177–194). Ottawa: University of Ottawa Press.

Carey, J.W. (1989). "Communications and the progressives." *Critical Studies in Mass Communications,* 6, 264–282.

Cheal, D. (1990). "Authority and incredulity: Sociology between modernism and post-modernism." *Cahiers canadiens de sociologie,* 15(2), 129–147.

Clarke, A., & Clarke, J. (1982). "Highlights and action replays: Ideology, sport and the media." In J. Hargreaves (Ed.), *Sport, culture and ideology* (pp. 62–87). London: Routledge & Kegan Paul.

Coakley, J.J. (1990). "Sport and the mass media," In *Sport in society* (pp. 277–301). St-Louis, MO: Mosby.

Cole, C.L. (1993). "Resisting the canon: Feminist cultural studies, sport, and technologies of the body." *Journal of Sport and Social Issues,* 17(2), 77–97.

Cole, C.L., & Rail, G. (1994). "La science comme pratique culturelle: vers une déstabilisation de l'objet des études du sport." In N. Midol, J. Lorant &

C. Roggero, *Sciences des activités physiques et sportives: Aspects épistémologiques, méthodologiques et impacts sociaux* (pp. 4–10). Paris and Nice: AFRAPS-LARESHAPS.

Crawford, R. (1984). "A cultural account of 'health.'" In J.M. McKinlay (Ed.), *Issues in the political economy of health care* (pp. 198–214). London: Tavistock.

Crowther, P. (1990). "Postmodernism in the visual arts: A question of ends." In R. Boyne & A. Rattansi (Eds.), *Postmodernism and society* (pp. 237–259). London: Macmillan.

Dator, J. (1989). "Highlight on culture: What do you do when your robot bows, as your clone enters holographic MTV?" *Futures*, August, 361–365.

De Wachter, F. (1988). "The symbolism of the healthy body: A philosophical analysis of the sportive imagery of health." In W.J. Morgan & K.V. Meier (Eds.), *Philosophic Inquiry in sport* (pp. 119–124). Champaign, IL: Human Kinetics.

Debord, G. (1983). *Society of spectacle*. Detroit, MI: Red and Black.

Derrida, J. (1967). *De la grammatologie*. Paris: Minuit.

Duncan, M., & Brummett, B. (1989). "Types and sources of spectating pleasure in televised sport." *Sociology of Sport Journal*, 6(3), 195–211.

Duncan, M., & Hasbrook, C.A. (1988). "Denial of power in televised women's sport." *Sociology of Sport Journal*, 5(1), 1–21.

Eastman, S.T., & Meyer, T.P. (1989). "Sports programming: Scheduling, costs, and competition." In L.A. Wenner (Ed.), *Media, sports, and society* (pp. 97–119). Newbury Park, CA: Sage.

Elias, N., & Dunning, E. (1986). *Quest for excitement*. Oxford, England: Blackwell.

Errais, B. (1991). "La planète sportive." In F. Landry, M. Landry & M. Yerlès (Eds.), *Sport . . . Le troisième millénaire—Actes du Symposium international* (pp. 579–585). Québec: Presses de l'Université Laval.

Faurschou, G. (1987). "Fashion and the cultural logic of postmodernity." *Canadian Journal of Political and Social Theory*, 11(1–2), 68–82.

Featherstone, M. (1983). "The body in consumer culture." *Theory, Culture and Society*, 1, 18–33.

———— (1990). "Postmodernism and the aestheticization of everyday life." In J. Friedman & S. Lash (Eds.), *Modernity and identity*. Oxford, England: Blackwell.

Fiske, J. (1986). "Television: Polysemy and popularity." *Critical Studies in Mass Communication*, 3(4), 391–407.

———— (1987). *Television culture*. New York: Methuen.

Foucault, M. (1970). *The order of things: An archaeology of the human sciences.* New York: Random House.

Frampton, K. (1986). "Some reflections on postmodernism and architecture." In L. Appignanesi (Ed.), *Postmodernism* (pp. 26–29). London: ICA Documents.

Glassner, B. (1989). "Fitness and the postmodern self." *Journal of Health and Social Behavior,* 30(2), 180–191.

Goodger, J.M., & Goodger, B.C. (1989). "Excitement and representation: Toward a sociological explanation of the significance of sport in modern society." *Quest,* 41, 257–272.

Gruneau, R. (1989). "Making spectacle: A case study in television sports production." In L.A. Wenner (Ed.), *Media, sports, and society* (pp. 134–156). Newbury Park, CA: Sage.

Guiraud, P. (1975). "Signification: Form and substance of the sign." In *Semiology* (pp. 22–44). London: Routledge & Kegan Paul.

Haraway, D. (1985). "A manifesto for cyborgs: Science, technology, and socialist-feminism in the 1980s." *Socialist Review,* 80, 65–107.

Hardison, O.B. (1989). *Disappearing through the skylight: Culture and technology in the 20th Century.* New York: Viking.

Harvey, J., & St-Germain, M. (1995). "L'industrie et la politique canadiennes du sport en contexte de mondialisation." *Sociologie et société,* 27(1), 33–52.

Hassan, I. (1987). *The postmodern turn: Essays in postmodern theory and culture.* Columbus, OH: Ohio State University Press.

Hilliard, D.C. (1994). "Televised sport and the (anti) sociological imagination." *Journal of Sport and Social Issues,* 18(1), 88–99.

Huyssen, A. (1984). "Mapping the postmodern." *New German Critique,* 33, 5–52.

——— (1986). *After the great divide: Modernism, mass culture, postmodernism.* Bloomington, IN: Indiana University Press.

Jameson, F. (1984). "Postmodernism or the cultural logic of late capitalism." *New Left Review,* 146, 53–92.

Jencks, C. (1987). *Post modernism: The new classicism in art and architecture.* London: Academy Editions.

Jensen, K.B. (1990). "The politics of polysemy: Television news, everyday consciousness and political action." *Media, Culture and Society,* 12, 57–77.

Kellner, D. (1989). *Postmodernism, Jameson, critique.* Washington: Maisonneuve Press.

King, S. (1993). "The politics of the body and the body politic: Magic Johnson and the ideology of AIDS." *Sociology of Sport Journal*, 10(3), 270–285.

Klotz, H. (1984). *Postmodern visions: Drawings, paintings, and models by contemporary architects*. New York: Abbeville.

Kroker, A., & Cook, D. (1987). *The postmodern scene*. New York, NY: St-Martin Press.

Kroker, A., & Kroker, M. (1987). "Theses on the disappearing body in the hypermodern condition." *Canadian Journal of Political and Social Theory*, 11(1–2), i–xvi.

Kuhn, A. (1985). *The power of the image: Essays on representation and sexuality*. London: Routledge & Kegan Paul.

Lefebvre, H. (1968). *La vie quotidienne dans le monde moderne*. Paris: Gallimard.

Lingis, A. (1988). "Orchids and muscles." In W.J. Morgan & K.V. Meier (Eds.), *Philosophic Inquiry in sport* (pp. 125–136). Champaign, IL: Human Kinetics.

Loret, A. (1990). "Du sport 'digital' au sport 'analogique.' " *Science et vie*, 172, 190–164, 168–170.

Lucaites, J.L., & Charland, M. (1989). "The legacy of liberty: Rhetoric, ideology, and aesthetics in the postmodern condition." *Canadian Journal of Political and Social Theory*, 13(3), 31–48.

Lyotard, J.F. (1984). *The postmodern condition: A report on knowledge*. Minneapolis, MN: University of Minnesota Press.

Lypovetsky, G. (1983). *L'ère du vide*. Paris: Gallimard.

Meier, K.V. (1984). "Much ado about nothing: The television broadcast packaging of team sport championship games." *Sociology of Sport Journal*, 1(3), 263–279.

———— (1988). "Embodiment, sport, and meaning." In W.J. Morgan & K.V. Meier (Eds.), *Philosophic Inquiry in sport* (pp. 93–101). Champaign, IL: Human Kinetics.

Mosco, V., & Wasko, J. (1988). *The political economy of information*. Madison, WI: University of Wisconsin Press.

Paoletti, J.T. (1985). "Art." In S. Trachtenberg (Ed.), *The postmodern moment* (pp. 53–80). Westport, CT: Greenwood.

Peters, J.D. (1989). "Satan and savior: Mass communication in progressive thought." *Critical Studies in Mass Communication*, 6, 247–263.

Rader, B. (1984). *In its own image: How television has transformed sports*. New York: Free Press.

Rail, G. (1992). "Physical contact in women's basketball: A phenomenological construction and contextualization." *International Review for the Sociology of Sport*, 27(1), 1–25.

———— (1991a). "Technologie post-moderne et culture: un regard sur le sport médiatisé." In F. Landry, M. Landry & M. Yerlès, *Sport: The third millennium—Proceedings of the International Symposium* (pp. 731–739). Québec: Presses de l'Université Laval.

———— (1991b). "The dissolution of polarities as a megatrend in postmodern sport." In F. Landry, M. Landry & M. Yerlès, *Sport: The third millennium—Proceedings of the International Symposium* (pp. 745–751). Québec: Presses de l'Université Laval.

Rail, G., & Harvey, J. (1995). "Body at work: Michel Foucault and the sociology of sport." *Sociology of Sport Journal*, 12(2), 164–179.

Rorty, R. (1979). *Philosophy and the mirror of nature*. Princeton: Princeton University Press.

Sarup, M. (1989). "Totality or fragmentation." In *Post-structuralism and postmodernism* (pp. 134–138). Athens, GA: University of Georgia Press.

Slowikowski, S. (1990, July). "Nostalgia, political ritual and the sport-festival flame ceremony." Paper presented at the annual conference of the International Association of Sociology, Madrid, Spain.

Wenner, L.A. (1989a). "The Super Bowl pregame show: Cultural fantasies and political subtext." In L.A. Wenner (Ed.), *Media, sports, and society* (pp. 157–179). Newbury Park, CA: Sage.

———— (1989b). "Media, sports, and society: The research agenda." In L.A. Wenner (Ed.), *Media, sports, and society* (pp. 13–48). Newbury Park, CA: Sage.

Whannel, G. (1984). "Fields in vision: Sport and representation." *Screen*, 25, 3.

Wood, P., Frascina, F., Harris, J., & Harrison, C. (1993). *Modernism in dispute: Art since the Forties*. London: The Open University.

8

Sex, Lies, and Videotape: The Political and Cultural Economies of Celebrity Fitness Videos

Margaret MacNeill

Celebrity fitness videos are popular mediums through which North Americans exert themselves physically, symbolically, and economically. In 1992, 8 of the top 10 selling videos in North America were workout videos. Although some male celebrities from the music, modelling and professional sports industries are distributing their own fitness videos—such as rapper Marky Mark, Fabio the model, and Sugar Ray Leonard, the former boxer—female celebrities have played a significant role in the development and growth of a multibillion dollar fitness industry over the past 15 years. The use of fitness as a celebrity photo opportunity is not a new phenomenon. Hollywood personalities have often staged feats of strength and flexibility as promotional events: Marilyn Monroe, for example, posed in erotic yoga positions; Lana Turner rowed for the cameras to demonstrate how she kept "sprite and trim"; and Jayne Mansfield was photographed being stretched by "Mr. Universe" to get public attention. More recently, numerous female celebrities, including Racquel Welsh, Zsa Zsa Gabor, Angela Lansbury, Heather Locklear, and Tanya Tucker to name a few, have sold systems of exercise and weight loss programs to boost sagging careers and to capitalize on their iconographic worth.

This chapter focuses on the political and cultural economies of the celebrity workout video genre in order to determine how celebrity bodies are culturally produced as historical ideals and how audiences are positioned, as well as to examine the slippery "boundaries of awe" between fans-stars and to question how contradictory discourses are legitimated. A central premise of this chapter is that fitness is not a state of body development alone. Rather, being "fit" is an embodied act, a social process, a product for sale, and a set of mediated relationships. Three case studies are done and the following videos are examined: (a) Jane Fonda's Step Aerobic and Abdominal Workout, (b) Cher's Body

Confidence, and (c) Cindy Crawford's Shape your Body. All three videos were released in 1992 and became best sellers that same year. This celebrity genre is found to be mediated by a series of contradictory discourses including healthism, heterosexual attractiveness, and consumerism.

Celebrity workout videos disrupt the usual boundaries of awe that normally separate fans from entertainment and sporting celebrities. The "untouchable" mass mediated distances between public figures and fans usually help to sustain the magic of their superstardom. The workout video's ability to lower the boundaries of awe by inviting the consumer into the celebrities' everyday life (or vice-versa, the viewer invites the celebrity into her or his home gym) is, paradoxically, a key reason for the popularity of this genre. However, disrupting the boundaries of awe also offers a tremendous opportunity for liberating people from oppressive ideals of bodily development, gendered beauty, and Hollywood celebrity appeal. Most often being consumed on the private domestic site, the video workout format offers an opportunity for resistance to media ideals and control over mainstream fitness options to the viewer/exerciser because of the technological potential for bricolage the VCR offers. Semiotic warfare can be pursued by editing images, fast forwarding videos over movements, creating a different sound track to accompany the visual instructions, and so on. This evolving genre of home media may offer participants a freedom to explore and express movement in ways that rigidly controlled studio aerobic classes often do not.

Fiske's (1987) classification of media codes[1] has been employed in this analysis to examine the networks of meaning weaving throughout these videos. This system permits an analysis of the layers of cultural discourses mediating the video text. Three levels of codes can be analyzed including: (a) social codes of reality, (b) conventional representational codes, and (c) ideological codes. The intent is to uncover the relationships of power uncritically reproduced under the guise of health and lifestyle programming. Media constructions of these codes are analyzed using feminist theoretical appropriations of concepts offered by Michel Foucault and Pierre Bourdieu in order to study the cultural and economic capitals of fitness videos. Overall, celebrity fitness video can be seen as a media genre in which audiences actively turn their bodies into a site for "practical, direct locus of social control" (Bordo, 1989, p. 13).

The Political Economy of the Home Video Market

Fitness videos have become an important consumer product for the weight loss and the fitness industries. The surge in the popularity levels of fitness videos has been due to a wide variety of factors, including the globalization of the media industries and technology companies, the globalization of the North American fitness and sporting goods industry, better access to cheaper home based opportunities compared to expensive private sector fitness clubs, the cocooning of North American families during leisure, health promotion initiatives in North America, and target marketing using celebrity endorsements to promote workout products and club memberships. In 1989, fitness supplies and products represented a $100 million a year business in Canada, and a one billion dollar a year industry in the United States (*Fitness Management*, 1990). In 1990, the National Sporting Goods Association reported that sports apparel sales for that year had reached $23 billion a year in sales; this represented an increased overall sales figure of 9.8 percent during the recession, and a 19.9 percent level of increased sales within the women's sport-fitness market compared to the previous year (*Fitness Management*, 1990).

The economic health of the home exercise video industry is due to a number of political, economic and cultural factors. Video recorder penetration into North American households has surpassed the 70 percent mark (Riddell, 1993). This technology has shifted from being a luxury appliance in the early 1980s to a typical household entertainment device in the early 1990s. Moreover, the television and VCR are particular social forms of late capitalist commodity culture (Seiter, 1989). The video technology offers a new twist in consumption power in that the viewer can seek out and select a text for consumption, rather than choosing from the limited choices of broadcast and cable programming on television at any one time (although new interactive and pay-per-view technologies are quickly expanding consumer choice). Canadian video market of sales and rentals has been estimated at $1.3 to $1.5 billion per year. Sales at Jumbo Video outlets jumped 10–20 percent annually during the recession of the early 1990s in North America (Riddell, 1993). Demographic shifts and fiscal restraint urging baby boomer families to "cocoon" explain in part the significant leaps in video sales and rentals in the 1990s. Videos offer an affordable and convenient source of entertainment and fitness programming. They can be rented or bought at a much cheaper rate than other forms of family entertainment or fitness pursuits in the community.

Since the mid-1980s, the exercise genre has been one of the most profitable and most consistently rising sales categories in the home-video sales industry (Goodtimes Entertainment, 1993). By July 1993, over 10 million units of Jane Fonda's "workout library" of tapes had been sold by Lorimar Home Video. Fonda's record breaking profits and unit sales levels have earned her the Video Software Dealers' Association "Visionary Award," which acknowledge her as the "originator of the exercise video" format.[2] While Fonda acknowledges that she did not invent the format, the home-video market was emerging in 1982 when she released her first video:

Hardware was crying out for software in order to make people want to
buy and use the hardware. I didn't realize that I was meeting a need.
Not just for exercise but for something that would help build a whole
home-video industry. This was the kind of product that was needed.
(Jane Fonda: The interview, 1993)

Currently her video library is sold to retailers through a variety of
categories: "Premiere Fonda," "Classic Fonda," "Unique Fonda," and
"Children's" segments, or through beginner, intermediate and advanced fitness
levels. Fonda's Lorimar Home Video Library is part of the global Warner
Entertainment media conglomerate.

Cindy Crawford's inaugural video, Shape Your Body Workout, was
released in 1992 and has sold over 3 million units at a suggested list price of
$19.99. It is the best-selling exercise program of the early 1990s. Crawford
retains the top sales position in North America for 35 weeks in the "Health
and Fitness" video home retail sales category (Video sales charts, 1993). Her
video was listed in the top 30 sales ranking for video sales of all genres
(Jeffrey, 1993).

Production and distribution companies for celebrity fitness videos often
use cross promotional campaigns to create consumer impressions and boost
sales. In the early 1990s, the fitness industry sells workout products at a rate
of $2.1 billion wholesale and $3 billion retail per year (*Inside Track*, 1993,
February 27). Typical cross-promotions for advertising fitness videos include:
print and television advertisements, extended infomercials for videos and
related products such as Fonda's plastic step platform, point-of-purchase displays and promotional materials, coupons, and advertisements on other fitness
videos. Bally Matrix Fitness Centres across North America employ Cher as
their celebrity spokesmodel. Cher warned the public in her advertisements:
"Excuses. They don't mean anything to your thighs, Okay? Excuses are not
going to lift up your butt."

Since the emergence of commercial television in the United States in
the 1950s, celebrities from the entertainment and fashion industries have been
hired to endorse products sold through television advertising and programming. Celebrities currently sell their own products and services through
televisual home shopping. Both Cher and Fonda have published books to
supplement and encourage the purchase of their video aerobic system. Cher
published a fitness book between her first and second videos. In 1991, she co-
wrote *Forever Fit: The Lifetime Plan For Health, Fitness and Beauty* with
Robert Haas. Fonda introduced her recent step aerobic video and step platform with an infomercial television program. This has become a highly effective way of increasing sales through both retail stores and telepurchasing.
GoodTimes Entertainment, the company producing Cindy Crawford, Marky

Mark and Richard Simmons exercise videos, is now diversifying into interactive media, computerizing their distribution, enhancing duplication facilities, and producing infomercials to boost sales of the home videos (Goodtimes
Entertainment, 1993). The National Infomercial Marketing Association recently reported that this new extended advertising program format has developed since 1984 to an estimated $800 million annually in 1991.

All three videos in this analysis also include formal advertisements
before or after the workout and educational sections. Cher's Body Confidence,
for example, stalls video participants from starting their warm-up with an
advertisement for her first workout video that display Fox/CBS and Equal
Sweetener corporate logos around her own title. Cher's workout tape concludes with an advertisement for rubber bands fitness gear by "CherFitness."
Similarly, Crawford's video contains a Revlon cosmetic advertisement while
her Trainer Radu advertises himself on his T-shirt. Before the Fonda video
workout concludes, the viewer is reminded to "stay tuned for a short review"
of her other products. At the end of the Step Aerobic and Abdominal Workout, an extended advertisement for the Fonda library screens like a commercial auto-biography. Every step of Jane's past aerobic history is still for sale.
She has not allowed her earlier media self to become obsolete in the fitness
genre.

Infomercials and point of purchase display successfully sell videos
because promotions explicitly invite the consumer into the celebrity workout
sphere. Video jackets often present both video snapshots of what will be seen
in the workout, signed invitations from the celebrity to the consumer, and
bodily images of the "end product": the fit celebrity. Crawford writes on her
cover:

> My career makes me take care of my body. So, over the last two years, I've
> been doing these total body workouts developed by my personal trainer, Radu.
> These workouts are tough, exciting . . . and they work. They don't take any
> fancy equipment—just two hand weights (3–5 lbs). There's great music and
> locations to keep your energy up, and it looks more like a music video than an
> exercise tape—so it's actually fun to watch. But the ultimate reward is that
> these workouts can help you look, and feel, better than ever.
>
> — Cindy

Cher's back cover assumes that she has captured the attention of her
former video classmates from her first-step video, and thus offers the potential buyers of Body Confidence a personal letter:

> If you've been thinking . . . "I like Tape One so much, I wish that Cher would
> make Tape Two . . ." Well, I have! My new tape teaches you the fundamentals

of cross training. If you're unfamiliar with this method of training you're going to find out that it actually cuts your workout time in half and you come out with the best results. Once again, I'm a student with you, but the good news is . . . there's no test at the end. You learn at your own pace. You just have to keep committed to it. Exercise should become a part of your life so you might as well become friends with it sooner, rather than later. I've done it, it works for me and I know it can work for you.

— Cher[3]

Jane Fonda's video packaging does not include a personal invitation. Rather, the video jacket suggests to the consumer that he or she can "Burn Fat. Sculpt hips, thighs and buttocks. Tighten abs. The workout challenges every fitness level." Fonda's promotion approach now involves clearly labelling videos for type and level of intensity for liability reasons, as well as advertising her entire range of video choices to segment both the body and the entire fitness market into niches. Fonda's approach to market fragmentation offers at least one video for each ability or age level and for a variety of movement styles: "Beginner Easy-Going Workout," "Fun House Fitness: The Swamp Stomp" for children, Fonda's "Pregnancy, Birth and Recovery," "Intermediate Lean Routine," Advanced Workout Challenge," the "Step Aerobic and Abdominal Workout," and the "Lower Body Solution." The promises of health, lean bodies and celebrity appeal are among the most successful promotional devices in a culture of strict gendered differences.

Video sales ratings by *Billboard* (a music industry trade journal) and fitness magazine reviews have become free promotional tools for celebrities who overshadow the products of professional fitness leaders. *New Body* (1993, November) magazine, for example, has helped boost the sale of Fonda's new "Step Aerobic and Abdominal Workout" by ranking it the "fifth greatest video of all times" despite the fact that Fonda does not actually "step" in the video and that the video had only been released for a few months. Controversy and bad press also increase the sales records of celebrity videos. After a debate in 1992 between magazine editors and Crawford's trainer on national newscasts about the failing safety ratings the Crawford video received from magazine reviews, sales of Crawford's video soared. In the *Shape* (1993, January) Annual Video Review for example, Crawford's exercise tape was rated "F+" and was summarized overall as:

Crawford generally uses terrific form to demonstrate risky, ineffective moves, and she doesn't seem to understand the word 'aerobic.' Her trainer, Radu, fails to provide even the most basic safety or alignment cues.

Radu defended his reputation calling his training a series of "natural movements . . . intended to improve strength" and that many styles and systems of training exist. Popular criticism is free advertising: it simply helps to target additional audiences' voyeurs. Sales soared in the wake of this controversy to extend the shelf life of this video; it remained in the top position for over six months following the media debate.

From Social to Video Realities

All fitness "realities," be they in the aerobics studio or within the domestic context of television viewing, have intersecting histories. The video realities of home fitness programming (and of the new cardio-TV rooms of fitness clubs) are mediated by the social relationships of economic, political and ideological power. According to Fiske's (1987) analytic framework, the technical presentation of the movements and the pledges of aerobic fitness form the social "reality" level of the videos. The danger of adopting Fiske's model literally is the danger of assuming the fitness level or Fiske's "reality level" of analysis to be the level of "truth." As Foucault observes:

> truth is a thing of this world: it is produced only by virtue of multiple forms of constraint. And it induces regular effects of power. Each society has its own regime of truth, its "general politics" of truth: that is, the type of discourse which it accepts and makes function as true. (1980, p. 131)

Since the celebrities studied here chose to position their videos within the fitness video category of the home video industry, this study positions and analyzes the "fitness" elements at the level of Fiske's social codes. The exercise video genre offers a format in which the audience is spoken to directly by the celebrity/trainer. Unlike cinematic traditions of placing the audience in the position of outsider, voyeur or witness, both participant and observer roles are constructed for the viewer of the fitness video: a kind of inverted Foucauldian panopticism in which subjects survey their bodily supervisors. The social reality of the consumer at home becomes mediated by the video realities of the celebrities who invite the exerciser into "their" cyberspace health club, onto their stage of performance, or beside them on the beach. What binds the celebrities together in these three top selling videos is that they all promise weight loss, healthy bodies and personal attention.

This collection of mass mediated "social realities" is evaluated using the standards of the National Fitness Leadership Advisory Committee (NFLAC, 1989) to deconstruct the aerobic level of scientific discourse and other dominant codes of representation from the perspective of health and safety standards recently negotiated within the fitness industry as state-of-the-art codes. Both Cindy Crawford and Jane Fonda act as instructors during select segments of their video, while Cher positions herself as participant. NFLAC standards have been adopted by most provincial fitness leadership bodies and the national Canadian Aerobic Instructor's Network as the blueprint for their certification programs. These standards are aligned with the International standards of such groups as the American Council of Exercise and the Aerobic Fitness Association of America.[4] The NFLAC recommended performance standards for basic fitness leadership define the leader as "an individual who leads a person or persons through a physical activity for the primary purpose of improving health and well-being and promoting active living" (Recommended performance standards, 1992, p. 1). In both Canada and the United States, no licence is required to teach fitness classes. Minimum standards for fitness instructor certification include the written, oral, and physical demonstration of "measurable knowledge, attitude and behavioral skills in the areas of physiology, biomechanics, nutrition and weight control as they are applied in the design, conduct and practice of safe and effective fitness programs" according to NFLAC guidelines. Fitness leaders are examined about the topics of physiology of exercise, movement mechanics, principles of conditioning, safety, basic nutrition, weight management, program planning, class organization and standards, use of music, individual progress monitoring, leadership and communication skills. Current standards of fitness technique and leadership are not universal standards, but rather, are historical attempts to declare ownership over the surveillance of bodily health in a population. Minimum standards of knowledge and skill instructors must demonstrate to be declared "fit to lead" a class are part of broader constraints on defining expertise and power over the knowledge of the body.

For Foucault, knowledge and power are inextricably linked. Health science and professional fitness organizations present themselves as the ultimate authorities on the appropriate state and use of the physical body. The authority is quintessentially political because scientific knowledge, particularly about energy costs of exercise, can be appropriated by fitness video celebrities and used to sell weight loss and stereotypically gendered images. Voices of authority and bodies of knowledge can be recirculated by the culture of marketing. Foucault argues that the embodied subject is both a site for the exercise of social power and an object of knowledge for the authorities. Thus, when the body of the celebrity is promoted as the product of her own workout system, the icon of the celebrity body becomes an economically and politically useful site for exerting power and for the embodiment of the "scientific" knowledge she espouses. The following chart summarizes the evaluation of the "fitness" reality presented in these videos using the NFLAC standards.

TABLE 8.1

Comparative Fitness Leadership Standards

	Fonda	Cher	Crawford
A) Class Design			
Warm-up			
circulatory movements	***	**	*
static stretching	***	*	x
Workout			
cardiovascular endurance	***	**	x
cardio warm-up	***	**	x
peak cardio	***	**	x
cardio cool down	***	**	x
muscular strength	*	***	*
muscular endurance	**	***	**
heart rate monitoring	***	***	x
Cool down			
static stretching	***	**	*
B) Teaching Skills			
flow	***	***	*
safety	***	***	x
communication	***	**	x
education	***	*	x
use of music	***	***	**
C) Leadership Skills	***	*	x
D) Program Planning	**	**	x
E) Overall Video Rating	***	**	x

Note: *** = Excellent; ** = Good; * = Marginal; x = Incomplete/unsafe

Official standards of fitness leadership are mediated by deeper ideological codes that organize our changing cultural world into a set of socially acceptable practices. Fiske's ideological code level of analysis prompts scrutiny of the celebrity experts and associated systems of exercise from a perspective that questions patriarchy, consumerism, and other forms of social power.

Ideological Levels of Meaning: Sex and Lies?

The home workout video is a multi-accentuated text that permits many levels of reading and relationship with the mediated personalities. Unlike the boundaries of awe created around supermodels and actresses during their regular work on screen or on magazine covers, the fitness video presents the viewer with the possibility of working out with the celebrity and achieving her state of fitness. In other words, the relationship constructed with the fitness audience allows for the possibility of cultural reperfussion. Reperfussion is the reattachment of the celebrity icon into a mediated reality of the "everyday" social lives of viewers. Cher, for example, is mainly videotaped by the camera operator using wide angle framing; this helps to create the social atmosphere of a dance class which the video consumer is invited to join. The boundaries of awe and envy around entertainment idols are polluted, thereby leaving spaces for viewers to construct strenuous/passive relationships with people they admire as well as recreational/sensual relationships of pleasures derived from acts of fitness and/or acts of voyeurism. In her video, Crawford is fully surveyed by the camera. The hip-circling, camera-grinding workout portrays Crawford in conflict with her own body while also being supervised by a male trainer. Radu, her trainer, is depicted hovering above Crawford, guiding her limbs through space, balancing her, touching, hugging and hoisting her above his head in celebratory rapture on the beach. In sync with the visuals, the master trainer commands her to move "brisker," "higher," "harder." The framing captures Crawford's consent to misogyny in motion. Through multiple frames of surveillance, Crawford is at once conquering her body, being loved for her bodily achievements, and being visually framed as dominated.

Crawford is the first celebrity fitness instructor to venture into postmodern aesthetics. Crawford has chosen production values with high jolts-per-minute. The bricolage of Cindy's body parts, fragmenting her to the beat of the music, is the semiotic heritage of MTV's referential frame of cybertime; a network she also serves as host to the House of Style show. Promotions for this video make bold claims about how it was to innovate in the fitness industry. Instead, the style combines and conforms to the dominant MTV dance track style for studio visuals, and to the soft-porn technique used in swim suit beach shots in the Sports Illustrated Swimsuit Edition annual video. The pageantry of images leaps from colour to black and white, from the beach to the warehouse studio, then to the industrial roof top, transferring the audience rapidly through time, space and colours. Visual texture changes so rapidly that Crawford is within reach, then she steps away from the viewer, turns her back, and appears on the roof. The edited shots are digitized to correspond with the music, movement phrases, and wardrobe changes.

A choreographed shuffle through time, space and wardrobe changes is presented. Realist filmic traditions have been disregarded to continually display a metamorphosis of Crawford. The music rapidly paces the workout consumer through the exercises, keeps the viewer enthralled, and occasionally anchors the visual statement. For example, there are close-up images of Crawford's chest during her rowing exercises, while the lyrics repeatedly demand "kiss me." She visually leaps from scene to scene: she appears in the evening light of a beach, then suddenly reappears in a brick-walled New York studio, then on an urban roof top. The opening graphics provide a video collage of fitness, anatomy and biomechanics diagrams in which the "body as machine" is presented. The urban industrial setting of the studio and the roof top "sweat shop" image process the industrial body. The camera catches some standard exercise techniques: biomechanically-safe body alignment is demonstrated in some exercise sequences such as during pushups and triceps kickbacks. Yet, failing to meet the NFLAC standards overall, the camera style and editing are privileged over fitness substance. Lacking a safe overall fitness repertoire of movement, the Crawford fitness video is predominantly offered as an exercise in voyeurism.

The cultural reperfussion of the celebrity into personal domestic spaces is the key to the profitability and ratings success of the fitness video genre. Celebrities are represented as "everyday" people working out to maintain and retain certain levels of fitness and visual appeal. The vision is still near "image-perfect," but the evidence of sweat, the sounds of exertion and breathlessness help to reposition the level of celebrity fitness within the realm of possibility for the consumer. Celebrity videos attempt to establish a workout relationship with the audience through dialogue and visual contact. Cher performs the exercises and "hot dance" routines beside her female trainer and choreographer while displaying no actual physical or visual contact with others on the set. While Cindy Crawford is instructed and handled by her trainer Radu throughout her video, Cher physically locates herself on an equal plane with her instructors, neither following nor being manipulated by a trainer. She centers herself independently in space. Coiffed and dressed in a bustier, Cher speaks directly to the audience between workouts to pledge her support for the viewer at home:

the most important thing that I'd like to get across, while I'm not up here sweating, is that to have a healthy mind in a healthy body, you've got to make a commitment to it, and don't think that it should be something that is so painful. And I hope that my effort, what I'm trying to bring to you, is to make it a little bit easier, so you're not doing it alone. We're doing it together, it's not—I don't want it to kill you. I don't really believe in no pain, no gain. And I just want to know, I just want you to know, I just want to be supportive. We're just trying to support you. That's what the tapes are about. It's about helping you get the best for yourself.

Ironically, in her fitness book, Cher admits, "I don't always feel connected to people. My whole life, even when I was little, was not what people would call normal ... I have always felt separate" (1991, p. 177). Video consumers are told to "mak[e] friends with exercise" in Cher's workout, as opposed to making friends with one's body or other people in her own video class setting. Cher and background dancers stare blindly forward as they move through their "hot dance" sequences. Cher claims that "we're right there with you," but home exercise is designed as a solitary pursuit. Laments about a lost love affair narrate the actions of the exercise as Cher sings along to her own hit song "If I Could Turn Back time." Most selections are upbeat, with lyrics that match the types of movements she is performing. During the muscle "sculpting" section, songs such as "Addicted to Love," "I Wanna Real Man," "Pretty Woman," and "Mr. Postman" provide a backdrop for an underlying narrative promising heterosexual relationships after achieving the shape and size of the celebrity body.

Fonda uses realistic filmic traditions and advice from exercise physiologists to present safe fitness programmes that will sell. Fonda's entire video series all begin by setting the aerobic studio scene. Participants arrive on set and hug. Fonda employs a multicultural mix of males and females in her video class to provide a character hook for a wide array of audience members with whom to identify. Moreover, her videos have moved from "no pain, no gain" philosophy of the intense "go for the burn" type of workout popular in her aerobic studio in the early 1980s to a 1990s "graded approach" designed by exercise scientists. While Fonda uses a variety of certified instructors and has shifted to a multi-intensity system to provide the audience with choice, like all of the celebrity video workout systems examined, her workout fragments the body and targets zones in need of "remaking." Fonda has hired a bevy of sport medicine doctors, exercise science advisors and fitness leaders to design her video content and the bodies of the nation. Fonda prides herself in "bare bones, no nonsense workout." The popularity of her video series according to her own market research, is due to the fact that exercise video consumers "trust" her for safety (Jane Fonda: The interview, 1993). The continuous introduction of new fitness videos into Fonda's "library" of home resources continually feeds the weight loss market with new options for "fat-burning" tools. Fonda now promotes personal empowerment through exercise, that is, she stresses the discovery of the "inner athlete" (Barrett, 1991, p. 46). Fitness is presented as a self-help movement.

In the North American culture of marketing, style still holds court over content. As a relative newcomer to the fitness video genre, Crawford employs the language of science to bolster her image of leadership, and the production techniques of music video to offer a mesmerizing visual montage of dangerous exercises. Personal trainer Radu Teodorescu, whom she calls the "killer whale," advocates a strict "no pain, no gain" approach. His credentials and training are never revealed in this video, which also carries a warning that the distributors are not responsible for any injuries. Radu's commands and counts abruptly set the pace of the workout; interestingly, it is Crawford who offers most of the body positioning information. Under Radu's tutelage, Crawford has become the "expert" and leaves her body mentor in the background. The current terminology of exercise physiology is infused to legitimate her anaerobic resistance workout, which she incorrectly calls "aerobic." This celebrity has been able to claim and subvert a language, package a vision of science, and resell an outdated system of physical development.

The main theme that emerged from all of these video case studies was that the workout video genre has created a mass mediated weight-loss club. Despite claims for holistic health promotion, the celebrity fitness genre tends to target female participants specifically to promote "the workout" as a method of weight reduction. As women venture into formerly untraditional modes of training the body (e.g., muscular strength and power training with weights), the new techniques and tools are quickly being commandeered for adaptation to gendered formats. Cher, for example, has a "mighty bands" rubber resistance workout for the purpose of "sculpting" the body. Cher promises a transformation in body shape: not strength, not power, nor size of musculature. Instead, unsubstantiated promises of "spot reduction" and of aerobics as an anti-aging antidote for the 1990s mingle with her own music. Cher's video is organized around 38 minutes of aerobic activity and a "fat-burning" section called "hot dance" (1970s-style modern dance). The video cover promises that the fat-burning section of aerobic fun will burn "calories and fat safely and effortlessly."

Body image disparagement messages are a common feature of celebrity fitness videos. Calling herself "wonder woman" while performing a chest exercise, Cher chastises herself for the fat on her back, which hangs over her favorite sun dresses. She promises, "with this [exercise and product] you can wear your sun dresses." During the seated row, Cher gleefully announces, "Ladies, this exercise will get rid of fat around the bra line." At age 45 she is proud of being fit and pulling a heavier band than her trainer. However, the pursuit of the lean image belies the language of health promotion she articulated in the introduction to the video. The lesson offered is that women's bodies are to be whittled via fitness for the purposes of being visually consumed by others. Fitness is not fully offered as a resource for health or a form of pleasurable movement. Spot reduction and body zone attacks are features of the other two videos as well. Crawford advocates sideways sit-ups to "get rid of the fatty area here" (as she points to her midriff). Abdominal roll-ups are performed to the lyrics of "I don't want to lose your love." Get fit, be loved. The quest for public and personal worth have been subsumed under the search for the desired body image. While all three videos offer a different kind of training regime, all are marked with an overall movement style based in traditional hetero-feminine patterns of fitness performed to music, and mediated with typical messages of weight loss and toning of the external surface of the female form. Fitness products, such as the video, are often best sellers in a patriarchal consumer culture that sells weight loss as an avenue to self-worth and social power for girls and women in North America.

Paradoxically, media and cultural ideals of the healthy and fit woman are often hazardous to women's health. The mainstream media culture represents only the overweight condition, not the underweight, as psychologically and physiologically risky. The current hegemonic vision of bodily health is presented by celebrities as a descending line of health for each increased measured increment of body mass. Many celebrity fitness programmes advocate the notion that "less size is better," "less size is healthier" and "more exercise is healthy." Cher's *Fit Forever* plan states, "the benefits of fat loss are progressive. For each pound of fat that you burn off, you gain a new measure of health and fitness" (Cher & Haas, 1991, p. 40).Yet both underweight and overweight states, according to the current medical consensus, represent physical health risks. In fact, the relationship between mortality and mass is not represented by an ascending line but rather a U-shaped curve (White, 1985, p. 13).

Workout videos are constructed with perverse economies of scale for measuring healthy success. Cher's *Fit Forever* book is a "lifetime health, fitness and beauty plan" offering permanent weight loss, weight maintenance and "anti-aging skin regime." Her print resources include a cookbook, a video guide, and a food composition index to help the reader become a "nutrition renegade." The body is meant to be measured, observed and tallied: calories in—amount of energy worked out. "Our bodies are like machines," she claims (Cher & Haas, 1991, p. 9).

The celebrity fitness video image of health is an unhealthy underweight state when the Body Mass Index (BMI) formula is applied. Healthy weight categories currently employed by the health care industry are based on the BMI. This BMI is based on the average weight of Canadian adults from 20–65 years of age. The formula is calculated by dividing weight in kilograms by height in metres squared. Medically acceptable ranges currently span an index of 20 to 27.[5] Having a body mass outside of this range places the individual in a health risk category. Individuals with BMI indexes between 20 to 27 have the lowest rates of disease and early death (Health and Welfare Canada, 1988). Physical health risks associated to obesity provide the medical rationale for dieting and societal pressures for slimness—but it is the psyche of the social that drives the desire to avoid this condition and promote the other unhealthy extreme. Behind Hollywood visions of fitness are overdieted and surgically reconstructed bodies. At 5'8", Cher has admitted to weighing as little as 106 pounds during her career, which is a seriously underweight and unhealthy level according to the BMI (cited in Brody, 1992). Likewise, Crawford at 5'9½" and 125 pounds is underweight for her height although she claims to be the first supermodel since Twiggy to break the ultra-thin "macro-neurotic" ideal. Moreover, in order to legitimate the worth of her product, Cher held press conferences with her plastic surgeon to admit facial and breast surgery, but to deny rumours of liposuction and ribs removal. The promise of weight loss through home exercise required medical testimonials to insure the fitness promises and sales ratings.

The promotion of the celebrity fitness video as a private sector weight loss system contributes to the widespread negative body image held by North American women and adolescent females. The percentages of Canadian women of healthy masses wishing to lose weight has increased since the early 1980s and during this time the celebrity video genre has risen in popularity. According to the 1985 Health Promotion Survey (Epp, 1985), 23 percent of Canadian women in the lowest weight category still wished to lose weight.[6] In the 1990 Health Promotion Survey (Health and Welfare Canada, 1993), it was found that 37 percent of Canadian women in the acceptable healthy weight ranges were trying to lose weight.

Body ideals presented in fitness media texts are fragile. For instance, the media ideal has shifted toward a more muscular body compared to earlier generations of women in North America. Thus, as best-selling celebrity videos go in and out of fashion, patriarchal panic about image cultivation is fed by shifts in body styles and popularity polls of celebrities in the entertainment industry. The 1980s Christy Brinkley outdoor athletic look shifted to the Cindy Crawford look in the early 1990s; now ideals are suddenly circulating back to a 1960s "waif look" such as 100-pound British model Kate Moss. Through commercialized fitness regimes, women of the 90s are being taught to dominate their bodies to move toward states of anorexic ideals while fitness programmes targeting men offer pumping up toward megarexic states.

At the same time that celebrity figures are promoted as ideal possibilities for video consumers to attain, the icons of fitness are dissatisfied with themselves. Crawford presents herself in the fitness video as the "real Cindy"— her runway professional personae is something she creates and calls the "The thing." Her self-objectification is an industry into itself that generates a $2 million modelling salary per year (Powell, 1993). As a long term company "spokesmodel" for Revlon Cosmetics, she must maintain herself as part of their line of "Unforgettable Women." To do this, Crawford admits that she diets and workouts more than she likes: "I have curves and boobs, I have to watch it" (cited in Powell, 1993, p. 97). Ideals of perfection offered by the entertainment and fashion industries cover up the celebrity as a human struggling to maintain that vision:

> There are days where I hate my body. Like when I'm doing a runway show and everyone else is a toothpick, and I feel like a moose. Or

when, I'm trying on a swimsuit in fluorescent lights with those three way mirrors—you know how it is . . . Cindy Crawford the model gets a lot of validation because she's on covers. But Cindy Crawford the person . . . I still need reassurance. (cited in Brody, 1992, p. 91)

The workout video breaks down the boundary of awe normally surrounding the celebrity icon, to sell the possibility of consumer success with the program. In her video, Crawford demonstrates that she works hard to attain a "natural" look, and video consumers can learn how to craft and dominate their bodies in the privacy of their home.

Obsession with exercise is presented as a positive habit rather than a vice. "Some people might say I'm fanatical or obsessed with exercise," Cher reveals, "But at least that's a healthy obsession" (Cher & Haas, 1991, p. 16). Cher believes women who workout are enamoured by the power they develop over their bodies:

It's the power to look in the mirror and like the changes you see, wear great clothes that show off parts of your body you couldn't show off at first, but they will only lead to a self-confidence you never had before . . . It never fails: to us, exercise is nothing short of a miracle. (Cher & Haas, 1991, p. 3)

Like Crawford, Cher believes that she is "really far away from physical perfection" and has her own celebrity body role model: "Bo Derek in the movie 10" is Cher's image of perfection (Cher & Haas, 1991, p. 191). The North American mainstream fitness culture treats bodily curves as if they are unnatural to the female form. Bodies are treated as a style, and styles go in and out of fashion. The body is continually reinvented.

Fonda technically avoids the erroneous spot reducing promises, but nonetheless markets her videos as "fat burners" and then fragments the body into battle zones. The Step Aerobic and Abdominal Workout jacket describes the video as a:

• Fat burning, low impact step aerobic workout
• Sculpts hips, thighs, buttocks and abs
• Separate abdominal workout.

After her absence in the "fat burning step workout," Jane alone teaches the abdominal workout session to the home viewer. She is presented in solitary confinement with her step bench product, displaying yet another use for the product. As instructor, she smiles incessantly at the consumer to keep the process pleasurable and to hook viewers on Fonda as their personal trainer.

In the "Fonda system," fitness has become a road to youthfulness to slow the tide of aging. Women over 35, she argues are "culturally missing people" (Fonda & McCarthy, 1984, p. 24), but she neglects to state that she remains on the public agenda by retaining an image of youth. Aging is a "partially negotiable" (p. 39) process according to Fonda because one can address the misuse and disuse of the body. While Cindy sells youth, Cher and Jane sell the promise of maintaining it. Video advice and systems offer mass produced solutions to individual problems and cultural obsessions. Indeed, the promises of health, lean bodies and celebrity appeal are among the most successful promotional devices in a physical culture of strict gendered differences.

Celebrity videos sell gendered promises of health, but our society confuses health and goodness by equating muscle tone and modern morality. As Ehrenreich suggests:

There's a difference between health as a reasonable goal and health as a transcendent value. By confusing health and virtue, we've gotten testier, less tolerant, and ultimately less capable of confronting the sources of disease that do not lie within our individual control. Victim-blaming, is an almost inevitable side effect of healthism. If health is our personal responsibility, the reasoning goes, then disease must be our fault . . . Somehow we need to find our way back to being healthy without being healthist. (1992, pp. 67–68)

Ironically, the media and audience-negotiated fitness ideals are offered as the end products of cyber symbiosis (the integration of manufactured technology and human bodies). The video consumers are offered a system for reproducing their bodies through fitness with their cyberspace instructors; yet many video celebrities have wasted their bodies and built curves with implants. In response to media criticism that she "bought" her body, Cher argues:

I've killed myself in the gym to have this body . . . If I have cosmetic surgery, does that mean I don't work out? My nose always bothered me since childhood. My teeth were crooked and pushed in too far. But they're mine . . . It's my body to do with what I want. Look, we're a visual society. I didn't make this society. I just live here. (Cher, 1991, p. 182)

But the public worth of the female body is to a large degree bound in the presentation of the celebrity form: Cher does indeed make this body culture. The celebrity video sells a culturally constructed "ideal" to the consumer-exerciser. But to be like the celebrity is to be different than yourself. Celebrities now have the power to cultivate and make particular meanings about the fit body "stick." Purchasing a popular celebrity video has become an ideological investment in patriarchy.

For Pierre Bourdieu, the central aim of social analysis is "to uncover the most profoundly buried structures of the various social worlds which constitute the social universe, as well as the 'mechanisms' which tend to ensure their reproduction or their transformation" (1989, p. 7). Fitness has remained an under-studied area of the sociology of sport and physical activity, yet the fitness video is a pervasive technology and mechanism of power. The video is a technology of power for the economy of techno-home leisure products, a technology of power for maintaining unequal gender relationships in sport and fitness pursuits as well as in society, and a technology of power over oneself. The promise is that observing the rituals of the celebrity body habitus will help the consumer transform her body and the disciplined relationship to this body. The current weight loss orientation of celebrity videos, cloaked as a self-help health promotion genre, is a technology for learning self-mortification practices.

Videos can and do offer home viewers access to active living options, but they offer little visual and social latitude for liberating the patriarchal body. As mediated weight-loss clubs and technologies of self-discipline— where one learns to measure and sculpt the feminine body habitus—celebrity workout videos promise rewards in the weight-loss payoff as opposed to health or pleasure in the process. Regardless of which celebrity icon is "in style," the fitness video breaks the normal boundary of awe around a celebrity, suggesting that you can work along side a celebrity and be mediated compatriots.

Reconstructing the Fitness Video Experience: Moving Beyond Textual Analysis to the Politics of Mediated Fitness

Celebrity workout videos are exchanged upon the contested terrain existing between popular consumer culture, entertainment, and self-help health promotion spheres. Celebrity fitness videos have been praised for transforming thousands of sedentary lives, and yet heavily criticized for perpetuating sexist stereotypes, dangerous systems of exercise, and perpetuating anorexic obsessions in the workout culture. Ownership of a video is license to observe and copy the celebrities remaking themselves through aerobic exercise. While some celebrity workout videos such as the recent Fonda video series offer safe basic fitness programs, most celebrities sell fitness primarily as a fat-burning and body-size reduction tool. The video serves many viewers as a technology of self-discipline. Celebrity fitness "experts" possess a high level of cultural capital. Professional models, singers and actresses—such as Cindy, Cher and Jane—carry auras of culturally defined gendered ideals of femininity and heterosexual appeal. The viewer is invited to remake her body and live along side her chosen icons of gendered leadership. The video, therefore has primarily been sold as a mediated weight-loss club. Manifestations of a capitalist and patriarchal culture are indeed etched deeply into the current consumer library of celebrities in motion. To break the grip of power that celebrity workout videos currently hold over North American home based fitness, requires that the audience move past the desire to attain celebrity body styles toward celebrating an ontology of difference.

Foucault argued that "where there is power, there is resistance" (1979, p. 154). Thus, the workout video can provoke a wide range of polysemic meanings and uses for audience members. Exercise videos can serve to reduce the boundaries of awe normally surrounding celebrity role models, and the workout format opens up possibilities for resistance to mass mediated visions (e.g., using home media technology to alter images) and for active relationships with one's own body. At the same time, the viewer is produced by the video and produces the meanings and experiences she has with the video in her home.

The workout video can be used to celebrate joyful movements alone or socially, and possesses the potential for offering activity as a resource for health and pleasure. Some possibilities for reconstructing the video experience to empower those wishing to workout and become healthy in a multidimensional sense include: (a) organizing media literacy programmes specifically about consumer, health and gender issues education; (b) employing new multimedia and interactive technology to reconstruct fitness meaning systems in order to empower the consumer to manufacture visual meanings about exercise suitable to their needs, circumstances and lifestyle orientations; (c) expanding the range of video leadership, redefining conventions of production and altering the movement repertoires to meet the needs of various audiences; (d) expanding the distribution system for access to video resources (e.g., public lending libraries) and access to technology to produce videos; and (e) promoting more social and communal uses of the video format in neighbourhoods, in addition to current individual home-based consumption, to cater to social as well as individual needs.

Fitness is not a shape or an ideal state of achievement. Fitness is ultimately an embodied act, a process, a relationship with one's own body habitus and a relationship to the social habitus.

Notes

1. According to Fiske's codes of television (see 1987, p. 5), an event to be televised is already encoded by *social codes* such as those of appearance, dress,

make-up, environment, behaviour, speech, gesture, expression, sound, etc. These are encoded electronically by *technical codes* such as those of camera, lighting, editing, music, sound, etc., which transmit the *conventional representational codes* that shape the representations of the narrative, character, action, setting, etc., which are organized into coherence and social acceptability by *ideological codes* such as individualism, patriarchy, race, class, materialism and capitalism.

2. Jane Fonda has been the most successful video series in terms of total sales, however, she is not the originator of the exercise video. Before her were Kathy Smith, Richard Simmons, Bonnie Pruden, and earlier public health and industrial health calisthenic films (see "Jane Fonda: The interview," 1993).

3. Her personal letter to the video consumer, is also her opening speech to the video, which is followed by an advertisement for her earlier step video which precedes the opening title for Body Confidence.

4. The National Leadership Advisory Committee set the performance standards for fitness leadership under the auspices of the Interprovincial sport and Recreation Council of the former Federal Ministry of Fitness and Amateur Sport. This committee was made up of representatives from The Canadian Association for Health, Physical Education and Recreation, the Canadian Association of Sport Sciences, the Canadian Council of University Physical Education and Recreation Administrators, the Canadian Parks and Recreation Association, Fitness Canada, the Interprovincial Sport and Recreation Council, the YMCA and the YWCA.

5. Because regular exercise and proper nutrition builds muscle and increases bone density (bone and muscle weigh more than fat per unit), as women become active in their lifestyles, the healthy weight range for women in the various height categories should be set at a heavier level. The current contradictions between slim celebrity visions of health versus physiological and nutritional possibilities for strengthening the body, lead women to seek culturally constructed ideals of body mass reduction when healthy pursuits should be physiologically making the measure heavier.

6. Unpublished data from the Health Promotion Survey, (cited in Health and Welfare Canada, 1988, p. 29). Underweight categories have greater risks of developing chronic fatigue, depression, anemia and eating disorders according to the Canadian Cancer Society BMI Index (Health and Welfare Canada, 1988).

References

Ang, I. (1985). *Watching Dallas*. London: Methuen.

Barrett, E. (March 1991). "Interview with Jane Fonda, Exercise Videos-Lifetime Achievement Award: Jane Fonda." *Self Magazine*, March, p. 46.

Bordo, S. (1989). "The Body and the reproduction of femininity: A feminist appropriation of Foucault." In A. Jagger & S. Bordo (Eds.), *Gender/body/knowledge:*

Feminist reconstructions of being and knowing (pp. 13–33). London: Rutgers University Press.

Bourdieu, P. (1989). *La noblesse d'État. Grands corps et grandes écoles.* Paris: Éditions de Minuit.

Bourdieu, P., & Wacquant, L. (1992). *An invitation to reflexive sociology.* Chicago: University of Chicago Press.

Brody, L. (1992). "Bella Cinderella: Cindy Crawford makes a fitness fairy tale come true." *Shape,* November, pp. 88–91.

"Canadian Fitness Survey highlights" (1984). *Physical Activity and Weight Control,* p. 23.

Cher, & Haas, R. (1991). *Forever fit: The lifetime plan for health, fitness and beauty.* New York: Bantam Books.

Ehrenreich, B. (1992). "The morality of muscle tone: Are we confusing health with goodness." *Utne Reader,* May/June, pp. 65–68.

Epp, J. (1985). *The active health report: Perspectives on Canada's Health Promotion Survey.* Ottawa: Health Services and Promotions Unit, Health and Welfare Canada.

Fiske, J. (1987) *Television culture.* New York: Methuen.

Fitness Management (1990). October, p. 3.

Fonda, J. (1991). Cited in "New fitness column." *Self Magazine,* March, p. 46.

Fonda, J., & McCarthy, M. (1984). *Women coming of age.* New York: Simon and Schuster.

Foucault, M. (1979). *The history of sexuality, Volume 1, An introduction.* London: Penguin.

———— (1980). *Power/knowledge.* New York: Pantheon.

"Goodtimes Entertainment" (1993). *Billboard,* July 17, p. 43

Gray, A. (1987). "Behind closed doors: Video recorders in the home." In H. Baehr & G. Dyer (Eds.), *Boxed in: Women and television* (pp. 38–54). London: Pandora Press.

Health and Welfare Canada (1988). *Promoting healthy weights.* Ottawa: Ministry of Supply and Services Canada and Health and Welfare Canada.

———— (1993). "Canada's Health Promotion Survey 1990—News release." Ottawa: Health and Welfare Canada.

Inside Track (Mary Hines, host) (1993). CBC Radio, Feb. 27.

"Jane Fonda: The interview" (1993). *Billboard,* July 17, pp. 90–91.

Jeffrey, D. (1993). "Video-on-demand looms." *Billboard*, June 12, p. 24.

Lauge, L., & Smith, C. (1993). "How thin is too thin?" *People*, September, pp. 74–80.

National Advisory Committee on Fitness Leadership Development and Recognition (1984). *Guidelines for the training and recognition of fitness leaders in Canada.* Ottawa: Fitness Canada.

"New body" (1993). *The Fifty Greatest Exercise Videos of All Time*, November, pp. 36–41.

NFLAC (1989). *Performance standards for the basic fitness leader.* Ottawa: Ministry of Fitness and Amateur Sport.

———— (No date). *Legal liability: Considerations for the fitness leader.* Ottawa: Ministry of Fitness and Amateur Sport.

Powell, J. (1993). "Cindy: A style all her own." *Redbook*, October, p. 97.

Quirk, L. (1991). "Totally unhibited: The life and times of Cher." *Cosmopolitan*, September, pp. 34–35, 78.

"Recommended performance standards for the basics fitness leader, NFLAC" (1992). *Ontario Fitness Council's Practicum Information Booklet*, April, p. 1.

Riddell, K. (1993). "Fall video surge expected." *Marketing*, September, p. 15.

Seiter, E. (1989). *Remote control: Television audiences and cultural power.* New York: Routledge.

"Shape annual video review." (1993). *Shape*, January, pp. 26–35.

Talbott, S. (1993). "The female athlete triad . . . Not for athletes only." *Fitness Management*, August, pp. 37–40.

Video: Cher (1992). "Body confidence." Beverly Hills, CA: CBS/FOX Video.

Video: Crawford, C. (1992). "Shape your body." Ajax, Ontario: Satellite Films-HGV.

Video: Fonda, J. (1992). "Step aerobic and abdominal workout." New York: Warner Home Video.

"Video sales charts" (1993). *Billboard*, June 26, pp. 24.

White, F. (1985). *The epidemiology of overweight in Canada in reference to the development of a health promotion strategy: Summary report.* Ottawa: Health and Welfare Canada.

9

Excavating Michael Jordan: Notes on a Critical Pedagogy of Sporting Representation

David Andrews

> We're living in a decade which has chewed up and spat out ideas so fast that most of us are reaching for the Rennie. Surely the only way to slow down this tide of information is to try and attach some meaning to it? And surely it's the only way to stay sane. Superficiality is the curse of the Nineties. We're too afraid to think, because the reality of our situation is simply too painful. And so we merely consume.

> — Craik

Perhaps better than any academic treatise, the above letter to *The Face* captures the swelling nihilism that threatens to engulf those whose subjectivities and experiences have been formed within the hypersemiurgic culture of postmodernity. Whether Generation X or the "slacker culture" to which the letter alludes actually exists as a collective entity (other than in the avaricious imaginations of opportunistic advertising executives) is rightly open to contentious debate. Yet, there does appear to be a significant backlash brewing in both popular journalistic and critical intellectual circles, targeted at countering the asphyxiating cultural stupor that has accompanied the rise to pre-eminence of the moribund "civilization of the image" (Kearney, 1989) in which we find ourselves presently ensconced. This chapter is intended to contribute toward the resistance against the creeping superficiality and meaninglessness of contemporary promotional culture (Wernick, 1991).

By developing a framework for what Kellner has called a "critical media literacy" (1991, p. 63), my aim is to offer an interpretive survival strategy for those bombarded with the mediated images, signs, and spectacles, that proliferate within, and indeed characterize, postmodern culture. This seductive and domineering empire of signs has stimulated the ascension of a "postmodern pedagogy of mass advertising" (Giroux, 1994, p. 2) that has invaded public spaces and threatens to engulf the fashioning and experiencing of daily life. According to Giroux (1994), cultural workers are compelled to counter the promotional colonization of everyday life by creating insurgent narratives that engage popular culture within the new technologies and regimes of representation. With this in mind, this chapter seeks to develop a progressive understanding of the hyperreal world of mediated sport as a key element of the popular promotional culture that radiated from the outgrowth of an American formation defined and dominated by semiurgic production.

As a number of cultural commentators have indicated, the postmodern culture of the image has subtly, but nonetheless fundamentally, restructured American politics (Clarke, 1991; Giroux, 1994; Grossberg, 1992; Luke, 1991; Rubenstein, 1989). The televisual politics of the American New Right explicitly located itself within the affectively charged sphere of mediated popular culture, and subsequently appropriated and mobilized the affective orientation of popular commodity-signs in the substantiation of Reaganism's reactionary agenda. In general terms, this chapter identifies mediated sporting texts as lustrous examples of this media-induced politicization of popular culture, which facilitated the inversion of the relative importance of ideology and affect in the construction and experiencing of everyday life. More specifically, this chapter develops upon my previous exposition of Michael Jordan (Andrews, 1994) as an affectively oriented [post-]Reaganite commodity-sign. Within this earlier paper, I focused on what Fiske (1992) has called the primary level of textual production; which in Michael Jordan's case represents Nike's initial substantiation and concerted elaboration of his mediated persona. Herein, my focus is the second level of textual production, and particularly the corroborative machinations of the numerous corporate armatures of the promotional culture industry, who, taking Nike's lead, have further embellished the affective identity and investments of Jordan's hyperreal identity according to the conjunctural imperatives of [post-]Reaganite popular cultural politics.

My intention is to engage in the type of critical pedagogy of representation vaunted by Solomon-Godeau (1991). This involves contextualizing specific practices of representation within particular historical and cultural circuits of power, and critically explicating how these conjunctural forms of representation secure affective investments that work to actively produce and mobilize our own desires and identities, in the construction of particular subject positions and the securing of specific forms of authority (Giroux, 1994). Hopefully this project will disrupt the superficial affective euphoria that has dominated the articulation and consumption of Michael Jordan's image, and excavate what the disinterred meanings and submerged political implications are of being, and perhaps more importantly, wanting to be like

Mike. Thus, within this chapter, I am taking up Craik's (1994) challenge. I am attempting to attach some meaning to Michael Jordan, with the hope of encouraging us to confront the reality of our situation in order that we can begin to change it. Or in Kellner's more expansive terminology, this theoretically and contextually grounded multitextual analysis of Michael Jordan is intended to stimulate the growth of "more autonomous agents, able to emancipate themselves from contemporary forms of domination and able to become more active citizens, eager and competent to engage in processes of social transformation" (1991, p. 63).

A Postmodern Cultural Studies in Process

I would concur with Giroux (1994) in the assertion that cultural theory is crucial to any pragmatic pedagogical practice. This is not to assert some incontrovertible and universal theoretical stratagem. Rather, it acknowledges that cultural theory, like the critical pedagogy it is designed to inform, is necessarily always in process. Theory must respond to history in order to legitimately expect to create conjuncturally informed agents of social transformation. Hence, the intrusive manifestations of postmodern culture confronting large sections of the American populace, represent a significant point of departure for the way American culture is lived and experienced. As a result, I find it increasingly difficult to accept (as I had done previously) that a mode of critical cultural analysis transplanted from a radically different historical and cultural setting (the cumbersomely labelled British cultural studies) has any analytic relevance to contemporary America. However, I have no wish to renounce cultural studies' post-Marxism en bloc; for instance, I am candidly committed to the political project of cultural studies, as well as to many of its theoretical and methodological orientations. Thus my goal, akin to those of Chen (1987, 1991) and Grossberg (1992), is to develop a post-Marxist philosophy positioned beyond, but also between, cultural studies and critical postmodern theorizing. In Anzaldúa's (1987), Chamber's (1990), or Kellner's terms (1989b), I intend to inhabit the borderland between these contrasting intellectual formations.

The advent of the postmodern era of televisual overload has neutered the interpretive potency of Hall's structural-conjuncturalist approach. Cultural studies has reached yet another intellectual impasse, for it no longer provides a cogent understanding of the relationship between the social formations of power and the lived experiences of everyday life within the postmodern mediascape. For this reason it is necessary to confront the proliferating discourse that interrogates the conditions of postmodernity. And yet, "it is not a matter of taking up postmodernism as a political and theoretical position but of engaging its description of the nature of contemporary cultural and historical life" (Grossberg, 1989b, p. 416). Grossberg's subsequent (1992) analysis of popular music formations in contemporary America involved an innovative synthesis of cultural studies and the post-structuralist philosophies of Gilles Deleuze and Félix Guattari, and to a lesser extent, Michel Foucault. My personal preference is to strategically incorporate elements of Jean Baudrillard's radical social philosophy, within the broad agenda of cultural studies, in order to generate a more insightful understanding of postmodern American culture.

On the surface there would appear little scope for, or worth in, converging the non-essentialist ideologism of Hall's cultural studies with the cybernetic determinism of Baudrillard's radical metaphysics. Nevertheless, by instigating a critical dialectic between them, an incisive new critical space can be formulated in the borderland between these markedly different intellectual projects. In order to establish such a hybrid interpretive position, it is necessary to identify the points of convergence, or divergence, at which it becomes possible, or in fact necessary, to cross over the epistemological and ontological boundaries which differentiate cultural studies from Baudrillard's postmodernism (Chen, 1991). Grossberg (1986) identified the postmodern moment as one dominated by emergence of contemporary forms of mass cultural dissemination, and the complex re-articulation of human agency in the light of this development. The problematic of mass communication captured the central point of intersection between cultural studies and postmodernism. Moreover, the result of strategically collapsing the elements of these discursive domains related to the electronic media would be a more adequate understanding of contemporary American society; a postmodern cultural studies.

Metaphysics refers to the creation of a conceptual universe within the subjective confines of an individual's imagination. In his later work, Baudrillard explicitly aligned himself with this tradition:

> Well, let's be frank here. If I ever dabbled in anything in my theoretical infancy, it was philosophy more than sociology. I don't think at all in those terms. My point of view is completely metaphysical. If anything, I'm a metaphysician, perhaps a moralist, but certainly not a sociologist. (Baudrillard, 1987a, p. 84)

Baudrillard's metaphysical position developed out of frustration with the political and intellectual inertia of post-1968 France, and was fuelled by a concern with the advent of postmodernity. It is less a source of practical knowledge grounded in material conditions, and more a highly personalized, often idealized, view of the world constructed around imaginary projections. His new-age metaphysics can be seen as a response to the redundant modernist preoccupation with the construction of theoretical metanarratives of social life.

Baudrillard's postmodern imagination became obsessed with the subject-object reversal of commodity-sign culture, and created a hyperreal universe in which the human subject no longer creates objects, but is in fact created by them. This "metaphysical world view" (Revill, 1990, p. 297) is a simulated model of reality that purports that the hyperreality of commodity-sign culture is more real than reality itself. As Kellner stated, "Like all metaphysicians, Baudrillard has thus constituted a world to his own measure and taste" (1989a, p. 180). Thus, Baudrillard's gaze is that of the narcissistic metaphysician whose blinkered vision stares smugly at a world which only projects the interpretive categories that dominate his imagination.

Although his earlier work was grounded in an eclectic synthesis of Marxist and post-structuralist theory, the turn to metaphysics was symptomatic of Baudrillard's recognition of social theories as being a simulation, rather than capturing the very essence of reality (Baudrillard, 1988b). Hence, Baudrillard's metaphysical sojourns into postmodern culture are purposefully constructed like vertiginous and metaphorical thought games, as opposed to empirically grounded and structured examples of modernist social theorizing. Despite the intriguing results of his innovative approach, Baudrillard's metaphysics is vulnerable to the charge of producing self-indulgent, un-grounded, and under-theorized descriptive narratives. According to Revill, "You can explain Baudrillard in his own terms, as a terrorist and a seducer, with no basis and no end" (1990, p. 293). Moreover, "His writing proceeds without example, without argument, in despondent and pontifical generalities" (1990b, p. 14).

The most celebrated and notorious example of Baudrillard's willfully sweeping and shallowly provoking (to borrow from Frith, 1988) metaphysics emerged in his pronouncements concerning the Gulf War:

> Just a couple of days before war broke out in the Gulf, one could find Baudrillard regaling readers of *The Guardian* newspaper with an article which declared that this war would never happen, existing as it did only as a figment of mass-media simulation, war-games rhetoric or imaginary scenarios which exceeded all the limits of real-world, factual possibility (Norris, 1992, p. 11)

Baudrillard's understanding of the Gulf conflict as a hyperreal war played out in the realm of televisual circuitry, rather than in the lives of everyday people, exhibited his blinkered preoccupation with the realm of hyperreal simulation. It is plainly ludicrous to purport that the Gulf War, which resulted in heavy military and civilian injuries and fatalities, exclusively inhabited the hyperreal realm of "purely fictive or illusory appearances" (Norris, 1992, p. 14). To put it bluntly, there seems to be something very real about being blown apart by an Iraqi landmine, or being butchered by the indiscriminate fire of the American forces.

Of course most Americans experienced the Gulf War by tuning in to Arthur Kent (the "scud stud"), Charles Jaco, Bernard Shaw and their colleagues, and the simulated war created by the mass media networks. And, there is little doubting the simulated and artificial nature of televised events such as this, which at times are more reminiscent of theatrical farce; the most vivid example of this being the American forces making their secretive landing on the Somali beaches, where they encountered an already landed Dan Rather and a battery of journalists, cameramen, and technicians, televising live pictures to the folks back home. Such was the parodic nature of the situation; it was little wonder that many of the invading task force dropped their aggressive deportment and responded to the friendly gaze of the television cameras with the customary "Hi, Mom." Nevertheless, as with any commodity-sign, neither did the Gulf War nor the Somalian crisis exclusively reside in the realm of hyperreal simulation. Interacting with Gulf War hyperreality had very real effects on the daily lives of the grieving relatives, anxious spouses, concerned Americans, and the thousands of Americans of Middle Eastern descent who were made to feel decidedly uncomfortable during the conflict. The predictably negative intellectual response to Baudrillard's exaggerated hyperontology is neatly expressed by Bauman:

> Personal experiences can be enclosed by the frame of the television screen. One doubts whether the world can. One suspects, pace Baudrillard, that there is life left after and beyond the television. To many people, much in their life is anything but simulation. To many, reality remains what it always used to be: tough, solid, resistant and harsh. They need to sink their teeth into some quite real bread before they abandon themselves to munching images. (Bauman, 1992, p. 155)

While Baudrillard's playful hyperontology overstated the importance of hyperreality, it seems equally troubling to deny any relationship between the hyperreal and the real (as Bauman seems to have). Within the postmodern mediascape, the consumption of hyperreal images can and does have real effects; images, visual texts, and signs continually shape people's everyday relations, experiences, and identities. As a consequence, it is necessary to de-essentialize both Baudrillard's hypermetaphysical discourse, and the reactionary critiques fabricated around an intentionally literal, and hence ultimately futile, reading of his project (see Bauman, 1992; Callinicos, 1990; Clarke, 1991).

This bifocal de-essentializing can only be achieved by acknowledging that the experience of contemporary culture is partially grounded in hyperreality, and hence it is important to recognize the realm of simulation as being "part of the real without reducing it to the only effect operating in the social world" (Chen, 1991, p. 42). This is perhaps the most significant point of convergence between cultural studies and Baudrillard's radical semiurgy. Where cultural studies has purported, but failed, to ground critical analysis in material existence, such a goal has not even dared surface within Baudrillard's metaphysical agenda. The irony is that a materialist reading of Baudrillard's theory of hyperreality provides a postmodern cultural studies with an invaluable analytical tool for linking the ideological realms of representation, signification, and articulation to the concrete level of human experience.

By the early 1980s, and through recourse to his Althusserian re-reading of Gramsci, Hall enabled cultural studies to negotiate its own critical space between the bi-polar schism of structuralist determinism and humanist essentialism. The result was a cultural theory of power that focused almost exclusively on the interrelationship between the conjuncturally specific values of representation, signification, and ideology, and their implications for the production, distribution, and consumption, of social identities and power. As Grossberg stated, "It is the specific articulation of social subjects into these circuits of value, circuits which organize social possibilities and differences, that constructs the structured inequalities of social power" (Grossberg, 1989b, p. 418).

By developing into a structural-conjuncturalist intellectual formation (Grossberg, 1989a), cultural studies became increasingly aligned with the neo-Kantian philosophical foundation of post-structuralism. This was founded on the assumption that social identities and meanings are wholly dependent upon their positioning within a conjuncturally specific system of differences (Easthope, 1991). The post-structuralist preoccupation with the realms of the discursive and the ideological, greatly influenced cultural studies research in the 1980s. Consequently, much cultural studies research privileged the metaphysical realm of ideology. Although never reckless enough to deny the importance of the non-discursive realm, Hall certainly sidesteps the issue by advancing the primacy of the ideological domain:

My own view is that events, relations, structures do have conditions of existence and real effects, outside the sphere of the discursive; but that it is only within the discursive, and subject to its specific limits and modalities, do they or can they be constructed within meaning. Thus, while not wanting to expand the territorial claims of the discursive infinitely, how things are represented and the "machineries" and regimes of representation in a culture do play a constitutive, and not merely a reflexive, after-the-event, role. This gives questions of culture and ideology, and the scenarios of representation—subjectivity, identity, politics—formative, not merely an expressive, place in the constitution of social and political life. (Hall, 1988, p. 27)

The metaphysical posturing of Hall's structural-conjuncturalism lays cultural studies open to the charge of neglecting its materialist roots in the critical analysis of everyday life. By exclusively concentrating on the ideological effects of cultural practices and circumventing other levels of effectivity, it becomes impossible to bridge the gap between ideology and everyday existence.

By privileging the ideological domain of existence, Hall produced a cultural studies rationalism in which cultural politics and cultural existence can only exist within the plane of signification (Chen, 1991). And yet, every cultural practice is embroiled in a complexly intertwined set of effects, which makes it extremely problematic to reduce cultural practices solely to their ideological effects. Thus:

the failure of cultural studies is not that it continues to hold to the importance of signifying and ideological practices but rather, that it always limits its sense of discursive effectivity to this plane. It fails to recognize that discourses may not only have contradictory effects within the ideological, but that those ideological effects may themselves be placed within complex networks of other sorts of effects. (Grossberg, 1986, pp. 72–73)

This is exactly the point that cultural studies can benefit from engaging with postmodern social theorizing. As Chen put it: "If postmodernism has emphasized non-ideological domains, then this is where cultural studies ought to come in" (1991, p. 40). Postmodern social theory highlights the diversity of effects that impinge upon cultural life, by stressing the importance of the discursive articulation of signs as well as their asignifying and non-discursive effects. Postmodernism has recognized that cultural practices are implicated in, and constructed out of their ideological, economic, libidinal, aesthetic, material, and emotional effects none of which are necessarily preeminent (see Baudrillard, 1983a, 1988a, 1990; Deleuze & Guattari, 1987; Grossberg, 1992).

The precise position of a cultural practice within the tangled economy of effects defines its conjunctural identity and influence. The constant making and re-making of lines of articulation between practices and their effects produces contextual maps of reality that link "this practice to that effect, this text to that meaning, this meaning to that reality, this experience to those politics" (Grossberg, 1992, p. 54). In this way, the economy of effects connects or articulates practices to the real level of everyday experience. The goal of a postmodern cultural studies, then, is to reconstruct the economy or network of articulations which create a historical conjuncture within which the effects of a cultural practice are determined and experienced. As Grossberg continues, "This analytic project might be described as a cartography of daily life which attempts to (re)construct at least a part of the complex texture of a certain terrain" (1992, p. 63); an interpretive strategy used to great effect by Hebdige (1981, 1987, 1988).

Grossberg advocated a return to a multi-dimensional study of popular culture that links the various effective levels of existence that may be mobilized at any particular position in space and time. In a sense, this represented a highly conditional reversion to Shuttleworth's (1971) integrated study of people and culture. Moreover, Shuttleworth's vivid allusion to the importance of emotion in the construction of everyday lives and experiences clearly related to the terrain of effectivity with which Grossberg has become so preoccupied. Whereas Shuttleworth used the notion of emotion to describe the domain which gives tone and texture to our everyday lives, Grossberg preferred the term "affect."

Identifying the differences and relationship between emotion and affect are complex problems. For the purposes of my (admittedly simplistic) understanding, I prefer to characterize the affective realm as an economy of different forms of emotional response and involvement to mediated ideological narratives. Affect is the energy we invest in particular cultural practices, emotions are the specific forms that this affective investment takes; affective investment therefore "anchors people in particular experiences, practices, identities, meanings and pleasures" (Grossberg, 1992, p. 82). Of the numerous vectors of effectivity that constitute the complex terrain of everyday life, Grossberg consistently argued for a consideration of the affective economy in order to counter the ideological rationalism of cultural studies (1984a, 1984b, 1986, 1988a, 1988b, 1988c, 1988d, 1992). In light of this, it is important to note that Grossberg (1988b, 1992) defined popular culture as those cultural practices and formations whose primary effects are affective. Hence, Grossberg entered into a false bipolarity between the affective and the ideological. This bewilderment by affect severely hampered his interpretive project, and lay him open to the same charge of effective exclusivity which he leveled at Hall's ideologism (Mellencamp, 1992). Mellencamp's solution to the problematic of theorizing affect lay in "[a]cknowledging the linkage between thought and affect, and the merger and crossover of the private, the public, the market, and state apparati" (Mellencamp, 1992, p. 234). In line with Mellencamp's (1992) thinking, I would contend that popular culture represents the intersection of affective and ideological vectors of effect.

Reaganism's Affective Mobilization of the Popular

Merely recognizing the link between the ideological and affective effects of contemporary cultural practices creates little more than an interpretive "shell without trajectories" (Chen, 1991, p. 41). As a consequence, it is essential to develop a conjunctural understanding of the inner logics, and internal dynamics, of the ideological/affective inversion that takes place in conditions of visual overload. While cultural studies can benefit from postmodernism's recognition of the non-signifying vector of effects that can determine the conjunctural articulation of cultural practices, Baudrillard's cybernetic determinism similarly needs to recognize and confront the multiplicity of determinate relations and effects that map the conjuncturally contingent social formation. Baudrillard conflated postmodern existence as being cybernetically determined by indeterminate hyperreal simulations. A conjuncturalist postmodern cultural studies, whilst never denying a sense of determinacy, would adhere to a more diverse, and substantively contextualized, theory of determination. One in which:

> Reality is always a construction of and out of the complex intersections and interdeterminations among specific conjunctural effects. Reality in whatever form—as matter, as history or as experience—is not a privileged referent but the ongoing (in Deleuze and Guattari's term, "rhizomatic") production or articulation of apparatuses. (Grossberg, 1989a, p. 143)

This approach represents a bridge between the overt ideologism of Hall's articulation theory and Baudrillard's theory of cybernetic seduction. Such a postmodern cultural studies involves the historicizing and localizing of Baudrillard's affective, but indeterminate, logic of symbolic seduction. According to this hybrid schema, the articulation of cultural practices, which determine the limits and possibilities of social existence (the potential for human agency), is a product of the complex relationship between conjuncturally specific ideological, political, economic, cultural, and affective vectors of effect; which are increasingly, but not always, communicated through the electronic media.

Contextualizing the postmodern mediascape within its own socio-historic effective context allows us to formulate a better understanding of politics and power relations, within the context of hyperreality (Luke, 1989, 1991a, 1991b). The process of articulation within the hyperreal mediascape involves the effective mobilizing of commodity-signs that promote and attempt to consensualize the dominant faction's quintessential view of reality. In as much as hegemonic practices always attempt to engage a politics of simulated consensus, the era of the commodity-sign has inaugurated a politics of hypersimulation:

> Power in hyperreality derives from controlling the means of simulation, dominating the codes of representation, and managing the signs of meaning that constitute what hyperreality is taken as being at any particular time. By setting the limits of what is hyperreal, and therefore at least temporarily "real", the managers of media, movements, and displays can set agendas, determine loyalties, frame conflicts, and limit challenges to the prevailing organization of what is taken as being real. (Luke, 1991a, p. 20)

The effective determination of what is real at any given conjuncture creates a hyperreal cultural context in which our senses of space and time, of the world, of the real, are largely (re)defined by the operations of the mass media (Chen, 1987). This simulated cultural politics constructs a complex network of commodity-signs that "determine whether and how meanings and subject positions are taken up, occupied, invested in and possessed" (Grossberg, 1989a, p. 143). Hence, analyzing the media's affective investment in strategic cultural practices deconstructs the simulated politics of postmodernity, and discloses a system of hyperreal power relations implicated in the real experiences of everyday life.

Baudrillard (1983a, 1988b, 1990) discussed how the explosive growth of the information industries created a simulated culture that symbolically seduced and fascinated the mediated populace. The contemporary mediascape coldly seduced the postmodern populace by merging ideological codes and affective investments within the proliferating system of hyperreal commodity signs. This implosive procedure was characterized by Chen (1991) as de-rationalization of ideology and the accompanying de-irrationalization of emotion, and it resulted in the commodity-sign culture of postmodernity historicizing the inner mechanisms, and articulating the conjunctural inflections, of the affective economy. The implosion of ideology and affect, within the multiplying circuitry of the mass media, created a network of hyperreal cultural practices and identities that mobilized affect and resulted in the increased encroachment of the [hyper]media into the experiencing of everyday life (Lefebvre, 1971). This occurred because:

> The power of affect derives, not from its content, but from the fact that it is always the vector of peoples investment in reality, that it is the plane through which (but not necessarily on which) articulations are accomplished. (Grossberg, 1992, pp. 104–105)

The complex tapestry of commodity-signs defined the sites, modes, and intensities of affective engagement with the cultural practices and identities that constitutively inhabit the socio-historic formation. In this way every conjunctural formation is defined, and indeed potentially reproduced, by an interwoven economy of commodity-signs that are inscribed upon the understandings and experiences of everyday life. Due to their relative discursive positioning, these commodity-signs were structurally distinct; they signified different things. But, as a result of their simultaneous inflection through the conjuncturally specific economy of affect, these structures of difference became politically implicated in shaping everyday existence. The televisual detritus of postmodern culture produced popular mattering maps which seductively directed people's affective investments in (and thereby their ideological understandings of) the world in which they live. As Grossberg stated:

> affect has a real power over difference, a power to invest difference and to make certain differences matter in certain ways. If ideology (and even pleasure) constitute structures of difference, these structures are unrealized without their inflection through an affective economy. For it is affect which enables some differences (e.g. race, gender, etc.) to matter as markers of identity rather than others (e.g. foot length, angle of ears, eye color) in certain contexts. (1992, p. 105)

The seductive capacity and affective influence of a given commodity-sign was determined by the conjuncturally specific direction of the affective vectors of televisual articulation. The mass media's affective investments in the cultural terrain mobilized, whether intentionally or otherwise, key elements of the ideological discourses that reflected the state of play in the struggle for a hegemonic cultural politics. Hence, the conjuncturally specific affective economy strategically directed popular investments in the material conditions of existence, and consequently made concrete connections between politics and everyday life. In this way, popular culture was centrally implicated in the organizing, disciplining, and mobilizing of daily life, in the service of particular political agendas (Grossberg, 1992).

Evidently, the popular emergence of the American New Right under the rather ambiguous umbrella of Reaganism, was an example of populist affective politics. Appropriating Bennett's (1989) understanding, Grossberg (1992) developed a spatial model of culture and power in a contemporary America dominated by the New Right, which viewed the terrain of popular culture as a spatialized field of social management. He argued that the new conservatism was put into place through the restructuring of our investments in the various sites of the popular (Grossberg, 1988b). In other words, the televisually oriented Reaganite project implicitly located itself in, and indeed mobilized, the formations of popular sentiment, taste, and culture. In doing so, Reaganism became an affectively oriented struggle in which popular culture led politics.

Given that the struggle for a new conservative hegemony in the United States was centered on an affective rather than an ideological politics of the popular, it follows that Reaganism sought to win over the nation's body and soul, rather than its mind. Throughout his presidential campaign, and during his tenure as American leader, Reagan disparaged the overt ideological discourse of his political adversaries, in favor of an outwardly apolitical stance that sought power by being seen to dissociate from conventional politics. Indeed, much of Reagan's popularity was attributed to his capacity for turning political into gut-level issues (Schneider, 1990). In contradiction to this avowed disdain for ideological politics, Reagan repoliticized and re-ideologized American society. This was achieved by covertly organizing a hegemonic project under the guise of regenerating popular affective investment in the American nation; a populist politics that explicitly keyed on a regressive and ethnocentric nationalism.

Reaganism articulated America's apparent decline in affective terms. According to Reaganite discourse, the corporatist consensus had, economically, politically, militarily, socially, and morally, weakened the affective resolve and commitment of the American people to their once great nation. The result was a developing crisis of nihilism within American society:

> The crisis is the product of a lack of passion, of the fact that people do not care about the values they hold to do "what is necessary" . . . Americans are not working hard enough—at their jobs, in their families, for their nation, or in the service of their values. (Grossberg, 1992, p. 256)

The aim of the new conservatism was to restore pride in the American nation by encouraging the public to care passionately about strategic aspects of their everyday lives; practices and values which the Reaganite hegemony articulated as being either pre-requisites of, or necessary rejects from, the project of creating a resurgent American nation. This hijacking and reconstruction of the terrain of American politics meant that political contestation was no longer waged in the sphere of ideological differences. Reaganism shifted the site of contestation to that of the affective mobilization of American national popular culture:

> Here the struggle for hegemony foregrounds popular culture and language; it attempts to transform popular mattering maps and the nature and sites of authority in contemporary life. It operates on the very ground on which affect and politics are linked together, rather than on the terrain of ideology and common sense. (Grossberg, 1992, p. 255)

Unlike Thatcherism, Reaganism was less concerned with the ideological meanings of popular practices than it was attentive to their material distribution within the socio-cultural formation, the specific ways they were appropriated, and most importantly, the disciplined mobilization of people's affective commitment to them.

The New Right's disciplined mobilization of affect encouraged positive popular investment in cultural practices that advanced the discriminatory logics of Reaganism; cultural logics (incorporating neo-liberalism, neo-conservatism, and moral traditionalism) which reasserted a vision of an America dominated by a white, heterosexual, and patriarchal, middle-upper class. The struggle for the hegemony of the New Right was organized around the installation of a postmodern frontier which, in the service of an explicitly reactionary political agenda, redistributed peoples' affective investment in key aspects of American popular culture. Reaganism's construction of affective epidemics territorialized popular existence by differentiating between those practices, values, and identities that fostered the new conservative agenda, and those that subverted it.

Reaganism constructed an affective frontier within American culture which restructured the mattering maps of everyday life, "redistributing the places that matter and redefining their political inflections" (Grossberg, 1992, p. 283). In a 1988 speech to a Republican rally in Illinois, Reagan cogently depicted this affective frontier that Reaganism had constructed in American culture:

> You must choose between, on the one hand, policies of tax and spend, economic stagnation, international weakness, and always, always "blame America first"; and on the other hand, limited government, economic growth, opportunity, strong defense, solidarity forever, and always, always "I pledge allegiance to the flag of the United States of America." (Reagan, 1989, p. 1449)

The battle waged over American history and everyday existence, for the control of this affective frontier, involved the selective appropriation from the residual, dominant, and emergent fields of popular culture. Or, as Grossberg mentioned, the New Right's objective involved "taking advantage—sometimes strategically entering into its construction—of this history, rearticulating what is already determined elsewhere" (1988b, p. 34). Accordingly, traditionally conservative American practices including the family, the church, the mythology of the American dream, nationalism, and consumerism, were enthusiastically appropriated and rearticulated into Reaganism's regressive nationalist politics. Conversely, cultural practices that opposed Reaganite doctrine, including the variant manifestations of youth culture, the gay and

lesbian subculture, left wing political activism, the emergent women's movement, and an increasingly assertive black population, were all aggressively
condemned as being anti-American. This organizing, disciplining, and mobilizing of people's affective responses to specific popular cultural practices, in
the service of the new conservative agenda, required work at the intersection
of politics, everyday life, and popular culture. In the postmodern mediascape,
this intersection is situated within the network of hyperreal commodity-signs
that dominate and define contemporary American culture. Postmodern
America's expansive economy of commodity-signs (the mediated objects,
practices, identities, and personalities associated with American life) constituted the locales of Reaganism's affective epidemics, from which the mattering maps of national popular culture were drawn.

The presence of a conjuncturally specific economy of affect, turned
Reagan's America into an affective experience, as opposed to an ideological
construction. Consequently, in conditions of postmodernity, Anderson's frequently cited (1983) notion of the modern nation as an imagined community,
is displaced by the nation as an affective community, experientially defined by
the commodity-signs that inhabit the simulated world of the televisual, video,
and cinematic networks. For this reason, the affective logic of American existence can be found within the profundity of commodity-signs that constitute the
extraordinary hyperreality of contemporary America culture (Rubenstein, 1989).
This has been particularly evident during the Reagan-Bush era, when American
popular culture has been dominated by a myriad of hyperreal commodity-signs,
including: Max Headroom; Spuds Mackenzie; Vanna White; Joe Isuzu; The
Dancing Raisins; and the Stealth Bomber Honda advertisements (Rubenstein,
1989). Arguably the most influential commodity-sign of recent times was Ronald
Reagan himself. As a "hyperreal object" (Rubenstein, 1989, p. 583), Reagan's
entire political/ film career and identity was built on his affective investment in
a simulated and celebratory model of American life. This virulent commitment
to a hyperreal and regressive American nationalism gelled the New Right into
a coherent political force. In doing so, the potent affective populism that pro-
pelled the Reaganite hegemony set the simulated politico-cultural climate for
the 1980s. As a consequence, the ability to infiltrate and mobilize the hyperreal
terrain prompted Merrill (1988) to describe Reaganite hegemony as being established on a simulated consensus.

At least temporarily, Reaganism successfully engineered a position of
hegemonic influence that engineered the connection of America's commodity-
sign culture to the discourses of the New Right. Consequently, the reactionary
codes of Reaganism dominated the American mediascape in the 1980s and
fashioned an economy of embodied commodity-signs whose simulated experiences of American existence bolstered the populist mattering maps cultivated by Reagan himself. As Reaganite commodity-signs, these hyperreal

American heroes corroborated and authenticated Reagan's strategic affective investment in a simulated America.

Reaganism's utilization of the American media networks (especially television) blurred the boundaries between actual historical figures, and their fictional companions. If Reagan was the first TV president (Merrill, 1988), then Reaganism was the first TV politics, and what it celebrated, through the TV narrative, was a:

> fin de siècle cult of supermen; those whose images rise above the inscrutable bureaucracy, the fragmentation, and frustrations of modern industrial society to get things done. This cult includes men—still almost always men—from business, finance, and government like T. Boone Pickens, Lee Iacocca, Carl Icahn, Oliver North, or H. Ross Perot and their characters is pre-defined and valorized by television heroes like Blake Carrington, J.R. Ewing, Sonny Crockett, or Lifestyles of the Rich and Famous. (Merrill, 1988, pp. 142–143)

Whereas Reagan's mediated image embraced the broad vista of new conservative politics, the attendant cult of supermen proffered numerous personalized commodity-signs such as Lee Iacocca, Oliver North, John Rambo (see Jeffords, 1994), and Bill Cosby (see Jhally & Lewis, 1992). These mediated heroes embodied, and thus vindicated, Reagan's affective investments in the substantive territories that fashioned the mattering maps of the New Right coalition; maps that represented simulated models for everyday existence in Reagan's America. Enter Michael Jordan, stage right . . .

Endorsing the Dream

In an earlier paper (Andrews, 1994), I identified how Michael Jordan's mediated identity, originated and primarily engineered by Nike, was borne out of, and subsequently vindicated, the reactionary racial climate of Reaganism. The hyperreal Air Jordan, like his mediated contemporary Heathcliff Huxtable (Bill Cosby's lead character on The Cosby Show), became a seductive simulation of the Reaganite project. By embodying the neo-liberal economics, neo-conservative politics, and moralistic cultural traditionalism of the New Right, the Nike-initiated Jordan narrative celebrated Reaganism's morally corrupt and criminally negligent vision of a colorblind American society. Within this hypermythological realm, individual agency was exulted as the primary determinant of individual success, and the socially inscribed experiences and identities associated with racially based discrimination and exploitation were viewed as distant and irrelevant remnants of the past. Consequently, after an extremely brief period at the vanguard of the intense contemporary mediascape, Jordan became an affective epidemic who vividly represented the Nike-wearing, Reaganite reincarnation of Horatio Alger. Jordan, the commodity-sign, celebrated for all to see that the American dream was alive and dunking. Hence, he became a site of popular affective investment that compellingly advanced Reagan's racially indifferent cultural hegemony, and seemingly vindicated the dismantling of a programmatic commitment to social welfare, much to the detriment of America's growing African-American underclass.

Despite his constitutive association with the affective topography of Reagan's America, more than half of Jordan's career in the promotional apogee of the N.B.A. has been spent in the post-Reaganite context of the Bush and Clinton administrations. Although Reaganite cultural hegemony did not immediately end with the handing over of governmental power to George Bush, the New Right occupied an increasingly diminished position of hegemonic leadership. This was primarily because the post-Reagan era has been dominated by a spiralling budget deficit that has had profound implications for the socio-economic well-being of the American populace, and consequently the state of play in American cultural politics. The influential American middle class experienced a noticeable decline in living standards, and large sections of the already dislocated working class were forcibly entombed in the expanding ranks of a permanent American underclass. Not surprisingly within this recessive climate, popular dissatisfaction undermined the hegemony of the New Right, and ultimately expedited Bill Clinton's rise to Presidential office. That is not to say a Clintonite hegemony has emerged, rather the terrain of American cultural politics, while still inclined toward the New Right, has been in a state of relative flux since the second half of the 1980s (Davis, 1993).

Michael Jordan's position within this turbulent historical conjuncture has been that of an increasingly residual (in the sense of residue used by Williams, 1977) component of new conservative popular culture. First and foremost, Jordan was Nike's child of Reaganism; a commodity-sign who strategically invested in the affective epidemics that constituted the mattering maps of new conservative cultural politics. Given the popular media's gleeful appropriation and unimaginative investment in this particular articulation of Michael Jordan, the post-Reagan epoch has been marked by its enduring repetition. The popular media has steadfastly continued to articulate Jordan as being exciting, successful, determined, engaging, affable, wholesome, and perhaps most importantly, ethnically and racially non-assertive and non-threatening. In other words, he has continued to be cast as the proto-typical Reaganite all-American hero of African-American extraction, who effectively denies the legitimate representation of African-American experience or identity. Having previously identified Nike's pivotal role in the formulation and circulation of the popular discourse that enveloped Michael Jordan (Andrews, 1994), the remainder of this chapter examines what Fiske has called the second level of textual production; the intertextually informed televisual vignettes fashioned by specific commercial interests, to corroborate and embellish Jordan's hyperreal persona, and in doing so, connect his substantial commodity-sign value to material commodities they wish to promote.

By articulating Michael Jordan's image to the dominant codes of Reagan's America, Nike set in motion the semiotic process that culminated in him becoming a prominent American commodity-sign who not only signified and promoted himself and Nike, but who also symbolically represented the preferred expressions of contemporary American culture. However, it should not be overlooked that on his entry into the N.B.A. in 1984, corporate sponsors were initially reluctant to follow Nike's lead and enlist Jordan to endorse their products. Predictably, after the phenomenal success of the Air Jordan campaigns (in tandem with the phenomenal performances of Jordan on the court) there was no longer a shortage of interested commercial suitors. As soon as Jordan's mediated persona had been given time to register with the American population, the all-American code associated with Nike's hyperreal Air Jordan became a free-floating signifier and store of promotional capital which was subsequently commandeered by the corporate leviathans of the American marketplace. As Patton stated, "The family image is attractive to McDonald's. The Olympic glow appeals to Chevrolet and Coca-Cola, trying, as always, to sell themselves as All-American products. And Jordan's modesty appeals to all of them" (1986, pp. 52-53). These, and other, manufacturers of the staple products of American existence appropriated Jordan's image in order to re-enforce their own American identity and appeal.

Having created and nurtured Jordan's hyperreal American image, Nike now saw it circulating around the commercial hyper-space. Nevertheless, the influence of Nike's promotional initiatives ensured that through both the print and electronic media, the Jordan narrative increasingly became synonymous with the American dream. Clearly, the company retained a fair degree of control over the promotion of Jordan, in its capacity as adjunct overseer of his commercial development. In fact, Nike appears to have greater influence upon Jordan's commercial dealings than ProServ, the sports marketing agency with which he is attached. ProServ's senior vice-president, David Bagliebter, freely admitted, "We confer with [Nike] on every deal that comes up . . . We like to get their input before we move ahead with these arrangements" (McManus, 1990, p. 66). Understandably, given its vested interest, Nike was concerned with actively consolidating Jordan's popularity by ensuring that the products he was associated with do not contradict the image it created for him. Hence, ProServ's (and Nike's) marketing strategy for Jordan involves selecting products "that are complementary and deliver a consistent message

... the products he is associated with are wholesome and all-American" (Falk, quoted in Dishneau, 1991, p. 114). Falk continues, "By matching him [Jordan] with some of the cornerstones of American marketing . . . we've created a real synergy which ties each of the companies together and further enhances his name recognition" (quoted in Sakamoto, 1991, p. 44).

Although Nike and Jordan are still synonymous with each other, Jordan's diffusion across the realm of the American commercial media has successfully linked him with, amongst others, Bigsby and Kruthers, CBS-Fox video, Chevrolet, Cleo calendars, Coca-Cola (latterly Gatorade), Electronic Arts computer games, ERO sleeping bags, Farley Candy Co., Hanes underwear, Hangtime bubblegum (a subsidiary of the Wrigley Co.) Illinois State Lottery, McDonald's, NBC ProStars television cartoon show, Ohio Art Co. (makers of Etch-A-Sketch), Upper Deck trading cards, Wheaties, and Wilson Sporting Goods (And he plays basketball too, 1992, p. D3). It would definitely seem that as a result of expanding his commercial interests, the onetime assertion that "Michael Jordan without Nike won't mean anything" (Phil Knight, the Nike chairman, quoted by Strasser & Becklund, 1991, p. 655) has been rendered a hollow threat.

The unceasing promotion and embellishment of Jordan's American identity across numerous commercial contexts turned Jordan into a multi and intertextual promotional construct. By implication, therefore, within what Goldman and Papson (1994) identified as the age of hypersignification, a Jordan commercial promotes not only Jordan and the product in question, but also the rest of the American commodity-signs within his expansive endorsement portfolio. This is because:

Promotion in different spheres, then, multiply interconnects—both in terms of the common pool of myths, symbols, tropes, and values which it employs, and through the way in which each of the objects to which a promotional message is attached is itself a promotional sign, and so on in an endless chain of mutual reference and implication. (Wernick, 1991, p. 187)

Hence, the multiple promotional sites associated with Jordan have generated a cybernetic system of promotional capital that spirals into ever increasingly pervasive and intrusive circuits of influence. Being associated with traditionally American products obviously corroborated Jordan's American aura. Equally as important however, was the way his personality was substantiated within these various commercial settings. Hence, it is important to illustrate representative examples of the commercial contexts in which Jordan's life and character were substantiated in a complementary fashion to the dominant cultural codes of the [post]Reaganite era. In order to facilitate such a discussion, it is appropriate to engage in a brief discussion of Langman's (1991) novel perspective on American national character as an important site of cultural reproduction within "the amusement society of unending disconnected simulacra" (Langman, 1991, p. 213).

Rejecting conventional approaches, Langman's understanding is based on the premise that national character consists of "patterned tendencies of feelings toward self, other and objects, together with affective investments in particular values" (Langman, 1991, p. 203). In specific terms, the American national character is a legacy of historically accumulated values and aspirations, manifested "in terms of affective investments in four basic value polarities" (p. 204), that have a profound effect upon the everyday practices and experiences of large sections of the American populace. The basic American value polarities identified by Langman are those of individualism-community, toughness-compassion, moralism-pragmatism, and utopian-nostalgia. While in earlier times these affective expressions were transmitted through rituals, myths, ceremonies, and later on printed and audio texts, today the primary mode of affective transmission is televisual communication. Thus it is my contention that the hyperreal narratives within Jordan's commercials exploit many of the basic values deemed by the New Right as fundamental aspects of traditional American existence. Particularly discernible is the way Jordan's mediated personality vindicates the paradoxical affective commitment to both individual and community which underpinned the Reaganite project.

The explicit investment in both individual and community concerns were central themes within the New Right's contradictory agenda. However, the celebration of individual responsibility, ambition, and agency, as the accepted means of securing collective advancement has been a residual aspect of American national character at least since it was identified by Tocqueville in the 1830s. The New Right merely appropriated this preoccupation with the individual within the context of the perceived crisis in American existence. The *Zeitgeist* of the 80s popular conservatism, the decade of the self, was best captured by Margaret Thatcher's vitriolic pronouncement that "There is no society, there are only people." In this way, individual responsibility and advancement was prescribed as the surest route toward collective development. Such a political philosophy renounced any sincere commitment to communal well-being. Abstracting individual experience from socially constructed identities and experiences, denied the significance or even the existence of socially constructed (and frequently disadvantaged) identities and experiences. Moreover, this political philosophy effectively reinforced the incumbent social relations of power, by seeming to legitimate the savage dismantling of America's social welfare structure. The result was an America in which some individuals could meet their responsibilities of social advancement with consummate ease, whilst others, the habitually discriminated and disadvantaged, were made to feel a burden to a social formation that was designed for their failure.

Returning to Tocqueville (1945), he identified how the apparent advance of equality in American society lead to a pervasive preoccupation with securing an elevated social status that differentiates individuals from the masses. More often than not, this American individualism manifests itself in the realm of economic accumulation and competition. Intriguingly, Tocqueville also noted how this cult of the individual induced a conformity to the communal structures that bind American society together. According to Collins and Makowsky, Tocqueville deduced that:

> the individualism of a mass society of equals goes together with the total power of the state. As the private individual seeks his personal gain in business or other purely private affairs, his political interests are reduced to a desire for tranquility—a government that will maintain order so that he can pursue his own affairs. The man of mass society is willing to give great power to the centralized state and in the process loses his freedom to oppose it. (1972, p. 58)

Although Tocqueville refers to conformity to the American nation-state, his point can be explicated to incorporate other popular conservative institutions (most notably the church and the family), which are viewed as the backbones of American society. For instance, the anxiety and insecurity created by the credo of individualism is assuaged by feelings of communal identity and solidarity that are purportedly engaged when conforming to the traditional patterns of American family life. Thus, the traditional institutions of American life, as extolled by the New Right, performed a similar function to the popular obsession with individual advancement; they inevitably reproduced the unequal social arrangements by providing stabilizing institutional anchors that seemingly legitimate the veracity of the American way. Bringing Tocqueville up-to-date, the hyperreal commercial narratives relating to Michael Jordan can be broadly classified into two aspects of the same American dynamic. They either extol the emancipatory virtues of American competitive individualism, or they assert a devoted allegiance to the family as a metaphor alluding to the simulated harmony of American society as a whole.

Through assorted promotional manifestations of the flight metaphor, Nike was instrumental in connecting Jordan to the American ideology of individualism. However, in the wake of its mass circulation, the Air Jordan flight symbolism was both explicitly and implicitly expropriated by other commercial interests. Displaying a concern for intertextual continuity, Coke duplicated the jump man logo in a commercial that pictures Jordan, in orbit and silhouetted against the moon, leaping for a bottle of Coke that hovers tantalizingly in zero-gravity. Jordan is reaching for the stars, and when he gets there what does he find? A bottle of America's favorite soft drink. Once again the flight metaphor exposes Jordan's decidedly individualistic demeanor, or what Langman has characterized as a "striving for agency, self determination, differentiation from others and freedom from control" (1991, p. 205).

The interconnection of promotional imagery is not confined to the products that constitute Jordan's endorsement inventory. Conditions of Jordan cyberblitz have allowed commercial interests, with no direct association with him, to indiscriminately borrow from the contemporary mediascape in order to promote their own products. Indeed, the ultra-American discourse symbolized by Jordan's flight metaphor has been best captured in a recent magazine advertisement for American Airlines; a company that Jordan does not endorse. In the advert, a picture of an anonymous basketball player, performing a dunk *à la* Jordan, is accompanied by the message:

"WHAT IT TAKES TO FLY—Instinct. Strength of will. Honest sweat. Unbridled desire. These are some of the qualities that mark the difference between an athlete and a competitor. Between those who compete. And those who rise above the rest. We have always valued the qualities that bring out the best in the individual and team performance. Because we've always understood what it takes to fly. We are, with pride, the official airline of the N.B.A."

American Airlines based this entire commercial strategy on the implicit recognition of the commodity-sign to which they are alluding, Michael Jordan. The intention is to capitalise on the vast store of promotional capital which Nike and others have generated around Jordan. Northwest Airlines adopted a similar strategy in a television commercial that also plays upon the Air Jordan flight metaphor. A series of carefully scripted basketball scenarios, evidently inspired by Jordan's airborne displays, is accompanied by a stirring song:

> Some people just know how to fly.
> They set a goal and the aim is high.
> They do it better than the other guys,
> Some people just know how to fly.

The "some people" to which the commercial refers, is an implicit reference to Michael Jordan. Hence, the viewer is encouraged to believe that, like Jordan, Northwest Airlines are the sole arbiters of their own destiny who have set and attained high standards of achievement that differentiate them from their competitors. American and Northwest Airlines are not alone in counterfeiting the image of an airborne Jordan. Dutch Boy Paints, N.B.C., and Sportschannel, have also skyjacked the image of an in-flight Jordan. Thus, time after time, commercial after commercial, Jordan is indirectly implicated in the individualistic discourse of American values, this time in terms of the obsessive pursuit of personal success.

As well as the pervasive flight metaphor, other strategies have been adopted in order to link Jordan to the American obsession with competitive individualism. One such promotion for the McDonald's McLean Deluxe involved an interaction between the person who is presumably assembling a sandwich on view, and affirmative responses culled from Jordan in game situations. The various stages in the production of the sandwich are filmed in color, whereas Jordan exclusively appears in black and white. The commercial opens with Jordan driving to the basket and dunking, and the anonymous voice asking "Hey Michael, you like lean beef?" The shot then shifts to a hamburger being placed on a bun. Jordan's emphatic response comes with him repeatedly punching the air (having made a game winning shot). "Ok, ok . . . What about fresh lettuce and tomato" counters the McDonald's spokesman, over a picture of a sandwich in its half finished form. This time, Jordan is seen turning around and putting his two thumbs up in the air, the reply being "I'll take that as a yes." "All the trimmings, alright": to this Jordan can be seen delightedly punching groundward *à la* ice hockey celebration. "What say we put it all on toasted sesame seed buns," and Jordan smiles and nods, as the picture focuses on the sandwich in all its glory. "McDonald's calls it the new McLean DeLuxe Michael. It's 91 percent fat free, 100 percent delicious. Say Michael, can we get you one?" Jordan points to his shirt and makes a V sign with his fingers, "Ha-ha, two is it?" The commercial ends with the following re-stating of McDonald's official status as an American symbol; as if being connected with Jordan was not enough, they created the "McDonald's McLean DeLuxe, the official sandwich of the N.B.A." What is interesting is the way the commercial makers appropriated Jordan's image from actual game situations and re-articulated it in order to augment their promotional message. Again, this gets back to the postmodern preoccupation with pastiche and parody. By juxtaposing Jordan's responses to game situations with the rather inane questions of the sandwich maker, a pastiche-like text composed from different media sources is created, a text that affectionately parodies Jordan's enthusiastic and passionate commitment to basketball and winning.

As well as championing the American yearning for self-determination, Jordan's hyperreal persona also demonstrates an unswerving allegiance to the family; the other extreme of the paradoxical American national character. Particularly within conservative popular discourse, the American family has become synonymous with the American nation. Zealously protecting the traditional family structure and values is thus viewed as a key element in safeguarding the nation's future. Since the commercial media repeatedly portrays Jordan as the consummate family man, his hyperreal image demonstratively underlines the importance of an institution that is habitually valued and fiercely guarded as a foundation of American existence. Both Coke and Wheaties paid homage to the American family in commercials involving Jordan, in the company of his mother, playing the role of obedient and loving son. Hanes took a slightly different approach to Jordan's familial conditions by introducing Jordan's father (since deceased) and wife. In a post-game family moment, presumably set in his home, Jordan walks into the front room and shoots a basketball, which conveniently lands on a pile of underwear lying on the coffee table. His father, having been distracted from his newspaper, initiates the following dialogue:

Father: Michael, are these your Hanes?
Jordan: Uh-huh.
Father: Son, is there a reason why you wear them?
Jordan: (Before he has a chance to enter, his wife enters the room and drapes her arms around him). Definitely.
Father: Think Mom would like me in these?
Jordan: Maybe.

A number of important themes are brought to light by this whimsical narrative. Most significantly, the structural solidarity of the Jordan family is portrayed beyond question. This is evidenced by Michael's easy-going relationship with his father, his willing compliance with his wife's wishes by wearing Hanes underwear, and his father seeking the approval of his wife by perhaps doing the same. The entire scenario depicts the Jordans as an ideal American family; one in which personal relations across generations and between partners display a pleasing and reassuring sense of understanding, fun, and mutual affection. Importantly, the humor of the commercial also detracts from any allusion to Jordan's sexuality. Jordan's carefully cultivated asexuality had been an important factor in this African-American male gaining the popular approval of a white American populace stricken by a moral panic (Cohen, 1972) created by the media's reactionary preoccupation with stereotypical images of the sexually threatening African-American male (Hall, 1993). Hence, the advert's concluding message "Hanes, nothing feels so right!" is as relevant to the underwear being marketed, as it is to the proto-typical [African] American family on display.

Appearing in harmonious commercials with members of his immediate family advanced Jordan as someone who upholds the importance of family values. This sentiment was furthered through promotional sketches during which he was seen to interact naturally and affectionately with children.

Jordan's refusal to allow his own children to appear in commercials has resulted in him being portrayed as an amiable older brother/uncle/neighbor type figure. In a Wheaties commercial he was seen playing tabletop basketball with a young friend. In a Coke commercial, he used his leaping ability to deliver a six-pack to his young friends in a tree-house. Both scenarios nurtured the idea that because of his evident affection for children, it is obvious that Jordan is a good person. While not intending Jordan to personally benefit, the setting up of the Michael Jordan Foundation by his mother in 1989, has furthered this aspect of his popular appeal. The very existence of the Foundation, a charity for disabled and underprivileged children, is yet another source of marketable intertextual promotional capital that will continue to be exploited by the avaricious entrepreneurial vectors of post-industrial capitalism.

Given the institutional importance of the American family, Jordan's mediated familial ties articulated him as a torchbearer of America's collective conscience and identity. Another vaunted aspect of Jordan's affective investment in American institutional structures is his commitment to education. Numerous corporate interests, seeking to enhance their own standing, have actively made connections between Jordan and education. Sharon Sleep, Director of the Illinois State Lottery, forcefully defended why the agency paid Jordan over $900,000 (Culloton, 1991) to headline a lottery promotion campaign constructed around the "Say Yes To Graduation" motif:

> The respect that Michael Jordan commands among all segments of our population makes him an ideal spokesman; the immense popularity he enjoys among today's youth makes him the ideal spokesman for the "Say Yes to Graduation" message. In short, if anyone can go on TV and help convince kids to stay in school, it's Michael. (quoted in Sharp, 1991, p. 12)

Coke also used Jordan in a similar role in their "No Brain No Gain: Stay in School" campaign, as did Nike when recently re-uniting him with Mars Blackmon in a schoolroom setting in which after a rather intense discussion about the principles of gravity, the two friends exclaim "Don't Be Stupid, Stay in School." In a further slot, Jordan is joined by Chicago Bulls teammates Bill Cartwright, B.J. Armstrong, and John Paxson, in an N.B.A. sponsored commercial. The story line, underscored by the rhythmic chanting of "One For All And All For One," stresses the importance of teamwork and co-operation in the Bulls' winning their second N.B.A. championship and translates it to an educational setting. Jordan wraps up this uplifting commentary with this modest admission: "I can't do it alone, neither can you. Stay in school!"

In yet another "Stay in School" promotion that aired during the 1991 N.B.A. Finals, Jordan joins forces with another of his endorsement portfolio, McDonald's. The commercial opens with Jordan dunking, driving for the basket with his tongue hanging out, and generally having fun playing the basketball superstar. Following this exciting introduction, the audience is introduced to a rather somber looking Jordan, dressed in a dark suit. Just in case we were in any doubt who this is, the accompanying legend reads:

MICHAEL JORDAN
Laney High School
Wilmington, NC Class of '81

Jordan then recounts a familiar tale: "Even when I went through the frustration of getting cut from the varsity team, I still had that driving force of competing in academics and I think you've always got to get something to fall back on, and that's what education is. Stay in school! It's your best bet." — This message "furnished by Ronald McDonald's Children's Charities, and the N.B.A. and its players."

By being seen to care about education, Jordan is demonstrating a concern for the children of America and hence America's future. This connection significantly enhances Jordan's popular image and appeal, and by association, those of the corporate interests who sponsor these messages.

Jordan's resolute advocacy of the American way has also been nurtured in commercials in which he is seen to map his own identity according to the cultural geography of the United States of America. In a Chicagoland promotion, McDonald's sold a burger with smoked bacon, cheese, barbecue sauce, onions, mustard, and pickles, predictably named the McJordan sandwich (Lazarus, 1991). McDonald's, a hugely symbolic American institution, recognized their's and Michael Jordan's prominence on the American cultural terrain, "It takes an extra special person for McDonald's to name a sandwich after him ... And Michael Jordan can definitely handle that honor" (Dean Govotis, vice president and advertising chairman of McDonald's Owners of Chicago and Northwest Indiana, quoted by Lazarus, 1991, p. 1). The McJordan sandwich was marketed as being personally designed by Jordan, and it was said to reflect his love of traditional southern barbecue food, a taste he acquired during his childhood in North Carolina. Thus both Jordan's culinary preferences and his upbringing were anchored in an explicitly American setting.

Another promotional campaign restricted to the Chicagoland area involved Chevrolet bringing Jordan's American up-to-date by having him state his affection for and affinity with his adopted city, Chicago. Driving the obligatory Chevy Blazer past the Chicago Stadium, Jordan muses:

I love that old building, I mean people were talking about doing a new . . . You know, to me that's home. Just because of the way that it's built. Every seat is a good seat. You feel all that appreciation from all the fans. And you know you got 18,676 cheering for every move that you make. You just can't have any other feeling. I love it because it gives you a good sense of home.

Jordan's scripted sentiments identify him as a man of the people; someone who appreciates his doting fans; someone who identifies with them sufficiently to refer to the place where they congregate as home. Accordingly, Jordan is considered to be a proud civic representative of Chicago and its people. He is construed as more than transient athlete peddling his wares to the highest bidder. Like Walter Paten, Ernie Banks, and even Harry Caray, Jordan is an important constituent of Chicago's (sporting) cultural identity. It could even be argued that he is the single most significant figure in contemporary Chicago, for as Madigan recounted, he is the "[c]ity's most valuable imagemaker" (1991, p. 1).

As an amalgam of a North Carolina past and a Chicago present, Jordan's collective identity is firmly located on the geo-cultural map of American society. This point is visually captured in a McDonald's newspaper commercial relating to the 1992 U.S.A. Olympic Basketball Team. The text reminisces over Jordan's exploits as a high school senior in the 1982 McDonald's All-Star Game, whilst the accompanying picture portrays him as he is today; like McDonald's itself, an all-American symbol of national popular culture. In this way, the dialectic of promotion ensures that as well as publicizing their own wares, the commercial narratives discussed in this section simultaneously authenticate Jordan's standing as a prominent all-American commodity-sign.

Endnotes on *Being Like Mike*

Perhaps the best summation of Jordan's affective investments and identity was captured in the recently retired "Be Like Mike" advertising campaign, which ushered Jordan's $18 million endorsement defection from Coca-Cola to Gatorade in 1991. The campaign was built around a lively television commercial that keyed on an infectious refrain:

> Sometimes I dream that he is me,
> You've got to see that's how I dream to be.
> I dream I move, I dream I groove
> Like Mike, If I could be like Mike,
> Oh if I could be like Mike,

Like Mike, if I could be like Mike,
If I could be like Mike, be like Mike, be like Mike.
Oh yeah I try, to seem to fly.
For just one day if I could be that way.
I dream I move, I dream I groove
Like Mike, if I could be like Mike,
I'm gonna be, I'm gonna be, I'm gonna be like Mike,
Like Mike, if I could be like Mike.
Be like Mike, if I could be like Mike.
Be like Mike, if I could be like Mike.

The commercial incorporated a mixture of voices, young and old, male and female, that simultaneously spoke to the viewer on three levels: unfulfilled desire ("I wanna be like Mike"); confident assertion ("I'm gonna be like Mike"); and explicit direction ("be like Mike, be like Mike"). If the aural text of the commercial articulated a common goal to emulate this cultural icon, then the visual narrative graphically explicated precisely what it meant to "be like Mike."

Between images of Jordan having his voracious thirst quenched by Gatorade, the commercial juxtaposed televisual vignettes incorporating the full range of his mediated personality. The opening sequence acknowledged his supreme basketball and athletic prowess through a slow motion replay of his stupefying lay-up, subsequently dubbed "The Move," executed in Game 3 of the 1991 N.B.A. Finals against the Los Angeles Lakers. From the sublime heights of basketball excellence, the visual narrative dove to the human imperfections of playground basketball. Here a small black child, tongue hanging out in true Jordanesque fashion, attempts to imitate one of Jordan's explosive moves to the basket. Subsequent scenes depict black and white, female and male, children likewise trying to emulate their common hero. This iterated that Jordan's popular appeal, and influence, crossed racial and gender boundaries.

By immersing him in settings where he interacts naturally with his youthful admirers, Jordan is portrayed as the down-to-earth basketball megastar who still has time for the common people, no matter how small or insignificant. These interactions also present him as a warm hearted man who enjoys being around children; a trait that endeared him to the population at large. In one such scenario Jordan playfully guards a small boy, who is wearing the same Air Jordan apparel as his mentor. Later in the commercial, the roles are reversed when Jordan, smiling and evidently enjoying himself, is pictured attempting to keep the ball away from a host of small children all eagerly trying to steal it from him. In another scene, Jordan dribbles across a basketball court being pursued by a hoard of children all faithfully copying what he does. Jordan then pulls up for a jumpshot, and the assembled throng dutifully, almost hypnotically, follows his lead. Although portrayed as relating easily with children, the commercial leaves the viewer in no doubt that to "be like Mike" is also a serious and adult business. Jordan is shown playing a determined and focused game of one-on-one. Yet, even in this highly charged competitive atmosphere, he is still able to laugh at himself when he loses control of the ball. The fact that Jordan is a fun person to be with is reiterated in the frequent interludes in which he laughs and jokes with the guys (women being noticeable by their absence) when taking that much needed Gatorade break.

Having stressed his lighthearted side, in winding up the commercial, the viewer is reminded of his fierce desire to win, this time through recourse to his last second pull-up jump shot in the 1989 play-off game against the Cleveland Cavaliers; a shot that won the series for the Chicago Bulls. After making the shot, Jordan repeatedly punches the air in unbridled ecstacy. Having visually summarized what it is to "be like Mike," the commercial then, in self-parodying tone, ends with Jordan drinking from a cup of Gatorade and turning to smile directly at the camera. The commercial then concludes with the following message: BE LIKE MIKE. DRINK GATORADE.

The parodic nature of this commercial underscores that, rather than being a contributory factor, drinking Gatorade is merely a by-product of being Michael Jordan. The intertextual self-referentiality of promotional culture (Goldman & Papson, 1994) has established a commonly acknowledged understanding that "Being like Mike" incorporated a series of more profound personal investments which Gatorade's marketers, ever aware of the phenomenon of commercial synergy, gleefully tacked their product on the end of.

Hopefully, this preliminary engagement with a critical pedagogy of representation has identified the superficiality of Michael Jordan's promotional ubiquity, and excavated the ideological foundations of his simulated affective identity, which actively produce and mobilize popular desires and identities and thus contribute to the construction of specific subject positions and forms of authority (Giroux, 1994). Being like Mike, throughout the range of his expansive televisual portfolio, entails investing in the affective epidemics that constitute the mattering maps of the [post]-Reaganite project. Within Gatorade's anthemic commercial, and throughout the rest of his corporate portfolio, Jordan's audience is confronted by an unerringly consistent narrative, dominated by his simulated investment in the competitive individualism and institutional markers of traditional American life. On the surface these would seem to be harmless personal investments. Yet, by digging below the affective surface, it is possible to expose the ideological underpinnings that problematize the sign of being, and hence the experience of wanting to be, like Mike. Most significantly, Jordan's hyperreal persona conclusively fails to be contextualized within the specific forms of culture and race in which it must inevitably make sense (Dyson, 1993). Or, developing upon Dyson's suggestive but rather impotently expressed theme, the contrived absence of any systematic reference to culture and race necessitates that Jordan is condemned to being a mediated agent of reactionary as opposed to progressive politics. Given the habitual downplaying and obscuring of his racial and ethnic identity, it is hardly a surprise that the sign of Jordan became the acceptable embodiment of the African American male to the white dominated mass culture industry. As such, Jordan's image effectively denies the legitimate representation of an African American identity within the popular media. Jordan, to use Willis' (1991) terminology, has been constructed as a black replicant of the [post]-Reaganite All American individual, and as Marable (1993) noted, the white hegemony of American popular culture conclusively asserts that to be an all-American is, by definition, not to be an Asian-American, Pacific-American, American Indian, Latino, Arab-American or African American. As a black replicant of a white model (Willis, 1991), Jordan's simulated image represents a preferred African-American identity, against which all others are measured. In this way, the racially exclusive hyperreal narrative constructed around Jordan has material effects upon the way many African Americans are perceived within, and thus experience, everyday life within contemporary America. The harsh realities and entrenched inequities of the American racial formation are conveniently obscured by the Jordan hypermythology, as white America congratulates itself for Jordan's very existence, and simultaneously demonizes the amassing victims of America's racial hegemony for not being like Mike.

Within this abbreviated excavation, I have attempted to advance a critique of postmodern culture that discloses and demystifies how power, position, and privilege are produced within an electronically mediated consumption community. The goal of any critical pedagogy of representation must be to provide people with texts for realizing their location within the contemporary structures of both individual and group domination and exploitation. Once people discern their positioning within the complex structure of power relations within postmodern America, then, and only then, they are in a position to consciously resist both individually and as part of a collective opposition. Of course, Baudrillard would condemn such a thought. After all, in his eyes, the only form of resistance open to the media-bombarded silent majority is the cynical privatism and mass apathy of hyperconformism (Baudrillard, 1983b, 1983c). Nonetheless, I would argue that contextualizing and de-essentializing commodity-signs such as Michael Jordan, opens up important semiurgic spaces for meaningful strategies of resistance. Moreover, if cultural politics is waged on the hyperreal terrain of everyday life, then it is my contention that political resistance and opposition can, and must, also be practiced on that level.

References

"And he plays basketball too" (1992). *Champaign-Urbana News Gazette*, December 13, p. D3.

Anderson, B. (1983). *Imagined communities*. London: Verso.

Andrews, D.L. (1994). Michael Jordan: A commodity-sign of [post]Reaganite times. *Working Papers in Popular Cultural Studies*, 2(1), 1–50.

Anzaldúa, G. (1987). *Borderlands/La frontera: The new mestiza*. San Francisco: Spinsters/Aunt Lute.

Baudrillard, J. (1983a). *Simulations*. New York: Semiotext(e).

——— (1983b). *Les stratégies fatales*. Paris: Grasset.

——— (1983c). *In the shadow of the silent majorities*. New York: Semiotext(e).

——— (1987). *Forget Foucault*. New York: Semiotext(e).

——— (1988a). *America*. London: Verso.

——— (1988b). *The ecstacy of communication*. New York: Semiotext(e).

——— (1990). *Seduction*. New York: St. Martin's Press.

Bauman, Z. (1992). *Intimations of postmodernity*. London: Routledge.

Bennett, T. (1989). "Culture: Theory and policy." *Culture and policy*, 1, 5–8.

Callinicos, A.T. (1990). *Against postmodernism: A marxist critique*. London: St. Martin's Press.

Chambers, I. (1990). *Border dialogues: Journeys in postmodernity*. London: Routledge.

Chen, K.H. (1991). "Post-marxism: Between/beyond critical postmodernism and cultural studies." *Media, Culture and Society*, 13, 35–51.

Clarke, J. (1991). *New times and old enemies: Essays on cultural studies and America*. London: Harper Collins.

Cohen, S. (1972). *Folk devils and moral panics*. London: Paladin.

Collins, R., & Makowsky, M. (1972). *The discovery of society*. New York: Random House.

Craik, L. (1994). "Letter to the editor." *The Face*, August.

Culloton, D. (1991). "Illinois lottery makes Michael Jordan richer." *Chicago Tribune*, January 21, section 2C, pp. 1–2.

Davis, M. (1993). "Who killed LA? A political autopsy." *New Left Review*, 197, 3–28.

Deleuze, G., & Guattari, F. (1987). *A thousand plateaus: Capitalism and schizophrenia*. Minneapolis: University of Minnesota Press.

Dishneau, D. (1991). "Is sport's top pitchman pitching himself out?" *Chicago Sun-Times*, July 31, p. 114.

Dyson, M.E. (1993). "Be like Mike?: Michael Jordan and the pedagogy of desire." *Cultural Studies*, 7(1), 64–72.

Easthope, A. (1991). *British post-structuralism since 1968*. London: Routledge.

Fiske, J. (1992). "British cultural studies and television." In R.C. Allen (Eds.), *Channels of discourse reassembled: Television and contemporary criticism* (pp. 284–326). Chapel Hill, NC: University of North Carolina Press.

Frith, S. (1991). "Art of poise." *Village Voice*, April 9, p. 74.

Giroux, H. (1994). *Disturbing pleasures: Learning popular culture*. New York: Routledge.

Goldman, R., & Papson, S. (1994). "Advertsing in the age of hypersignification." *Theory, Culture and Society*, 11(3), 23–53.

Grossberg, L. (1984a). "Another boring day in paradise: Rock and roll and the empowerment of everyday life." *Popular Music*, 4, 225–258.

——— (1984b). "I'd rather feel bad than not feel anything at all." *Enclitic*, 8, 94–111.

——— (1986). "History, politics and postmodernism: Stuart Hall and cultural studies." *Journal of Communication Inquiry*, 10(2), 61–77.

——— (1988a). "Rockin' with Reagan, or the mainstreaming of postmodernity." *Cultural Critique*, Fall, 123–149.

——— (1988b). "It's a sin: Politics postmodernity and the popular." In L. Grossberg, A. Curthoys, P. Patton & T. Fry (Eds.), *It's a sin: Essays on postmodernism, politics & culture* (pp. 6–71). Sydney, Australia: Power Publications.

——— (1988c). Putting the pop back into postmodernism. In A. Ross (Ed.). *Universal abandon? The politics of postmodernism*. Minneapolis: University of Minnesota Press.

——— (1988d). "Postmodernity and affect: All dressed up with no place to go." *Communication*, 10, 271–293.

——— (1989a). "The formations of cultural studies: An American in Birmingham." *Strategies*, 2, 114–149.

——— (1989b). "The circulation of cultural studies." *Critical Studies in Mass Communication*, 6(4), 413–420.

——— (1989c). "MTV: Swinging on the (postmodern) star." In I. Angus & S. Jhally (Eds.), *Cultural politics in contemporary America* (pp. 254–268). New York: Routledge.

——— (1992). *We gotta get out of this place: Popular conservatism and postmodern culture*. London: Routledge.

Grossberg, L., Nelson, C., & Treichler, P. (1992). "Cultural studies: An introduction." In L. Grossberg, C. Nelson, & P. Treichler (Eds.), *Cultural Studies* (pp. 1–22). London: Routledge.

Hall, R.E. (1993). "Clowns, buffoons, and gladiators: Media portrayals of African-American men." *Journal of Men's Studies*, 1(3), 239–251.

Hall, S. (1988). "New ethnicities." In *Black film, British cinema* (pp. 27–31). London: ICA.

Hebdige, D. (1981). "Towards a cartography of taste 1935–1962." *Block*, 4, 39–56.

——— (1987). "Digging for Britain: An excavation in 7 parts." In *The British edge* (pp. 35–69). Boston: ICA.

——— (1988). *Hiding in the light: On images and things*. London: Comedia.

Jeffords, S. (1994). *Hard bodies: Hollywood masculinity in the Reagan era*. New Brunswick, NJ: Rutgers University Press.

Jhally, S., & Lewis, J. (1992). *Enlightened racism: The Cosby Show, audiences, and the myth of the American dream*. Boulder, CO: Westview Press.

Kearney, R. (1989). *The wake of the imagination: Toward a postmodern culture*. Minneapolis: University of Minnesota Press.

Kellner, D. (1989a). *Jean Baudrillard: From marxism to postmodernism and beyond*. Stanford: Stanford University Press.

——— (1989b). "Boundaries and borderlines: Reflections on Jean Baudrillard and critical theory." *Current Perspective in Social Theory*, 9, 5–22.

——— (1991). "Reading images critically: Toward a postmodern pedagogy." In H. Giroux (Ed.), *Postmodernism, feminism, and cultural politics* (pp. 60–82). Albany, NY: State University of New York Press.

Langman, L. (1991). "From pathos to panic: American national character meets the future." In P. Wexler (Ed.), *Critical theory now* (pp. 165–241). London: Falmer Press.

Lazarus, G. (1991). "McDonald's looks to score on a fast break by McJordan." *Chicago Tribune*, March 19, section 3, pp. 1, 4.

Lefebvre, H. (1971). *Everyday life in the modern world*. London: Allen Lane.

Luke, T.W. (1989). *Screens of power: Ideology, domination and resistance in informational society*. Urbana, IL: University of Illinois Press.

McManus, J. (1990). "It's a dream team: Jordan, Jackson, Gretzky eye cartoon show." *Advertising Age*, May 14, p. 66.

Madigan, C.M. (1991). "Michael: City's most valuable imagemaker." *Chicago Tribune*, June 2, section 1, pp. 1, 18.

Mellencamp, P. (1992), *High anxiety*. Bloomington: Indiana University Press.

Merrill, R. (1988). "Simulations: Politics, TV, and history in the Reagan Era." In R. Merrill (Ed.), *Ethics/aesthetics: Post-modern positions* (pp. 141–168). Washington, D.C.: Maisonnever Press.

Norris, C. (1992). *Uncritical theory: Postmodernism, intellectuals, and the Gulf War*. Amherst, MA: University of Massachusetts Press.

Patton, P. (1986). "The selling of Michael Jordan." *New York Times Magazine*, November 9, pp. 48–58.

Reagan, R. (1989). "Ronald Reagan, 1988." In *Public papers of the Presidents of the United States*. Washington, DC: United States Government Printing Office.

Revill, D. (1990a). "Report: Jean Baudrillard." *Paragraph*, 13, 293–300.

——— (1990b). "Star in love triangle." *Times Higher Education Supplement*, December 21, p. 14.

Rubenstein, D. (1989). "The mirror of reproduction: Baudrillard and Reagan's America." *Political Theory*, 17(4), 582–606.

Sakamoto, B. (1991). *Michael Jordan: MVP and NBA champ*. Lincolnwood, IL: Publications International.

Schneider, W. (1990). *The in-box president*. Atlantic Monthly, January, pp. 34–43.

Sharp, S. (1991). "Voice of the people: Jordan and lottery a good team." *Chicago Tribune*, February 6, section 1, p. 12.

Shuttleworth, A. (1971). "People and culture." *Working Papers in Cultural Studies*, 1(1), 65–96.

Solomon-Godeau, A. (1991). *Photography at the dock*. Minneapolis, MN: University of Minnesota Press.

Strasser, J.B., & Becklund, L. (1991). *Swoosh: The unauthorized story of Nike, and the men who played there*. New York: Harcourt Brace Jovanovich.

Tocqueville, A. (1945). *Democracy in America* (2 vols.). New York: Knopf.

Wornick, A. (1991) *Promotional culture: Advertising, ideology and symbolic expression*. London: Sage.

Williams, R. (1977). *Marxism and literature*. Oxford: Oxford University Press.

Willis, S. (1991). *A primer for daily life*. London: Routledge.

10

Baudrillard, "Amérique," and the Hyperreal World Cup

Steve Redhead

This chapter critically considers the work of Jean Baudrillard on "America" and suggests possible uses of this, and other literature, for those wishing to adopt a popular cultural studies approach to the World Cup and especially to U.S.A. '94.

To begin, I want to set this chapter in its popular cultural studies context by briefly referencing a selected group of previous, mainly British, analyses of the soccer World Cup as an event over the last 30 years. Most of these have concentrated on the extent to which "reality" has been displaced by the televisual or cinematic "image." Since England's home victory over West Germany in 1966, the World Cup in soccer as a global television event seems increasingly constructed by, for, and in the mass media.

The Reel Thing

The articles and books written around the subsequent World Cup Finals, which reflect this apparently incremental process of "mediatisation," include the following list which is set out here in recent World Cup Final historical order[1]:

West Germany 1974. The first piece of work I want to refer to is a pamphlet called *Football on Television* (Buscombe, 1975) which comprised a study of television coverage of the 1974 World Cup eventually won by the hosts in the Final against the "total football" of Holland. In it, Buscombe and his colleagues at the British Film Institute (BFI) and elsewhere concentrate on football on television, focusing on the debates about the problem of "mediation." The crux of the contemporary debate in the mid-1970s—and as Whannel (1992) has shown ever since—was the extent to which television programmes in general, and sports coverage in particular, were not so much a record of events as socially constructed phenomena. A major focus, too, was the exploration of the values and ideologies generated in the process of social construction.

Argentina 1978. As the venue moved to South America, I want to cite two contrasting European perspectives: an influential article in the film theory journal *Screen* (Nowell-Smith, 1978/9), and an essay by Umberto Eco (1987) before he achieved global fame as a (postmodern) novelist. Nowell-Smith, focusing on Argentina 1978, explicitly built on the BFI study, theorising television as "never exactly a reproduction of" an event but "always, in some way or other, a representation," recognising nevertheless that "the prejudice dies hard that television is there to reproduce; that its subject is given reality" (1978/9, p. 46). He notes the irony of holding the World Cup in a country where terror reigns and citizens frequently "disappear." Eco's piece on the World Cup in Argentina in 1978 stressed that this faraway global television event was taking place in the year of the Red Brigade's kidnapping and killing of the former Prime Minister of Italy, Aldo Moro. Eco's chapter in "Reports From the Global Village," a most appropriately named section of his collected essays *Travels in Hyperreality*, is concerned as much with the wave of terrorism then sweeping late 1970s Italy as with football. It discusses the way that the "World Cup has so morbidly polarised the attention of the public and the devotion of the mass media" arguing further that "public opinion, especially in Italy, has never needed a nice international championship more than it does now" (1987, p. 170). In other words, in Eco's judgment, the global televising of an event like the World Cup deflects attention from other, harsher "realities."

Spain 1982. The tournament in Spain took place against the backcloth of a recently finished war over the Falklands/Malvinas in the South Atlantic, involving three of the competitors, England, Northern Ireland and Argentina. In "The World Cup—A Political Football" Clarke and Wren-Lewis (1983) develop the ideas of both the BFI study and Nowell-Smith (Eco's account though written in 1978 was not published in English until 1986) in an article for the then recently launched journal *Theory, Culture and Society*. They examine the "ways in which political discourses did and did not intrude on to the footballing world as seen on television in June/July 1982" (Clarke & Wren-Lewis, 1983, p. 123), that is, the period of the World Cup in Spain. The claim by Clarke and Wren-Lewis is that "the footballing world is a well developed site that does not easily appropriate discourses outside itself," and one which "indeed has its own politics" (1983, p. 131).

Mexico 1986 In an edited series of papers published under the title *Off the Ball* (Tomlinson & Whannel, 1986), various references to the mass media and the World Cup appear. The relationship between modern media and global soccer culture is especially evident in one of the papers entitled "Tunnel Vision: Television's World Cup" and written by Geraghty and Simpson (who were then connected to the BFI) with the increasingly important media and sport theorist Whannel. The essay ranges across the history of the World Cup and the related history of the televising of the event. The three authors' incisive discussion shows how "television football became a global phenomenon" but also emphasises that a "western oriented view of the sport has become the norm in much of the world" (1986, p. 20).

All of the essays I have briefly referenced so far reflect a concern that, incrementally every four years, the televising of the World Cup from the 1960s onwards displayed a trend more generally seen in the electronic transformation of Western culture, a trend which was producing an increasing domination of the "image." For some commentators, however, the (post)modern world was fast becoming more than just a more visual culture; it was seen instead as a fully fledged post-literate culture of television images with no, or at least little, reference to something previously known as "reality." The coverage of global sport by the time of the 1990 World Cup Finals was seen by a few critics as having already reached this stage. The critical analysis made by these writers was of a qualitatively different kind to that reviewed so far. It drew on the controversial perspectives of postmodernism, even where its authors denied the definitions and assumptions assumed to be behind such a label.

Italy 1990. The best example of such a different perspective is found in *All Played Out*, Davies' (1991) book on Italia '90. Following on from his earlier forays into mass market fiction (e.g., *The Last Election*, 1987; *Dollarville*, 1990), the book is a "postmodern-ish" travel/theory journey through the World Cup Finals in Italy 1990, implying that events such as this have become part of a media saturated (hyper)reality designated by Davies as "Planet Football." Planet Football is described as an unreality zone of media and marketing mayhem, a land of hysterical fantasy, much of which relates, as Davies skillfully shows, to the ever present impending doom of soccer related violence. My own idiosyncratic discussion about Italia '90 is contained in a chapter called "Ninety Minute Culture: E for England Party Mix" in *Football With Attitude* (Redhead, 1991). This chapter re-presents the hysterical media stories of English hooliganism at the World Cup Finals in Italy in such a way that it is as if the (hooligan) event that had been widely predicted in the mass media hardly took place, a conclusion which Davies also independently reaches. His analysis—or mine—does not suggest that there is no "real" fan violence at World Cup finals, but it does stress the important role of news/media expectations and their often self-fulfilling prophecies. More controversially, along with much postmodern theorising, Davies' book hints that an event like hooliganism which is not covered in the media has not fully occurred at all—in other words it is not "real." Davies' title phrase is taken up throughout his book suggesting the "death" or "exhaustion" of all kinds of aspects of football and media culture including the post-colonial English national football team, former winners of the Jules Rimet trophy in 1966.

Channel Surfin' U.S.A.

In summer 1993, a year prior to the World Cup being staged in the U.S.A. in 1994, Davies (1993) published a post-Italia '90 article on America and soccer's biggest prize. Following hard on the heels of more mainstream football writers (e.g., Barclay, 1993; Glanville, 1993), Davies takes a careful look at the implications of the U.S.A. being the host nation for the development of soccer in America. He focuses on the crucial dimensions of space and time in a country the size of America, and the likely impact of the global telecommunications industry on the internal consumption of the event. The "new" experience of having the World Cup in the U.S.A. for the first time despite the country having entered the inaugural finals in Uruguay in 1930, and qualified for several more of the last stages in the intervening years, is prominent in the article, giving rise to an optimistic view of both how the World Cup will be staged in '94 and the likely impact on the playing of soccer in the future in the United States. However, there is pessimism in Davies' (1993) account too, as he notes the potential for the World Cup to "disappear" when he claims:

The baffling vastness of America presents all manner of difficulties both for organisations and for fans ... So it may be that the World Cup will be huge in nine cities, and that in Kansas or Idaho they won't give a cuss. Eleven weekend games will be live on ABC and the other 41 will be on ESPN—a 24 hour sports cable network reaching 70 million homes—but whether anyone will watch outside those nine immediately concerned media markets remains to be seen ... we should ... be watching with some fascination to see what they do with it; but if there's one country on this earth where the World Cup can happen and a whole bunch of people not even notice or care, then this is the one.

Another writer who has cultivated the idea of "disappearance," is the infuriating and reluctant guru of the "post," Jean Baudrillard. Baudrillard has proclaimed the complete meaninglessness of the term postmodernism in his statement that "there is no such thing as postmodernism"[2] (Gane, 1993, p. 22) and denied being anything approximating to a postmodernist. His own biographical trajectory, and eventual rise to academic superstardom, can be usefully compared to that of Umberto Eco (see Rojek & Turner, 1993). Both authors, interestingly, are fascinated by America and the fake/hyperreal, but Eco retains a "respectable" gravitas inside and outside the academy whereas Baudrillard provokes the most extreme hostility as well as uncritical celebration. Let us consider the commentaries of Baudrillard on the areas which I have already covered with regard to Eco.

Although he has written very little about sport, Baudrillard has mused in a collection of essays "on extreme phenomena" called *The Transparency of Evil* (1993) about the extent to which media coverage displaces the "real" event. For Baudrillard, in the essay entitled "The Mirror of Terrorism":

The most striking thing about events such as those that took place at the Heysel Stadium, Brussels, in 1985, is not their violence *per se* but the way in which this violence was given currency by television, and in the process turned into a travesty of itself. (1993, p. 75)

He comments further that:

The Romans were straightforward enough to mount spectacles of this kind, complete with wild beasts and gladiators, in the full light of day. We can put on such shows only in the wings, as it were—accidentally, or illegally, all the while denouncing them on moral grounds. (Not that this prevents us from disseminating them worldwide as fodder for TV audiences: the few minutes of film from the Heysel Stadium were the most often broadcast images of the year.) Even the 1984 Olympic Games in Los Angeles were transformed into a giant parade, a worldwide show which, just like the Berlin Games of 1936, took place in an atmosphere of terrorism created by a power's need to show off its muscles: the worldwide spectacle of sport was thus turned into a Cold War strategy—an utter corruption of the Olympic ideal. Once wrenched away from its basic principle, sport can be pressed into the service of any end whatsoever: as a parade of prestige or of violence, it slips . . . from play founded on competition and representation to circus like play, play based on the pull of vertigo. (1993, p. 77)

Baudrillard follows this point later in the essay by commenting on a post-Heysel European Cup tie in 1987 between Real Madrid and Napoli which was ordered by the European Union of Football Associations (EUFA) to be played behind closed doors. He writes that:

the match took place at night in a completely empty stadium, without a single spectator, as a consequence of disciplinary action taken by the International Federation in response to the excesses of Madrid supporters at an earlier game. Thousands of fans besieged the stadium, but no one got in. The match was relayed in its entirety via television. A ban of this kind could never do away with the chauvinistic passions surrounding soccer, but it does perfectly exemplify the terroristic hyperrealism of our world, a world where a "real" event occurs in a vacuum, stripped of its context and visible only from afar, televisually. Here we have a sort of surgically accurate prefigurement of the events of our future: events so minimal that they might well not need take place at all—along with their maximal enlargement on screens. No one will have directly experienced the actual course of such happenings, but everyone will have received an image of them. A pure event, in other words, devoid of any reference in nature, and readily susceptible to replacement by synthetic images. The phantom football match should obviously by seen in conjunction with the Heysel Stadium game, when the real event, football, was once again eclipsed—on this occasion by a much more dramatic form of violence. There is always the danger that this kind of transition may occur, that spectators may cease to be spectators and slip into the role of victims or murderers, that sport may cease to be sport and transformed into terrorism: that is why the public must simply be eliminated, to ensure that the only event occurring is strictly televisual in nature. Every real referent must disappear so that the event may become acceptable on television's mental screen. (1993, p. 80)

Baudrillard's various comments quoted above from *The Transparency of Evil* come in the context of the "live" televising of the deaths of 39 Italian fans at the Heysel Stadium football disaster at the European Cup Final in May 1985[3] rather than a World Cup Finals, but any analysis of mass media presentations of the U.S.A. '94 World Cup will need to accommodate the extent to which the "real referent" has in fact disappeared over recent years and how far audiences, both "live" and television, have been transformed by the increasing domination of the "mental screen."

Veneer and Loafing in Los Angeles

The 1994 tournament was held in the U.S.A., the land of the mediascape, with Japan waiting in the wings to host the first Finals following the year

2000 after France, Baudrillard's home country, has staged them in 1998. The 1994 event may well symbolise a watershed in the mediatising of this ultimate example of global popular culture. A more "passive," as opposed to "participatory," audience for football is one possible outcome as soccer is globally consumed more and more through the mediation of television. American "live" audiences for U.S.A. '94 were possibly the least committed and knowledgeable of any World Cup held so far. There is also widespread criticism that the lack of informed, technical knowledge amongst broadcasters led to a reduction in the generally high quality coverage of sport on TV in the U.S.A. The commercial and media aspect to the event was assumed by large sections of football fans in Europe to be the reason for the award of the staging of the competition in a country where soccer has such a low profile compared to baseball, basketball and American football. The U.S.A. was generally perceived by commentators as an eccentric choice for the 1994 Finals. Certainly, European sports journalists reacted cynically—with a few exceptions such as Patrick Barclay (1993)—when the news of the U.S.A. as the venue was announced. For instance, Michael Parkinson noted in the context of writing about some sporting ideas he wanted to send to the Federation Internationale des Football Associations (FIFA): "I hope they will take my suggestions seriously in Zurich. I am hopeful. They might sound barmy but the people at FIFA are used to that. It was they after all, who gave the next World Cup to the yanks" (Parkinson, 1992).

Nevertheless, sports journalists' sarcasm notwithstanding, the final of the 1994 World Cup was held in the same city that hosted the Olympic Games, and this in itself was a new moment in the globalisation and commodification of sport. It was played in the Pasadena Rose Bowl in Los Angeles, California, where a large crowd witnessed the Olympic Soccer Final in 1994. Germany, the holders of the World Cup after defeating the 1986 winners (Argentina) in an acrimonious final in Italy in 1990, opened U.S.A. '94 at Chicago stadium at Soldier Field. The 24 finalist teams were put in groups of four at the final draw in Las Vegas in December 1993. Many of the widely predicted changes to the actual on-field playing of the game of football as a consequence of the staging of the tournament in the television-saturated U.S.A. did not come forth. For instance, the president of FIFA, Joao Havelange, declared in November 1992—after much previous speculation to the contrary—that his plan to split matches into four quarters would not be implemented in time for the 1994 Finals. However, the ever faster changes in new communications technologies at the end of the millennium inevitably coincided with the televising of the 1994 World Cup and its aftermath. For instance, in early 1992, it was proclaimed (Soccer Fans Get Choice of TV Shot in Cable's "Next Best Thing To Terraces" headlined *The Guardian* on February 12, 1992) that armchair British football fans would soon be able to select their own television pictures following the launch of a new cable service. Interactive television was seen by the providers, the Videotron cable company, as enabling viewers to select from four cable channels all covering a match simultaneously with different facilities such as camera angles and statistical information. At the time, Greg Dyke, London Weekend Television chief executive, called the Videotron experiment "a big, big message for the 21st century."

To go back to Baudrillard, I want to argue in this chapter that we can use his work in a more complex way than merely reproducing what he has written about the hyperreality of modern media culture, some of which is based upon his extremely controversial contention that "TV is the world." As a contribution to what the disciplinary field that I have elsewhere labelled as "Popular Cultural Studies"[4] can now bring to the analysis of "U.S.A. '94," the remainder of this chapter critically appraises Baudrillard's travel/theory/ adventure book *America* (1988) and assesses its implications for the study of the hosting of the World Cup by a country Baudrillard describes as "(un)culture" and "born modern"[5] or as "the original version of modernity" which "has no past and no founding truth" and that "lives in a perpetual present . . . in perpetual simulation, in a perpetual present of signs" (1988, p. 76). In his role as a European tourist travelling to the U.S.A., Baudrillard proclaims that Europe has disappeared into America, or more accurately, into California ("in Los Angeles, Europe has disappeared," says Baudrillard, 1993, p. 81). In a book of essays on Baudrillard (see Rojek & Turner, 1993), Smart and Turner argue legitimately that the Europe/America couplet which Baudrillard uses, is located in a more general historical critical transatlantic tradition. Baudrillard merely pushes this tradition to its limit in his comparing and contrasting of "modern" America and "traditional" Europe; the New World and the Old World.

Apart from the contributors to the above collection of essays, perhaps the scholar most critically sympathetic to Baudrillard has been Gane. In Gane's (1993) book of selected interviews with Baudrillard, one of the sections is entitled "America as Fiction" and reproduces a previously little known interview with Baudrillard about his views on America at the time of the French publication of the book *Amérique*. Baudrillard comments in this interview that the last thing he wants to suggest "is that America is some sort of paradise. It is precisely its rawness which interests me and its primeval character, although one shouldn't confuse it with some sort of primitive society" (quoted in Gane, 1993, pp. 131–135). He goes on to specify that America should not be read as a realist text, its subject matter being a fiction itself. For Baudrillard, the difficulty in the book had been to evoke this transpolitical, transhistorical reality of an American society which "is not a society of appearances" (p. 135). According to Baudrillard, America has no counterpart to the games of seduction with which he sees Europe as being so familiar. For him Americans "experience reality like a tracking shot" which is why they succeed so well with certain media, particularly television. This fascination with the object of his post-tourist inquiry does not mean that Baudrillard "likes" what he sees. He is, simultaneously, seduced and repelled. His view is that "America is hell" and that it is, as a whole, a "matter of abjection." But Baudrillard adds that "such criticisms are inconsequential" because at "every instant this object is transfigured. It is the miracle of realised utopia . . . America is a place where utopia was realised by a geographical displacement and conservation of the ideas of the eighteenth century" (p. 135).

Nevertheless, looking back a few years after the book was first published and realising that the utopia he mentions has a historical referent in 1950s America, Baudrillard claims that the United States has "changed since I wrote *America*. It now functions only in the mode of protectionism, survival" (quoted in Gane, 1993, p. 187). He confesses, in a separate interview in the collection, to having lost his "exaltation over America," a confession which itself perplexed some critics on the Left who had thought they had perceived in *America* a Baudrillard who was condemning the dehumanising influence of America. Nothing could be further from the truth. Even in *America* there is a hint of the "disillusionment" with even an achieved utopia when Baudrillard argues that "today the orgy is over" and that the United States, along with everybody else, "now has to face up to a soft world order, a soft situation" where "power has become impotent" and de-centred (p. 107). Baudrillard, here at least, certainly articulates the experience of many European tourists of America as an empire at the end of its tether.

For some critics, the publication of *Amérique* was worth taking seriously, though not without a very rigorous critical reading as an exposition of elementary errors and prejudices in Baudrillard's writing. For many others (e.g., Kellner) it was a sign of how far Baudrillard's once Left wing credentials had slipped around the head of just another "lazy" French academic. For yet others, the "panic" theorists of postmodernity, Baudrillard's vision was, if loaded in manic fashion onto other examples of French intellectual production, a paradigm case of the hyperreality of postmodernity (the idea of Disneyland being the "real" America, for instance) and also evidence of a wider connection between Europe and America. For Kroker (1992) especially, almost all of the leading contemporary French social and cultural theory—most explicitly Baudrillard, but Lyotard, Foucault and others too— is integrally related to "America." Kroker asks (rhetorically):

And why the fascination with French though? Because its discourse is a theoretical foreground to America's political background: fractal thinkers in whose central images one finds the key power configurations of the American hologram . . . French thought, therefore, as a violent decoding and recoding of the American way, which is to say, of all the world, since America is today the global hologram. (1992, pp. 1–3)

The comparative (economic) failure of Euro Disney in France may call into question such ubiquitousness of the American hologram, and also some of the wilder elements of Kroker's own "panic" appropriation of Baudrillard, but the different versions/visions of *America* are there for all to see. For Baudrillard himself, *America* was:

a book I wrote in a flash of inspiration. I loved that country. The book is talked about a lot, but there was nothing but negative reactions. On the one hand, I've been treated like the last of the Europeans, stuffed with prejudices and self satisfaction, who had understood nothing about the reality of America. It was impossible to connect that by saying that I was not presuming to judge American reality. My critics were reading the wrong book. On the other hand, some people read it another way. (quoted in Gane, 1993, p. 189)

Baudrillard's "astral" America is clearly distinct from the economic and social "reality" of America and there are obviously many different Americas; as Smart and Turner have pointed out "Baudrillard arrived already in possession of America, possessed by it, a colonised subject of its empire of cinematic signs" (1993, p. 55). Personally, I am convinced that any popular cultural studies criticism of the 1994 World Cup in America (and beyond) needs to take Baudrillard's version of America seriously but with a good deal of caution, too. As Gane has contended about Baudrillard's work in general:

He is not always capable of surprising and provoking us to the degree he would wish, and some of his analyses are vulnerable to the most harsh of judgments. Yet the overall impression we are left with is of a consistency and persistence of critical imagination which produces, sometimes, remarkable insights. Some of his work is utterly self defeating, even hypocritical. But there is an undeniable vitality and creativity coupled with an undying fidelity not to a utopian vision in a passive sense, but to a passionate utopian practice in theory. (1991b, p. 1157)

This judgment by Gane, with which I concur, serves also as a useful summary of Baudrillard's writing in *America* specifically. It means, though, that when using such a text as one way into the consideration of U.S.A. '94 as a global media event, the precise angle of the "flight" to America needs elaboration.

My own "America" is a less cinematic one than Baudrillard's. In a way, some of my previous works on soccer's mediatised culture from a popular cultural studies perspective (Redhead, 1987, 1991) combine elements from what was once called the "new journalism," the beat poetry of Jack Kerouac and several decades of American rock culture with an iconoclastic use of theories of the so called "postmodern condition." A subtitle such as "The Last[6] World Cup" has, for me at least, the distant echoes of an empire of pop culture signs including Hunter S. Thompson's *Fear and Loathing in Las Vegas* and *Fear and Loathing: The Campaign Trail '72*, Jack Kerouac's *On the Road*, Bob Dylan's Highway 61 Revisited and Blonde on Blonde, and R.E.M.'s Automatic For The People. In my fictional journey to "America" and U.S.A. '94, Baudrillard (with his French sidekick, Paul Virilio, armed with the "aesthetics of disappearance") meet the above characters on their way to the World Cup Final in L.A. Both Baudrillard and, say, Hunter Thompson, in their very different ways, have, during the last 25 years, provided insights into the American (or "Western" or "Capitalist') condition; when the spirits of these two mavericks meet up (one a visitor from the outside, one a visitor from within), the product may be something of a postmodern travelogue entitled *Veneer and Loafing in Los Angeles* perhaps, or *Fear and Loathing in Pontiac* as the self-styled "half decent football magazine" *When Saturday Comes* (September 1993) suggested in its preview of U.S.A. '94.

A number of travelogues, besides Baudrillard's own, have in fact been written on the U.S.A. Recently this has been done by utilising genres such as American popular music (e.g., Brown, 1993; Bull, 1993; Davies, 1992; Heath, 1993) and popular crime fiction (e.g., Williams, 1991) as a way into American popular culture, as a journey to the heart of the contemporary American dream. I have suggested in this chapter that the search also might be done through soccer, and the event of U.S.A. '94, and that a critical reading of Baudrillard's *America* might be a helpful guide. But soccer is in many ways alien to American popular culture, an originally European cultural form inserting itself into the psyche (or sign) of America. Baudrillard's series of distinctions and contrast between a modern, deculturated America and an older, more historical, "cultured" Europe is one possible frame for analysing the media presentation of the summer '94. Nevertheless, for conventional academic researchers, the way to study the production, consumption and regulation of a globalised TV event like the soccer World Cup is more likely to be by "zapping" the channels ("surfing") on as many television sets as can be found in as many countries as possible. Such research design may not necessarily even entail visiting the United States of America during the period that the event takes place at all. In this sense the methodology and theoretical apparatus that lend themselves most easily to such cultural analysis are the sort exemplified by the BFI study of the televising of the 1974 Finals (see Buscombe, 1975). Such an approach does resolve some difficult research problems (such as how to fund travel from other countries to the U.S.A.) though to eschew any form of ethnography in these cases is likely to lead to only a very partial view of an event. Conventional ethnographic study could and should be done to supplement media and textual analysis of what occurs on television screens. To rely simply on the semiotic analysis of TV signs in accounting for an event such as the U.S.A. '94 is to risk ignoring how the event is differentially consumed by a variegated (live and television) audience and to accept the dangerous logic of the complete disappearance of the "real referent."

What can finally be said about the event of U.S.A. '94? Even though Havelange's plan to divide the 90 minutes of play into four quarters—to better accommodate television advertising—was shelved, many effects of the World Cup being staged in the home of the ultimate landscape of the media manifested themselves. In fact, it could be said that before even starting, the World Cup '94 had "already taken place" in terms of its contribution to the global media coverage of soccer, especially in Europe. The transformations of the football audience—from more participatory to more passive—were advanced. The "disappearance" of the audience, which Baudrillard toys with, has not, of course, literally taken place, apart from isolated games (like the one Baudrillard reviews) where indiscipline by supporters led to governing bodies ordering the playing of matches behind closed doors. Nevertheless, it is clear that the reorganisation of the business side of many of the world's biggest soccer clubs (e.g., AC Milan, Barcelona, Manchester United) is proceeding in such a way that "live" paying spectators will not necessarily be required in order that these entities survive in future as economically successful corporations. Television revenues, sales from various commercial exploitation of related commodities, and sponsorship already count for far more than spectator income. The drive for more passive (at the ground or at home watching television) rather than more participatory spectators risks, of course, diluting the spectacle itself, which for many critics depends on the enthusiasm generated by participatory football fans. Whether the "resistance" movement amongst fans in many countries succeeds in fighting this modernisation and rationalisation of global soccer is at present unpredictable, but in Britain, for instance, clubs (e.g., Arsenal) have already experimented (albeit during ground reconstruction) with the "simulation" of a participatory crowd. Artists' impressions of a terrace crowd and piped chanting/cheering were part of the simulation of a whole "end" of terrace culture.

However, the implication of Baudrillard's work for popular cultural study of the World Cup is even more fundamental than this. The problem posed by Baudrillard is how to make sense of something that is so "mediatised," so hyperreal, that it can be said: (a) to have already taken place; or (b) that it will not take place; or (c) that it will hardly take place.

For Baudrillard (1991), the Gulf War was such an event to be analysed in these terms. For some of his harshest critics (e.g., Norris, 1991), this approach to a local/ global war was ludicrous, and worse, politically dishonest in view of the terrible loss in Iraqi, and other populations' lives. At first, Baudrillard's position on the Gulf conflict, before any military hostilities began between Iraq and the "allies," seemed to be a fairly straightforward prediction that there would be no war—merely simulation of war—but once there was fighting in early 1991, this argument had to be clarified. In the context of the aftermath of a global event such as Italia '90, I argued in a footnote on the Iraq war that "within months the world was plunged into ultra high-technological warfare in the Gulf where video games replaced dead bodies as the products of war" (Redhead, 1991, p. 107). As Gane points out in his analysis of Baudrillard's writings on the war once it had begun, Baudrillard could have easily outlined the "novelty of war in which computer simulation played . . . a major part in the technological armoury of both sides" (1993, pp. 7–8). But, Gane rightly points out, "Baudrillard went considerably further" suggesting that "everything was unreal: the war, the victory, the defeat" (pp. 7–8). Baudrillard rarely, in fact, goes this far in his varied writings and interviews—that is, implying total simulation and the complete disappearance of the event/referent—and as can be seen from his analysis of Heysel and subsequent soccer events, the theoretical desire to do so is often limited in practice, giving way to a more balanced account of the "hyperreal." It is debilitating to follow Baudrillard at his most extreme—he sets up, as many have pointed out, his own "disappearance"—and clearly, the World Cup really did take place in the U.S.A. in 1994. Nevertheless, the event, as a global media show, may well have been foreshadowed in the changing face of television driven, media mogul dominated world soccer culture. The 1990 tournament in Italy brought howls of protest that, in playing styles, "we are all Europeans now" and that as a result of most of the world's best players being collected into the Italian league, soccer difference and spontaneity were in danger of being squeezed out of the world football game. Maybe this European football culture has disappeared in America as Baudrillard's tourist gaze implies. Or maybe not. Is the memory of U.S.A. '94 set to become a watershed of a different kind; of renewal in global and local soccer culture? Perhaps now that U.S.A. '94 has taken place we will be able to look back on the event as a World Cup that brought something more than fatalism and embodied some shreds of an optimism for the future of certain popular cultural forms.

Notes

1. There are many histories of the World Cup. For one very comprehensive and readable volume, see Glanville (1993).

2. For a thorough discussion of Baudrillard's large body of work in the context of the debate about postmodernism, see also Gane (1991a, 1991b). All three of Gane's books on Baudrillard make out an extremely good case for regarding Baudrillard as anti-modernist and anti-postmodernist.

3. For my own satirical account of the youth cultural context of the Heysel disaster, Thatcherite politics and the mass media, see Redhead (1987).

4. For a history and outline of the possible field designated by the label "Popular Cultural Studies" and how it might be seen to grow out of, but also differ from, previous formulations such as "Contemporary Cultural Studies," see Redhead (1994).

5. Baudrillard's view in America is that "you are born modern, you do not become so" (1993). See, in contrast, for a 1990s Marxist-oriented sociology of "(post)modern" America, Woodiwiss (1993). Woodiwiss sees postmodernism (which he defines to incorporate Baudrillard) as having made a contribution to a more adequate sociology, without accepting the onset of a qualitatively different and new "postmodern" world which has replaced a pre-existing condition of modernity. He is sceptical about the generalisation of hyperreality/postmodernity "amongst even the advanced capitalist nations of the world" and specifically rejects "post-Marxist" contentions.

6. The idea of the "last" is deliberately jokey. It does not suggest that I think there will literally be no new World Cup Finals after 1994 in the U.S.A. There is, though, a serious implication of such a phrase as "the last." I used it in the subtitle to *The Last Football Book* (Redhead, 1987) as I do here to draw attention both to the specific historical deterioration in the genre (either football writing or the World Cup as a spectacle) and the more philosophical idea of "end of . . ." See Kroker and Kroker (1993) for a similar use in the different context of sexuality.

References

Barclay, P. (1993). "A family at war in the land of hype and glory." *The Observer*, June 20.

Baudrillard, J. (1988). *America*. London: Verso.

———— (1991). "The Reality Gulf." *The Guardian*, January 11.

———— (1993). *The transparency of evil: Essays on extreme phenomena*. London: Verso.

Brown, M. (1993). *American heartbeat*. London: Michael Joseph.

Bull, A. (1993). *Coast to coast*. London: Black Swan.

Buscombe, E. (Ed.) (1975). *Football on television*. London: British Film Institute.

Clarke, A., & Wren-Lewis, J. (1983). "The World Cup—A political football." *Theory, Culture and Society*, 1(3), 123–133.

Davies, P. (1987). *The last election*. Harmondsworth, England: Penguin.

——— (1990). *Dollarville*. London: Vintage.

——— (1991). *All played out*. London: Heinemann.

——— (1992). *Storm country*. London: Heinemann.

——— (1993). "Tomorrow the world." *The Guardian*, June 26.

Eco, U. (1987). *Travels in hyperreality*. London: Picador.

Gane, Mike (1991a). *Baudrillard: Critical and fatal theory*. London: Routledge.

——— (1991b). *Baudrillard's bestiary*. London: Routledge.

——— (1993). *Baudrillard live*. London: Routledge.

Glanville, B. (1993). *The story of the World Cup*. London: Faber and Faber.

Heath, C. (1993). *The Pet Shop Boys versus America*. London: Viking.

Kroker, A. (1992). *The possessed individual: Technology and postmodernity*. London: Macmillan.

Kroker, A., & Kroker, M. (Eds.) (1993). *The last sex*. London: Macmillan.

Norris, C. (1991). *Uncritical theory*. London: Lawrence and Wishart.

Nowell-Smith, G. (1978/9). "Television—Football—The world." *Screen*, 19(4), 45–59.

Parkinson, M. (1992). *Sporting lives*. London: Pavilion.

Redhead, S. (1987). *Sing when you're winning: The last football book*. London: Pluto Press.

——— (1991). *Football with attitude*. Manchester, England: Wordsmith.

—— (Ed.) (1991). *The passion and the fashion: Football fandom in the new Europe*. Aldershot, England: Avebury.

——— (1994). *Unpopular cultures*. Manchester, England: Manchester University Press.

Rojek, C., & Turner, B. (Eds.) (1993). *Forget Baudrillard?* London: Routledge.

Tomlinson, A., & Whannel, G. (Eds.) (1986). *Off the ball: The football World Cup.* London: Pluto Press.

Whannel, G. (1992). *Fields in vision: Television sport and cultural transformation.* London: Routledge.

Woodiwiss, A. (1992). *Postmodernity USA: The crisis of social modernism in postwar America.* London: Sage.

Williams, John (1991). *Into the badlands.* London: Paladin.

PART IV

SPORT AND POSTMODERN BODY INVADERS

11

INSTRUMENTAL RATIONALIZATION OF HUMAN MOVEMENT: AN ARCHEOLOGICAL APPROACH

JACQUES GLEYSE

This chapter seeks to break away from the histories of human physical activities, especially games and sports. It endeavors to establish the premises of discourses on human physical activities, games and sports for their archeological history, along the lines of the type of analysis developed by Michel Foucault (1966, 1969) for other areas of study such as punishment, sexuality, insanity or clinical medicine (1975, 1984, 1961, 1963). As Foucault underlines:

> Archeology analyzes the ground rules by which are formed a set of paradigms ... it analyzes the extent and the form of a discourse's permeability: it establishes the principle by which its various components are Expressed throughout a sequential chain of events; it defines the operative processes by which in paradigms, events manifest themselves. (1969, p. 218)

My point here is, therefore, not only to identify and describe the discursive structures pertaining to human physical activities, but to grasp their interconnections and to endeavor to rediscover the fundamental tropisms[1] that permitted their genesis in a given historical period. Following Foucault, it would be appropriate to go so far as to speak of "chains of inference" (1969, p. 132). Within this perspective, I will endeavor to link together the threads of the various discourses to a central and material point which seems to condition them fundamentally: namely, the point regarding the modifications over time of "praxis," that is, of the structure of "labor" in the broadest sense of the term.

"Labor," which has been defined by Marx in his *1844 Manuscripts* as "the act by which man [sic] defines himself" (1962, p. 122)—that is, as an action exerted by an individual as a culturally defined being, upon a human being understood as human nature—seems to me to be decisive in the understanding of the transformations in the various discourses on human physical activities and games, as well as in the understanding of the transformations of these same activities.

Three tropisms and three archeological watersheds seem to be fundamental to the analysis of the metamorphoses of discourse as well as to the forms and structures of physical activity from the Renaissance period to the end of the 20th century. The first one, which comes about in the 16th century, has its earliest origins in the form defined as the factory. The second one develops primarily from the end of the 18th century and the beginning of the 19th century onwards and operates on the basis of the two related models of the mill/plant and its precursor (the steam engine), and the thermal energy engine which replaces the basic natural energy machine (i.e., the water wheel) of the early factories. As pertains to theories of work analysis, their corollaries are the discursive currents of the works of Ford, Taylor and Fayol. These currents are still widespread today, but are quickly losing ground ever since the beginning of the post-industrial (Touraine, 1969) and especially postmodern (Lyotard, 1979) periods. The third one comes about with the gradual de-reification of labor as well as its gradual shift towards a service sector based economy as is well described by Fourastié in *Les Trente Glorieuses* (1979). This de-reification is especially related to the anthropomorphism of capital, to paraphrase Guigou (1987, 1992), and to the constitution of a third and virtual conception of human nature and of its prominence on a mechanistic level, through the computer and computer sciences.

In this chapter, I endeavor to sketch out the interconnections of these general structures with the lines of discourse specific to human physical activities, games and sports. I will especially delve into the process of the instrumental rationalization of bodies and movements, from the viewpoint of physical activities, through the study of authors and texts.

From Craftsmanship to the Factory, from Games to Physical Exercises

It is undoubtedly useful to remember that the form of activity known as the factory first develops in Italy at the end of the 15th century. It quickly imposes its forms and structures upon the world of work, and the powers that be just as quickly focus their attention on this system. In France, notably, as early as 1531, King François the 1st, by granting a royal charter to the Fontainebleau Royal Manufacture, demonstrates the importance the French crown attaches to this model of labor practices.

As Cornaert (1949) points out so well, the factory fundamentally modifies the routines and habits of craftsmanship and promotes a type of rationalization of work heretofore unknown. Moreover, Borkenau (1934), emphasizes that the factory imposes precision motion, standardization, repetition and efficiency. It radically transforms the world and as such attests to a total modification of the "*épistémé*" (Foucault, 1966) maybe even instigating that modification.

Stipulating the severe punishment of any type of failure to meet norms and rules of precision concerning finished products, the orders proclaimed by the French King's minister Colbert in 1669 give additional proof of the tropistic force of this structure and the potential effects it can engender in fields of study other than work practices. With the factory, the imprecise work and the non-standardized movements of the craftsman are banned. The factory worker can no longer be satisfied with the medieval world "of give or take an inch, of hit or miss" (Koyré, 1973, p. 78).

This move towards more precision, normalization, rationalization and mechanization recurs throughout the *épistémé* and notably in the field of human physical activities and discourses about the body.

The Factory's Impact on Anatomy: The Motionless Body

> My efforts at learning would have fallen through, if during my medical studies in Paris, I had not personally applied myself to the task at hand and if I had been satisfied with the few internal organs which in the course of a public dissection or another were superficially and without insistence shown to me and my comrades by barbers of incomparable incompetence. Such was the carelessness with which anatomy was then taught. . . . During the third session . . . I performed the dissection myself, and did it more correctly than was generally the case. In the course of the second one I undertook, I applied myself to displaying the hand muscles as well as to displaying a more careful anatomical view of the internal organs. Indeed, except for the eight muscles of the abdomen, shamefully lacerated and presented in an erroneous order, no one had ever, to speak truthfully, shown me any specific muscle, nor for that matter any particular bone whatsoever, and even less a network of veins or arteries. (Vesalius, 1555, p. 33)

This quotation perfectly demonstrates the "ordering" ("*mise en ordre*" according to Foucault, 1966) which the factory is in the course of achieving as concerns knowledge of the body. The body is put on exhibit; it is divided into sections, cut up methodically and precisely. Behind the complexities of the bodily microcosm, Vesalius searches for the universal laws and guiding principles of anatomy. Subscribing to a "taxinomical" point of view (Foucault, 1966), he meticulously classifies all of the components of the human body. Though maintaining as an ideological backdrop the idea of a body created by God and the product of nature or the great "opifex" (master crafts-man), Vesalius endeavors through dissection to construct another concept of the body: a body as object, as a product of man, as a product of human technology. This duality can be perceived particularly well in the entire set of plates of *De Humani Corporis Fabrica* (1555). The human sectional views are at the same time so realistic as to seem alive (they seem cut open *in vivo*), and as being already even then quantified and standardized by the exactness of anatomical science.

Such is also the case with Estienne's (1545) *De Dissectione Partium Corporis Humani.* Toward the end of his book, already looms the foundations of an understanding of anatomical science seen from a viewpoint influenced by geometry; a viewpoint which into the world of corporeality borrows ele-ments from the world of the factory.

In the beginning of the 17th century, the various representations of the human body are henceforth fundamentally at odds with those of the previous century. The bodies in the drawings of sectional views of the human body have become neutralized, sanitized, de-reified and standardized, as if they were products of a factory. Such is also the case with several other authors. For instance, Roberto Fludd constructs his "Anatomiæ Amphithéatrum" (1623) on the basis of the Renaissance viewpoint of classical similarities between man and the world, and he proposes dissection plates of representations of human sectional views, which already follow the model of the neutralized viewpoint of the body. Joanis Velingi drafts his "Syntagma anatomicum" (1663) in a way similar to the treatises of anatomy of the 19th century: the body is divided into sections and the human sectional views are de-reified, sanitized and neutralized. A last example is René Descartes' "De homine figuris" (1664) which was to tip the scales in the world of anatomy toward Galilean outlooks on that science. In so doing, it subscribes to an understand-ing of corporeality based on the physical sciences (i.e., a mechanistic view-point) and to the demands of the factory. In Descartes' book, the human body is constantly compared to a simple machine and described by means of a geometric interpretation of anatomy, as if it were something unreal.

Mercurialis and Borelli and the Imprint of the Factory on Human Movement

It would be a major error to confer solely upon Hieronimus Mercurialis the honor of being the father of modern gymnastics for at least two reasons. On the one hand, Mercurialis is not the first to write on this topic even though he is the first to explicitly entitle a book *De arte gymnastica* (1569). Before him, Hierome de Monteux de Méribel (1559, the first Latin edition being in 1557) had devoted an important chapter of his *Commentaire de la conserva-tion de la santé et prolongation de la vie* to physical exercise and idleness, as well as to their respective effects. In this text, he re-establishes the reputation of Galenic thought and the exercises of the ancient Greeks and Romans. His position of advisor and official medical doctor to the French King Henri II is such that one can assume that his treatise will have been known about among the powerful and the intellectuals. Interest in this topic is also to be found in the works of another advisor to the King, Du Choul, who in 1567 drafts *De la religion des anciens romains, de la castrémation et discipline militaire d'iceux. Des bains et antiques exercitations grecques et romaines*, in the works of Simon de Valembert, who in 1565 writes on the subject of the education of children, and lastly, after the publication of Mercurialis' book, in the works of Petri Fabri (1592) and Laurenti Jouberti (1582). Understood in this context, Mercurialis is not the precursor he is thought to be. Though Mercurialis' text is truly an attempt at ordering the movements of the body in an exhaustive inventory fashion, it remains in its foundations and descriptions more imbued with the spirit of the medieval world or of ancient Greece and Rome than with that of the Renaissance or modern world. The body, like in Vesalius' or Estienne's conceptions of anatomy, remains a subject within the world. In contrast to the plates of the human body in *De Homine*, which express a geometric, de-reifying viewpoint of the body, those from *De Arte Gymnastica* do not and are simply representations of the body. In this respect, they are in keeping with the prevailing forms in portraiture and, generally speaking, with the pictorial arts of the Renaissance. From this point of view, Johan Alphonse Borelli totally rocks the world with his *De Motu Animalium* published in 1685, which opens the door to biomechanics.

In this work, mechanistic schemes of understanding the world, be they Galilean, Cartesian, even Newtonian, lay claim to the field of corporeality. The tropism of the factory invests the universe of the muscles, the body, of human movement, of games. Borelli quantifies with the maximum precision possible the forces produced by muscles, as one would quantify work produced by machines in a factory. His object here, is to establish norms and, to this end, to come up with mathematical theorems by which the quantification and standardization of movement might become possible. In this respect, the title of chapter four in the first volume speaks loudly: "Theorem useful to ostentatiously showing the muscles' immense possibilities of movement" (Borelli, 1685, p. 15). Within the text, human movement is de-reified, expressed abstractly and mathematically, in short, it is expressed in terms of the factory. It is no longer, as it was in the previous historical period, an element of humanity, a part of the microcosm constituted by man and nature, but rather a set of forces, of vectors and their angles; a whole quantifiable along the model of the machine. All forms of motor-learning activity, including games, are subjected to a factory-type of instrumental rationalization. Such is the case for movements exerted outside like walking, foot racing, jumping, hurdling and swimming. This paradigm will come to its apogee and to a certain extent, the culmination of its theoretical improvement in 1798 with the book *Nouvelle mécanique des mouvements de l'homme* by Barthez. When he writes that "explanations I give of movements are solely grounded on facts known by Anatomy as well as on the basic laws of Mechanics" (1798, p. I), Barthez adds the crowning touch to the ideological system of this field of study. The paradigm of the factory-like understanding of human movement has come to its ultimate logical conclusion. The spontaneous approach to games characteristic of the medieval period has passed on to give way to "physical exercises." To this day, this constitutive strata of modernity remains one of the substructures of human physical activities. It persists, by absorbing other ulterior forms, in practices such as aerobics, body-building or stretching. The factory-like alignments and the externally visible manifestations of these forms of activities are the most apparent factors of these practices. As pertains to the first and the last of these forms of physical activity (i.e., aerobics and stretching), music is often a means to pace the body's activity. Its primary function is not musical expression, but rather to impose rhythm, to impose a standardization of time.

The Mill/Plant, the Thermal Energy Engine, and "the Animal as a Machine"

A Brave New World?

> To bend the will of this reticent, indocile workforce, used to being master of its own work processes, to the regularity of hourly schedules and work rhythms, to the respect of order and hierarchical relations, to an economy of motion and speech, to the immobility of the body, is truly to subject that workforce to an industrial training through discipline.
>
> —Perrot (1979)

This quotation, in and of itself, perfectly summarizes the kinds of mutations the modifications of work entail for human physical activities. The gymnasium and the structurally broken down physical exercises that emerge at the end of the 18th century in Europe are truly applications of the mill/plant model to the human body. As for modern sports, they are founded on the model of industrial capitalism, as much in their premises as in their structures, as has been perfectly demonstrated by Brohm (1976).

As early as 1832, Charles Babbage, in his book *On the economy of engines and factories,* establishes a paradigm purporting to establish the productivity of men and the scientific organization of human labor in factories as a fundamental element of industrial success. In 1855, Jean Gustave Courcelle-Seunneuil publishes the first real treatise on the organization of industrial enterprises. But the final result of this line of thought is Frederick Winslow Taylor's "Scientific management" and "Time and motion" studies which, as of 1890, promote a rational and scientific organization of human labor that will, for instance, make it possible to increase the quantity of smelted iron handled by a workman within one working day from 12.5 to 67.5 tons. In these studies, human movement is minutely de-composed and "dissected." Any waste of time is eliminated for the purpose of increasing productivity. Furthermore, the best laborers are selected to work at the tasks at which they are the most efficient. This is the same process that is implemented in sports and in human physical activities toward the end of the 19th century. At the same period, and since the leitmotiv of the newly developing industrial world is productivity and machines, a new model is imposed upon the human body: that of the steam engine. This new model comes about via the application of theories of thermodynamics to human movement. Such application is the logical repercussion of the application of Charles Babbage's theories to labor in mills and plants.

At this point, it is possible to follow a historical thread of thought from the functional improvement of steam engines to the application of the underlying concepts of this improvement to the "human machine." One author sets the tone within this perspective and it is Hirn (1862, 1887).

The Paradigm of the Steam Engine

I will not here harp back on what I have expounded upon at length in previous articles (Gleyse, 1991, 1992). Let me say, however, that a discursive thread can be brought to light. This thread begins with Denis Papin's engine in 1690 (when the first steam engines were then only in their infancy), then follows with the granting in 1698 of an inventor's patent to Savery, by the Royal Society of London, then leads to the theoretical refinements of Thomas Newcomen at the very beginning of the 18th century, and to the first applications to the study of the human body, of the physical and chemical conceptualisations resulting from these inventions, notably with Lavoisier's experiments in 1774.

In 1824, the theories of Sadi Carnot in *Réflexions sur la puissance motrice du feu* establish the scientific basis of this paradigm and, at the end of the 19th century, become what was to be known as the technology of the body. The viewpoint of the human body rationalized as a fuel-powered machine comes about from the invention and development of the steam engine technology, but also from the need to produce more quickly and precisely than had been done in the factory of the previous historical period. The model of the steam engine is henceforth used for the improvement of both machines and the human body.

Hirn and the Prominence of the "Steam Engine"

At its very basis, this paradigm is simple and can be found concretely in the world of sports; a world that comes about and develops throughout the 19th century, while the world of calisthenic exercises, by sort of coasting along, goes on promoting the previous model of the factory and biomechanics. As Hirn writes: "There exists . . . a mechanical equivalent to work and a calorific equivalent to heat" (1862, p. 30). Having so theorized, nothing stands in the way of applying this theory to the human body. That is exactly what Hirn does in his *Analytical and Experimental Exposition of the Theory of Heat*. For instance, he writes: "that which is at this point obvious to us today, from the point of view of the mechanical theory of heat . . . is that when by the use of our bodily members we execute such and such external work, we are functioning like a motor" (1862, pp. 604–607). A year after drafting this text, he was to expand upon this point of view even more in his book *Mechanical Theory of Heat*.

With Hirn, the paradigm of the steam engine which started out with craftsman-like groping is perfected by science, then, turns back against man, by means of a process of mechanization, reification, and instrumental rationalization of his own body. Man, within the tropism of the mill/plant, comes to be seen as a steam engine, then later, a motor. Indeed, as René Thom (1990) points out, an unavoidable logic unfolds: the techniques of the steam engine make possible the establishment of a science of that invention, and that science—expanding beyond its primary scope of application or expanding by being transposed to other fields—brings about the development of a technology and even, in certain cases, a technocracy (when the human body and especially human physical activities are the object of that technology).

Auguste Chauveau (1837–1917), Hirn's precursor, had previously outlined the implementation of a physiology of work and a science of ergonomics. Hirn consolidates this paradigm and transposes it to human physical activities, broadly speaking, extending it beyond the sole scope of the world of industrial production.

In an article entitled "Thermodynamics and work in living beings" appearing in the May 1887 issue of *Revue Scientifique*, Chauveau very clearly explains how his theories came together and how they may be applicable to all of the fields of human physical activities. In this article, he particularly recounts the experiments he performed in the Spring of 1857, and based on these experiments, he demonstrates what "work is, properly speaking, for the human motor" (p. 679). These experiments lead him to state that:

what we have just ascertained as pertains to our man made motors of the physical world is also necessarily and literally applicable to motors made up of living organs, and . . . to the motor that is man, which for us is the easiest one to study exactly and scientifically. (Chauveau, 1887, p. 678)

At this point, we have come full circle. Man is being understood in terms of a machine while the combustion processes of the body serve as a basis for the understanding of machines. In these few words, Chauveau expresses the essence of Hirn's outlook on man, an outlook excessively grounded in the physical sciences. Without even bothering to stop and question his assumptions, he leaps from nature to man, from physics to physiology, from inanimate to animate, from what is mechanical to what is alive. According to Canguilhem (1989) and Thom (1990), this is indeed the most monumental error of modern physiology. Following Hirn, the paradigm of the animal as a machine will only gather strength and breadth in discourses.

Paul Bert's development of the physiology of work paradigm in his book *The Human Machine* (1867) will gather speed because of other research conducted at the same period by Etienne Jules Marey. Marey's introduction to his book *The Animal Machine, Terrestrial and Aerial Locomotion* (1873) is enlightening in that regard:

Very often and in every historical period, living beings have been compared to machines but it is only in our day and age that we are able to understand the soundness of this comparison. . . . comparing animals to machines is not only legitimate, it is also of an extreme usefulness from various points of view. (Marey, 1860, pp. v vi)

The third chapter of this same book deals with the topic of "animal heat" (1860, p. 17) and effectively confirms that the thesis of the body as a fuel-powered machine has become a dominant one, and that, such being the case, the entire gamut of human movements can be analyzed as one would analyze a machine. In this text, we find practically *in extenso,* what Hirn wrote in his 1887 article. The same theses can be found in *Physiology of the Exercises of the Body* (1888) by Fernand Lagrange, particularly in Chapter III, which deals with the "human motor and thermal energy machines" (p. 28) and in Chapter IV, which deals with problems of "combustion" (p. 36).

Georges Demeny (1902), as a spiritual disciple of Bert and Marey, will also pursue the development of this line of thought, which is particularly dominant at the end of the 19th and the beginning of the 20th century. It is however more surprising to discover this same analysis in the first chapter

("Physical education and race. Work, health and longevity") of Philippe Tissié's book *The Human Motor in Calisthenic Function* (1919). The last texts of the period preceding the Second World War to function along this model are those which can be found in an anthology edited by Labbé (1930) and entitled *Physical Treatise*. Especially interesting in the anthology is the article by Dechambre entitled "The training of animate motors"[2] and the article by Labbé himself entitled "Energy processes in muscles."[3]

This interpretation of human movement persists strongly today but its explanatory strength has been considerably weakened in comparison to other explanations since the beginning of the development of a post-industrial society in the Western world (Touraine, 1969). In spite of this, the triathlon and the majority of athletic races and major road sporting events (e.g., cycling) are still based on such an understanding of human movement, of corporeality.

Transformation Toward a Service-Based Economy and Society: The Information Age and Postmodernism

The third paradigm I wish to expound upon has its origins in the computer and in the transformation of the means of production toward "a service-based economy." Once again, it entails effects upon discourses about the body and human physical activities in general.

After the Second World War, along with the theses of Von Neumann (1958) and Wiener (1951), machines that will considerably modify the industrial world see the light of day. With hindsight, we know that these are, of course, computers (see Breton, Rieu & Tinland, 1991). Subsequently, at the end of the 1960s and the beginning of the 1970s, work becomes of a tertiary nature (Fourastié, 1979), even de-reifying itself (Durand & Merrien, 1991), and gives rise to new information-based conceptions of the body (Parlebas, 1987). Under the influence of these new models, both the body and sport come to be understood in terms of information/data. Data are used to explain the motionless body, biology, and in France, theories of data processing are applied to the field of human physical activities. In this world of "beyond labor" (Durand & Merrien, 1991) and of "postmodernity" (Lyotard, 1979), is there room for play, for playfulness, for hedonism (can postmodern subjectivism replace the instrumental rationalization of bodies)?

Post-Industry, Postmodernity, or a Hypertrophy of Modernity?

In 1969, by highlighting the transition to a "post-industrial" society in France, Alain Touraine points out the deep-seated upheaval in "praxis" and in "poïésis" that had already been anticipated by Joffre Dumazedier in 1962 when he wrote *Towards a Leisure Civilization*. This is also to some extent what Herbert Marcuse stressed from another point of view in his *One Dimen-*

sional Man (1964) and when he affirmed that "automation in its broadest meaning, means that one is no longer concerned with measuring work" (1968, p. 54). This also means that we are, in part, no longer concerned with measuring the body, or more particularly the movement of the body. Indeed, and as a corollary to the upheavals that took place in almost all Western nations in 1968, a deep groundswell shook up the mode of existence "of words and of things" as in the title of Michel Foucault's book (1966). Jean Fourastié expresses this in a very explicit fashion:

> Out of changes in the nature of economic activity, there springs forth for man, a whole range of changes in work and daily life . . . service sector occupations are indeed less demanding in physical force than are other ones—they are more alienated from the hardness of volumes, from considerations as to weight, temperatures, climates. On the other hand, they require (generally speaking, may I mention once again), more care, and often more delicacy of execution . . . industrial machines become easier and easier to operate and with minimal physical strength while yet being smoothly precise . . . the tendency is for primary and secondary sector employments to become subject to the domination of the prevailing tertiary (i.e., service) sector. Everything happens as if human work were in a transition period from physical effort to intellectual effort . . . today [what's essential] is the contact of the mind with information/data. (1979, pp. 82–84)

Fourastié could not have been clearer. And, obviously he is not the only sociologist to defend that point of view. It is also found in the writings of Georges Fougeyrollas (1991) and those of Jean-Pierre Durand and François Xavier Merrien (1991). Durand and Merrien even go so far as to more or less pick up where Dumazedier left off, since they describe "The end of this century" as "an era beyond work." A society and a world in which work had heretofore been the cardinal virtue and which is also deeply shaken cannot help leaving its stamp in the field of discourses on the body and human physical activities. This point of view is also shared by Jean Lojkine in a book entitled *La révolution informationnelle* (1992). In it, he shows that a world where information rather than matter dominates, implies a questioning of the entire structure of the social order ("socius"). In the final analysis, this would mean the toppling of all of the value systems of modernity. There could then come about a new era for man, as was the case at the time of the Renaissance, during the classical period.

Alain Touraine in his *Critique de la modernité* (1992) fine tunes this analysis by demonstrating that while modernity is built on an equilibrium between "rationalization" and "subjectification," the former pole of this continuum has dominated the latter for at least two centuries. Indeed, this manifests itself in discourses on human physical activities through the domination of the instrumental rationalization of the body. The present period, which some have characterized as postmodern, could potentially balance out the system by swinging the pendulum toward subjectification.

In fact, to the extent that modernity structures itself around a few strong lines of logic—such as, according to Fougeyrollas (1991) "the reign of reason" and "the domination over nature," including domination over the nature of the body—one can understand that human physical activities in general, as an analytical component of the "socius," would be grounded in this value system. It is possible to push this reasoning a bit further as does Touraine and to see that modern society's model for knowledge is "evolutionism" while its moral models are "energy, work and self-control" (1992, p. 289). It then becomes patently clear that these moral systems are the same ones that have been part of the constitution of the discourses on the body, the education of the body, and human physical activities, since at least the beginning of the 19th century.

Certain thinkers holding positions that are contrary to the one above or who go beyond them, believe that they can discern a rupture in value systems, a rupture that could, in Foucault's terms, be characterized as "epistemic." The postmodern era would be taking shape according to something of an antithesis and a line of fracture against modernity.

In this new axiologic universe, indifference and narcissism would replace collective rebellion, the logic of de-standardization and seduction would replace that of standardization, humorous forms of expression would replace the solemnity of ideology. Such is at any rate how Gilles Lipovetsky (1983) characterizes this swing. Michel Maffesoli (1985) goes further by arguing that in this new world, expressions of sentiment and emotion replace the ideals of the reasoning mind, and the logic of affective factors replaces the logic of identity. In fact, according to Maffesoli, we have already fully entered the era of tribes, the latter having replaced the large-scale systems of social rationalization. Along the same line of thought, an era that can be said to be Dionysian, faces off against the Promethean universe of the industrial era. Everywhere, a social fabric, which can be said to be irrational, driven by instinct, boisterous, un-comprehensible, irrepressible—which puts into question all prior lines of logic—insinuates itself into the cracks of the last gasps of socialization. Jean François Lyotard writes:

> Postmodernism could be seen as that which within modernity, in its own manifestation, alleges not to be liable to being presented (i.e., is "not-presentable"); that which refuses to take part in the consolation of "good forms," i.e., of culturally sanctioned norms—that which denies

to partake of the consensus of prevailing tastes which would allow it to experience the nostalgia of that which is impossible together; that which delves into and explores new modes of expressions, not for the purpose of enjoying them, but rather, to better get the message across, that there are things which are not-presentable. A postmodern artist or author is in the position of the philosopher: the text he drafts, the work of art he accomplishes, are not, as a matter of principle governed by pre-established rules, and they cannot be judged on the basis of a verdict putting them into such and such known category by which they might be pigeonholed. These rules and classificatory criteria are precisely that which the work of art or the text strives towards. (1988, pp. 26-27)

Whereas modernity was structuring, postmodernity is de-structuring, without any real re-construction, re-composition. Elsewhere, the same author explicitly comments on that:

Postmodern knowledge is not only the instrument of the power struc-tures: it also attunes our sensitivity to differences and reinforces our capacity to endure the inconceivable. Postmodernity itself does not draw its self-justification from the homology of experts, but rather from the paralogy of inventors. (1979, cover)

In short, even though it is impossible to clearly side with one or another of the hypotheses, it is patently clear that the axiologic world that was the framework of the industrial era is, in the Western world, in the process of passing away, to the benefit of a world that can be characterized as "praxic," "epistemic" and "poiétic."

Toward another Conception of the Body?

The model of the body as a biological computer replaces everywhere the previous discourses that were prevailing at the time when the industrial sector, revolving essentially around the model of man as motor, was domi-nant in the Western world. From this point of view, it is certain that the invention, during World War II, of this machine known in English as the "computer," is a determining element in the understanding of the genesis of this transformation process. For lack of space, I will not recount its history (I refer the reader to the various histories of computer sciences and computers to have been authored in the past several years). However, it is necessary to refer to two important authors, namely Norbert Wiener and John Von Neumann. It must be emphasized that after the publication of his important book *Cyber-netics* (1948), Wiener authored a later work entitled *Cybernetics and society* (1951) in which he transposed to the entire social sphere (and to man) his earlier theory destined for the maximization of the use of computers: "When I give a machine a command, the situation is not fundamentally different from that which exists when I give a person an order" (1971, p. 44). This was possible because the social sphere was analyzed essentially in terms of rational information: "Living efficiently, essentially means living with adequate information" (p. 47). If Wiener was able to make such propositions, it is because he was deeply imbued with the modifications in the modes of production brought about by the computer. This is particularly demonstrated by his expressing his distances on the subject of an energy consuming body, his viewpoint being that "We degrade man by chaining him to an oar to use him as a source of energy, but we degrade him just as much by assigning to him in a factory, a task consisting solely of repetitive motions and which demands barely one millionth of his intellectual capacity" (p. 157).

As can be seen in Wiener's writing, the interpretation of the body has changed and this change will affect all subsequent analyses of the body. Von Neumann, starting from a less humanistic position than Wiener's, applies the same analogical transposition of the computer, but this time, to the mind and the entire human being. In so doing, he fundamentally confuses reason with thought, rationality with existence. To do this, it was necessary for him to liken objects to living things. For instance, he writes that a "clear and revealing comparison can be arrived at by likening the logically active part of the living cell to a vacuum tube or to a transistor" (Von Neumann, 1992, p. 52). Just as was the case at the end of the 19th century, the leap here from technological artefact to the human being, is disconcerting. Even though one can see a certain similarity between the functioning of reason and the computer, one can hardly understand how this model, mechanistic in terms of its input, throughput and output, can be postulated in the cognitive sciences as an operational model for the entirety of thought processes (and not solely of rationality), and further, how this same model, via the science of ergonomics, could possibly have been transposed to the study of the body in motion. However, that is precisely what happened. In France, psycho-motor scientists in the field of human physical activities (e.g., Le Boulch, 1971; Picq & Vayer, 1960) will all analyze a considerable part of educational bodily practices within educational institutions, in terms of information processing. In these discourses, the body is de-reified along a new model based on the structure of labor/work. For example, Le Boulch mentions: "At various stages of the learning process, stress must be placed on the input of information in relation with the corresponding motor response" (1971, p. 189). Such outlook will become omnipresent in the field of human physical activities and one could quote an infinite number of sentences that apply this transposition. However, on this score, the most caricaturist discourse can be found in a 1987 text entitled *The child and sports* in which the author, Marc Durand, defines the child practicing a sport as a type of microprocessor, a type of computer:

> We will here resort to the analytical approach of data processing processes underlying the child's performances. The human processor is a type of channel through which information flows and whose capacity is limited. These limits are such that only a small quantity of information can transit simultaneously through the channel. The information flowing in the channel is treated, i.e., it is the object of transformations due to the application of certain processes. These processes are operations of coding, selection, regrouping, identification . . . (1987, p. 142)

In so speaking, Durand is not here talking about a "computer," nor about data processing, but about a child practicing a sport! Astonishing as this may seem, some of the early 1990s discourses go even further along this line, since it is either "expert systems" or "highly advanced computer languages" that are applied to sporting practices and more broadly to physical practices.

Such discourses are also legitimated in the sense that sporting practices of the Western world are the object of symposia said to be about the "psychology of sport" in which the overwhelming majority of the papers presented is forged on this paradigm. In short, instrumental rationalization in the form of the computer has left its stamp everywhere. Along the same vein, human physical activities have undergone deep changes since the 1960s, and as Parlebas (1987) and Pociello (1982) emphasize, for some time now practices that are said to be "Californian" or "computational" are more and more replacing practices based on man as a fuel-consuming being. Here, of course, the point is no longer one of adaptation of these practices to the model of the computer, but rather one of conformity of these "techniques of the body," to the new world of labor. This new world is characterized by a phenomenon of "cognomorphism," that is, an overall de-reification of human practices as well as their specular-ization and spectacularization.

Over and above this, in a good number of works, the body and movement become transposed into language, discourse; into systems of symbols and meanings. The body is marked by the new universe of labor; a universe of tertiary sector production which has been dominant since the end of the 1960s and in which it is essential to gather information, to communicate, to express oneself, to give meaning to one's actions.

These types of studies are possibly the latest forms of rationalization of the body and movement. Alternatively, they may be forms tending toward the pole of subjectification or perhaps postmodern forms of human physical activities.

The End of Rational Instrumentalization: A Postmodern Body

For the past several years, discourses in the field of subjectification have come about. Such is the case for sport critics (e.g., Brohm, 1976) and more generally for critics of the body (e.g., Bernard, 1976). Alain Touraine clearly defines what he means by subjectification:

> It is the act of refusal, of resistance, which creates the subject. On a more limited basis, it is the ability to step outside of one's social roles, it is the fact of not belonging to any group whatsoever, and it is the need to challenge such and such, all of which breathes life into each and every one of us as subject. And, subjectification is always opposed to socialization, to adaptation to statutes and social roles, but, only as long as one does not shut oneself off in a counterculture of subjectivity, and that one instead, wages a struggle against those forces which actively destroy the subject. (1992, p. 318)

Criticism of the overarching systems that constitute sports and more generally of the models of intelligibility applying to corporeality is entirely consistent with this perspective. In France, the 10 books published between 1974 and 1979 in the Delarge collection, the issues of the journal *Quel corps?* published since 1975, as well as a good number of recent books seeking to bring to light the systems of norms and of coercion imposed on the body and on movement through the phenomena of sports and physical education, are also consistent with this perspective. At the very least, in discourses, there is a critique of the logic of modernity, of its universalist and rationalizing dominant axiologies, and a consideration of the subject, of subjectification. Furthermore, such innovative discourses are appeals to the creation of new practices, appeals to hedonism, to playfulness, to a return to that which is Dionysian. They improve the image of the paralogy of postmodernism which lays claim to tribalism as opposed to systems, which promotes the individual in the face of institutional bodies. The call to marginal, non-conformist practices, and to radical neo-Marxist critiques of large systems such as that of the modern sporting system is quite closely related to postmodernism.

On another level, the more and more frequent emergence of marginal, multi-disciplinary and unofficially sanctioned practices that negate the logic of sporting federations, attests to the profound modification of the *épistémé* and may be seen as postmodern. For instance, bungee-jumping, a sporting practice that has developed in France at the end of the 1980s, perfectly corresponds to the idea of postmodernism. At its very beginning, this activity was not controlled, which actually brought about a number of fatal accidents. It can, by this fact, be said to be a form consistent with postmodern axiology.

The goal is internal to the subject and not liable to being presented to a public. All of the jumpers of *la petite mort* are speechless when it comes to the sensations they experienced during their leap. Bungee-jumping represents that which is not presentable, not expressible. It makes sense only for the person who does it. The development of new and informal activities like off-road cycling (in its non-official forms) and dance-climbing also demonstrate a challenge to the great values of modernity.

The fact that in the sporting world, a greater number of voices are raised to call for a system of ethics, could give credence to the idea of a passage to the era of postmodernity. The simple fact, for example, that the 100-meter World Athletic Record was canceled because of the use of illicit drugs or that an athlete like Sergei Bubka puts the priority on income as opposed to sporting ideology (i.e., he continuously beats his own world pole-vaulting record, parsimoniously, centimeter by centimeter, while in certain competitions he could have improved it all at once by 10 or 15 centimeters), attests to this distortion of the system, to this transmutation of values. In France, this leads to ever stronger voices against the concept of performance at any cost, and to challenges to programs of "Early Childhood Intensive Training." All these critiques and challenges attest to the profound and raging debate on the modernist ideology of evolutionism and instrumental rationalization of the body. In the infancy of postmodernity, the quintessential epitomy of modernity that the sporting world represents is challenged in terms of its value system. I could accumulate example after example of this cleavage, but we will stop here, leaving it up to the reader to conduct her or his own investigations.

Conclusion

In the space of this chapter, I could not truly engage into an authentic work of archeological discourse. I am satisfied with having pointed out and paved the way for various lines of analysis. I do hope that the tolerant reader will be so kind as to accept to believe me when I affirm that the structures I present are grounded in a very considerable degree of historiographic research which I could only go so far as to give an inkling of in this chapter. The archival collections of the University of Montpellier College of Medicine, which I continue to explore to this day, and which were of considerable help in this research, are an inexhaustible store of knowledge.

The essential components of modernity, analyzed through discourses, have consisted of corporeal and technical "artefacts." The overwhelming majority of discourses defended up to the 1960s have as their purpose the instrumental rationalization of the body. Postmodernity, inasmuch as this era and this axiology can be said to exist, challenges this dynamic. However, discourses on the body remain fundamental components of society in and of themselves. From an archeological perspective, then, it is possible to reconstruct a society on the basis of vestiges, of scattered fragments of such discourses. Consequently, the latter remain conspicuous and analytical examples of epistemic, praxic and poiétic lines of fracture.

Notes

1. As concerns the concept of "pregnance" (translated in this text as "tropism"), we use this term as it is defined by René Thom (1990, p. 56): "certain forms have an immediate biological importance as regards their subject: Such, for animals, is the case for such forms as preys, predators and sexual partners. These forms could be said to be 'tropistic,' tropism, being the corresponding defining characteristic. They lead to important modifications in motor and affective behavior in the subject, along with hormonal changes of a long term duration on his physiology." Here, Thom's point of view partly coincides with Jürgen Habermas' (1987), in his theory of "L'agir communicationnel."

2. As a matter of fact, this text starts off with a strange comparison: "In animated motors like in man, training is the faculty which makes it possible for the individual to supply the maximum muscular effort with minimum fatigue" (Dechambre, quoted in Labbé, 1930, p. 159).

3. "Man is a producer of energy. Tapping in his food, the fuel that he needs, he transforms it, as a steam engine does with coal—he takes from that fuel, its latent energy and liberates it in the form of heat and in the form of movement" (Labbé, 1930, p. 292).

References

Arnaud, P. (1983). *Les savoirs du corps*. Lyon: Presses Universitaires de Lyon.

Arnaud, P. (1987). "Les athlètes de la république." In *Gymnastique, sport et idéologie républicaine, 1870–1914*. Toulouse: Privat.

Babbage, C, (1832). *On the economy of engines and factories*. London: S.N.

Barthez, P.J. (1798). *Nouvelle mécanique des mouvements de l'homme*. Carcassonne, France: Pierre Polère.

Beltran, A. & Griset, P. (1990). *Histoire des techniques au XIXe et XXe siècles*. Paris: Armand Colin.

Bernard, M. (1976). *Le corps*. Paris: Presses Universitaires de France.

Bert, P. (1967). *The human machine.* Paris: Félix Alcan.

Birrien, J.Y. (1990). *Histoire de l'informatique.* Paris: Presses Universitaires de France.

Bloch, M. (1936). "Les techniques, l'histoire et la vie." *Les Annales,* 32, 513–515.

Borelli, J.A. (1685). *De motu animalium* (two volumes). Lugduni (Lyon): D. Gaesbeck, C. Boutiesteyn, J. et P. De Vivie.

Borkenau, F. (1934). *De Ubergang vom Feudalen zum Bürgerlichen Weltbild.* Paris: C. Douniol.

Breton, P., Rieu, M.A., & Tinland, F. (1990). "La techno-science en question." In *Éléments pour une archéologie du XXe siècle.* Seyssel, France: Champ Vallon.

Brohm, J.M. (1976). *Corps et politique.* Paris: Delarge.

Canguilhem, G. (1989). *La connaissance de la vie.* Paris: Vrin.

Carnot, S. (1824). *Réflexions sur la puissance motrice du feu.* Paris: Veuve Valat la chapelle.

Chauveau, A. (1887). "La thermodynamique et le travail chez les être vivants." *Revue scientifique,* 22, 673–684.

Collectif (1979). *Collection Histoire générale des techniques* Volumes III and IV. Paris: Presses Universitaires de France.

Collectif (1986). *Dictionnaire encyclopédique d'histoire.* Paris: Larousse.

Coornaert, É. (1949). "Les manufactures de Colbert." In *Information historique* (volume II). Paris: La découverte.

Defrance, J. (1987). *L'excellence corporelle.* Rennes, France: Presses Universitaires de Rennes-AFRAPS.

Demeny, G. (1902). *Les bases scientifiques de l'éducation physique.* Paris: Félix Alcan.

De Monteux de Mérybel, H. (1559). *Commentaire de la conservation de la santé et prolongation de la vie.* Lyon. Ian de Tournes.

Du Choul, G. (1567). *Discours de la religion des anciens romains, de la castrémation et discipline militaire d'iceux. Des bains et antiques exercitations grecques et romaines* (two volumes). Lyon: G. Roville.

Durand, J.P., & Merrien, F.X. (1991). *Sortie de siècle.* Paris: Vigot.

Elias, N. (1969). *La civilisation de mœurs.* Paris: Flammarion.

Estienne, C. (1545). *De dissectione partium humani corporis.* Parisus (Paris): S. Collinaeus.

Fabri, P. (1592). *Agonisticon. De re athletica ludisque, veterum gymnicis, musicis at que circensibus spirilegiorum tractatus.* Lugduni (Lyon): F. Fabrum.

——— (1984). *L'usage des plaisirs.* Paris: Gallimard.

Foucault, M. (1963). *La naissance de la clinique.* Paris: Presses Universitaires de France.

——— (1961). *Histoire de la folie à l'âge classique.* Paris: Gallimard.

——— (1966). *Les mots et les choses.* Paris: Gallimard.

——— (1969). *L'archéologie du savoir.* Paris: Gallimard.

——— (1975). *Surveiller et punir.* Paris: Gallimard.

Fougeyrollas, P. (1991). *L'attraction du futur.* Paris: Méridiens Klienksieck.

Fourastié, J. (1979). *Les trente glorieuses, ou la révolution invisible de 1946 à 1975.* Paris: Fayard.

Friedman, G. (1950). *Où va le travail humain?* Paris: Gallimard.

Gleyse, J. (1991). "Corps et technologie. Approche épistémologique des concepts." In N. Midol (Ed.), *Actes du colloque de Nice, santé et performance* (pp. 83–89). Nice: AFRAPS.

——— (1992). "Corps, techniques et sciences. Quelques éléments d'archéologie, de l'âge classique à la postmodernité." *Revue des S.T.A.P.S.*, 29, 43–55.

Guigou, J. (1987). *La cité des égo.* Grenoble: L'impliqué.

——— (1992). *Critique des systèmes de formation des adultes (1968–1992).* Paris: L'Harmattan.

Habermas, J. (1987). *La théorie de l'agir communicationnel, volume I—Rationalité de l'agir et rationalisation de la société.* Paris: Fayard.

Hirn, G.A. (1862). *Exposition analytique et expérimentale de la théorie de la chaleur.* Paris: Mallet Bachelier.

——— (1863). *Théorie mécanique de la chaleur.* Paris: Lieber.

Jouberti, L. (1582). *Operum latinorum.* Franckfurti (Franckfort): Heredes Andrea Wecheli.

Koyré, A. (1973). *Études d'histoire de la pensée scientifique.* Paris: Gallimard.

Labbé, M. (1930). *Traité d'éducation physique* (two volumes). Paris: Doin.

Lagrange, F. (1888). *Physiologie des exercices du corps.* Paris: Librairie Scientifique Internationale.

Le Boulch, J. (1971). *Vers une science du mouvement humain*. Paris: E.S.F.

Leroi-Gourhan, A. (1964). *Le geste et la parole*. Paris: Albin Michel.

Lipovetsky, G. (1983). *L'ère du vide*. Paris: Gallimard.

Lyotard, J.F. (1979). *La condition postmoderne*. Paris: Minuit.

Maffesoli, M. (1985). *Le temps des tribus*. Paris: Méridiens Klienksieck.

Marcuse, H. (1964). *One dimensional man*. London: Sphere.

——— (1968). *Automation and major technological change*. London: Sphere.

Marey, E.J. (1868). *Du mouvement dans les fonctions de la vie*. Paris: Baillères.

——— (1873). *La machine animale. Locomotion terrestre et aérienne*. Paris: Germer Baillères.

Marx, K. (1962). *Manuscrits de 1844*. Paris: Editions sociales.

Mercurialis, H. (1573). *Libri sex. De arte gymnastica*. Venetiis (Venice): Iuntas.

Mumford, L. (1973). *Le mythe de la machine*. Paris: Seuil.

Parlebas, P. (1985). "La dissipation sportive." *Culture technique*, 13.

——— (1987). *Éléments de sociologie du sport*. Paris: Presses Universitaires de France.

Picq, L. & Vayer, P. (1960). *Educations psychomotrice et arriération mentale*. Paris: Doin.

Pociello, C. (1982). *Sport et société*. Paris: Vigot.

Rauch, A. (1982). *Le corps en éducation physique*. Paris: Presses Universitaires de France.

Russo, F. (1986). *Introduction à l'histoire des techniques*. Paris: Blanchard.

Thom, R. (1990). *Apologie du logos*. Paris: Fayard.

Tissié, P. (1919). *L'éducation physique et la race. Santé, travail, longévité*. Paris: Flammarion.

Touraine, A. (1992). *Critique de la modernité*. Paris: Fayard.

Vallambert, S. (1565). *Manière de nourrir et gouverner les enfans dès leur naissance*. Poitiers: De Marnefz et Bouchetz Frères.

Velingi, J. (1663). *Syntagma anatomicum comentaris illustratum*. Amstelodami (Amsterdam): Joanum Janssonium.

Vesalius, A. (1555). *De humani corporis fabrica*. Basilae (Bâle): J. Oporinus.

Vigarello, G. (1978). *Le corps redressé*. Paris: Delarge.

Von Neumann, J. (1992). *L'ordinateur et le cerveau* (2nd ed.). Paris: La découverte.

Wiener, N. (1951). *Cybernétique et société*. Paris: Les deux rives.

12

ADDICTION, EXERCISE, AND CYBORGS: TECHNOLOGIES OF DEVIANT BODIES

CHERYL L. COLE

Prior to the emergence of what we call crack, drugs posed questions of control, legalization, and containment. Their usage seemed to belong to the socio-juridical precincts of civil disobedience. Ever since its inception as legal category, this all-American crime has earned its dose of moral defensibility from a link to anti-war activities. But crack when it brought the War to drugs, brought war unto the law. Civil disobedience split away from constitutionally sanctioned habits: this war unlike others, permits no dissent. Destructing a civil constitution based on difference, crack introduces narcopolemics as total war.

—Avital Ronnel

Postmodern America: Bodies, Drugs, and Exercise

During the 1980s, United States national popular culture became saturated with images of hard, addicted, and cyborg bodies. It was a conjunctual moment in which conservative forces manufactured the war on drugs, AIDS, the rise of Nike and the NBA, The Cosby Show, Rambo, new reproductive politics, the fitness boom, urban deterioration, and the incarceration of black men and poor women—all framed through the popular and modern categories of recovery, will, and opportunity. The body/anti-body trope was a discourse on the loose marking (and unmarking) patriotism, race, gender, sexuality, poverty, contamination, and threat, and producing an affective economy populated by images of free-floating fetuses, hard bodies, productive bodies, bodies working out, bodies by Nautilus, bodies marked as morally superior, patriotic bodies, soft bodies, welfare bodies, crack bodies, AIDS bodies, anorexic bodies, deteriorating bodies, and erupting bodies. As Jeffords (1994) argues, it "was an era of bodies" motivated by a search for bodies that contained free will and that, by extension, contained national interests. Cultural anxieties around "will" were captured in and provided the motivating force behind the two advertising campaigns that defined the national imaginary in the 1980s: Nike's signature "Just Do It" and the New Right's "Just Say No" campaign for the war on drugs. Physical transcendence and free will became America's hottest commodities.

The Reagan administration capitalized on the logic of will by redeploying an amplified individualism and will that located America's decline and uncertain status in bodies and historical moments that it marked through the lack of will: the social and countercultural movements of the 1960s and the feminized Carter administration. Addiction was made most visible in and through the figures produced and circulated by mediated moral panics imbricated in the war on drugs. Racially-coded images of crack, embodied by crack houses, crack addicts, crack mothers, and crack babies became inextricably bound with everyday lived experience and fears: threat and fear were heightened through the image of a criminal masculinity inscribed on the bodies of black male youth. Such images affectively masked the multiple consequences of late capitalism: the heightened unemployment and poverty produced through dynamics associated with hyperindustrialization and globalization and Reagan's defunding and repressive policies. As racial inequalities and tensions escalated in America's urban areas, inner cities reinvigorated their economies by promoting an urban, worldclass lifestyle (restaurants, shopping districts, stadiums, sport events, and sport superstars). Nike and the NBA claimed prominent places in national culture and in our everyday lives. As the Los Angeles Lakers would have it, it was "Show Time" in America's inner cities.

While Reagan sought to recover the nation's lost masculinity and Rambo searched for MIAs in Vietnam, the performativity of Michael Jordan and other African American sport celebrities was contained within the space of sport in inner cities. (After all, how could America accommodate the image of an African-American Rambo complete with a machine gun strapped across his chest scouring the jungles of Vietnam to save the U.S. from a soft, feminized past?) Although clearly complicated by racial inscriptions of the black body (how else could we understand Jordan's ability to fly?), Michael Jordan and other prominent African American male athletes exemplified the healthy body, the athletic body, the pure body, the body distanced from the threatening black masculinity inscribed on the other predominant inner city figure—the addict. During the summer of 1993, a *Chicago Tribune* headline announced that Nike's premier icon, Michael Jordan, was worth over $1.5 billion to the city. Nike Town, the store that sells "Just Do It" to thousands of tourists, became Chicago's leading tourist attraction, located only a few miles from one of the most infamous housing projects in the United States—Cabrini Green.

Racially coded images of athletes (Just Do It) and addicts (Just Say No) remained intertwined in the national imaginary. Especially effective in the heightened racism that surrounded the war on drugs were images of professional athletes ruining careers or dying young from drug-related complications. Len Bias's cocaine-induced death, 48 hours of being drafted by the Boston Celtics, was central to the war on drugs campaign. In fact, Bias's image was so powerful that it was invoked to help make sense of Magic Johnson's association with AIDS. As they have been articulated in the United States, AIDS and drug narratives turn on a logic of addiction—a logic that depends on "free will" and locates insufficient free will in the bodies of Others. Both discourses rely on a logic that produces and differentiates between deteriorating bodies and the hard, productive body of the general public.

The rhetoric of recovery was directed at America's spirit, its economy, its place in the world order, and the multiplying numbers of individuals who were labelled and labelled themselves addicts. Addiction is a term that implies a substance, licit or illicit, and a subject, a compulsive subject, who can be managed. Although identities produced through the logic of addiction cannot be separated from the conjunctural forces through which they gain momentum and meaning, and while "drugs" is a preeminent sign in America's affective economy, it would be a mistake to limit the critique of the logic of addiction to conservative forces such as Reagan's war on drugs and neo-conservative discourses around AIDS. In other words, the affective purchase and discursive significance of the sign "drugs" exceeds the hysteria generated around inner-city crack use.

Featherstone (1982), Gitlin (1990), and numerous others have depicted the postmodern human condition as one structured through a dynamic of insatiable consumption. As Ehrenreich suggests, despite the ubiquitous images of drug addicts, "the addiction that most of us have most to fear is not promoted by a street-corner dealer. The entire market, the expanding spectacle of consumer possibilities has us in its grip, and because that is too large and nameless, we turn our outrage toward something that is both more powerful and concrete" (1989, p. 247). This "something" is the normalization and routinization of:

> the high-intensity consumption of commodities but also the idea that the self is realized through consumption. It is addicted to acquisition. It cultivates the pursuit of thrills; it elevates the pursuit of pleasure to high standing; and, as part of this ensemble, it promotes the use of licit chemicals for stimulation, intoxication, and fast relief. The widespread use of licit drugs in America can be understood as part of this larger set of values and activities. (Gitlin, 1990, p. 45, cited in Reeves & Campbell, 1994, p. 133)

The sign "drugs" then gives concrete form to the anxieties generated through the dynamics of late-capitalism and its apparent preoccupation with a transformed self through consumption, a self understood to be even more authentic than the pre-transformed self. The promise of transformed self is perhaps made most visible in Rambo's trickle-down and everyday counterpart: the hard, muscular body produced in fitness clubs. As America's borders became increasingly permeable, the body with firm boundaries promised social mobility and U.S. recovery. During the 1980s and now in Clinton's America, promises of trickle-down social mobility and increased consumption power were and remain intertwined with ideologies of working out and biological self-betterment.

Appropriately, but still oddly enough, the promises of exercise (which spawned America's corporate celebrity "Nike") found a prescriptive counterpart in America's first celebrity drug—Prozac. The small green and white capsule was the first anti-depressant introduced through advertising hype, and has been hailed as a yuppie drug, a drug that increases creativity and productivity, a late-capitalist steroid. The hype around Prozac's possibilities and the promises made in its name are virtually identical to those made in the name of exercise: the transformation of the self, increased concentration and productivity through neurophysiological effects. Both were widely promoted in the 1980s: "change your body," "change your personality," "change your life." Exercise, framed through the natural and the unnatural, was oxymoronically dubbed "nature's Prozac"—and was identified as addictive and potentially dangerous. The exercise addict became a reality as psychologists sought to render visible a new deviant subject.

Addiction is both the logic of postmodern culture: a culture not necessarily beyond modernity but aware of the limits and the failure of modern logic, and a culture aware of the failed promises of the enlightenment. After all, could a "deviant-type", called the "exercise addict", exist within the boundaries established by the binaries that structure modern thought? This is finally the question that is threaded throughout this chapter. In order to address the question, I engage a debate that also reveals several of the problems with traditional and dominant formulations of the relations among sport, bodies, and exercise.[1]

The exercise addict and addiction-in-sport generally are most properly understood as products of the discourse of addiction whose contemporary currency suggests that we have become a "society under the influence . . . always on the edge and yet somehow susceptible to management" (Schor & Weed, 1993, p. iii). Addiction-attribution is typically understood through a passive-subject/demonized-object relation, a formulation I challenge in this chapter. I want to suggest that the discourse of addiction is a mechanism of classifying and producing both the normal and the pathological/deviant/

excessive, and as such, is a technology of the body. As I have already suggested, the contemporary epidemic of addiction seems to suggest that something else is going on—it is perhaps a sign of the cultural preoccupation with
and desire to return to the space of wholeness.

My project is aligned with Jacques Derrida's contention that the "general logic" of the "drug problem" can be understood neither as singular nor
isolated, but is intertwined with the "discourses on the subject of, for instance, artificial insemination, sperm banks, the market for surrogate mothers,
organ transplants, euthanasia, sex changes, the use of drugs in sports, and
especially, especially on the subject of AIDS"[2] (Derrida, 1993, p. 17).

Taking up Derrida's observation of the challenge that AIDS presents to
the metaphysics of the subject, in the context of works by Michel Foucault
and Eve Sedgwick, I explore the affronts to the metaphysics of presence
apparently brought about by technological advances. While all three critics
(Foucault, Derrida, and Sedgwick) share a concern with the relations among
language, power/knowledge games, and "the will," and while all interrogate
modernity, subjectivity, the body, representation, and desire, their trajectories,
principles, and strategies differ. Drawing on genealogical and deconstructive
strategies, I argue that popular understandings of drug-use and addiction build
on two manifestations of the metaphysical insistence of presence: a search for
origins and the "presences" produced by modern technologies of power.
Genealogy and deconstruction share a concern with the authentic subject and
the relation of truth and the subject; however, Derrida's concern is with the
epistemological imperative that the subject produce truth, while Foucault's is
with the subject as a product of truth.

Next, I consider both the modern invention of the addict and the contemporary epidemic of addiction, especially the significance of the articulation of addiction and exercise/sport. Here, I argue that drugs/addiction and
exercise/sport, as networks and strategies of power, are normalizing practices
constitutive of a political corporeality. In part, my concern is with their relation to the crisis of the modern subject and its corresponding organic, discrete, unitary body, and how the discourses of drugs and addiction
(re)territorialize the sporting body and the exercising body. Given this, my
interrogation of "addiction"/drugs, even in sport, is related to a Foucauldian
project that examines the production and organization of deviant bodies and
pathologized subjectivities.

I end the chapter by briefly discussing the increasing failure of abso-
lutes (e.g., the logics of the natural, the will, and the body) foregrounded by
this epidemic and its relation to questions about sport in general and its
relation to drug use. I finally conclude with a discussion of bodily-prosthetics,
the crisis of the modern subject, and their relation to and implication for
sport. I argue that the epidemic of addiction-attribution is symptomatic of a

crisis of modern logic: while the modern body and subject have become the objects of disciplinary strategies, they have necessarily become pathologized because the conceptualizations of the organic body and free will are no longer viable.

On Deconstruction and Genealogy

Both genealogical and deconstructive logics present challenges to Western reason and the modern subject (the subject of liberal-humanism, the unitary, self-authorial subject). Both can be understood as critical gestures that unmask and refuse the continual reinvention of nature. By Derrida's view, Western thought is centered around logos requiring both a rational subject and referential language.[3] Deconstruction is a strategy that interrogates and disrupts the grammar of Western reason: this grammar presents itself as a metaphysics of presence through a series of oppositions where a privileged term always emerges but relies upon and repeats itself in hopes of recapturing an original trace of meaning. Deconstruction presupposes that the metaphysics of Western reason is at once inescapable but always incomplete and unstable: first, in the sense that language can never capture the present, and second, in the sense that binary terms are always interdependent. The deconstructionist works by attaching him/herself to the binary logic in order to unravel it or to show how it unravels itself from within.[4]

Deconstruction asserts that meaning is produced through *différance:* the double process of difference and deferral. Meaning is deferred in the sense that it is produced temporally, through the trace, and produced through difference (in that each unit derives its meaning through its difference from others). Language is structured through the forced dependence of categories that constitute hierarchized binaries in which the first term announces itself as presence while the second term, on which the first relies, is always absent. While Western logic at once depends upon a phantasmatic center, it continuously relies on its periphery to establish the center. Because it is relational, Western thought cannot posit any central self-identical ideal upon which it is founded. Just as deconstructive logic is parasitic on an already given text, terms that are apparently primary to logos, such as free will, parasitically relies on the term that precedes and opposes it (for example, free will relies on compulsion).

Whereas Derrida is concerned with the force relations among terms that distinguish and dismantle the difference between intention and utterance, a critique he extends to both Freud and Lacan's formulation of the subject in psychoanalysis (presence of the subject), Foucault is more interested in the knowledge systems that produce the cognitive subject itself than he is in the force of difference in cognition.[5] In other words, Foucault is not examining cognition as a phenomenon of history, nor does he ask how a person is cognitive, for example, how a person is satisfying an absence. Foucault is interested in the relations of power that produce the speaking subject as object and subject of knowledge. In the same way, while both Derrida and Foucault examine the way the origin resonates semantically, Foucault looks at how the origin resonates historico-discursively. Foucault's work is not a search for origin stories or essences, but is concerned with the historical production of essences.

For example, the operating terms that presume originality in the discourse of addiction are free will and compulsion. Derrida and Sedgwick examine, in different ways, the force relations between the terms: the constant exertion of pressure at their boundaries, the constant policing required to maintain those boundaries, the incompleteness of the category of the will and the violence it does. Deconstructionist strategies emphasize the constant motion of the boundary, placing emphasis on the transgression always already taking place at the border. Foucault names such binary relations "dividing practices"; his work recognizes their mutual dependence but emphasizes the production of the self's border as a social process of producing and policing the other. In other words, the construct of free will, partly constitutive of the normal, is dependent upon what it excludes, the marking of the compulsive, abnormal and the deviant. Those mechanisms deployed to "fix" the deviant simultaneously stabilize the norm. Sedgwick explains the imperative to propagate free will:

> So long as an entity known as "free will" has been hypostatized and charged with ethical value—a situation whose consolidating moment in the Reformation already revealed the structure of its dramatic foundational fractures and their appropriability to the complex needs of capitalism—for just so long has an equally hypostatized "compulsion" had to be available as a counterstructure always internal to it, always requiring to be ejected from it. (1992, p. 586)

Given this, free will requires continual policing to firm up its boundaries because free-will requires limits, borders, and the marginal. Foucault understands the production and continual policing of this border that demarcates the norm from the deviant, as a mechanism of modern power.

While deconstructionists and genealogists agree that there can be no truth without untruth, Foucault's central concern is with the historical and philosophical effects of power and truth. Rather than operating through repression, which presumes that power can be accumulated and possessed by people or particular economies, Foucault understands power as exercised through and productive of truth. Whereas deconstructionists expose the logic of self-production to be impossible, genealogists show how the self-productive self is an effect of power, the effect of an *épistémé*, the effect of a power/truth game.[6] The genealogical critic places him/herself simultaneously at the side of and in the "discursive traffic" to show how the subject and the will are productive effects of power.[7]

Derrida's and Sedgwick's Addicted-Bodies

> Discipline and addiction. Practice your scales. Repititions. Bach on coffee. Berloiz on hallucinogens (but also on coffee and cigars): The Witches' Sabbath, a concoction of Faust and the opium deams that Berloiz read in De Quincey's *Confession of an English Opium Eater*. Mussorgsky's wine, Stravinsky's cigarettes.
>
> —Avital Ronnel

Despite the illusory correspondence between the word "drug" and particular substances, the concept of "drug" cannot be reduced to a fixed referent or drug use to practices or behaviors; instead, the concept of "drug" is inscribed historically, culturally, evaluatively, and normatively through particular understandings of the body, the will, consciousness, truth, and the social bond (Derrida, 1993). While there may be no drugs in nature, the discourse of addiction is one that continually reasserts and reinvents the natural. Derrida initiates this critique through denaturalizing gestures: destabilizing the "nature" in "addiction" and the presumed natural referent or toxic or harmful substance that corresponds to the sign "drugs." The central concern for Derrida is the discourse of "drugs" and the concept's historical and cultural inscriptions as well as its moral-ethical valuation. As Derrida explains: "There is not in the case of drugs any objective, scientific, physical (physicalistic), or 'naturalistic' definition . . . [drugs] carries in itself both norm and prohibition" (p. 2).

The invention of "the addict" (or the "toxicomaniac"—the pathologized subject of drug use) was, like the homosexual, predicated on the modern epistemic regime in which particular acts and behaviors like sodomy and drug-taking were transformed into criminalized and pathologized bodies through the positive effects of power (Berridge & Edwards, 1981; Derrida, 1993; Foucault, 1980; Sedgwick, 1992). The modern regime organized itself through a division between the normal and the pathological; producing a deviance and threat located in the body—corporeal identity. That is, in a disciplinary society, power operates by subjecting individuals to practices of normalization: strategies and operations through which bodies are endlessly subjected to detailed surveillance, including medical and psychological examinations, in the forms of measurement and standardization.[8] Unlike premodern regimes in which power was possessed by the sovereign and enacted spectacularly and violently against bodies, modern power works by disciplining and subjecting bodies to the subtle and benevolent regulation of life.[9] The techniques deployed by science and law are central to the marking of that border and the production of deviant subjects. As I have already suggested, Foucault argues that dividing relations work through the production of deviance, which then produces and stabilizes the norm. Like the modern subject of sexuality described by Foucault, the addict, in its multiple forms, can be understood as the confessing subject, especially the one involved in 12-step programs. The subject of the 12-step programs initiates recovery by admitting s/he has an addiction and turning his/her own authority to a higher power; that is, by acknowledging that s/he has no free will (which is a moral failure) and relinquishing and preventing free will in the future.

Similar to Foucault's repressive hypothesis, the general discourse of drugs, which includes the only apparently contradictory ethico-political liberationist and prohibitive position, presumes a relation between the natural body and a repressive power located in institutions. As such, the dominant positions comply with and mystify power by transforming addiction/drug use into an individual matter and a problem for science, medicine, and the police. Drug advocates appeal to a series of naturals (body/desire) that are repressed by artificial regulations. Prohibitionists appeal to what they presume to be a benevolent power necessary to protect the juridico-rational subject, the natural and self-contained body, and the social bond. Both positions bracket the technological condition asserting both the original body in opposition to an exterior, pathogenic, foreign, Other from which it needs protection.

Derrida contends that the crime of drug use is not so much about the individual and isolated act of a drug user nor the ingestion of harmful substances; instead, it is a crime because drug users devalue and challenge rationality, productivity, responsibility, and health by privileging an alternative reality. In other words, by Derrida's view, drug use is criminal because it threatens the social bond, that which links us as subjects together and management of which is "almost always presented as protection of a 'natural' normality of the body, of the body politic and the body of the individual member" (1993, p. 14).

Sedgwick (1992) contends that the multiple articulations of addiction that exceed the foreign object (such as substances like food, and behaviors like refusal) suggest that the discourse of addiction posits some abstract space that governs the relation between the body and a substance.[10] Quoting Sedgwick:

> To the gradual extension of addiction-attribution to a wider variety of "drugs" over the first two-thirds of the century has been added the startling coda of several recent developments . . . the telling slippage

that begins by assimilating food ingestion perceived as excessive with alcoholism—in the founding of say, Overeaters Anonymous. . . . From the pathologizing of food consumption to the pathologizing of food refusal (anorexia), or even of intermittent and highly controlled food consumption (bulimia) . . . the demonization of "the foreign substance" that gave an ostensible coherence to addiction . . . "substance abuse" is deconstructed almost as soon as articulated. (1992, pp. 582–583)

Still, addiction appears to be governed by a subject-object relation in which a diseased-self relies or becomes dependent upon an object inscribed with mystical qualities (whether consumed or not) to fulfill the subject, or addiction can be understood as freely choosing health—the healthy free will.[11] In this sense, addiction attribution is embedded in and motivated by the cognitive logic of modernity and its presumed correspondence between "free will" and the healthy body—what Derrida identified as the basis of the social bond.

Sport and exercise are not simply addressed by Derrida and Sedgwick as afterthoughts nor are they simply listed as yet other examples of addiction; instead, both address sport and exercise as special cases. As Sedgwick describes exercise:

Healthy free will would belong to the person who had in mind the project of unfolding these attributes (consolation, repose, beauty, energy) out of a self, a body, already understood as containing them in potentia . . . [in this view] now a staple of medicalized discourse both lay and clinical . . . the exerciser [not the dieter] would be the person who embodies the exact opposite of addiction. (1992, p. 583)

Because sport and exercise are removed from the subject/object relation governing addiction/drugs, because sport and exercise appear to be the anti-addiction, in both arguments sport/exercise occupy pivotal points as extreme and complicated examples of the failure of modern logic.[12]

Derrida explains the authoritative condemnation of chemical prosthetics in sport through his discussion of writing as drug and of the drug-addicted writer. Drawing from his essay "Plato's Pharmacy," in which he discusses the Phaedrus, Derrida argues that since Western logic presupposes an "im-mediacy" of presence, speech rather than writing has been privileged across philosophical thought as the ideal moment of presence, associated with the unmediated, the transparent, and pure consciousness. Writing has been debased as an inferior form of signification that alters rather than reports truth: writing has been viewed as a second order of reality, simulacra, and is associated with imitation, bad memory, and the pharmakon. Out of the epistemic problem of writing, Derrida distinguishes between the Automatic writers, those authentically inspired by God or spiritual sources, and those inspired inauthentically by drugs. "Authenticity" insists on production through effort: automatic and similar writers are excepted from this moral claim because their spirit remains understood as authentic. Writing, like drugs, is a question of truth or imitation; like the pharmakon, writing and drugs are poison and antidote.[13] According to Derrida, sport, like some writing, is inscribed as a zone of authentic work: even more, sport is the anti-drug: "the education of the will as in the overcoming of the self" (Derrida, 1993, p. 18).

Derrida's interests lie in revealing how disease, drugs, and addiction are always already on the inside of sport and in demonstrating how the drug-related "experience" cannot be reduced to a particular substance, form of ingestion, or even ingestion itself. He points to sport as a drug—intoxicating and depoliticizing—but he also complicates the presumed naturalness of the body (the persistent elision of the technological condition) by problematizing the use of "artificial natural prosthetics" to enhance the naturalness of the body. He amplifies the crisis of the natural by pointing to problems with drug-tracking, in making visible the so-called unnatural in the body.

Sedgwick approaches the question of addiction noting what she calls "the rise of the exercise addict in the 1980s" by asking what it means that we have become addicted to this drug called exercise. Here, I want to make several observations: first, exercise became implicated in the discourse of addiction at least as early as 1967; second, during the 1970s, the exercise addict increasingly became an object of scientific knowledge as scientists and psychologists sought to make visible, discernable, and quantifiable a newly produced and pathologized identity; and third, as the category of the "exercise addict" gained popular currency in the 1980s, a recommendation was made for the exercise addict to be included in the *Diagnostic and Statistical Manual IV* (DSM-IV) as an official psychological disorder.

For Sedgwick, exercise addiction is the super-addiction; it is a limit-case because the object is purged from the discourse of addiction. The subject/object relation differs in exercise: mystical properties are not projected onto an object but unfold within the self, the potential to fulfill the lack lies with the subject. That is, the case of the "exercise-addict" evacuates any necessary substance from addiction attribution. In this case, the subject is addicted to the idea of free subjectivity, addicted to the repeated act of freely choosing health—that act which is supposed to be anti-addiction.

Again for Sedgwick, the articulation of exercise and addiction produces a discourse of addiction on the loose; a discourse no longer delimitable, but that can mark all bodies, all behaviors, and all exchanges, even those most revered, as diseased. Similar to the modern search for pathology, multiple forms of bodily inspections are produced that traverse work, consumption, and sexuality in the form of the workaholic, shopaholic, and codependent. In these cases, addiction "resides only in the structure of a will that is always somehow insufficiently pure" (1992, p. 584).

The End of the Organic (Modern) Body

Drugs are excentric. They are animated by an outside already inside. Endorphins relate internal secretions to the external chemical.

—Avital Ronnel

In conclusion, I want to draw together the two "presences" I have discussed throughout this chapter by concluding with a few of the problems they raise in and for a configuration of practices called "sport."

Sedgwick's and Derrida's arguments converge around the critiques of the metaphysics of presence and the contemporary crisis of the categories that repeat that presence. Both suggest that the conceptualization of the body as natural, organic, discrete and of free will are outmoded. Both turn to sport as a critical site in this crisis, and both are interested in how prosthetic devices challenge our understanding of the body. Both argue that since free will and the natural are always already contaminated by their outside, such a crisis is unavoidable; Sedgwick argues that the taxonomic frenzy of addiction signifies the crisis and attempts to construct outdated unities. Sedgwick turns to steroid-man as a metonym for the contemporary cultural condition—steroid man is not Foucault's organic body but Donna Haraway's cyborg who refuses the dividing lines or at least destabilizes binaries along multiple axes: body/machine; human/animal; healthy/unhealthy body; pure/impure; satiable/insatiable desires; natural/prosthetic; and democracy/communism.

Derrida suggests that it is the crisis of "naturalistic metaphysics" that extends beyond drugs and that is amplified in the age of biotechnologies. Derrida examines the scopic regime of drug-testing and its attempts to discern, render visible, and measure the natural and the foreign, the pure and the impure. Derrida turns to the politics of corporeality on offer in sport, which is highlighted by the simultaneous destabilization and reinvention of nature and the natural required by the attempt to track and classify what counts as drugs. He asks: where does drug use begin? "How can we classify and track its products? And by what authority do we condemn this drug use or such-and-such a chemical prosthesis? And what about women athletes who get pregnant for the stimulating, hormonal effects and then have an abortion after their event?" (1993, p. 18). And I would add: How do we classify (as foreign) blood doping? Pregnancy doping? Fetal tissue implants?

My goal is not to provide an answer to the question about the appropriateness of drug use in sport; to engage that question would be to miss the point of the paper. Neither Derrida nor Sedgwick present their analyses as solutions. Both work from positions that locate change and movement in strategies other than the resolution of contradiction: genealogy and deconstruction are different kinds of strategies that do not seek resolution of contradictions. Derrida's and Sedgwick's critiques make apparent the fundamental problems with the regulations and rules governing sport—especially prohibitive drug legislation and its politics of and nostalgia for an organic corporeality and the moral valuations inscribed through its diagnostics. In this sense, drug-testing can be understood as an attempt to police and restore the boundaries of an outdated modern, organic body.

Notes

1. For example, Hoberman's (1992) interrogation of drug use in sport is constrained by his failure to question the "natural body" on which the drug-use debates rely and by the "performance enhancement" emphasis. The premises on which both categories rely bracket out the broader discourses on drugs and addiction.

2. The understanding of addiction and its production of pathologized bodies/ subjects requires a conceptualization of "sport" that destabilizes the familiar boundaries and connotations. Addiction-attribution, exercise, and sport are particularly in teresting sites because of their ubiquity in contemporary Western culture; all seem to be signs of a contemporary cultural condition that is simultaneously out of control and manageable.

3. "Referential" describes a function of language that presumes that language refers to the real.

4. Deconstruction works through a logic of grammar (the economy of signs, pressures, pulls, and a diffusion that produces meaning through difference) in which binary terms depend on, and fold on themselves.

5. The works represent two different spheres of the dialectic of enlightenment: (a) an understanding of the subject and the will to truth as positive, and (b) a notion of the subject understood as having a will over the body (the question of subjectivity from within the criteria of modernity) and the subject. Derrida's position on drugs as yet another manifestation of rational man and the social bond may address the effects of the discourse of drugs on one level, but it has clear limitations. For example, the technological regimes that produce the addict or that produce traces of deviance in the body are articulated with other relations in different ways in different historical moments.

6. In relation to this, his work is concerned with the modern subject as a discursive production generated by the effects and "truths" of knowledge/power. The modern subject, at least as articulated by Foucault in the *History of Sexuality*, is the confessing subject, the subject of the examination and confession.

7. For an excellent discussion on how the genealogist works, see Jennifer Terry's (1991) "Theorizing Deviant Historiography." The term "discursive traffic" is taken from Terry's work.

8. Given this, it is more useful to conceptualize sport as a cover term for a network of normalizing practices (including science and law) that produce multiple bodies and identities (raced, sexed, classed, heterosexualized, national, reproductive, prosthetic, cyborg, etc).

9. Of course, the body interrogated in this paper—the drug or prosthetic body—cannot be understood apart from these other bodies nor apart from the addicted-body in contemporary culture. In the case of "drug-tracking," the other relations are dissolved and re-articulated through the examination of the "suspicious"/drug-using body (see Cole, 1993, for a discussion of the suspicious body in sport).

10. The multiplication of sites and types of addiction parallels Foucault's argument regarding power and sexuality in which perversions multiplied from the invention of the category of "unnatural" sexuality. "Power in bourgeois society did not act mainly to repress or to silence a sexuality which nonetheless expresses itself as all instincts must. Rather such power resulted in the 'multiplication of singular sexualities'" (Foucault, 1980, p. 47).

11. The significance of addiction attribution exceeds the quantitative, its production through different mechanisms, and the multiple subjects it produces.

12. While the guiding logic of sport and exercise is one in which the body is understood as self-produced, Foucault's work, again, is concerned with the self as produced.

13. Derrida considers the drug-user's body over and against that of the athlete's body. Derrida views the athlete as having disciplinary power over his body. He understands sport as the site in which man can work on himself to be superman, the superbody, the athletic body. He sees sport as a practice representing the essence of man in concentrated form, the capacity to transform oneself. The question he poses is what happens when the athlete's body becomes infected with drugs.

References

Berridge, V., & Griffith, E. (1981). *Opium and the people: Opiate use in nineteenth-century England*. New York: St. Martin's Press.

Boyne, R. (1990). *Foucault and Derrida: The other side of reason*. Boston: Unwin Hyman.

Canguilhem, G. (1966). *The normal and the pathological.* New York: Zone Books.

Cole, C.L. (1993). "Resisting the canon: Feminist cultural studies, sport, and technologies of the body." *Journal of Sport and Social Issues,*17, 77–97.

Derrida, J. (1976). *Of grammatology.* Baltimore: John Hopkins University Press.

———— (1981). *Dissemination.* London: Routledge.

Derrida, J. with Autrement (1993). "The rhetoric of drugs: An interview" (M. Israel, trans.), *differences,* 5, 1–25. (Original published in French, 1989)

Dreyfus, H.L., & Rabinow, P. (1982). *Beyond structuralism and hermeneutics.* Chicago: The University of Chicago.

Ehrenreich, B. (1989). *Fear of falling: The inner life of the middle class.* New York: Pantheon.

Foucault, M. (1979). *Discipline and punish: The birth of a prison* (A. Sheridan, trans.). New York: Vintage Books. (Original published in French, 1975)

———— (1980). *The history of sexuality, Volume I: An introduction* (R. Hurley, trans.). New York: Vintage Books. (Original published in French, 1976)

Gitlin, T. (1990). "On drugs and mass media in America's consumer society." In H. Resnick (Ed.), *Youth and drugs: Society's mixed messages.* Washington, DC: United States Department of Health and Human Services Prevention (Office of Substance Abuse Prevention, Prevention Monograph-6, DHHS publication no. ADM-90-1689).

Haraway, D. (1985). "A manifesto for cyborgs: Science, technology, and socialist-feminism in the 1980s." *Socialist Review,* 80, 65–107.

Hoberman, J. (1992). *Mortal engines: The science of performance and the dehumanization of sport.* New York: The Free Press.

Kimbrell, A. (1993). *The human body shop: The engineering and marketing of life.* San Francisco: Harper San Francisco.

Reeves, J., & Campbell, R. (1994). *Cracked coverage: Television news, the anti-cocaine crusade, and the Reagan legacy.* Durham, NC: Duke University Press.

Schor, N., & Weed, E. (1993). "Editor's note." *differences,* 4, iii.

Sedgwick, E.K. (1990). *Epistemology of the closet.* Berkeley, CA: University of California Press.

———— (1992). "Epidemics of the will." In J. Crary & S. Kwinter (Eds.), *Incorporations* (pp. 582–295). New York: Urzone.

Terry, J. (1989). "The body invaded: Medical surveillance of women as reproducers." *Socialist Review,*19, 13–45.

———— (1991). "Theorizing deviant historiography." *differences,* 3, 55–74.

13

POST-SPORT: TRANSGRESSING BOUNDARIES IN PHYSICAL CULTURE

BRIAN PRONGER

This chapter considers the re-presentation of bodies in modern physical culture. It looks at modern sport as a mode of re-presenting, and thus making, modern human bodies. It also considers what we as academics in the sociology, history, and anthropology of sport and physical culture can do in our own representational domains, in publishing, in teaching, administrating, and coaching, to make the realities of cultured bodies a little freer. I will try to accomplish this by appealing to the ironic "wisdom" characteristic of postmodern moods.[1]

Ironically enough, it is pro forma for scholarly papers on postmodernism to begin by indicating that there are as many postmodernisms as there are postmodernists and scholars of the same. That said, I will situate myself in the hurly burly of postmodern studies by naming three authors: Donna Haraway (1985, 1988), Scott Lash (1990), and Linda Hutcheon (1989), all of whom frequently cite the works of others who have given us "the canon(s) of postmodernism(s)": Jean-François Lyotard (1979), Michel Foucault (1979, 1980, 1982), Jean Baudrillard (1983), Jacques Derrida (1976), Umberto Ecco (1976), Gianni Vattimo (1988), and Fredric Jameson (1984), among others. And while I owe a great debt to all these authors, borrowing from their work liberally, I bring to the postmodern climate some thoughts which these writers would consider decidedly un-postmodern. But then again, isn't eclecticism part of the "postmodern aura" (Newman, 1985)?

Prolegomena

I will begin by describing modern sport as a project of socio-cultural boundary maintenance. Many boundaries are negotiated in sport. The following list of oppositions is partial: man and woman; heterosexual and homosexual;

white and "other"; healthy and sick; animal, human and machine; legitimate play and illicit sex; rationality and irrationality; order and chaos.

It has become common in postmodern, socialist-feminist, and queer circles to document and encourage various means of transgressing these boundaries (see for example, Cole, 1993; Haraway, 1985; Jackson, 1991). Gender bending, for example, transgresses the boundaries of manhood and womanhood. The justification for such transgression is the belief that it liberates people from the restrictions of oppositional boundaries, giving them some measure of control over them. I will argue that while such "pollution" of boundaries (Haraway, 1985) does indeed offer some measure of freedom within the parameters of modern discourses, it does not go far enough.

I will suggest that for a strategy to be postmodern, it needs to stand in a more fundamental opposition to the modern than does transgression within the spheres of boundary projects. To make this argument, I will first attempt to explain what is modern in the competing boundary projects of maintenance and transgression. Scott Lash (1990) characterizes the modern as the achievement of the fullest possible autonomy of cultural spheres; a notion which he takes from Weber's concept of the self-legislation of cultural spheres, *Eigengesetzlichkeit*. Autonomy here lies in the fact that in modernity, socio-cultural spheres[2] come to refer only to themselves for their justification, legitimation, or to use an old-fashioned word, truth.

Taking our cue from Foucault, we can see that cultural spheres have come to dominate modern human life, indeed to subject human bodies to discourses of power (Foucault, 1982). In *The History of Sexuality Part I* (1978), *The Birth of the Clinic* (1973) and *Discipline and Punish* (1977), Foucault shows how it is that people are constituted by their embodiment of various programmes of power such as sexuality, madness, and criminality, and how their lives are ordered according to the power relations that these discursive programmes legislate. People's understanding of their bodies, of what is right and wrong, of what is socially permissible or anathema, comes to be defined in terms of such discourses of power. Life is thus lived in accordance with such discourses, effectively legislated by discourses.

What is distinctly modern here is that the various realms of modern culture ground themselves not by appeal to some "reality" that is more authoritative (e.g., deities) or original (e.g., Heidegger would say that Being is the origin of reality) than itself, but by appealing to itself. The source of legitimacy, indeed the common sense of, for instance, what men and women are and ought to do, how their bodies ought to move and relate to each other, lies in the logics through which the boundaries between them are created, reinforced, or perforated. The meaning of manhood and womanhood is entirely socio-cultural—this is the message of most modern feminisms. Many postmodern critics will argue that human bodies are simply there as vehicles for socio-cultural discourses; the logics of these oppositional relations are considered autonomous from the body, simply carried out upon it. Michael Feher, for instance, in his introduction to the three-volume collection of essays *Fragments for a History of the Body*, says:

> the history of the human body is not so much the history of its representations as of its modes of construction. For the history of its representations always refers to a real body considered to be "without history"—whether this be the organism observed by the natural sciences, the body proper as perceived by phenomenology, or the instinctual, repressed body on which psychoanalysis is based—whereas the history of its modes of construction can, since it avoids the overly massive oppositions of science and ideology or of authenticity and alienation, *turn the body into a thoroughly historicized* and completely problematic issue. (Feher, 1989, p. 11, emphasis mine)

Here we have the total appropriation, the colonization, the "resourcing" (Haraway, 1988) of the body by cultural history. In a similar fashion, the modern "natural" sciences of the body (e.g., physiology, anatomy, psychopharmacology, etc.) claim the body for a host of modern political discourses, understanding it as a machine, manipulable, productive, hierarchically organized and so on. Interestingly enough, this is accomplished by disguising the particular politics at work on the body by claiming that it is just "natural." There is a flourishing "body" of research on the politicization of the body by science. Foucault is perhaps the founding father. Some who have followed in his footsteps are: Mike Featherstone (1991), Nicholas Fox (1994), Chris Shilling (1993), Barbara Stafford (1991), and Bryan Turner (1992).

In the process of modernization, a completely modern body becomes a completely cultured body, a body which is defined, indeed circumscribed by the inscriptions upon it of cultural discourses, such as the oppositional boundaries mentioned above. There is nothing primordial about the modern body; it is, as it were, completely up to date with what is happening to it culturally. In the modernizing process, the primordial body becomes differentiated from the cultural body, even to the point of the disappearance of the primordial body. Lyotard says that modernity takes place in the withdrawal of the real. Similarly, the modernized body is processed in the withdrawal of the primordial body. In fully developed modernity, the primordial is eclipsed (or erased) by culture; in fact to speak of the primordial at all would be to raise considerable suspicion. It is crucial to keep in mind that this differentiation of the primordial body is not a *fait accompli;* it is a process. Modern sport, I will argue, contributes to this process. And as hegemony theory suggests about such processes, there is potential for change.

Modernization is not only an epistemological and ontological process, it is also a highly political process. The socio-cultural realm, differentiated from and autonomous of "the primordial body," takes control of the body, setting its possibilities and limits. This establishes a political regime in two respects. The first is the insinuation of relative stability—sometimes called "civilization" by the Western imperial (i.e., modern) gaze—in the wild ways of the primordial body. The second follows from the first: with the primordial body silenced, the political play of various boundary negotiations can proceed on its surface.

After explaining more fully the above argument on modernization as a process of differentiating the primordial body from the socio-cultural body, a process that culminates in the total eclipse of the primordial body, I will discuss the postmodernization of sport. Some postmodernists speak of transgression as a mode for loosening dominant boundary maintenance projects (Haraway, 1985). I will briefly discuss some transgressive options for sporting physical culture. But I will also argue that because these transgressions still work/play within the modern project of the differentiated legislation of the body from autonomous socio-cultural discourses, they are in fact trapped in the modern project. Indeed, they are arguably more modern than postmodern.

Linda Hutcheon (1989) describes postmodernity as "complicitous critique." This is an idea that is well tuned to "progressive" political sensibilities of the 1980s and 90s, sensibilities that were initially formed in the new Left optimism of the 1960s and 70s. But now, with the collapse of communism (and along with it hope for effective Leftist politics), with the seemingly unbounded expansion of consumption (at least in the so-called "first world"), with the disappointingly modest gains of "women's liberation," with the cooptation of much of lesbian and gay liberation politics into the mainstream of North American culture, with the continued oppression of Blacks and Native people, not to mention the dreadful destruction of the environment, and so on, optimism seems less and less appropriate. Foucault's analyses of discourses of power, moreover, have demonstrated the ways in which we are deeply embedded in the same social relations which critical theory has taken as its critical object. Hope for substantive social transformation has been seriously undermined, not least of all by widespread realizations of the complicity in such relations by those who are deeply dissatisfied with and critical of those relations: feminists, anti-racists, queer activists and so on. While the hope is disappearing, the critique is not. Given this situation, Hutcheon's focus on complicitous critique is appropriate.

Teresa de Lauretis is aware of the above sort of paradox in feminism, arguing that feminism lies both inside and outside the ideology of gender, aware of the "double pull," which is to say, critical of the patriarchal structure of gender while attempting to find some comfortable space for the category of "woman" (de Lauretis, 1986, p. 10). But as Hutcheon points out: "Complicity is not full affirmation or strict adherence; the awareness of difference and contradiction, of being inside and outside, is never lost in the feminist, as in the postmodern" (1989, p. 14). An appreciation of such contradictions, and therefore of irony, is crucial both to critique and political action in these post-optimistic times. Transgressive strategies are best understood in terms of complicitous critique.

After exploring the concept of modernization as a process of the differentiation of "the real" and the socio-cultural, such that for bodies the socio-cultural becomes their autonomous legislator, I will argue for postmodernization as a process of de-differentiation, wherein the modern body is ironically diffused by a postmodern body. Whereas the thoroughly modern body would be a completely cultural body, a postmodern body is at once a cultured body (gendered, raced, cyborged, etc.) and a wild body (primordial, erotic, transcendentally beyond culture). And so, whereas modern sport is a project of differentiation and socio-cultural boundary maintenance, postmodern sport (post-sport) is a wild event of de-differentiation and boundary pollution. Which is to say that postmodern sport should employ both (a) transgressive strategies in the essentially modern domain of cultural boundary negotiations, and (b) diffusion of the dominance of the modern in the erotic ecstasy of the primordially moving body.

My hope is that this will open doors for various scholarly investigations and political actions in physical culture. How modern are various sporting events? To what extent are some sports already engaged in postmodern bodily experience? What can we as physical educators, sport scholars or coaches do to further the postmodernization of sport?

Modern Sport as a Project of Boundary Maintenance

Modern sport has played a very important socio-cultural role, representing, creating and challenging numbers of important social relations. For instance, modern sport has contributed to the production of gender difference (Birrell & Cole, 1990; Greendorfer, 1983; Hall, 1993; Lenskyj, 1986, 1991; Messner & Sabo, 1990; Sabo & Runfola, 1980); masculine hierarchies (Connell, 1987, 1990; Kidd, 1987; Whitson, 1990); experiences of homosexuality and heterosexuality (Dewar, 1990; Pronger, 1990); ethnic and racial difference (Messner, 1992); class (Donnelly, 1988; Gruneau, 1983; Hargreaves, 1986) and the cultural difference between healthiness and sickness (Cole, 1993). These social relations are negotiated; through sport, boundaries are variously created, maintained, transgressed or destroyed.

The boundaries that constitute manhood and womanhood are negotiated through sport. An emerging body of literature explores the role of sport in the development of masculinities among men (Connell, 1987; Kidd, 1987; Messner, 1992; Messner & Sabo, 1990; Pronger, 1990; Sabo & Runfola, 1980). This work demonstrates how sport helps men set the boundaries for appropriate masculine behaviour, sense of self, and body production. Sport helps set the limits beyond which men should not venture if they are to achieve the status of man as opposed to woman, and maintain that difference through life. But the boundaries between manhood and womanhood are not the only ones negotiated in sport; sport also contributes to the subtler boundaries that establish masculine hierarchies among men. Connell (1987) introduced the notion of hegemonic masculinity. He says that masculinity is not one monolithic structure that all men share in equally; it is hierarchical, with some forms of masculinity seen as more valuable or powerful than others. Generally speaking, sportsmen are seen as more masculine than their nonsporting brothers. And within sport, men competing in violent team sports are more masculine than those in non-violent individual sports. Messner (1992) describes the ways in which class and education contribute to positions within these hierarchies of competing masculinities.

Sport as a site for the negotiation of gender boundary maintenance for women is even more complex than it is for men. The ideal woman in traditional patriarchy would not participate in sport at all. Helen Lenskyj (1986) gives an historical account of the ways in which women's involvement in sport challenged the boundaries of femininity. Resistance to women playing sport in the early part of this century came from fears that these boundaries would be transgressed. There are still fears of women becoming too masculine. As Cheryl Cole points out, the semidocumentary film "Pumping Iron II," in which a clearly larger and more masculine looking woman loses a bodybuilding competition to a smaller and more feminine woman, explores "the transgressive potential of the gender ambiguity of women bodybuilders" (1993, p. 88). And numerous authors have pointed out the ways in which the aerobics industry, rather than transgressing the boundaries of gender, making women both physically and symbolically stronger and therefore more masculine, actually emphasizes femininity, thus maintaining the boundaries (Bordo, 1991; Featherstone, 1991; Schulze, 1990; Singer, 1989). Whereas traditionally, women were not supposed to train their bodies in sport in order to maintain their femininity, contemporary Western consumerist patriarchy stresses:

> a new feminine aesthetic, versatile, athletic, hard, and slick. [This] represents a new dimension in the historical-cultural map of gender body-styles, the health/beauty/exercise complex, and commodity production. (Cole, 1993, p. 87)[3]

Not unrelated to the negotiation of gender boundaries in sport is the negotiation of the boundaries of heterosexuality and homosexuality. In *The*

Arena of Masculinity, I explored the ways that many sports marginalize gay men, while at the same time offering homoerotic opportunities for men and boys who prefer not to see themselves as gay. Here boundaries are drawn between explicit and implicit homosexuality. Women athletes, while often suspected of lesbianism, are encouraged to distance themselves from such suspicion by overt displays of heterosexual femininity: the ubiquitous presence of pony-tails in women's volleyball being a case in point (Dewar, 1990; Lenskyj, 1991).

Sport not only gives expression to the maintenance of the boundaries between man and woman, masculinities and femininities, heterosexualities and homosexualities, it also contributes to the production of these boundaries by bestowing on those who participate in sport and those who are fans of sport, manhood and womanhood, masculinity and femininity, the aura of explicit heterosexuality and the opportunity for implicit homosexuality. The boundary projects of sport thus participate in the sexual boundary projects of the larger society.

Race is another boundary project that takes place in sport. The fact that blacks predominate in some sports, for instance track and field and basketball, while whites predominate in others, such as swimming, rowing and equestrian riding attests to sport as a place that gives expression to racism and thus helps to consolidate racial difference. And the tendency for whites to play the higher status positions in some sports, quarterback in football for instance, while blacks typically play lower status positions such as lineman, also attests to the creation of boundaries that exist as hierarchies. That these boundaries are not fixed, that they are indeed negotiable is attested to by the fact that there are now some blacks in previously white only positions (e.g., the manager of the Toronto Blue Jays Baseball team).

Cheryl Cole (1993) has written about sport as one of the sites at which the boundaries between being sick and being healthy are set. Magic Johnson is the most famous case in point, instantiating through sport both the boundaries between homosexuality and heterosexuality and between health and sickness. Immediately after his announcement of his HIV status, he made a point of his heterosexuality. His career however, was cut short, when other basketball players refused to continue playing with him for fear of contagion—even though the risk of contagion by playing basketball is extremely low (Pediatrics, 1991). Sport separates the healthy from the sick, making the boundary ostensibly clear. In the Magic Johnson affair, Johnson became a marker of sickness, separated out from the majority of the athletes who are thus marked as healthy. Sickness is thus rendered as other. Cole says "sport serves as society's uncontaminated-immune system" (1993, p. 89).[4]

Donna Haraway's work on cyborgs introduces the boundaries that are traditionally drawn between animal, human and machine, arguing that in the late 20th century, these boundaries are becoming ever more porous. What better example is there of the cyborg than a modern athlete: they are experimented upon in much the same way as rats in kinesiology laboratories; they are exploited for their "animal aggression" by the producers of sports spectacles such as hockey and football; they are fine-tuned and chemically manipulated by techno-science; they are circuits in the network machine of the high performance sport system.[5] With the exception of Cheryl Cole, few have taken up Haraway's work on cyborgs and applied it to the many facets of sport and physical culture. To do so in depth is beyond the scope of this chapter, but it is worth noting that a fascinating politics for sport and physical culture is waiting to be developed in light of Haraway's "Manifesto for Cyborgs," which introduces a socialist-feminist postmodern political sensibility for cyborgs.[6]

Sport is also important for the modern project of the rationalization of the body. Writers such as Alan Guttmann (1978) have praised the modern project of bodily control by the forces of "reason." He lauds the rationalization of sporting technique and physiology. He is also very keen about the rationalization/ universalization of the rules and regulation of sport by international sports-governing bodies. But his praise of modern rationalization is far from the high moral ideals of modernists such as Jurgen Habermas (1983), who defends reason and the "unfinished project of modernity." Habermas argues that the power of reason is to be extolled because it is only by the rules of reasonable discourse that humanity can be saved from the cruel abyss that followed from passions such as those aroused in Nazi Germany. For Habermas, acceptance of the rules of reason and civilized debate make possible a democratic society based on consensus.[7]

Guttmann's interest in rationalization has nothing to do with commitment to the moral principles or political theories of freedom. For Guttmann, rationalization is good because it is efficient. Such modern fetishization of efficiency is criticized by Lyotard in his discussion of the "performativity principle," in which he says that a performance is accepted as good when it augments the power of the social system in which it takes place. Extrapolating from Lyotard, the most efficient athletic body, the most perfectly rational body, is one which serves sport best; it increases the socio-cultural power of sport. Modern sport is best served where its various boundary projects and economic and political interests are enhanced. This is why it is important, according to this logic, that coaches and physical educators become better and better versed in the scientific rationalization of the body: they help the system shape bodies so that the modern social system is rendered ever more efficient and ever more powerful. The irrational wilderness of the erotic body is the other side of the boundary of the rationalized body. Kinesiology and sport sciences are important contributors to the ever tightening boundaries of the modernized body.

Modern sport also negotiates the boundaries between order and chaos. The establishment of official rules for games and bodies that govern and control games, and the segregation of pleasurable physical activities from other aspects of life effectively keeps the chaos of erotic play within very specific boundaries. This is not unrelated to the generalized phenomenon of the rationalization of most of modern life. In the case of sport and physical culture, this is in effect a matter of controlling Eros by setting the boundaries beyond which Erotic experience is not allowed to venture. I this sense, sport has much in common with the discourse of sexuality described by Foucault (1980, 1985). Eros is acceptable if it is properly contained by the appropriate athletic setting, conducted at the appropriate time, within the rules of the game and interpreted as just another contributor to the productive, economic body. This last point is important. The eroticism of physical activity is a well-kept secret. Physical play is legitimate if and only if it is not explicitly erotic. Modern sport sets the legitimate boundaries for the erotic experience of the moving body. This is not unrelated to the homosexuality of sport, another well-kept secret. It is culturally forbidden for homosexuality to enter into the athletic arena; athletes may parade about naked in the showers, or in skimpy outfits on the playing field, playing with their own bodies and the bodies of others, only so long as a boundary is maintained between doing that and "having sex."

Transgressing Boundaries

Donna Haraway positions the political strategy and experience of transgression at the forefront of her "Manifesto for Cyborgs" (1985). She says that transgression allows for multiple perspectives which reveal both dominations and better possibilities. Transgression takes into account the ways in which we are embedded in, indeed created by, the discursive boundary projects of our time. In the post-optimistic 1990s, it is clear that we cannot simply opt out of boundary projects such as race, class, gender, sexuality, ethnicity, regionality and so on. As Hutcheon (1989) points out, we are complicitous in them, and simply progressing beyond them is out of our range. Transgression does not escape boundary projects *per se;* but because it crosses boundaries it allows us to see and experience the ways in which boundary projects dominate and control our lives. By moving into prohibited realms, we begin to confuse the lines and take ever more control over such socio-cultural experiences. While this is not an escape, a digression from such projects, it is a matter of taking responsibility (Haraway, 1985) for the way they work and the extent of their control.

Haraway (1985) points out that transgression is not just a new strategy that might now be deployed. It is part and parcel of the late 20th century condition. The cyborg, for instance, is not just a fantasy of science fiction, it is a fact. Cyborgs, being hybrids of animal/human/machine, transgress the formerly discreet boundaries of animal, human and machine. We are cyborgs: evolutionary theory, the hegemonic origin myth of modern culture, transgresses the old distinction between humans and animals. And the vast range of techno-scientific devices such as electro-magnetic resonance scanners and computer-manipulated television images have rendered our vision cybernetic. The production of the human body through biomechanics, exercise physiology, not to speak of the surgical installation of pacemakers and artificial joints, is evidence of the machine nature of our bodies. In urban, late industrial capitalism, it is impossible to deny our cyborg existence. The politics of transgression, rather than pining nostalgically for a pure human body, a body innocent of techno-scientific culture, opens up the possibility of people seeing themselves as cyborgs and taking some control over the ways in which they are cybernetic.

Haraway speaks of "pleasure in the confusion of boundaries and . . . responsibility in their construction" (1985, p. 72). In sport, this could mean that athletes wrest responsibility for their own cybernetic construction from the sport-industrial-techno-science-nationalist complex. Rather than being blindly manipulated into regimes of training, drugs and surgeries, regimes that serve only the performativity of the complex, transgressive athletes can take the wonder drugs of science, can technologize their bodies on their own terms, pollute the boundaries of animal/human/machine, for their own pleasure, responsibly determining for themselves what is best. Drugs are part of our cybernetic existence; what is important is that athletic cyborgs take responsibility for them in the production of their pleasures as animal/human/machines. The transgressive politics of athletic cyborgs does not engage in nostalgia for a pre-technological, pure human body in "Just Say No" campaigns against drugs, but gives control over the taking of drugs to the athlete who plays with the cybernetic boundary pollution of the body. While this transgressive game may bring pleasure, it does not guarantee safety; drugs can be dangerous. But as Haraway says, "Cyborg myth is about transgressed boundaries, potent fusions, and dangerous possibilities which progressive people might explore as one part of needed political work" (1985, p. 71). In sport this means encouraging people to experiment with the cybernetic boundaries of their bodies, thus resisting the boundary project of a sports system that requires athletes to technologize their bodies but punishes them if they are caught doing so, which is to say caught transgressing the boundaries of a nostalgia for an innocent, human, pre-cybernetic body.

Acknowledging the fact of our cyborg bodies can also have an impact on our contemporary regimens of the "healthy body," regimens that are intended to return the body to a more innocent way of being, in which it is natural, unpolluted. This regime of the healthy body Kroker and Kroker call "body McCarthyism" (1987). It is a body policed by the health professions, and ever more effectively, ever more proactively by the burgeoning physical fitness industry and physical education profession. It is important to note that the recruitment of physical education into the health sciences—often seen as a progressive move away from the sport paradigm that has produced athletes such as Ben Johnson—is also a move into the policing profession. Health-oriented, boundary-maintaining, physical education programmes preach against the pollution of the body with drugs, both recreational and performance enhancing. And many in the physical education profession are not only developing cunning ways of catching athletes who use drugs but also maintain vigilant, moralistic social campaigns that are meant to limit the pleasurable cybernetic drug options that might otherwise be open to athletes and other physically active people. An anti-policing, transgressive physical education programme, on the other hand, would incorporate the responsible use of drugs in the transgressive experience of the body.

The fact of our cyborg existence is not the only evidence of the reality of transgressed boundaries. Haraway says that the "fractured identities" of Third-World-women-of-color attest to the confusion of boundary projects such as "woman." She criticizes feminists such as Catherine MacKinnon for "appropriating, incorporating and totalizing" the vast variety of women's experiences under the coherent sign, "women's experience" (1988, p. 77). MacKinnon's version of radical feminism is a boundary project that sets the limits of women's experience in terms of white, First World women. This boundary is in actuality transgressed by the fractured, multiple identities of women. In the sociology of sport, this has important implications since there is a considerable literature that attempts to define and explain women's experience of sport under the totalizing sign of "women's experience." Helen Lenskyj's call for a girl-friendly sport, assumes a stable sense of the experience of girls and women. Most writings on women in sport assume a fairly stable object, namely "women." Moreover, the academic focus on sport rather than alternative forms of physical activity is also a boundary project, hegemonizing sport (a Western bourgeois phenomenon) over other aspects of women's physical cultures, usually to the exclusion or at least denigration of the others. The physical cultures of women already transgress the narrow boundaries of "sport," as they physically negotiate for instance child-rearing, violence, and poverty. Modern sport is primarily a First World enterprise. The physical cultures of women whose identities are multiply fractured along the lines of race, sexuality, ethnicity, economic status and so on, already transgress the boundaries of sport. If the sociology of sport were to seriously consider the transgressed boundaries implicit in the fractured identities of women, it would end its focus on sport (itself a boundary project) and address the multiplicity of women's physical cultures.

The socio-cultural phenomenon of transgressed boundaries not only already exists, it should be actively pursued. For those involved in the study of physical culture and the practice of physical education, this means pursuing the transgression of sport as a global project of boundary maintenance. As I said earlier, sport participates in the negotiation of a variety of boundary projects: gender, race, health, rationality, order, and so on. But the category of sport itself and its preeminence in physical culture and physical education programmes is a matter of sealing the boundaries of what it is to be embodied, of limiting the possibilities of the active body in the late 20th century. Those who take an active role in the creation of physical culture need to take an active role in the transgression of the privilege of sport. This means not only transgressing the various boundary projects within sport (e.g., encouraging pleasure in the confusion between the boundaries of heterosexuality and homosexuality, masculinity and femininity, or health and sickness), but also transgressing the privileged status of sport as a socio-cultural practice. We need to introduce into the world of modern sport the very things modern sport has tried to keep out: chaos, inefficiency, irrationality, sex, and other illicit pleasures. These transgressions bring us into the possibility of postmodern physical culture, to the making of postmodern bodies. For it is here that we transgress the boundaries of modernity itself.

Differentiation and the Project of Modernization[8]

The modern process of differentiation has its origins in the history of the separation of the sacred and the profane. Piaget periodized this development through three phases: "primitive," "religio-metaphysical" and "modern" (Lash, 1990). In the primitive phase, the sacred and the profane are immanent in each other; life is permeated with the sacred; nature and the spiritual remain undifferentiated in animism and totemism. At the religio-metaphysical stage, the sacred and profane begin to be differentiated; sacred matters belong to the churches, synagogues, mosques, temples, and to clergy, monks and nuns; while the everyday becomes the major concern of everyman, there is a tension between sacred and profane matters; the degree to which the sacred influences day to day life fluctuates. In the modern phase, the sacred and profane have been completely differentiated; the everyday is no longer governed or in anyway influenced by sacred matters; the profane is autonomous, setting its own rules for the conduct of society and culture.[9]

Martin Heidegger (1954) described a similar development in Western intellectual history in his essay on modern science. The dawn of modernity was a movement away from understanding grounded in the revelation of the sacred through holy writ and sacrament to a mode of understanding that grounds itself in itself. Modern understanding is self-contained; it needs no grounding from beyond the power of human thought. Man moves into the position of God. Descartes' famous cogito ergo sum expresses this modern change. In this way human understanding is differentiated from anything beyond itself; it is autonomous.

Lash says that "modernism . . . means a break with 'foundationalism' (1990, p. 9). Foundationalism is the opposite of self or autonomous legislation. It is heteronomous legislation from another, universalist "instance" such as nature, or reason, or God. Similarly, modern physical culture has no foundation in the primordial body. Modern culture legislates the body autonomously. Simply put, modern culture does not listen to the body, it simply legislates what it is and what it is to do.

In his essay entitled "The Question Concerning Technology," Heidegger (1962) explores what is particularly modern about our modern technology, namely the way it approaches beings. Ancient technology approached its objects with deference, the idea being to help beings become more fully what they are. This attitude is expressed in the Greek sense of sculpting. The artist did not turn a chunk of marble into the statue of a man; rather, he chiselled away at the marble to bring the statue out of the marble; the figure was already in the rock and the sculptor helped it appear. The modern attitude is quite different: we take raw materials and turn them into something they are not. The modern way, according to Heidegger, is to treat beings as resources— he calls it *gestell,* meaning "standing reserve." What is particularly modern here is the aggressiveness of the stance, of making something into something else. Modernity is technological in this sense: the aggressive taking up of things as resources, a move that allows them to be made into something which they originally were not.

Aggressive resourcefulness characterizes the relationship of modern socio-cultural discourses, of modern boundary projects to the body. Modern socio-cultural discourses appropriate the body to their own ends. Donna Haraway describes this relationship between nature and modern culture: "Nature is only the raw material of [modern] culture, appropriated, preserved, enslaved, exalted, or otherwise made flexible for disposal by culture" (1988, p. 592). One instance of such resourcing, Haraway says, is the boundary project of gender: male and female bodies are appropriated by the power relations of gender. "Sex is 'resourced' for its representation as gender, which 'we' can control" (1988, p. 592). The same could be said for the whole range of the boundary projects I have mentioned above. And sport, because it so explicitly takes up the body, is a perfect technique for the exploitation of the body as a cultural resource.[10]

The theme of control is very important to modernity. It is closely related to the historical shift in which humans move to the centre of life as the arbiters of what is and what should be. Indeed, the success with which humans have come to control nature and each other is the justification of modernity. Boundary projects have been very successful at controlling our lives; it is this story of control that Foucault told in his histories of Western discourses, such as medicine, psychiatry, criminality and sexuality. It is the thoroughly modern promise of being able to control society, the modern hope for creating a just society that keeps many Left-leaning intellectuals and political activists going. This human capacity for social control, whether it be to positive or negative ends, is an historical phenomenon, emerging out of the Enlightenment and the development of industrial capitalism. Even where it is benign, the quest for control is constructed in the logics of human domination.

The aggressive socio-cultural resourcing of the body is made possible by the modern process of differentiation. In this process the body is rendered a passive object for culture. The body, whose eroticism (which is to say whose very being, i.e., primordiality) is sacred, in the process of modernization is differentiated from culture, which is profane. The sacred, primordial body in no way informs modern culture, whereas modern culture literally shapes the body. In this way modern culture is autonomous, appealing only to itself for its authority in the socio-cultural construction of the body. The modern body is the body completely appropriated, completely resourced for modern boundary projects. Which is to say modern culture legislates itself, without reference to the body, even though the body is the subject of modernity. Clearly, modernity is not a democratic exercise when it comes to the relationship between the body and its socio-cultural governance. Through its myriad discourses and boundary projects, modern culture sets out to rule the body like a dictator. It is crucial at this point to remember that modernization is not a static state, not a *fait accompli;* it is a process.

We can look at physical cultures, at various sports, at bodies and ask, how modern are they? How modern is your body? How thoroughly have bodies been staked out by myriad boundary projects? To what extent do bodies resist their modernization? Or, to what degree do our bodies embrace, indeed, eroticize their modernization?

The thoroughly modern body is the thoroughly profaned body; it is a body whose sacredness has been eclipsed. This is the body completely resourced by the negotiations of boundary projects. Modern human beings find their "identities" (man/woman, white/other, gay/straight, etc.) in these projects, in their maintenance and in their transgression. Modern sport consists of physical activities that resource bodies at a highly differentiated level, which is to say at an autonomous level. Within this analytical framework, research on modern physical culture asks questions not only about border disputes (e.g., the masculinizing vs feminizing of sports, the possibilities of making sport "queer," the setting and contesting of racial and class boundaries, etc.) but also about the process of differentiation, of the resourcing of bodies and the extent of their modernization.

The Postmodern Body and Post-Sport

Modernity is a fact of late 20th century existence. For all but infants, an "innocent," pre-modern body is now impossible. We are cyborgs, gendered, raced, classed and so on. Transgressive strategies within boundary projects, such as women masculinizing themselves in sport or gay men playing up the homosexual aspects of sport, are still fundamentally modern strategies, working only on the differentiated modern body. Sport, being part of the modern project of differentiation, is created along modern lines and scholarly analysis or political action can no longer afford to neglect the production of the modern body as a resource for socio-cultural discourse. While transgression through boundary projects is a necessary political project, because it is limited to the autonomous and differentiated realm of modern culture and does not challenge modernity's resourcing of the body, it is not sufficient.

If we are to find some relief from the aggressive resourcing of the body that is characteristic of modern sport, a resourcing that takes place in the differentiation of the primordial and cultural body such that the body is rendered purely cultural, we need to look for practices in physical culture that are de-differentiating. This search will be both a matter of discovering to what extent physical practices already stand in a de-differentiating position in modernity, as well as a matter of engaging in the development of "new" postmodern physical activities.

If modernity, in physical culture, is essentially a process of differentiating the sacred from the profane, the primordial body from the resourceful, cultured body, then postmodernity is a process of de-differentiation of the same. I would like to underline here that this is not a nostalgic return to an "innocent" body. This is not an earnest romantic quest for the liberation of the "natural body" from the tyrannies of the socio-cultural. It is an ironic exploration of the body and its possibilities for pleasure in a highly modernized socio-cultural setting. A primary strategy for de-differentiation, for postmodernization, is erotic, primordial pleasure-seeking. Erotic pleasure is a de-differentiating postmodern strategy because pleasure can be limitless. As Deleuze and Guattari (1983) would say, pleasure can offer a "line of flight" from the overdeterminations of the cultural . And because pleasure sets out to optimize itself—an expert pleasure-seeker can find it anywhere—pleasure can work through the intransigence of boundary projects. The body is a surface upon which the texts of boundary projects and socio-cultural discourses are inscribed. But the body is also primordial, Erotic. Foucault showed how pleasure is used, indeed resourced, by socio-cultural discourse. But while this resourcing of pleasure has eclipsed the light of Eros, obscured the primordiality of the body, it has not annihilated the sacred possibilities of the body.

The de-differentiating, postmodernizing body seeks pleasure in the transgression of modern differentiation. Which is to say that it plays not only with the texts that are inscribed upon it—such as the playful transgressions of gender and sexual boundaries in events like the Pink Flamingo Relay at Gay swim-meets (see Pronger, 1990). The postmodernizing body also transgresses the body's textuality as such; it opposes the body's differentiated, autonomous legislation from socio-cultural discourse. The postmodern body seeks pleasure in the irony of resisting the limits of discourse, in the wild eroticism that moves passionately through discourse, through boundary projects. This is the ironic, erotic pleasure that sometimes perforates bodily markers such as man, straight, white, middle-class, and high-performance athlete.

The moving body has the capacity to see through its inscriptions and break the autonomous legislation of it from socio-cultural discourses. This is a matter of re-reading the body. For us moderns, ecstasy is the quintessential transgressive experience. Ecstasy literally means to stand out. The ecstasy of the primordial body stands out from the limits of its socio-cultural boundaries. The postmodern turn here, lies in letting ecstasy position us as complicitous critics of the modern project.

There is pleasure in sport: there is ecstasy in a good run, a hard swim, cycling up a hill against the wind. The modern reading of that pleasure casts it in the socio-cultural discourses of competitive sport, the building of masculinities, the production of a healthy, economically efficient body and so on. Whereas a postmodern reading allows the experience to stand out from these discourses. Running in high tech shoes, or riding a fast road bike—both prosthetic extensions of the cybernetic body—we can go through the order and rationality of modern athletic experience (created in the technologies of shoes and bicycles) and into the wilderness of Eros. This is a transgression of the modern project of resourcing the body, reasserting it as a being in its own right, while still being complicitous in its socio-cultural construction. The postmodern promise here is dwelling in the modern (our complicity) while seeing through it (our critique). This is the embodied version of Hutcheon's (1989) concept of postmodernity as complicitous critique. The postmodern body is one that experiences itself in a complicitous, yet critical relationship to its resourcefulness for modernity. The postmodern body slips about within the grasp of modernity—it does not escape, but neither is it fixed in the modern project.

The experience of ecstasy (the de-eclipsing of the sacred) doesn't always take the postmodern turn. This is not surprising.given that there is little or no encouragement for such a turn in our physical culture. Certainly, sport does not encourage it. And physical fitness culture is more about the forever unrequited pleasure of consumption, or the instrumentality of the physically active body in the production of economically viable bodies and the shaping of body surfaces along fashionable socio-cultural lines, than it is about the postmodern experience of embodiment as complicitous critique. And seeing through culture is not part of the activity of most (mainstream) physical education programmes. Nor is there yet any evidence of this postmodern turn in the annals of the sociology of sport. It would seem, therefore, that the postmodern turn in sport and (Western) physical education has yet to occur.[11]

I would like to close this chapter with a call for such a turn.[12] If physical education and physical culture are to be positive social forces, they need to aid in the postmodernization of the modern body. Cultural studies that concern themselves primarily if not purely with the body as a text, are in this analysis, quite modern; because these studies see the body and write its politics completely from the differentiated autonomous realm of modern culture's resourceful appropriation of the body. The emerging cultural studies thrust in the study of sport and physical culture should move through its fetishization of culture and the inscribed body (a modern body) and into an embodied complicitous critique of the cultured body. Schools of physical education need to move their curricula out of the modern sport and health paradigms and into the postmodern pleasure paradigm. This means that physical activity needs to play with the pleasure of chaos. This will be an innovative, educational form of erotic play whose anarchic, indeed wild tendencies are both socially/psychically dangerous and full of positive potential—because it brings people to the edge of the existential abyss that lies just beyond the confines of modernity. Rather than buoying socio-cultural discourses and the stability of modern boundary projects, physical education could become a destabilizing socio-cultural force. While this disruptive strategy will not provide an escape from modernity and the modern production of the body, it will at the very least help people see through modernity and explore the possibilities of opening up its boundaries.

Notes

1. See Haraway (1988) on the sensibilities of the coyote, taken from the tradition of the Plains Indians. On postmodernism and irony, see Linda Hutcheon (1989).

2. Lash does not speak of the "socio-cultural"; in fact his "*modus operandi* deals with, and through, eminently modernist distinctions between 'the cultural' on the one hand, and the economic and social on the other" (1990, p. 3). Its modernity aside, this traditional distinction between the cultural and the social strikes me as false in very important ways. If "culture" is seen as the domain of meaning, and "society" as the domain of material and human relations, it seems to me to think of either of them

having separate existences is if not utterly false, then at least analytically useless, except perhaps in the minds of anthropologists (culture) and sociologists (society) who have professional interests in seeing these things as discreet. There are no human relations devoid of meaning; indeed, many would say it is meaning that makes them human. Likewise there is no culture where there are no social/economic relations. To avoid the artificiality of this distinction, I will use the word "socio-cultural."

3. Of course, there are many other ways that sport contributes to the production of gender difference, too numerous to explore in this paper. The list certainly would include the historical development of sport as a predominantly male practice with masculine values and standards, sex-segregated sport, sex-testing in women's high performance sport, differential funding, facilities, and opportunities for women and men, national priority given to winning at international championships, rather than to issues of gender equity.

4. This purity, however, is only ideological. For in actuality, sporting bodies are vastly "contaminated" by both licit and illicit drugs, not to speak of "unnatural" and "unhealthy" training regimens.

5. Their resulting diminished humanity is mourned by modernist sport scholars such as John Hoberman (1992).

6. I will explore these politics briefly later in this paper.

7. Postmodern critics of Habermas—and there are many of them, for example, Jean-Francois Lyotard, Douglas Crimp, Craig Owens, Fredric Jameson, Jean Baudrillard, Edward Said—say that Habermas' hope for consensus is actually a totalitarian desire for unanimity and social control. The important questions that Habermas does not answer are: Who sets the rules of debate, the limits of reason? Who enforces them? What is the cultural specificity of such rules? Who decides when consensus is reached?

8. The following discussion of modern differentiation borrows from Scott Lash's work on the sociology of postmodernism, but departs from that work in a number of important ways. Lash maintains the modernist distinction between the social and the cultural, arguing that differentiation is a cultural phenomenon. I, on the other hand, following Foucault's insights regarding the culturally discursive nature of social power relations, take as my starting point the unity of the social and cultural. Also, Lash's analysis focuses on differentiation and autonomy between cultural spheres (i.e., in Weberian fashion which accounts for differentiation between ethics and natural law, for example). Whereas, I am concerned about the sources of authority, which is to say the nodes of legitimation, for modern society/culture itself. And finally, I am applying the concept of differentiation to the study of the body, specifically the differentiation of the primordial body and the cultural body; whereas Lash makes no mention of the body, whatsoever.

9. For an interesting ontological existential discussion of the separation of the sacred and profane see Hatab (1990, pp. 17–29).

10. Cheryl Cole says that "Sport . . . is most usefully understood as technology in the Foucauldian sense, an ensemble of knowledges and practices that disciplines, conditions, reshapes, and inscribes the body through the terms and needs of a patriarchal, racist capitalism" (1993, p. 86).

11. I am not sure if non-Western activities such as Tai Chi and yoga work with this postmodern potential. But it would be interesting to investigate.

12. A postmodern turn in sport and physical culture studies does not leave behind the important insights of more traditional critical theories (e.g., Gruneau, 1983; Whitson, 1984). Indeed, postmodern analysis follows through on the cultural implications that were raised in conjunction with materialist analyses, bringing insights on the nature of political consciousness more fully to the fore. One of the things postmodernism brings is an appreciation of disenchantment, disenchantment with the Enlightenment belief in human liberation and the possibilities for unified knowledge (see Lyotard, 1984, p. xxiii).

References

Baudrillard, J. (1983). *Simulations* (P. Foss, P. Patton & P. Beitchman, trans.). New York: Semiotext(e).

Birrell, S., & Cole, C. (1990). "Double fault: Rene Richards and the construction and naturalization of difference." *Sociology of Sport Journal*, 7, 1–21.

Bordo, S. (1991). "'Material girl': The effacements of postmodern culture." In L. Goldstein (Ed.), *The female body: Figures, styles and speculation* (pp. 106–130). Ann Arbor, MI: University of Michigan Press.

Cole, C. (1993). "Resisting the canon: Feminist cultural studies, sport and technologies of the body." *Journal of Sport and Social Issues*, 17(2), 77–97.

Connell, R. (1987). *Gender and power: Society, the person and sexual politics.* Cambridge: Polity.

Connell, R.W. (1990). "An iron man: The body and some contradictions of hegemonic masculinity." In M. Messner & D. Sabo (Eds.), *Sport, men and the gender order* (pp. 83–96). Champaign IL: Human Kinetics.

de Lauretis, T. (1986). "Feminist studies/critical studies: Issues, terms, and contexts." In T. de Lauretis (Ed.), *Feminist studies/critical studies* (pp. 1–19). Bloomington, IN: Indiana University Press.

Deleuze, G., & Guattari, F. (1983). *Anti-Oedipus: Capitalism and schizophrenia* (R. Hurley, M. Seem & H.R. Lane, trans.). Minneapolis, MN: University of Minnesota Press.

Derrida, J. (1976). *Of grammatology* (G.C. Spivak, trans.). Baltimore, MD: Johns Hopkins University Press.

Dewar, A. (1990). "Oppression and privilege in physical education: Struggles in the negotiation of gender in a university programme." In D. Kirk & R. Tinning (Eds.), *Physical education, curriculum, and culture: Critical issues in the contemporary crisis* (pp. 67–90). London: Falma.

Donnelly, P. (1988). "Sport as a site for popular resistance." In R. Gruneau (Ed.), *Popular cultures and political practices* (pp. 69–82). Toronto: Garamond.

Ecco, U. (1976). *A theory of semiotics.* Bloomington, IN: Indiana University Press.

Featherstone, M. (1991). "The body in consumer culture." In M. Featherstone, M. Hepworth & B.S. Turner (Eds.), *The body: Social process and cultural theory* (pp. 170–197). London: Sage.

Feher, M. (1989). Introduction. *Zone: Fragments for a history of the body,* 3(1), 11–17.

Foucault, M. (1979). *Discipline and punish: The birth of the prison* (A. Sheridan, trans.). New York: Vintage.

——— (1980). *The history of sexuality* (R. Hurley, trans.). New York: Vintage.

——— (1982). "The subject and power." In H. Dreyfus & P. Rabinow (Eds.), *Michel Foucault: Beyond structuralism and hermeneutics* (pp. 208–226). Chicago: University of Chicago Press.

——— (1985). *The uses of pleasure: The history of sexuality* (R. Hurley, trans.). New York: Vintage.

Greendorfer, S. (1983). "Gender differences in play and sport: A cultural interpretation." In J. Loy (Ed.), *The paradoxes of play* (pp. 198–204). West Point, NY: Leisure Press.

Gruneau, R. (1983). *Class, sports and social development.* Amherst, MA: University of Massachusets Press.

Guttmann, A. (1978). *From ritual to record: The nature of modern sports.* New York: Columbia University Press.

Habermas, J. (1983). "Modernity: An incomplete project." In H. Foster (Ed.), *The anti-aesthetic: Essays on postmodern culture* (pp. 3–15). Port Townsend, WA: Bay Press.

Hall, M.A. (1993). "Gender and sport in the 1990s: Feminism, culture and politics." *Sport Science Review,* 2(1), 48–68.

Haraway, D. (1985). "A manifesto for cyborgs: Science, technology, and socialist-feminism in the 1980s." *Socialist Review,* 80, 65–107.

———— (1988). Situated knowledge: The science question in feminism and the privilege of partial perspective." *Feminist Studies*, 3, 575–99.

Hargreaves, J. (1986). *Sport, power and culture*. Cambridge: Polity.

Hatab, L. (1990). *Myth and philosophy: A contest of truths*. LaSalle, IL: Open Court.

Heidegger, M. (1954). "The question concerning technology." In D.F. Krell (Ed.), *Martin Heidegger: Basic writings* (pp. 283–318). New York: Harper and Rowe.

———— (1962). "Modern science, metaphysics and mathematics." In D.F. Krell (Ed.), *Basic Writings* (pp. 243–282). New York: Harper and Rowe.

Hoberman, J. (1992) *Mortal engines: The science of performance and the dehumanization of sport*. New York: Free Press.

Hutcheon, L. (1989). *The politics of postmodernism*. London: Routledge.

Jackson, E. (1991). "Scandalous subjects: Robert Gluck's embodied narratives." *Differences: A Journal of Feminist Cultural Studies*, 3(2), 112–34.

Jameson, F. (1984). "Postmodernism or the cultural logic of late capitalism." *New Left Review*, 146, 53–92.

Kidd, B. (1987). "Sports and masculinity." In M. Kaufman (Ed.), *Beyond patriarchy: Essays by men on masculinity* (pp. 250–265). Toronto: Oxford University Press.

Kroker, A., & Kroker, M. (1987). "Panic sex in America." In A. Kroker & M. Kroker (Eds.), *Body invaders: Panic sex in America* (pp. 10–19). New York: St. Martin's Press.

Lash, S. (1990). *Sociology of postmodernism*. London: Routledge.

Lenskyj, H. (1986). *Out of bounds. Women, sport and sexuality*. Toronto: Women's Press.

———— (1991). *Women, sport and physical activity: Research and bibliography* (2nd ed.). Ottawa: Government of Canada.

Lyotard, J.-F. (1984). *The postmodern condition: A report on knowledge* (G. Bennington &B. Massumi, trans.). Minneapolis, MN: University of Minnesota Press.

Messner, M. (1992). *Power at play*. Boston: Beacon.

Messner, M., & Sabo, D. (Ed.) (1990). *Sport, men and the gender order: Critical feminist perspectives*. Champaign, IL: Human Kinetics.

Newman, C. (1985). *The post-modern aura: The act of fiction in an age of inflation*. Evanston, IL: Northwestern University Press.

Pediatrics, A.A. (1991). "Human immunodeficiency virus in the athletic setting." *Pediatrics*, 88(3), 640–641.

Pronger, B. (1990). *The arena of masculinity: Sports, homosexuality and the meaning of sex.* New York: St. Martin's Press.

Sabo, D., & Runfola, R. (1980). *Jock: Sports and male identity.* Englewood Cliffs, NJ: Prentice-Hall.

Schulze, L. (1990). "On the muscle." In J. Gaines & C. Herzog (Eds.), *Fabrications: Costume and the female body* (pp. 59–78). New York: Routledge.

Shilling, C. (1993). *The body and social theory.* London: Sage.

Singer, L. (1989). "Bodies-pleasures-power." *differences,* 1, 45–65.

Stafford, B. (1991). *Body criticism: Imaging the unseen in Enlightenment art medicine.* Cambridge, MA: Massachusetts Institute of Technology Press.

Turner, B.S. (1992). *Regulating bodies: Essays in medical sociology.* New York: Routledge.

Vattimo, G. (1988). *The end of modernity: Nihilism and hermeneutics in post-modern culture* (J. Snyder, trans.). Cambridge: Polity.

Whitson, D. (1984). "Sport hegemony: On the construction of the dominant culture." *Sociology of Sport Journal,* 1(1), 64–78.

——— (1990). "Sport in the social construction of masculinity." In M. Messner & D. Sabo (Eds.), *Sport, men, and the gender order: Critical feminist perspectives* (pp. 19–30). Champaign, IL: Human Kinetics.

PART V

PHYSICAL CULTURE, CONSUMER CULTURE, AND POSTMODERN GEOGRAPHY

14

In Search of the Sports Bar: Masculinity, Alcohol, Sports, and the Mediation of Public Space

Lawrence A. Wenner

> Humankind cannot escape the territorial dimension of existence, and cocktail waitresses learn this by firsthand experience. The ebb and flow of social life in every society occurs in the context of place: a cave, an open campsite, a village square, a convent, an adobe house with kitchen and sleeping room, a locker room, a home, an office, a bar. An always we live under the territorial imperative: to give meaning to space, to define the places of our lives, large and small, in cultural terms. (Spradley & Mann, 1976, p. 101)

In this chapter, I search modern and postmodern America for the sports bar. The search will take us to men's places. The tour will be a cultural geography of some of the key places and spaces of men's leisure. It will take us to the neighborhood tavern at the turn of the century. It will take us to the post-World War II corner pub where television is introduced into local community life. It will take us to the place of sports in male identity. It will take us to the progressively public spaces of sports: locker rooms, playing fields, large public stadia. Our last stops will be at sports bars. We will hit one in the local neighborhood and we will hit one out at the mall.

With one hand on this tour, I join Oldenburg's (1989) search for the "great good place." Here we find a world that is sadly "more jangled and fragmented" and an America that modernity has handed a perplexing "problem of place" that "manifests itself in a sorely deficient informal public life" (p. 13). Oldenburg searches for the vanishing "third place," a term he uses to describe the many public places that host "regular, voluntary, informal, and happily anticipated gatherings of individuals" (p. 16) beyond the home (the first place) and work (the second place).

Third places may take many forms—cafes, bars, beauty parlors, main streets. Oldenburg (1989) sees third places functioning in response to industrialization, having virtue in relieving stress and providing identity. They do so, according to his thesis, by providing a home away from home. The third place provides an accessible, socially-level neutral ground to facilitate a playful mood for regulars to engage in their main activity: conversation.

With the other hand, I join in Soja's (1989) search for "postmodern geographies." Here we find skyscrapers, urban renewal, suburban planned communities, highway strips, malls, amusement parks, and hyperkinetic media environments. Here is a commodified schizophrenic world, a bricolage of constructions and juxtapositions begging for interpretation. This is the world of Jean Baudrillard's *America* (1988). This is a world where the social production of space becomes the new frontier.

This part of the tour joins with Michel Foucault (1980) on his project of what might be thought of as the spatialization of history, on what Soja (1989, p. 18) characterizes as the "structuring of a historical geography." In calling for the reassertion of space in critical social theory, Soja builds on Foucault's observation that a history of spaces, "from the great strategies of geopolitics to the little tactics of the habitat" (1980, p. 149), needs to be written because space is essential to all exercises of power.

At first glance, Oldenburg's and Soja's searches would seem to be very dissimilar voyages into the American present tense. However, there are some basic similarities to their gazes. Both recognize that there is a critical dimension to geography, one that is triggered by going beyond the physical to the social, going from "space" to "place" (what Foucault calls "social spaces"). Oldenburg (1989) recognizes that something more than mere "place" is lost when third places disappear from the landscape, and that fueling that "loss" is an inherent shift in cultural sensibilities. In tracing Western Marxism's "spatial turn" to what he calls the "postmodernization of Marxist geography" (1989, p. 64), Soja sees the organization of space as a social product, a "socio-spatial dialectic" (p. 76) that directs spatial realignments as signals of changes in cultural relations.

In this chapter, I consider the physical place and social space of the sports bar in light of both the searches of Oldenburg and Soja. I am reliant on the development of two arguments. First, I will argue that the cultural logic of sports bars functions at the nexus of a high holy trinity of alcohol, sports, and hegemonic masculinity. Second, I will argue that the sports bar is partly modern and partly postmodern, partly the "great good place" and partly a commoditized construction of bricolage on the highway strip or mall.

In assessing how these variant cultural streams come together at the site of the sports bar, it is necessary to consider two pre-existing sets of relations, both of which hinge on the notion of "sexual geography" (Reiter, 1975). First, consideration will be given to the concept of the public drinking place and its relations to gender. Second, consideration will be given to sports—its cultural place as well as its places and spaces—and relations to gender.

These two elements will fuse in a third set of considerations: the sports bar as uniquely "super-gendered" public space and transformation of the sports bar from a modern "third place" into what I will characterize as a postmodern "fourth place" that is at its core "hypermediated." It will be argued that the evolutionary path of the sports bar can be seen as an attempt to seamlessly bridge the modern with the postmodern by constructing a "physical culture museum" (Slowikowski, 1993) filled with "imperialist nostalgia" (Rosaldo, 1989). A closing argument will be made that the power of the postmodern can be seen as the "rupture" of the postmodern sports bar simultaneously leaves traces in the modern sports bar, and that this is archetypal of the hegemony of the postmodern working on the modern.

The Place of Public Drinking and Gender

Masculinity and the Place of Drinking

In beginning to think about public drinking and sports as the two dominant social streams that go into the making of the sports bar, one must consider two striking parallels, both of which contribute to the social functioning of male hegemony. Not only do both public drinking and participation in sports serve as masculine rites of passage, their spaces and places often serve as refuge from women.

For adolescent boys, the first drinking experience is typically "one of the fundamental activities by which a boy is initiated as a man, perhaps because more formal rituals have dwindled" (Lemle & Mishkind, 1989, p. 214). Most importantly, it is commonly a public rite that takes place away from home in the company of peers. And beyond the first drink, a boy's first heavy drinking experience and intoxication frequently occurs outside the home, often within public view, such as in a parking lot, park, or car (Fromme & Sampson, 1983; Harford, 1979; Snow & Cunningham, 1985; Waller & Lorch, 1977).

Male adolescent public place drinking has been characterized as a male bonding rite that helps smooth a perplexing stage in the life cycle, the "threshold" state between boy and man where one is expected to act as a "real man" but finds the "family head" and "provider" roles are as yet inaccessible. As Burns notes:

until attaining that stage in the life cycle, as best he can he and his fellows must participate in whatever masculine activities are open to them to assert themselves as men. This is accomplished by "being rowdy." When young males are together, their conversations are filled with references to street fighting, acting "tough," and "being rowdy"—activities usually involving large amounts of beer. (1980, p. 280)

The young male's public consumption of large quantities of alcohol may be thought of as part of a triad of interrelated activites that demonstrate masculinity. With the companion proofs that "one can hold his liquor" and that one is "generous" by buying rounds of drinks comes fighting as proof of toughness and character and intentionally putting oneself in dangerous situations to prove courageousness (Wilsnack & Wilsnack, 1979).

Beyond alcohol as a rite of male passage, alcohol serves as a larger symbol of masculinity. Public transactions—ordering, being offered, consuming, and sharing alcohol—are seen to enhance one's manliness. Not only do men drink more often than women, they consume more often and in greater quantities with same-sex friends in public places (e.g., bars) and particularly at "male activities" (e.g., sporting events), than do women (Lemle & Mishkind, 1989).

The male ritual of "drinking each other under the table" is rooted in heavy drinking as a symbol of greater masculinity. Operant in the public exercise are men's concerns over how their masculinity is evaluated by other men. As Lemle and Mishkind (1989, p. 214) have commented: "This 'drinking with the boys' has two mutually reinforcing effects: it furthers the male image of alcohol, and it makes the men engaged in the activities seem more manly." So naturalized is alcohol in masculine identity that not "drinking like a man" (i.e., drinking beer or hard liquor, drinking it "straight," not drinking sweetened alcohol, drinking without hesitation and "holding" one's liquor) calls into question one's masculinity.

Public perception of drinking and masculinity lends support to these notions. Men who drink at a higher rate than their peers are considered manly, while those drinking less (or more slowly) risk peer rejection (Bruun, 1959; Burns, 1980). Similarly, drinking more and "getting drunk" is judged as "typical" and even "desirable" for males, but not for females (Orlofsky, Ramsden & Cohen, 1982).

The gendered "social space" of drinking alcohol is different in one final way for men and women. Rubin notes that men often use alcohol as "an inchoate wish to relax some the constraints that bind [men] in their human relationships" (1983, p. 140). Fundamental to the new men's studies has been the problematic of how the "competitive" nature of men's relations with each other has placed an emphasis on the suppression of feelings, particularly those associated with "weakness" such as sorrow or hurt (c.f., Brod, 1987; Fasteau, 1975; Kaufman, 1987; Kimmel, 1987; Kimmel & Messner, 1989).

Alcohol gives men "permission" to "open up" and break the standing verbal and physical limits on expressive displays of empathy, caring, and nurturance (Messner, 1992). Thus, alcohol not only separates the men from the boys but fuels the quintessentially male propensity to voice "I'm really drunk, so I can tell you this."

Masculinity, Sexual Geography, and the Public Places of Drinking

Given the standing relationships between masculinity and the social place of drinking, it is not surprising that public drinking places—German beer gardens, English pubs, French cafés, and American taverns—dominate Oldenburg's (1989) case studies of the "great good place." Oldenburg recognizes that an underlying feature of the "third place" is its sexual segregation. For Oldenburg, most and the best of third places "are the haunts of men or women, but not both" and the "joys of the third place are largely those of same-sex association, and their effect has been to maintain separate men's and women's worlds more than to promote a unisex one" (1989, p. 230).

The power structure of village life could always be seen clearly though its "sexual geography." In studies of the French village, there were two categories of public space in women's domain: shops (i.e., grocery, bakery, and butcher) and the church (Reiter, 1975; Roubin, 1977). Reiter characterizes the shops by their "domain-ance" or relationship to household duties and the church to the dominance of a moral imperative presided over by men (from the local priest to the Pope) but enacted at a place "where no self-respecting man is likely to be seen" (1975, p. 256). Men's places were either work (in the fields) or third places (the town square or cafés) where the links to the first place (the home) or the moral imperative were more tenuous. Men were fond of commenting: "The church is for the women, but we have our own chapel on Sunday mornings—the café" (Reiter, 1975, p. 256).

Similarly, Oldenburg found few "great good places" for women in mid-twentieth century America and these broke with the "hangout" or "do nothing" typal characteristics of the taverns, lodges, and clubs that were men's third places. Even the most sex-segregated hangout for women, the beauty shop, was about getting something done, "getting beautiful" to hold one's place in the social order. Other third places visited by women, general stores and post offices, were far less sex-segregated and related to being "eternally on duty" in the domestic setting. This has lead Oldenburg to conclude that "third places seem to be mainly a male phenomenon" (1989, p. 232). He mourns their passing and the losses (mainly of refuge, but also identity construction) that come with the sexual integration of the public place in contemporary times but has sympathy with the women's voice: "A third place! God! I don't even have a second place!" (p. 230).

It is likely that that the third place character of the public drinking house—as a "man's place" where nothing much got done when much remained to be done at home—added much subconscious fuel to the moral order campaigns against alcohol by the Women's Temperance Movement in the 1800s in America (Banner, 1974). The interaction of the public drinking house and its challenges to the moral order has a long history dating back to the days of the Greek and Romans (c.f., Ade, 1931; Field, 1897; Firebaugh, 1924a, 1924b; Hackwood, 1909). Cavan synthesizes the sentiments of this longstanding moral imperative and its relation to the licensing and regulation of contemporary public drinking places:

> The precarious status attributed to the public drinking community by the law presumably reflects the judgment of the conventional community. Historically, the patterns of behavior taken for granted in such settings as a matter of course have often been viewed not only as the antithesis of the general standards of propriety of polite society, but as destructive to the moral fiber of those engaged in them and ultimately to society as a whole. (1966, pp. 37–38)

Historically, there has been a good deal of cultural ambivalence over the public drinking house (Campbell, 1991). Its virtues as an "unserious behavior setting" (Cavan, 1966, p. 8) where an informal and social "time-out" provide a recreational break from everyday responsibilities have counterbalanced its character as a site for deviance and the manufacture of an "overly permissive" subculture (Pittmann, 1967).

Such ambivalence about drinking and particularly about the "social space" of the public drinking place, allow for the neighborhood tavern at the turn of the century to be characterized as Oldenburg's "great good place," a bastion of (male) sociability idealized much like "Cheers" where "everyone knows your name." Yet, when women were "allowed" in, the moral order called for them to be escorted in the company of men. After all, this was the "outside world," a man's world, a world where strength was needed to "drink like a man" and a "decent" woman needed protection. And thus it was that women who entered the tavern without an escort were cast as morally questionable. Even women who worked "legitimately" at taverns as cocktail waitresses were seen in the shadow of that moral order. Not only were they complicit servants to (and observers of) "boys being boys," but their roles were only a step away from other women's roles (e.g., B-girls and prostitutes) in the sexual geography of the tavern (c.f., Cavan, 1966; Roebuck & Frese, 1976; Spradley & Mann, 1975).

The neighborhood tavern in America was a decidedly modern phenomenon. In early industrial and postfordist times, men felt entitled to a "reward" at the tavern after a long, hard day at the factory. Women were at home and their work day went on long after the factory's whistle had blown. The coming of television—one of many post-war postmodern intrusions into the modernist landscape—was ushered in by sports programming, often boxing and wrestling, that provided low-tech and low-cost ways to fill air time. With television not yet in many homes, this tended to give men one more "natural" reason to visit the third place, and televised sports reinforced the masculine identity of the neighborhood tavern. It is not surprising then how the public drinking place has come to be naturalized as masculine. As such, the neighborhood bar carries a male "territorial imperative":

From the moment a man crosses the threshold into the bar he assumes territorial rights. This is his place, created expressly for men like him. He exudes confidence and ownership. It can be seen in the way he surveys the bar, orders his drinks, or looks over the women. All these belong to men. His presence here announces to everyone that he has come of age; no longer a boy, he can do those things reserved for adult males. And if he has doubts about his masculinity he can come to the bar where the very air seems to reassure him, giving him courage. After all, this is a place for men, evidence enough that all is well. (Spradley & Mann, 1976, p. 106)

The sexual geography of the tavern can be seen along many fronts. One basic area might be taken as a division of labor amongst tavern employees. Men mix drinks, serve customers at the (physical) bar, tend the cash register, and conduct business transactions with vendors. Women service tables, carrying drinks to customers and cash to the bartender. Yet, it may be more accurate to say that what is created is a "division of geography rather than a division of labor" (Spradley & Mann, 1976, p. 32). Observational research suggests that: "With few exceptions, what the females did in one part of the bar, males did in another—taking orders, serving drinks, wiping off table surfaces, receiving tips, cleaning ash trays, visiting with customers" (Spradley & Mann, 1976, p. 32).

This sexual geography mirrors that of the clientele of the public drinking place. Just as the area behind the physical bar is a man's place, the area in front of the physical bar is a man's place. This is true both of the standing area in front of the bar and the seating on stools at the bar. Indeed, many observational studies have found that women, together or alone, tend to avoid the physical bar and head to seating at tables (c.f., Cavan, 1966, Cloyd, 1976; Katovich & Reese, 1987; Spradley & Mann, 1976). This sexual geography is not benign; at taverns, seating at the bar is generally preferred, often indicative of high status as a "regular" or higher status as a friend of the house (Cavan, 1966; Spradley & Mann, 1976). When women are seated at the bar, it is typically in the company of a male escort. This role, called a "ride" (as riding on the coattails), confers little status in the ideoculture of the tavern as compared to any of the variants of the "regular" client type (Katovich & Reese, 1987).

In the world of the tavern, women are infrequently counted among the regulars who use the bar in "third place" fashion as a "home away from home." Similarly, women tend not to populate the categories of "irregular regular" (a regular who doesn't come around much anymore) or "regular irregular" (a frequent customer who doesn't mingle or fit in with the regular group). More frequently, in this status hierarchy, women are "irregulars"— something unnatural in this male preserve (Katovich & Reese, 1987).

One study (Spradley & Mann, 1976) goes even further and suggests that being female and being a "regular" (or a "friend of the house") are contradictory. In the hierarchy of customers in this study, "female customers" comprise a separate category from the other broader category of non-regular customers, "people off the street" (e.g., loners, couples, businessmen, drop-ins, and drunks). At this bar, "female customers" were often characterized as indecisive "dumb bitches" who are cheap, don't tip, and make confused requests for difficult-to-make "girl's drinks." So it is that women come to take the role of "Other" in the sexual geography of the public drinking place. The many parallels of this role to the role of women in sports will be seen in the next section.

The Place of Sports and Gender

Masculinity and the Place of Sports

The socio-spatial dialectic of sports works beside and on top of the public face of drinking as a cultural stream that goes into the making of the sports bar. As is the case with alcohol and public drinking, much of the cultural power of sports is linked to its functioning as a male rite of passage and the role sports spaces and places play as refuge from women. Sports explicitly naturalize "man's place" in the physical. Implicitly, it also appropriates "woman's place" as "other," inherently inferior on the yardstick of the physical, and thus life. These dynamic elements allow sports to play a fundamental role in the construction and maintenance of patriarchy (Kidd, 1987; Sabo, 1985; Messner, 1992; Messner & Sabo, 1990)

Sports as a broad-based male rite of passage is a "modern" phenomenon of early industrial and postfordist times. In earlier eras, sport was in the main a peculiarly male institution, but one that did not cut across social class. Thus, wealthy Greek males were the athletes at Olympia, exploited males became the gladiators in Roman times, and upper class males with leisure time populated the sporting clubs of mid-nineteenth century Britain and America (Coakley, 1990).

As industrialism progressed, there came concerns both over the problematic leisure of the working class and over the "feminizing" of the (male) middle- and upper-middle class work force. With regards to the first concern, the strategy was that sports was supposed to build "character." At the time, this meant building an appreciation and acceptance of the "gentlemanly" and "civil" dominant upper classes, although working class interpretations of sport often exposed the workings of this agenda (Messner, 1992). Ironically, the strategy with regards to the second concern also vested sport with an ideological dimension that was wound around a counterbalancing framing of "desirable" (male) character. Here, a society becoming too "gentlemanly" was judged as problematic to the churnings of modern industrialism:

> With no frontier to conquer, with physical strength becoming less relevant in work, and with urban boys being raised and taught by women, it was feared that males were becoming "soft," that society itself was becoming "feminized." Many men responded to these fears with a defensive insecurity which manifested itself in the creation of new organizations such as the Boy Scouts of America (founded in 1910) as a separate cultural sphere of life where "true manliness" could be instilled in boys by men. The rapid rise and expansion of organized sport during this same era can similarly be interpreted as the creation of a homosocial institution which served to counter men's fears of feminization in the new industrial society. (Messner, 1992, p. 14)

In short, the premise moved quickly beyond the building of men's bodies. If men were to be both the natural leaders and backbone of the postfordist industrial economy, then there would need to be some mechanism by which consent was manufactured between leaders and workers. Sport was one such mechanism. It brought these men together to celebrate their shared manliness and develop strength, competitiveness, efficiency: attributes and beliefs that were "natural" to their differences with women and beneficial to the "greater good" of the economy.

Just as not all males participate in the rite of the first public drink "with the boys," not all boys take in the rite of sports first hand. In many ways the "event" of sports participation that signifies the boy becoming a man varies and is more difficult than the drink to pinpoint. The significant "event" of sport may indeed be an event (e.g., the first officially competitive game in Little League Baseball or Pop Warner Football) but that need not be. In fact, the critical "event" of sport for the boy often comes earlier. It comes at that time when he begins to identify with sport and its values as being "manly";

when he begins to recognize that sport is a "natural" typal characteristic of the adult male. This may commonly come with a significant spectating experience, one that marks the sport's hold on the boy.

The "critical event" of spectating may involve going to the stadium for the "big game," often with one's father or in the larger company of significant elder males. Or this may occur in the domestic setting, where the "big game" transforms the household. Here the boy often witnesses a "territorial invasion." The congregation of men who come together to "do what men do" and watch the "big game" bridges the drawing room relationship of the men's social club with that of "regulars" at the neighborhood tavern. That the household agenda moves easily aside to accomodate men's needs to transform space for such a social event is significant. The lesson marks this decidedly male celebration of male athleticism as dominant.

In that transformation of space, it is important to take note of how the roles of women parallel those of women in the bar subculture. Women may be "regulars," but this is an atypical role, and just as is the case with women regulars at the tavern, women are a special class of regular and are often "protected" by regular men. In the case of the bar, regular men protect women regulars from untoward advances from nonregulars (Katovich & Reese, 1987). In the case of television spectating, men "protect" women and themselves by displaying complex mastery and "insider information." This display serves dual purposes: showing superior knowledge to other men and setting men apart as superior to the women (Duncan & Brummett, 1993).

Beyond regular status, women take on other roles. If women stay in the household during the event, they may be cast as regular irregulars who don't quite fit in. By fleeing to other territories in or out of the home, women may be cast as nonregulars. In the particular instance of taking up territory in the kitchen, women may find themselves "working the tables" as cocktail waitress to the male host who plays the role of bartender.

Although the "critical event" of sport may differ amongst boys, the lessons of sport are common, and these lessons define the social place of sports. These lessons may be seen as the "promises" that sports makes in boyhood to the man (Messner, 1985, 1992). While sports work in a vast array of ways in the construction of male identity, these may be reduced to the interlocking promises that as a male: (a) you are strong, therefore dominant; and thus (b) you are special, therefore superior to women (Whitson, 1990). The first promise is related to sport as male practice, the second to sport as male preserve (Kidd, 1990). The first is keyed to the connection between manliness and the use of the body in "forceful and space-occupying ways" (Connell, 1983). The second is keyed to sport as a segregated site of "male solidarity" where men can "rehearse" their identification with other men (Dunning, 1986; Whitson, 1990).

Like public drinking, public displays of male athleticism function as a larger symbol of masculinity. As will be discussed in the next section, the places of sports not only serve as refuge from women, but they also serve as stages for the performances of men. Just as one does not walk onto stage without rehearsal or a role, there is a set of "fundamentals" (core values) and much practice that go into male role performance in sport. As a result, the first promise of sports to boys is largely a backstage phenomenon, learning fundamentals that will later be applied on stage with equal fervor in sports and life.

Much in a boy's life is seemingly supervised by women. Therefore, because the fundamental lessons of sport are typically taught by men, they may often be taken as more than lessons about sports and as lessons about life. The young boy's ears may perk up because these lessons are important enough to be taught by men. While scrutiny exposes the homily "it's not about sports, it's about life," it may be a tad more accurate to say "it's about the dominant way many men prefer to think about men's lives" (Coakley, 1990).

A central lesson of sports is about male physicality (that is, one's strength and muscles) and how this relates to one's moral stock. Sport helps link the notion that through physicality the male is naturally dominant, with the notion that courage in the face of pain is archtypal of the male. The promise is that physicality and pain will bring gain. This may be the central promise of male sports. It fuels the naturalization and terms of both competition and aggression. Playing through pain means that "real men" naturally use physicality in combination with working through pain to compete, and one bothers with this because one competes only in order to win. Playing aggressively, and even employing one's body (or a sports tool) as a violent weapon, are natural aids that help one be competitive. By learning to play through pain and adversity, one can aggress or take advantage of others who cannot. And in the spectre of sports, those who "cannot" are tainted as "weak" males (Kidd, 1987; Messner, 1992; Nixon, 1992; Whitson, 1990).

Still "weak" males compete and do not call into question the central logics of sports. In the hierarchy of sport, there are lesser classes beneath the weak males who "cannot": those who "will not" and those who "are not." Those males who "will not" compete or as spectators will not acknowledge the value and lessons of sport are cast as "sissies" or "nerds" or "spoiled sports." This "queer" behavior may fuel having their sexuality questioned by marginalizing them as "feminine" (or "less than masculine") and probable homosexuals. With heterosexual identity firmly entrenched in the male patriarchy of sports, there is little room for the "other," whether that other be gay or female. Both of these groups fall into the "are not" category, so inferior by definition that their "feminine" traits deny admittance (Messner, 1992).

Sabo has cast this dynamic between the teachings of sport and fears of femininity as central to male identity:

> Sport teaches males to think that men are better than women. Men learn to avoid what the culture defines as feminine activities or traits. Much of boys' and men's drive to conform to masculine stereotypes, moreover, is fueled not so much by the desire to be manly, but the fear of being seen as unmanly or feminine . . . Finally, because male athletes possess a clear and unequal advantage over women as regards social status and prestige, males learn that "being like a women" can jeopardize their social standing and reputation. For these reasons, male socialization in sport can be said to be just as much an outgrowth of men's flight from feminity as it is an expression of the desire to fulfil the masculine ideal. (1985, p. 4)

The "other" role of girls, women, and anyone else who might be cast as feminine also tends to give the sexual geography of sports places a special character. In the next section, the interaction of sexual segregation, gender identity, and male solidarity will be considered in the framing of sports places as male preserves.

Masculinity, Sexual Geography, and the Places of Sports

The second promise of sport builds on how it has come to be a naturalized refuge from women. The lessons about sport move through a variety of real life places. These places become progressively more public, but remain in what is a fundamentally male preserve. The early stages, in the locker rooms and on the playing fields or courts, are marked by overt sexual segregation with women in absentia. The later stages, played more broadly in large public stadia and in the media, are marked by covert sexual segregation with women as the "other."

The segregation of men and women in sport was no historical accident. By design, modern sport was fashioned as a male entitlement. To keep it so, a moral imperative was invoked to naturalize a state of affairs that kept women out of sport. This went well beyond merely discouraging girls and women from participating in sport by handing them inferior facilities and resources or deriding their efforts. Here, the moral imperative was fueled by science. "Scientific" arguments of physicians and physical educators backed the position that women who engaged in athletic activity would be harmed, and thereby harm society. Not only would women undermine their own delicate health, but larger social damage would be inflicted if they "used up" precious energy needed for reproduction. These prejudicial beliefs were widely held and contributed, along with other economic and social conditions, to the exclusion of girls and women from sport (Kidd, 1987).

The legacy of this logic can be seen today. Indeed, participation and opportunities in sports have increased for girls and women with recognition of health and other developmental benefits. However, this has come about largely by changes in law, and more importantly, litigious action rather than by any "open-armed" acceptance by the male sporting establishment to offer equal opportunities and resources to girls and women in sport. The situation remains today that sport is a "right" for men, and a "privilege" for women (Loppiano, 1992).

Much of the efforts for "equity" have aimed at developing comparable programs for girls and women. This maintains a division of labor that, much like that in the neighborhood tavern, might be better seen as a division of geographical space. Integrated girl-boy sport, when and where it exists at all, tends to stop in anticipation of puberty. At this juncture, continued sport participation develops the "man," and raises questions for the girl. When girls have "special" (i.e., male level) talents, they are "allowed" on the boys' team. The sexual geography of sport is largely maintained. As Kidd points out, the effects of this relate directly to the workings of power and dominance:

> The effect of sports is also to perpetuate patriarchy by reinforcing the sexual division of labor. By giving males exciting opportunities, preaching that the qualities they learn from them are "masculine," and preventing girls and women from learning in the same situations, sports confirm the prejudice that males are a breed apart. By encouraging us to spend our most creative and engrossing moments as children and our favorite forms of recreation as adults in the company of other males, they condition us to trust each other much more than women. By publicly celebrating the dramatic achievements of the best males, while marginalizing females as cheerleaders and spectators, they validate the male claim to the most important positions in society. (1987, p. 255)

These effects may be traced to the socio-spatial dialectic of sports. The segregated sexual geography of sports places facilitates a larger social logic that is readily imported to the sports bar as a public space.

A basic "rehearsal" hall for sport may be found in its locker rooms and dugouts. The locker room, by its very definition, is a sexually segregated place. Thus, even the regulated presence of women reporters in the locker rooms of male elite sport becomes highly controversial. In youth sport, the locker room is a "dressing" area and the private place where boys receive inspirational talks about how they must show they are "real men" in the game. The "preparation" aims to turn slogans into reality. These slogans may be told, but are often posted as maxim or official ideology. These slogans focus the central goals of sport: aggressiveness and winning, mental and physical fitness, hard work, discipline, and subordination of self to the team (Snyder, 1972). Commonly voiced are aphorisms such as:

- Winning is not everything, it is the only thing.
- Defeat is worse than death because you have to live with defeat.
- No one ever learns anything by losing.
- A quitter never wins, a winner never quits.
- When they are drowning, throw them an anchor.
- You're as good as you want to be.
- The harder I work, the luckier I get.
- When you're through improving, you're through.
- If you can't put out, get out.
- Live by the code or get out.
- The way you live is the way you play.
- There is no I in team.

What the focus on slogans such as this misses is that these goals must be framed in reference to something that the ideal athlete is not. Often that something is women.

In a study of the locker room discourse of "big-time" intercollegiate male athletes in a contact sport, Curry (1991) suggests that the relating of talk in the areas of competition and women may be seen as situational, a product of the locker room. Talk about competition was hostile, sarcastic, and offensive. Athletes used it to provide distance from others with whom they were competing on the team or on an opposing team, and enhance their status as better, read less feminine. Second, talk about competition was demonstrative of the emotional control needed to be a successful athlete, and much of this focused on overcoming the adversities of pain so as not to be construed as feminine. Talk more directly about women and sexuality focused on conquest stories that positioned women as objects. Here the talk was aggressive and hostile toward women; talk that promoted rape culture. All of this aggressive talk aimed at defining "real men" by what they were not—women and homosexuals. Athletes' talk expressed dislike for femaleness and homosexuality. Mockery of stereotyped gay behavior helped athletes distance themselves from such categorization, helping them to establish more firmly a traditional male identity. Evidence shows that such talk does not wait until interecollegiate levels to show its head. Pre-pubescent boys in Little League Baseball are as active in expressing sexist, racist, and homophobic attitudes through their talk and jokes (Fine, 1987).

Experiences in the locker room and dugout prepare the athlete for the more public stage of the playing field or court. Here the male learns that his performances, not just on the playing field but in life, are open for judgment by the "crowd" (Messner, 1985, 1992). On display is one's competitiveness; at issue is one's ability to win; and at risk is one's masculinity. The downside of the risk may come with poor performance, something that is often synonymous with failing to win. The upside of the risk comes with winning and the adoration of the the crowd. While that crowd is diverse, what the boy learns is that his performance is most carefully being judged by other significant males on the central criteria of manliness. One of the central lessons of the playing field is that the boy's rightful place is on public display, and the performance must yield results. And winning once is not enough. To keep one's masculinity intact, one must keep winning. On the playing field, in front of the crowd, the lesson teaches that you're only as good as your last game. Thus, the playing field as a place helps construct the masculine trait of conditional self-worth (Messner, 1992).

As the level of play goes higher, there is no familiar crowd in the bleachers. The place of sport moves to the public stadium. The largest of public stadia are usually the largest structures in a community. The physical space that they demand is huge. There is parking and seating for 50,000 to 100,000 people. The amount of community resources and contributions that go into the building of such stadia run into the hundreds of millions of dollars, dwarfing almost any other development or priority in society. Kidd's comments about the development of the Toronto SkyDome suggest that cultural workings behind such public stadia are often seamless, but the effects on male identity are considerable:

The architect calls it "a secular cathedral." I suggest it be called the Men's Cultural Center. . . . Its primary tenants will be . . . the Blue Jays and the Argonauts, which stage male team games for largely male audiences. The other major beneficiaries will be . . . corporations, which sell the predominantly male audiences to . . . advertisers. . . . At the ideological level . . . it will celebrate male privilege, displaying male prowess while leaving the gendered nature of sport unchallenged. . . . Women . . . will be either rendered invisible or exploited as sex objects (cheerleaders) along the sidelines. Males who identify with the athletes on the field are also basking in the privilege that sports bring them and in the "symbolic annihilation" of women. . . . The stadium will even look like a Men's Cultural Center. Standing at the foot of the world's tallest free-standing telecommunications tower, it will be a gigantic Klaes Oldenberg-like sculpture of the male genitals. (1987, p. 256)

The SkyDome is not unique in this regard. The entrance to Texas Ranger Stadium frames the baseball experience with an imposingly tall "phalogenic" likeness of the folk hero pitcher Nolan Ryan as the "official greeter" (Trujillo, 1991). These symbols help us see the larger notion of "phallocentric" sculpted space and how it is archtypal of sport's masculine imprint on cultural life. It is important to recognize that this space is not casually constructed. It may be seen at almost every turn of the public stadium "experience." The stadium experience may be seen as a carefully manufactured "physical culture museum." It is a shrine where the items on display, from the players to the souvenirs to the cheerleaders to the "cutie" shots on humongous "Diamondvision" screens, speak to a naturalized set of relations that celebrate the male as dominant.

The most public stage for this male physical culture performance is in the museum of media. As a series of studies shows, women are nearly invisible in this museum (Duncan, 1993). On television news, women receive only 5% of the sports coverage. When seen, women in televised sports coverage are marked as "other." First, a "man-as-the-measure-of-all-things" norm prevails, seen by the "nomination" of women's basketball and "ex-nomination" of the men's game merely as "basketball" or the competition. Second, while coverage of men's athletics tends to focus almost exclusively on athletic abilities, women athletes are "others" who are fawned over for their beauty, "feminine" attributes, and romantic developments.

Given the stacking of the social deck of the place of sports and the sexual geography of its places, it is not surprising that the spectating of sports on these various stages is a special experience for the male. Perhaps because it is so fundamentally male, sports, like drinking, gives men "permission" to "open up." As Fasteau observed:

> Sports is one of few things men feel they are allowed to become emotional about. Sitting in a bar, grunting, groaning, elbowing each other in the ribs and exclaiming over the ebb and flow of a football game on the owner's TV is the closest a lot of men come to sharing strong feelings with another man. (1976, p. 110)

Made long before the sports bar was a "concept," this comment taps the intersection of drinking and sports as important in the construction of male identity and elemental to male hegemony Alcohol and sports are such a successful mixture that they have naturalized what might be taken as a cultural irony, a juxtaposition of imbibing and athletic performance (Wenner, 1991). The constructed mixture fuels many sport venues, from tailgating parties in stadia parking lots, to the concession stands at games, to the sponsorship of sports events and televised sports. The next section looks at the site of one such construction, the sports bar, and explores its socio-spatial dynamic as public space.

The Sports Bar

Toward a Definition

The sports bar brings together the cultural streams of drinking and sports at a place. But what is the nature of that place? On a basic level, the sports bar is a public drinking place. On another, sitting at the intersection of drinking and sports, it is masculine. But is it sexually segregated as "great good places" are prone to be? Is it a third place? Or is it no place, somewhere on the postmodern geographical horizon? How does its mediation relate to its sense of place? Is its use of media a modernist retrofit? Or is it an exercise in postmodern hyperreality as motif?

One thing is clear, the sports bar concept is hot. At least the trade publications that surf the conceptual merchandising waves think so. *Restaurant Hospitality, Nation's Restaurant News,* and *Top Shelf: Barkeeping at Its Best* see the sports bar as a recession proof replacement for the neighborhood tavern that is rich with promotional opportunities (Keegan, 1990; Lyke, 1990; "Sports Triumph," 1991). The recipe is fairly simple: start with a large and well located place, seed it with beer, sports, and television, stir with nostalgia, then add activities for a young sporting crowd. On the surface of it, the concept appears merely derivative of the television set tuned to a game in the corner of a neighborhood tavern. But the differences in the new concept are more than those that would come about through lineal descendance. This can be seen by looking at neighborhood taverns that have been "retrofitted" as local sports bars. These retain a local identity, with local owner/managers, with allegiance to local teams, and most importantly "regulars." The new concept sports bar is a new genre, a "hyperreal" hybrid with family background that does not quite allow it to fit into the categories of public drinking places that have come before it.

There are two main typologies of public drinking places, both useful in assessing the nature of the local and new genre sports bar. The first typology is based primarily on geographic location, but also considers the physical structure, type of clientele, and social function of the tavern. Here there are five types: cocktail lounges (and downtown bars), drink-and-dine taverns, nightclubs (and roadhouses), skid row taverns, and the most numerous neighborhood taverns (Campbell, 1991; Clinard, 1962; Macrory, 1952).

Cocktail lounges are usually centrally located in business districts (often downtown) or shopping centers. They offer higher priced liquor, limited food and modest entertainment (television, jukebox, games) to diverse, but transient, white collar patrons who use the bar for convenience and to transact business in late afternoon and early evening peak hours. The dine-and-drink tavern is located in central districts or often along commuting paths near city limits. Here a wider menu of fine food is the draw for convenient business transactions at lunch or dinner, although music is sometimes featured through the long dinner hours. Because nightclubs exist primarily to present "shows," they situate either in entertainment districts or as roadhouses along a main highway. With the "show" as primary focus, nightclubs are organized differently. Patrons may enter only at specific times before shows and are escorted to tables, while often there is only a service bar with no physical bar for seating. Tickets provide revenues, "minimums" are enforced on drinks, food is limited, and the clientele is generally "respectable." In contrast, the more "notorious" skid row tavern located on city center side streets provides little entertainment apart from cheap drinks and "dealings" (of gambling, drugs, sex, and stolen merchandise) to a "down on their luck" local clientele of male regulars (Campbell, 1991; Clinard, 1962; Macrory, 1952; Roebuck & Frese, 1976).

Finally, there is the neighborhood tavern that is archtypal of Oldenburg's great good place. Situated in a residential district, the neighborhood tavern serves primarily locals, some of which form a hard core of regulars who use the place as a "home away from home." Often located on a side street like the home, it is a "basic" place. The physical space is simple—a long bar along one side, some tables, and perhaps a back room and some games. It features a local proprietor, regular bartender and help, low cost liquor, and a limited menu (often only packaged food). Its main attraction is a friendly, homogeneous, cohesive social culture, often formed along the lines of ascribed characteristics of race, ethnicity, sexual preference, country of origin, language, or occupation. However, achieved subcultures, such as those formed around interests in sports, politics, gambling, or literature, can also bring a cohesiveness to the character of the tavern (Campbell, 1991).

Overlapping with geographic locale, a second typology—convenience bar, nightspot, marketplace bar, and home territory bar—focuses on the primary uses to which the tavern is put. Thus, some cocktail lounges, drink-and-dines, skid row bars, and neighborhood bars may be convenience bars, used primarily because they are around the corner or on the way home. Similarly, cocktail lounges or drink-and-dines used primarily for business transactions or as a "meat market" would qualify as marketplace bars. Home territory bars are most likely neighborhood bars, being put to use by a special group who "claim" the place as the base of its mostly social operation. Home territory bars are "third places." While the home group usually adopts the neighborhood bar, cocktail lounges, drink-and-dines, and skid row bars may also be adopted as a home base. The night spot, because its primary use is for entertainment, is largely synonymous with the nightclub/roadhouse category in the first typology (Cavan, 1966).

While local and new genre sports bars share an identity as "men's cultural centers," sucking at the core of male hegemony, the two typologies provide a way to see that their social geographies are fundamentally different. Yet, what is striking is that there is much surface similarity to their decors. They share multi-satellite driven television sets, pictures of sports stars and sport paraphernalia that line the walls and hang from the rafters, sporting games, and of course, alcohol. Certainly all these say "this is a man's place." But, when the typologies are added to the vantage points of Oldenburg and Soja, a fundamental "rupture" between the two places can be seen.

The Modern Sports Bar

I suspect that Oldenburg (1989) would be very comfortable in visiting the local sports bar. The two local taverns I observed for this study suggest this is the case. By collapsing the social geographies of these places, a profile of the local sports bar emerges. The local sports bar is located in a place, a neighborhood where people live, work, or regularly congregate for leisure. When regulars walk through the door they are greeted by the owner or a long-time bartender. The cocktail waitress inquires about recent health developments or how someone in the family is doing. Their regular drink shows up without any formal placement of an order.

The regular is far more likely to be a man than a woman. When women come to the local sports bar, they often come as "rides." During everyday "non big-event" times women are not a large presence, constituting perhaps 10 to 15% of the clientele. More women show up for "big games," but still it is unlikely that more than 20% of the patrons are female. At these peak times, two or three women sometimes "ride" with one man. And often larger groups of women come together. At any time, women are unlikely to come alone. Men often come alone, intentionally meeting a pal, or with the expectation of finding a familiar face or accomodating ear.

The geography is fundamentally that of the neighborhood bar. The physical plant is much of what always was. A long bar, seemingly an original installation, sits in a familiar place along one wall. Beat-up stools line the physical bar. A worn checkers set and a deck of cards sit in their place at one end of the bar. Tables with mismatched chairs populate the milling areas and the outer rooms. Trophies and pictures honoring the regulars who play on the "home" team are on prominent display. The walls are plastered with photos of local sports heroes, many of them signed, wishing the best to the owner. A television set sits in a familiar place in a corner high above the more interior end of the bar. The only thing different is that televised sport has invaded this environment in excess. That one television set in the corner has a lot of technological company.

The local sports bar distinguishes itself by its going beyond its main identity to demonstrate self-reflexiveness in calling attention to its sporting identity "beyond the hyphen." Thus, we have Red's Place: A Sports Bar, The Watering Hole: A Sports Place, or O'Shaunnessey's: Home of the 49er Club. The local sports bar is somebody's place or at least "some place" before it is a sports bar. Yet sport as a mediated decor shapes the identity of that person's place. But the "decorator" is a "do-it-your-selfer" and not a pro. The best analogy to the decor of the local sports bar might be the bedroom of an athlete in boyhood. Posters and pictures of favorites from local teams cover the walls of the room. Souvenirs and found objects are on display, but there is no showcase. The souvenirs are personal: signed balls, photos with the boy gleeming next to his favorite player, hand-me-downs from other men in the boy's family. The boy's own trophies may be added to the mix. In total, the sports decor is uneven, happenstance, and chaotic, and this could easily be mistaken for bricolage. But the room is a story of the boy. It is his room. It is his construction. It is his place.

Similarly, the local sports bar is someone's room. For it to be a "third place" is has to be "some place." To be "home territory" it must have some character of the home. And while the local sports bar is not the bedroom of the boy, it is more public extension of that private place. Thus, one might consider it a living room, or even a "family" or "recreation" room that was added in remodeling. But these are rooms of domestic living. The local sports bar is not a domesticated place. The local sports bar carries the sensibilities of one of man's few remaining places in the home, the place where much "do-it-yourself" home remodeling work is done: the garage workshop. The garage workshop is an "unfinished" place, where "real men" do "real work," except of course when they sit around and shoot the breeze with "the boys."

The mediated photo blitz on the walls of the local sports bar blends the aesthetic of boy's room with the garage workshop. The media montage is not so much decoration as it is a coat of paint or wallpaper. It covers the same walls of the same contours that formed the neighborhood tavern. The new "wallpaper" reflects the same ambivalence about women and gender identity seen in studies of public drinking places and sports places. Images of "real men," real heroes, local heroes, those "like us" are juxtaposed next to those who are "not like us." And those who are not like us are women.

Less than 5 percent of the local sports bar photo "wallpaper" featured women. The male images were largely local athletic heroes engaged in sports action, newspaper headlines of things that actually happened "here" and to "our people." Most of the women on the walls were not athletes. An archtypal montage featured a history of *Sport Illustrated's Swim Suit Issue* covers. Posters for movies featured women stars, like Rachel Welsh or Bo Derek, and mixed in traditional ideals of feminine beauty along the largely local male hero landscape. The few women athletes featured could be seen on the back room walls. These pictured champion figure skaters and gymnasts, sports most often typed as feminine. Just as is the case with media treatment of women, these walls cast women as invisible or "other," as objects of no challenge to male hegemony.

To the mediated wallpaper, 10 or so television sets are added to pre-existing room arrangements. Furniture is not rearranged (at least not much) to see the new sets, rather televisions are arranged to be visible from old comfortable spaces. Two or three sets are within easy view of most places. Sitting at the physical bar, the center of the regular man's base of operation, one may view as many as five sets, sometimes tuned to as many as five games. The regulars who are serious drinkers sit at the far corner of the bar near the original television set, drinking and making friendly wagers. The sociable regulars sit at the opposite corner of the bar near the entrance, rolling dice or playing cards, chatting with bartender and cocktail waitress, and greeting other regulars as they enter. Regular men regularly put in requests to change channels. Irregular men and women do not. And only regular men get to "borrow" the remote control from management, using the "ultimate power tool" to control what game to watch.

There is a large rear screen television set hoisted up on a stage in the back room. This is where women congregate. This is where men pass through on their way to men's places away from the bar: the pool table, the basketball challenge game, the dart board, the men's restroom. Men sometimes sit with women or groups of women in the back room. And sometimes "irregular" men sit there as well, commenting about sports across tables to other men, and attempting small talk with women.

When regular men (or irregular regulars) come with women to the local sports bar, they sit at bar height tables along the wall opposite the physical bar. These men traverse the milling areas behind the physical bar to visit with the hard core regulars in their rightful places (without women). The women stay at the tables, generally avoiding the physical bar. Occasionally a regular irregular comes in alone, or even with a woman companion, and sits at the physical bar for a short drink or two. The regular irregular does not mix in amongst the regular regulars and is more task oriented and less sociable.

On the very rare occasions that women sit at the physical bar, they do so in larger groups, often of five or more. These younger women are irregu-lars, who tend to be unaware of the geographical norms of the local sports bar. They show up only when a "big game" is on, and they are adorned in sports clothing that identifies them as fans of the home team (Wenner, 1990). The women bar sitters hold tight, watching the home team game until the end, but watch as much for others who never arrive. When they are gone, they are gone. When they leave, some regulars huddle together to reclaim the territory with a wisecrack or two about conversations overheard from these women.

All of these workings of the local sports bar cast it as a modern place. To be sure, at this point, it is a transition institution. The changes of the neighborhood tavern into the contemporary local sports bar may be seen in terms of an evolving response to modernity. The local sports bar is a "retrofit," a remodel, a new coat of paint on the turn of the century tavern that functioned as a man's "third place," a place man visited in part as a response to industrialization. In the later stages of post-Fordist industrialization, with the rise of the suburb and television, the tavern as masculine public space evolved. With television, it went from modernist response to the integration of technology into that response. Some neighborhood taverns responded further. They added more televisions tuned exclusively to male sports as a coat of new paint. As Oldenburg (1989) has explained, the classic male "third place" was dying. Suburbia played a role. Time to do nothing disappeared. Women entered the workforce. With increased outside responsibilities, spouses started seeing less of each other and began to make time to spend together. Combined with increased mobility, spouses became best friends, replacing same sex friends. In such a climate, one way for a male "third place" to survive would be to add a level of masculinity. While the neighborhood tavern as third place offered one level of male identity and sports offered another, the local sports bar was "hegemonic masculinity squared." As such, it offered one survival path for traditional masculinity. It offered one more response to modernity for males, a way to play masculine myths out on a last hybrid frontier of alcohol and sports.

On the surface, the new genre sports bar looks like a continuation of that response to modernity. However, upon closer examination, a rupture of spatiality has occurred and with it has come an essential change in sexual geography. While a visit to the local sports bar may be characterized as a last gasp celebration of the remaining possibilities of being a "real man," the new genre sports bar is a visit to a physical culture museum where the authenticity of being a "real man" is a construction of the past.

The Postmodern Sports Bar

If the local sports bar is an evolved neighborhood tavern that serves as home territory for regulars, the new genre sports bar is a hybrid. In those I studied first hand and through trade press characterization, its permutations suggest something that is part drink-and-dine tavern, part cocktail lounge, and part night club. However, it is really something different than the sum of these parts. More clearly, it is a marketplace bar, and more than a marketplace for either business or sex, it is a marketplace for the consumption of cultural performance. If the local sports bar was low concept, merely being the extension of the television set in the corner at one end of the bar, the new genre sports bar is a high-concept theme park. If Oldenburg (1989) would have been at home visiting the local sports bar, he would have rejected the new genre sports bar out of hand. And it is hard to say just what exactly would have bothered him the most.

While the local sports bar is a place to go talk to friends, have a drink, and catch part of a game, the new genre sports bar is designed as an "experience" as opposed to a real place. If the local sports bar is "retrofitted" in response to advancing modernity, the new genre sports bar is "new construction" built on the foundation of the postmodern. Here we have Bleachers, "Philly's real sports bar," a 20,000-square-foot place where

> customers can sit and watch one of 56 television sets, dance inside a hockey-rink dance floor that's surrounded by 92 speakers, or play one of 15 sports-video games, six pool tables, four mini basketball games, four dart boards, two skeeball games, a golf driving range, shuffle board, football toss, or test their jumpshot on a half-court basketball setup. (Lyke, 1990, p. 122)

On weekends, with a cover charge, Bleachers turns into something closer to a nightclub, although one that has many shows. It is a "scene," almost psychedelic, but set in the climate of sports. There is music, dancing, lighting, live sports competitions on stages throughout the "arena," vendors parading the floor "hawking" stadium food and ice cold beer, action occurring on every imaginable scale and plane. Not surprisingly, few customers are watching the games being broadcast on the many sets.

Another 20,000-square-foot "happening" is the Pittsburgh Sports Garden. The Garden does $5 million a year in sales at its entertainment complex comprising 40 television screens, video games, pinball, air hockey, basketball, pool, darts, three bars, food service for over 300 people, and an overall capacity for 1,800 people. A regulation boxing ring doubles as a dance floor, and the bleachers that surround it allows viewing of people who belt it out to either tune. The bars are not just bars. One is a nostagic brick "replica" of the wall at Pittsburgh's yesteryear baseball stadium. Another is a representation of the "end zone" at the local football stadium. Significantly, there is an "owner's box" that allows the proprietor and celebrity VIPs to view the action far from the madding crowd ("Sports Triumph," 1991).

The sport as theme park concept seems to be working. People apparently like playing out sports fantasies on a stage in front of others, and to watch such cultural performances. People are knocking down the doors to get in. There is a cover charge everyday, and a larger one on the weekends. Some 17 percent of the Garden's sales come from these entry tariffs. The clientele

is young, upscale and college educated. And it is not just men coming to a
men's place to play men's games. The key to the new genre success seems
to be related to the appeal it has to women. Some 43 percent of the Garden's
customers are women. This key difference hints at the rupture of these sports
palaces from the local sports bar ("Sports Triumph," 1991).

Some basic elements of sexual geography go a long way in explaining
how the postmodern sports bar has more appeal to women. It works on the
following apparent contradiction: the postmodern sports bar is and is not a
man's place. There are a number of constituent elements in understanding
this. First, the local sports bar is someone's place. Sports is "beyond the
hyphen," a secondary element in reference to the primary one that defined the
local sports bar as being some man's place. The postmodern sports bar is
"nobody's place." Beyond the Bleachers and the Sports Garden, names of
these postmodern places are Champions, Challenges, The Ballpark, The Bottom
of the Ninth, Sports City Cafe, The Sporting Club, and All Stars American
Sports Bar.

In their largesse, these places transcend the plausibility of being owned
by "somebody." In losing plausibility of the merely mortal, we move from a
man's place to the denuded corporatized constructed environment. The scale
and nature of the physical space of the postmodern sports bar reinforces this.
The basic physical box is just that, a box. Some postmodern sports bars, like
Bleachers or the Sports Garden, are gutted warehouses. Their transformation
signifies the coming of the postmodern. These places move from the storage
of the products of industrialization to empty spaces where industrialization
has died—to new sites for the production of commercialized culture. Even
when placed in the alternate site of the mall or highway strip development,
the postmodern sports bar speaks to the empty spaces of industrialization and
just as importantly, to the new cultural economy. The product in store is a
cultural bin of simulations, a bunch of "important real things" that are put
together for us to deconstruct by a helpful corporate sponsor.

In the constructed environment, the vastly "superior" array of souvenirs
and memorabilia goes well beyond those found and dear-to-the-heart objects
seen in the more modest collection at the local sports bar. What we have
instead of "do-it-yourself" decor in a man's house are objects of art managed
by the curator of a corporate physical culture museum. As a report on Champions founder Michael O'Harro noted:

> O'Harro is emphatic about what goes on the walls and other display
> areas of Champions. "We don't put up decorations in our bars, we put
> up original sports memorabilia," he says. O'Harro and staff make weekly
> purchases of collectibles that now fill two warehouses and manage to
> keep a framer busy full-time. (Keegan, 1990, p. 126)

The sheer tonnage and the lack of personal affinity with this memorabilia marks it much differently than the personalized or found objects that line the personal space of the local sports bar owner. And the collection strategy reinforces this. The postmodern sports bar does not seek to simulate the "authenticity" of a local place. Designed as much for "out-of-towners" to catch the game and for the realization that fewer and fewer people live in the places they were from, the postmodern sports bar offers memorabilia "in the generic." A wide net is cast so that there is some identity hook for everyone, no matter their favorite team, level of fanship, or geographic past (Keegan, 1990; Lyke, 1990).

This distancing from the "authentic" and the "something for everyone" pluralism of the postmodern sports bar defines a rupture point between it and the local sports bar. The local sports bar brings together two homosocial cultures as its site. It marries drinking place culture with "ownership" of sports culture. Men who drink and men who play, and have played sports, are "like us." The postmodern sports bar is a heterosocial culture, one that transcends both place and "authentic" identity with regards to sports. Here sport moves beyond "men's place" to a "heterotopia" of consumer culture. As Foucault has explained:

> The heterotopia is capable of juxtaposing in a single real place several spaces, several sites that are in themselves incompatible . . . they have a function in relation to all the space that remains. This function unfolds between two extreme poles. Either their role is to create a space of illusion that exposes every real space, all the sites inside of which human life is partitioned, as still more illusory . . . Or else, on the contrary, their role is to create a space that is other, another real space, as perfect, as meticulous, as well arranged as our is messy, ill constructed, and jumbled. The latter type would be the heterotopia, not of illusion, but of compensation . . . (1986, pp. 25, 27)

The postmodern sports bar serves both functions of the heterotopia in relation to the local sports bar. First, it exposes the hegemony of masculine sports culture by self-consciously reordering and reappropriating its artifacts. Second, the rearrangement of these artifacts in the multi-media setting of the postmodern sports bar is perceived as a more meticulous, perfect space than that created by the "do-it-yourselfer" down at the local sports bar.

As heterotopic, these physical culture museums scattered across the landscape suggest the infinitely reproduceable and interchangeable nature of these collections. Still even though their objects are moved from warehouse to the stages of the postmodern sports bar, these are simulations of personalized objects and simulations of "real men's" games. It is a "designer" multi-media mix symbolic of the best that the hegemony of male sports has wrought. "Important" uniforms, equipment, trading cards, banners, press coverage of championships being won, and other such cultural artifacts are all in the collection. The collection marks a time in the past when "men were men," when heroes were "authentic." The juxtaposition of this particular physical culture museum collection next to perpetual playing of corporatized sport by "spoiled" players who "play for money" as opposed to the "love of the game" works against the present day authenticity of the ideology of the items in the museum.

As a result, the nostalgic affinities that the postmodern sports bar attempts to build are based on "imperialist nostalgia" (Rosaldo, 1989). As Slowikowski has explained: "Imperialist nostalgia is a yearning for a past that no longer exists or never existed; a yearning for something destroyed by the very ones nostalgically musing for that destroyed" (1993, pp. 27–28). Thus, the physical culture museum housed in the postmodern sports bar may be seen as a nostalgic assault on the underpinnings of the masculine hegemony of sports. As a museum, it is a monument to a past, one that no longer exists. It offers an experience that does not require personal experiences and the masculine history of a sporting identity, it merely requires a spectator identity. Just as appreciating a military shrine does not require a stint in the military, the postmodern sports bar minimizes the past of the spectator.

Heterogeneous populations visit museums, but will avoid a first hand tour of homogeneous subcultures that may dominate or threaten them. If the postmodern sports bar is a museum, the local sports bar combines the homosocial subcultures of the neighborhood tavern and the men's locker room. Museums provide signs and guided tours in a socially sanctioned sanitary environment. Thus, it is that essential character of the new genre sports bar as a postmodern museum that breaks down the hold of masculine hegemony on sports, and allows ease of entrance for women.

As heterotopia, the postmodern sports bar not only exposes the local sports bar through the reappropriation of nostalgia but through the creation of a more meticulous, constructed, more "perfect" sexual geography. If the local sports bar is a "basic" place with worn furniture, the postmodern sports bar is an extention of domesticated mall design. The space is airy, bright, lively, clean, and smells good. This is no men's locker room or garage workshop. When you enter, you do not enter a "do-it-yourself" remodel, you enter the designer model in the new suburban development.

Space here, if not gender neutral, is more user friendly to the woman. The bar may be a good case in point. Largely gone from the postmodern construction is the long physical bar located along one wall. In replacement for this "penile extender" (Fiske, 1987) is the more vulvic, vaginal bar "in-the-round." Bars now are like big tables, with a rectangular perimeter of bar running around a "wet area" in the middle that is serviced by bartenders. The new bar has four "corners" instead of two, and the more "perfect" arrangement allows a wider range of spectating and social opportunities.

In contrast to the local sports bar, the sexual geography of "servicing" the postmodern sports bar is much more equal. Both men and women serve the outlying crowd. Both men and women wait tables and serve food and drinks. While still uncommon, women do occasionally tend bar. Men do occasionally just deliver drinks. Gender diversity in staffing facilitates women "having the run" of the postmodern sports bar, without fear of invading the space of "regular" men. Space is used as it is at an amusement park. You wait your time in line, and then you can take the ride. And just as some rides at the amusement park may be gender typed, certain activities may be favored by men and women. Gendered consequences do not go away. Thus, at the postmodern sports bar, women may sit at the bar without reproach, although "approach" remains very much a part of the gendered script. Yet, there is no "back room" that is appropriate for women, while at the same time being a place that "regulars" avoid.

Concluding Comments

The postmodern sports bar exposes the dual male hegemonies of alcohol and sport by forming a physical culture museum that is a "more perfect union" for commodified contemporary times. Perhaps as a consequence of being "out in the world" more, women are both drinking more and participating in sport more. As a result, the postmodern sports bar is archtypal of what I will call "the fourth place," a new kind of public place that caters to a changed set of gender relations. The fourth place is a corporately produced public space that contains the past in a museum and reappropriates nostalgia into a new landscape of power (Zukin, 1991). The new landscape is not so much politically correct as it is a heterotopia that is "perfect" only in its goodness of fit to maximizing the market. Male hegemony does not go away, it is merely transformed by its reframing.

Such a strategy marks the rupture between the modern and postmodern sports bar. What at first appears as continuity of logic, as mere extension of largesse, is much more than that. As Jameson has pointed out:

> Postmodern (or multinational) space is not merely a cultural ideology or fantasy, but has genuine historical (and socio-economic) reality as a third great original expansion of capitalism. . . . We cannot return to aesthetic practices elaborated on the basis of historical situations and dilemmas which are no longer ours. (1984, pp. 88–89)

This situation—a changed and uncontrollable reappropriation of space and the historical connections we have with it—fuels a sense that we cannot go back. In response, the "authentic" begins to mirror the "simulation" and the blurring of the genres becomes overwhelming. Just as the mall has left cultural "traces" on main street, the local sports bar moves to accomodate the shift in logic articulated by the postmodern sports bar. And just as main street could never quite "retrofit" the mall on to its geography, the local sports bar is faced with grappling with the hegemony of the postmodern on its modern landcape. Certainly, it has been far easier for the postmodern sports bar to reinvent and configure the main street of sports onto its landscape. The twin issues—the modern not moving as fast as the postmodern and the modern's fundamental concern with understanding its own origins as an "authentic" point of departure—have served as essential ingredients in the modernist departure from the contemporary scene and the consequent tension between the "democratization" and the "commodification" of postmodern public space.

References

Ade, G. (1931). *The old time saloon.* New York: Ray Long and Richard Smith, Inc.

Banner, L. (1974). *Women in modern America.* New York: Harcourt Brace Jovanovich.

Baudrillard, J. (1988). *America.* London: Verso.

Brod, H. (Ed.) (1987). *The making of masculinities: The new men's studies.* Boston: Allen and Hyman.

Bruun, K. (1959). *Drinking behavior in small groups.* Helsinki: The Finnish Foundation for Alcohol Studies.

Burns, T.F. (1980). "Getting rowdy with the boys." *Journal of Drug Issues*, 10, 273–286.

Campbell, M.A. (1991). "Public drinking places and society." In *Society, culture, and drinking patterns reexamined* (pp. 361–380). New Brunswick, NJ: Rutgers Center of Alcohol Studies.

Cavan, S. (1966). *Liquor license: An ethnography of bar behavior.* Chicago: Aldine.

Clinard, M.B. (1962). "The public drinking house and society." In D.J. Pittmann & C.R. Snyder (Eds.), *Society, culture and drinking patterns* (pp. 270–292). New York: John Wiley.

Cloyd, J. (1976). "The marketplace bar." *Urban Life*, 5, 293–312.

Coakley, J.J. (1990). *Sport in society: Issues and controversies.* St. Louis: Mosby.

Connell, R.W. (1983). *Which way is up? Essays on class, sex and cullture.* Sydney: Allen & Unwin.

―――― (1990). "An iron man: The body and some contradictions of hegemonic masculinity." In M.A. Messner & D.F. Sabo (Eds.), *Sport, men and the gender order* (pp. 83–96). Champaign, IL: Human Kinetics.

Curry, T.J. (1991). "Fraternal bonding in the locker room: A profeminist analysis of talk about competition and women." *Sociology of Sport Journal*, 8, 119–135.

Drucker, S.J., & Gumpert, G. (1991). "Public space and communication: The zoning of public interaction." *Communication Theory*, 1, 294–310.

Dubbert, J.L. (1979). *A man's place: Masculinity in transition*. Englewood Cliffs, NJ: Prentice-Hall.

Duncan, M.C. (1993). "Representation and the gun that points backwards." *Journal of Sport and Social Issues*, 17, 42–46.

Duncan, M.C., & Brummett, B.(1993). "Liberal and radical sources of female empowerment in sport media." *Sociology of Sport Journal*, 10, 57–72.

Dunning, E. (1986). "Sport as a male preserve: Notes on the social sources of masculine identity and its transformation." *Theory, Culture, and Society*, 3(1), 79–90.

Fastau, M.F. (1975). *The male machine*. New York: Dell.

Field, E. (1897). *The colonial tavern*. Providence, RI: Preston and Rounds.

Fine, G.A. (1987). *With the boys: Little league baseball and preadolescent culture*. Chicago: University of Chicago Press.

Firebraugh, W.C. (1924a). *The inns of Greece and Rome*. Chicago: Pascal Covici.

―――― (1924b). *The inns of the middle ages*. Chicago: Pascal Covici.

Fiske, J. (1987). *Television culture*. London: Methuen.

Fromme, K., & Samson, H.H. (1983). "A survey analysis of first intoxication experiences." *Journal of Studies on Alcohol*, 44, 905–910.

Foucault, M. (1980). "Questions on geography." In C. Gordon (Ed.), *Power/knowledge: Selected interviews and other writings 1972–1977*. New York: Pantheon.

―――― (1986). *The use of pleasure*. New York: Vintage Books.

Gumpert G., & Drucker, S.J. (1992). "From the agora to the electronic shopping mall." *Critical Studies in Mass Communication*, 9, 186–200.

Hackwood, F.W. (1909) *Inns ales and drinking customs of old England*. London: T. Fisher Unwin.

Harford, T.C. (1978). "Contextual drinking pattern among men and women." In F.A. Seixas (Ed.), *Currents in alcoholism: Volume IV* (pp. 287–296). San Francisco: Grune & Stratton.

———— (1979). "Ecological factors in drinking." In H.T. Blane & M.E. Chafetz (Eds.), *Youth, alcohol, and social policy* (pp. 147–182). New York: Plenum Press.

Jameson, F. (1984). "Postmodernism, or the cultural logic of late capitalism." *New Left Review*, 146, 53–93.

Kaufman, M. (Ed.) (1987). *Beyond patriarchy: Essays by men on pleasure, power, and change.* Toronto: Oxford University Press.

Katovich, M.A., & Reese, W.A. II. (1987). "The regular: Full-time identities and memberships in an urban bar." *Journal of Contemporary Ethnography*, 16, 308–343.

Keegan, P.O. (1990). "Sports bars." *Nation's Restaurant News*, June 18, pp. 33–36, 40.

Kidd, B. (1987). "Sports and masculinity." In M. Kaufman (Ed.), *Beyond patriarchy: Essays by men on pleasure, power, and change* (pp. 250–265). Toronto: Oxford University Press.

———— (1990). "The men's cultural centre: Sports and the dynamic of women's oppression/men's repression." In M.A. Messner & D.F. Sabo (Eds.), *Sport, men and the gender order: Critical feminist perspectives* (pp. 31–44). Champaign, IL: Human Kinetics.

Kimmel, M.S. (Ed.) (1987). *Changing men: New directions in research on men and masculinity.* Newbury Park, CA: Sage.

Kimmel, M.S., & Messner, M.A. (Eds.) (1989). *Men's lives.* New York: Macmillan.

Lemle, R., & Mishkind, M.E. (1989). "Alcohol and masculinity." *Journal of Substance Abuse Treatment*, 6, 213–222.

Loppiano, D.A. (1992). "Colleges can achieve equity in college sports." *Chronicle of Higher Education*, December 2, pp. B1–B2.

Lyke, R. (1990). "The sporting life: New wave sports bars lure patrons with a dizzying mix of high-tech video and soft-touch nostalgia." *Restaurant Hospitality*, March, pp. 122–129.

Macrory, B.E. (1952). "The tavern and the community." *Quarterly Journal of Studies on Alcohol*, 13, 609–637.

Messner, M.A. (1985). "The changing meaning of male identity in the lifecourse of an athlete." *Arena Review*, 9(2), 31–60.

———— (1987). "The life of a man's seasons: Male identity in the life course of the jock." In M.S. Kimmel (Ed.), *Changing men: New directions in research on men and masculinity* (pp. 53–67). Newbury Park, CA: Sage.

———— (1989). "Sports and the politics of inequality." In M.S. Kimmel & M.A. Messner (Eds.), *Men's lives* (pp. 187–190). New York: Macmillan.

———— (1992). *Power at play: Sports and the problem of masculinity*. Boston: Beacon.

Messner, M.A., & Sabo, D.F. (Eds.) (1990). *Sport, men, and the gender order: Critical feminist perspectives*. Champaign, IL: Human Kinetics

Nixon, H.L. II (1992). "A social network analysis of influences on athletes to play with pain and injuries." *Journal of Sport and Social Issues*, 16, 127–135.

Oldenburg, R. (1989). *The great good place: Cafes, coffee shops, community centers, beauty parlors, general stores, bars, hangouts, and how they get you through the day*. New York: Paragon House.

Orlofsky, J.L., Ramsden, M.W., & Cohen, R.S. (1982). "Development of the revised sex-role behavior scale." *Journal of Personality Assessment*, 46, 632–638.

Pittman, D.J. (1967). "International overview: Social and cultural factors in drinking patterns, pathological and nonpathological." In D.J. Pittman (Ed.), *Alcoholism* (pp. 3–20). New York: Harper and Row.

Reiter, R.R. (1975). "Men and women in the south of France: Public and private domains." In R.R. Reiter (Ed.), *Toward an anthropology of women* (pp. 252–282). New York: Monthly Review Press.

Roebuck, J.B., & Fresc, W. (1976). *The Rendezvous: A case study of an after-hours club*. New York: The Free Press.

Rosaldo, R. (1989). *Culture and truth*. Boston: Beacon.

Roubin, L. (1977). "Male space and female space within the provencial community." In R. Foster (Ed.), *Rural society in France*. Baltimore: Selections for the Annales Economies, Societies, Civilization.

Rubin, L.B. (1983). *Intimate strangers: Men and women together*. New York: Harper and Row.

Sabo, D.F. (1985). "Sport, patriarchy, and male identity: New questions about men and sport." *Arena Review* 9(2), 1–30.

Sabo, D.F., & Runfola, R. (Eds.) (1980). *Jock: Sports and male identity*. Englewood Cliffs, NJ: Prentice-Hall.

Slowikowski, S.S. (1993). "Cultural performance and sports mascots." *Journal of Sport and Social Issues*, 17, 23–33.

Snow, R.W., & Cunningham, O.R. (1985). "Age, machismo, and the drinking locations of drunken drivers: A research note." *Deviant Behavior*, 6, 57–66.

Snyder, E.E. (1972). "High school athletes and their coaches: educational plans and advice." *Sociology of Education*, 45, 313–325.

Soja, E.W. (1989). *Postmodern geographies: The reassertion of space in critical social theory*. London: Verso.

"Sports triumph: The Pittsburgh Sports Garden" (1991). *Top Shelf: Barkeeping at Its Best*, May/June, pp. 22–27.

Spradley, J.P., & Mann, B.J. (1975). *The cocktail waitress: Woman's work in a man's world.* New York: John Wiley & Sons.

Trujillo, N. (1991). "Hegemonic masculinity on the mound: Media representations of Nolan Ryan and American sports culture." *Critical Studies in Mass Communication*, 8, 290–308.

Waller, S., & Lorch, B.D. (1977). "First drinking experiences and present drinking patterns: A male-female comparison." *American Journal of Drug and Alcohol Abuse*, 4, 109–121.

Wenner, L.A. (1990). "Therapeutic engagement in mediated sports." In G. Gumpert & S. Fish (Eds.), *Talking to strangers: Mediated therapeutic communication* (pp. 221–242). Norwood, NJ: Ablex.

———— (1991). "One part alcohol, one part sport, one part dirt, stir gently: Beer commercials and television sports." In L.R. Vande Berg & L.A. Wenner (Eds.), *Television criticism: Approaches and applications* (pp. 388–407). New York: Longman.

Whitson, D. (1990). "Sport in the construction of masculinity." In M.A. Messner & D.F. Sabo (Eds.), *Sport, men, and the gender order: Critical feminist perspectives* (pp. 19–30). Champaign, IL: Human Kinetics.

Wilsnack, S.C., & Wilsnack, R.W. (1979). "Sex roles and adolescent drinking." In H.T. Blane & M.E. Chafetz (Eds.), *Youth, alcohol, and social policy* (pp. 183–224). New York: Plenum Press.

Zukin, S. (1991). *Landscapes of power: From Detroit to Disney World.* Berkeley: University of California Press.

15

Rap and Dialectical Relations:
Culture, Subculture, Power, and Counter-Power

Nancy Midol

This chapter brings us to the heart of postmodern cities to explore a different element of physical culture: the Hip-Hop movement—a popular American street and Black movement. Elements that were determinant in the making of the Hip-Hop movement are discussed as well as the way in which this form of artistic expression emerged out of an environment marked by illiteracy, poverty, despair and violence. It is shown how and why, in the 1980s, wars between rival gangs sometimes gave place to artistic works that became acknowledged and copied on a global scale. The analysis brings us from New York City to Paris, where the Hip-Hop movement quickly made inroads. The American policy of repression is contrasted to the French policy of integration and control. Artistic, intellectual, political and commercial appropriations of the Hip-Hop movement are presented as evidence of the transformation of this movement in a major postmodern cultural form.

The Birth of the Hip-Hop Movement

The Hip-Hop movement comprises three related forms of expression: graphic art (i.e., tag), music (i.c., rap), and dance (i.e., break dance, smurf, electric boogie). This movement began in the Bronx, New York City's notoriously deprived suburb, where an important fraction of the population literally lives in the streets, and where verbal and physical challenges between youngsters have become a way of life. Violence is everywhere in the Bronx, the result of poverty, social rejection, the clash of cultures, and of the almost criminal nature of police repression. Gangs have also taken over the Bronx and organised battles between rival gangs are deadly.

In the 1970s, gangs such as the Black Spades, with its 20,000 members, were already challenging other important gangs such as the Black Assassins, the Savage Nomads and the Seven Immortals. Essentially, the rappers are the direct heirs to these gangs and to the political movements of the 70s (e.g., the Black Panthers, the Puerto Rican Young Lords, etc.). The rappers are the younger brothers and the sons of those who went to "war," those who fought in the "rumbles," these organised battles between gangs of several hundred members. In the late 70s and early 80s (and still today, it could be contended), in these times of constant and deadly fighting, to be 20 years old and alive was an achievement since heroin often finished off the "war" survivors. Snoop Doggy Dog, a famous rapper (who has also been involved in a gang-related murder case and been sued for selling narcotics), has mentioned, for example, that when looking at the photograph of his old school's football team, he noted that out of 28 young men, 12 were dead, seven were in jail and three were now drug addicts. Such a testimony speaks to the climate of violence, murder and death out of which the Hip-Hop movement emerged.

Two main conditions, a political one and a cultural one, enabled the Hip-Hop movement to evolve toward artistic expression in the Bronx. The first condition was a type of *renaissance* of the Black political consciousness that had left such a crucial mark on the 1960s. Martin Luther King, Malcom X, Angela Davis and others, in different ways, all pointed to systemic racism and the social problems it engendered in African American communities. These leaders allowed African Americans to see their oppression, to "dream" a better future and to join the protest movement. In the 1980s, some rappers, particularly the younger ones, were similarly interested in raising consciousness; facing an epidemic of death among young Blacks in the American inner-cities, they needed to speak up, denounce, and hope for social change. Some of the young rappers joined the Black Panthers, who taught them that fighting should be left to others (Loupias, 1982). Africa Bambaataa is one of these rappers and he has been seen as a contributing force in the effort to stop the gang wars (Loupias, 1982). Bambaataa is in fact a central figure in rap; a political as well as an artistic hero, he substituted dance for the fights. Young men "breaked," which meant "letting loose, having a wow of a time," and this letting loose involved dance or "when your body, in following the music, goes wild; it goes off in all directions; you spin on your head and your body flies away" (Zekri, 1982).

The second condition that enabled the Hip-Hop movement to evolve toward an artistic expression concerns the cultural capital of the African American community in New York. A number of cultural practices have been passed on from one generation to the other and dance and music, for instance, have continued to evolve in spite of the often sordid social conditions. In the 80s, for example, an observer witnessed "all these children lined up in school corridors, in hallways of council houses and unlit half-standing buildings. . . . [Their foot steps,] taught to others, became a succession of steps that could last for hours" (Barrat, quoted in Morgado, 1983). African American culture has always been dynamic and rich, and has been particularly remarkable in its ability to express a perception of the environment through music, singing and dancing. In that regard, if blues and jazz represented modernity, rap seems to express a form of post-modernity.

Hip-Hop: Between Arts and Riots

The Hip-Hop movement breaks with traditional art in three main fields: musical, pictorial and choreographic. With respect to the musical field, rap is a type of dance music produced by disc jockeys (DJs) from a variety of music. Rappers have perfected three techniques: (a) editing, which entails producing music from different pieces of music, (b) mixing sounds, where different kinds of music are superimposed, and (c) "scratching," which is obtained by scratching records in order to make the needle jump, thus producing small disconnected bits of music. As a consequence of these techniques, rap sound is hacked, rhythmic, dissociated, jerky, all of this being caused by pastiche or the recycling of deformed music—this gives it its first postmodern characteristic. During an interview, Mondino stated enthusiastically: "It's wonderful, you can write a whole song. When grey matter and electronics meet, thousands of people can make music. It's exciting because the possibilities are limitless"(quoted in Dufresne, 1991, p. 139). The DJ makes use of the breaks in the sound not only to blab, keep up the mood, bring the dancers to a state of trance, promote his self-image just like in an advertisement, boast to the girls, but also to speak of his problems and hopes and to deliver a political message. For example, "Africa Bambaataa, undisputed leader of the urban tribe 'Zulu Nation' (40,000 members in 1984) edits and mixes recordings, defaces them, interrupts them and passes from one recording to another without losing the rhythm. . . . [He] scratches them . . . to the point of hypnosis" (Loupias, 1982, p. 14). As for the political message, a good example is Grand Master Flash who has launched "The Message," a scream of war against life in the Bronx, which has become the Rappers' Hymn. The following excerpt from The Message is quite telling:

> Broken glass everywhere
> people pissing on the stairs
> you know they just don't care,
> can't take the smell
> can't take the noise,
> got no money to move out,
> guess I got no choice,
> rats in the front room,

roaches in the back,
junkies in the alley with a baseball bat.
Tried to get away, but I couldn't get far
cause a man with a tow-truck
repossessed my car.
Don't push me
cause I'm close to the edge,
I'm trying not to lose my head.
It's like a jungle sometimes
it makes me wonder
how I keep from going under.
(Grand Master Flash, 1982)

From a pictorial standpoint, rappers are also taggers, and they lay claim to city spaces with aerosol paint (as is done with graffiti), spraying it stealthily in open places. At first, kids aged between 10 and 13 years old found their way into the subway depot at night, seeking a good plain surface on which they could spray their names in huge letters. From then on, the spray painting has become more refined. From the taggers' perspective, "A train is alive, it has flanks, a head, eyes, and breathes like a monster. We paint over its body" (Loupias, 1982, p. 14). The taggers' challenge is to impress members of their own and of rival gangs. The thrill is to be impudent enough to go and spray in the most daring places such as a police vehicle, knowing that if one is caught, one will at best be beaten, or at worst killed. Although the taggers' works of art have style, are well finished and are perfectly controlled, public opinion sees them as pollution of public places; hence the hunt for taggers. Fines, beatings or more simply the obligation to clean up and repaint the trains in white fuels these youngsters' rebellious will to extend their territory even further. The taggers' acts of disobedience can be understood as a search for identity and recognition. From a psychological point of view, one could say that the authors are attempting to achieve an image of themselves by projecting themselves out of indifference and anonymity. The call is well heard, and at times, existence of the *oeuvre* is even recognised when artists and Soho intellectuals rise up against a public opinion that condemns taggers, classifies them as delinquents, and calls their art a "degradation." In the 1980s, a few spray paint artists were helped and found fame in galeries and fashionable night clubs.

Finally, from a choreographic perspective, if the dance presents new figures and imposes style and rhythm, above all it effectively exploits trance. Inseparable from rap, trance comes from television, from the streets, and from night clubs. It is a body language coming out of cartoons, comics, mime, combat, smurf, break dance, electric boogie, stroboscopic slow, and so

on. In th eearly 80s in Manhattan, a night club called "Roxy" became famous
for its effective exploitation of rap and trance. A Friday night at the club is
described in the following way:

> after midnight the dance floor is separated in two by a wall, for the
> graffiti makers to paint on with thick markers. Then a music of mixed
> sounds starts up. The rappers come on later: a crowd of young black
> girls, wearing white socks, white shorts and tee-shirts, invade the dance
> floor; they rope skip and are followed on by a mad youngster who
> dances on his head and turns wild somersaults. (Conrath, 1982, p. 12)

Shusterman (1992) emphasises the fact that there is a hypnotic aspect
to the dance, the possessed body, the trance, and that this a reminder of
Voodoo and African religious supernatural. Famous DJ Queen Latifah, for
instance, performs and at the same time asks the dancers again and again to
"dance for me." It is as if rappers were spell binding dancers covered in sweat
and seemingly possessed by the rhythm of the music. In fact, rappers must
lead their audience into dance by virtue of their own talent. In this sense, the
Hip-Hop movement became a political and spiritual guide under the influence
of many DJs. For example, DJ Kool Moe Dee suggested entrance into a
hypnotic state; a state of trance linked to a new God, a microphone God who
bewitches all other Godsand who can be described as a black friend wearing
glasses.

Diffusion and Appropriation of Hip-Hop

In the 1970s, rap tapes were already exchanged among aficionados, and
this, to the total indifference of the media and the general population. The
hostility of the parents, the teachers' associations and the media became visible
when rap music began to garner interest among white teenagers. Obviously,
opponents were quite perturbed by the commercialisation of music containing
obscene and violent language. However, DJs such as D. Chuck of the group
Public Enemy questioned whether "pornography should be the prerogative of
Marines and white racial extremists" (quoted in Dufresne, 1991, p. 98). Despite
opposition, rap made its way to various night clubs and the Roxy night club
became famous worldwide. This last club is interesting in that its story speaks
to the transformation of rap. As the reputation of the Roxy grew, Blacks and
Puerto Ricans who had made it successful were marginalised in that the club
refused them admittance to make room for the (whiter) middle class. The
simple setting used up to then by DJs and rappers was replaced by a professional one. Slowly, rap as it had been known up to then became less present.
Commercialisation further lead rap to lose its origins. At the same time, some

forms of rap became quite controversial granted their ultra racist and sexist values. For some groups, rap also became a vehicle for political expression and incitement to political fighting. Established sectors thus developed a vested interest in the Hip-Hop movement. The movement was thereby transformed and its influence extended to other social spheres.

In the political sphere, the appropriation of rap was wholly controversial in the United States. The political influence of rap was a concern for the highest governmental quarters who asked the F.B.I. for a report on "Rap music and its effects on national security" (Dufresne, 1991, p. 98) to be presented to Congress in June 1990. Some F.B.I. actions were taken, notably in the case of the group Ice-T who's song "Fuck tha Police" resulted in the F.B.I. writing to the recording company N.W.A. to warn the group. Prior to the 1992 U.S. presidential election, there was also a public argument opposing Republicans and Democrats on the subject of "Cop Killer," the song of the group Ice-T related to the Los Angeles incidents. David Hinckley, Ice-T's singer, even wrote an open letter to President Bush. The letter ended with the observation that "if [President Bush] had solved the problem, 'Cop Killer' would never have existed and now the problem remains: the conclusion is that Ice-T does its job better than you" (Behar, 1992, p. 14).

Internationalisation of Hip-Hop

As in the case of jazz, rap music influenced other communities separate from those which created it. Mainly youths took it over, transforming it according to their own culture and environment. Hip-Hop became crucial for a number of institutions, and the various appropriations of the movement were responsible for it losing its ground. Let us look here at the artistic, intellectual and commercial appropriations of the movement, and let us also look at its political repression in the United States and its integration and control in France.

The Movement in France: An Outer-Suburban Culture

In 1982, Zulu Nation, the Dutch Girls, Phase 2 and others groups left the Bronx for Paris, where the "Europe 1" radio station and the AZ recording company had organised "La grande nuit du rap" (the great rap night). The show made headlines in the press despite an unenthusiastic reporter who found the music "as boring as an American suburb" (Loupias, 1982, p. 14). Still the reporter promotes "lesson N°1 in rap," which is "paint the walls of the town, the underground trains everywhere, make your own music, the one you need, invent your own dance, on your hands, upside down, belly up. Rap is pleasure in a kit" (Loupias, 1982, p. 14).

In France, although the imported Hip-Hop movement changes tone and now finds its followers in the outer-suburbs, the original attitudes (i.e., hate for the police and administration, but no to drugs and violence) are retained. The "we want to exist" claim brings together the second generation of immigrants. Saliha, a rapper from Bagneux sings:

Children of the ghettos of the world
bound by this desert of pain
of misfortune of sadness and steel,
the children of the ghettos only want love
to see more, farther,
make their dream come true. (quoted in Mezouane, 1989, p. 79)

The revolt is also expressed in tags like this one: "Hey mister, stop. The rules and laws of blabbing will not govern our world. Tagging is better than having your photo taken, it's that mister Nobody, the local no-good has something to say, on the walls [. . .] The power of suburbia is great and limitless" (Tox 1, 1992).

An Outer-Suburban Culture Subjected to Socio-Political Control

In December 1990, Michel Rocard, the French Prime Minister, proposed measures to renovate the outer-suburbs. Each administrative area was to receive the help of a project manager to change the way of life. As much as U.S. $11 million would be used to set up 100 music cafés as early as possible. These cafés would be open in the evening for young rock and rap buffs (M.A.R., 1990). In the newspaper *Libération*, it was specified that this programme assumed an investment in the little things in life and that the State had faith in the citizens (Gaspard, 1990). Further evidence of the political recuperation of rap is the fact that in December 1990, the group "Clan Actuel" gave a rap concert in the Fleury Mérogis prison, near Paris. Similarly, in May 1991, the deputy mayor of Massy-Palaiseau (South of Paris) welcomed groups of rappers and dancers. The deputy mayor publicly recognised their culture and was supported by the President of France Plus Association, who actually appealed to prospective recording agents present at the meeting (Politicorama, 1991).

In 1991, Jack Lang, Minister of Culture, went further and said that he "believe[s] in this culture" and was prepared to assume the responsibility of providing financial aid for rap. As a consequence, rappers put together files, received grants and passed examinations. A content analysis of the written press is clear: all the articles for the years 1982 and 1983 speak about art, music and dance, but most of those for the years 1990 and 1992 speak of the social aspect of rap. In June 1992, the Contemporary Dance Theater in Paris, with the support of the Ministry of Culture, of the Social Action Fund, and of the Ministry for Youth and Sport, even organised a show devoted to Hip-Hop. In France, then, rap was appropriated by politicians who used it as a means of communication with those youths whose dissidence and violence they feared. "Better to control than repress" was the motto of the French State, and this, in spite of the fact that rap did not only have a good rep— for instance, the *France-Soir* newspaper (1990) referred to a Public Enemy concert as an "anti-white scandal."

The Movement in the United States: Repression from the American Powers

In the United States, the reaction of those in power at different governmental levels leant more toward opposition to, than integration of, the Hip-Hop movement—although we have to keep in mind that very different movements had developed on both side of the Atlantic. Nevertheless, 40,000 taggers in the Los Angeles region (9 million residents) were listed as gang members on police files. Police officers with degrees in ethnology and pretending to be journalists infiltrated the groups. Sometimes witnessing themselves the tagging operations, they were able to arrest taggers who later sentenced. The large number of arrests broke the solidarity between gangs as some of those arrested chose to become police informers to obtain a reduction of their sentences (Filloux, 1993). Police also confused taggers with criminals: while large numbers of taggers considered themselves as artists, police officers considered them as members of gangs dealing in drugs. In fact, police reports linked tagging with the rise in criminality, and differences between groups were not considered. Violence increased following the actions of the local authorities and getting rid of the graffiti costs the local collectivities $4 billion a year (Filloux, 1993).

Repression and Commercialisation

The repression, which from the French point of view, appeared excessive, was somewhat "counterbalanced" by the commercialisation of the movement. In September 1993, the Time Inc. Group (editor of *Time*, *People* and *Sports Illustrated*) established the magazine *Vibe*, and hoped to sell 500,000 copies within five years. *Vibe* was to give a voice to the black community and proposed to oppose violence. As its project manager explained: "Our principle is that in the absence of political leaders, today's blacks express themselves through rap: Hip-Hop is the CNN of the street. We must listen and we must not ignore the fact that NWA issued an album forewarning the riots" (Douadi, 1993, p. 6).

Conclusion: Hip-Hop and the Problems of Social Integration

In France and in the United States, being able to find one's identity and to say "I am" appears as the main problem facing those deprived of access to the media. More importantly, outsiders such as journalists and intellectuals often pretend to be spokespersons for those who are marginalised. In France, the media were quick to disseminate the idea that outer-suburbia was a place of despair; to tell suburbians that they had "missed the boat" in this century and that they did not exist but through violence. In the United States, similar things were being said about the Bronx and other ghettos. Interestingly, it is in these marginalized (and racialized) spaces that Hip Hop was born. The movement initiated aspirations common to this marginalized youth, enabling them to make contact at the speed of light. The movement also spread to commercial, intellectual and political spheres. Like jazz, it awakened needs and wants, and revealed something of our times. Rap became a terrain for the struggles between various social groups (e.g., youths, politicians, the police), all seeking, in their own ways, to territorialize their means of expression and identification.

If Hip-Hop can be seen as a postmodern way of continuing the jazz tradition, it has to be acknowledged that dancing, making music in the streets, and "blabbing" in rhythm have never been absent from the Black American community's way of life (Kochman, 1972; Midol & Pissard, 1986). It is the commercial appropriation of Hip-Hop that has transformed it into acknowledged forms. Like for jazz, the music remains unchanged, but the dance now follows a set of rules; like for jazz, the original creative and controversial expression is waylaid by the double game of artists who wish to succeed within the "system" and the wish of the dominant classes to corner this form of expression for their own benefit.

From an anthropological perspective, we can underline the needs of those living in large cosmopolitan cities, particularly those who are economically under-privileged, to express their culture in terms of their roots and to establish an ancestral, historical, ethnic, geographical and spiritual identity.

From an educational perspective, it would be interesting to study in greater detail why these teenagers, shut out of the school system, are motivated to express their creative drives elsewhere, thereby rising above the mainstream institutions where they failed. Compared to the Hip Hop movement (where youth can raise their consciousness of the systemic racism and oppression, can develop their bodies through dancing, and can express themselves creatively, etc.) the school system can be seen more clearly as one of subjugation, control and standardisation. Why make teenagers accept (white supremacist) values that they neither recognise as their own nor find compatible with their ambitions? Perhaps this is the first question a school administration should ask itself. Of course, the issue is more complex than this and returns to the political terrain. But one should nevertheless remember that uprooting does not diminish the feeling of belonging but on the contrary seems to increase it. In France, particularly, all town dwellers who came either from the provinces or a foreign country face what Italian writer Paolo Virno calls "the incurable lack of roots" (1991, p. 35). And in postmodern societies where electronic messages, signals and images become "hyper-reality," citizens come to experience a life of dispersion: "Exile or migrant, our sense of identity is put to a strong test, precisely because our unsettled feeling of self consciousness grows incessantly" (Virno, 1991, p. 33).

Finally, from an aesthetics point of view, the Hip-Hop movement seems to be the perfect answer to this quest for roots. It expresses a popular fulfilment in this postmodern age. It has renewed the link between arts and politics, a link that had been severed since the late 1960s. It has been placed on a par with art, not only because its protagonists lay a claim to artistic status but also because philosophers like Shusterman (1992), sociologists like Lapassade (1990), plastic artists and others recognise it as such.

Minor art or major art? Intellectuals argue over the movement, give their own interpretation of it, and transform it to give it importance. On the American side, Shusterman (1992) has suggested that it is a major postmodern art form, having roots in popular street groups, and Pareles (1990) has pointed out the dependence of rap upon media techniques, its unstructured nature (e.g., the song could possibly end in mid-air), and the omnipresence of inconsistencies. On the French side, Lapassade and Rousselot have stated that rap's artistic expression depends on commercial necessity: "Rap's entry into the record industry is somewhat unnatural; like the toast-master, rap was invented to last but an evening. Recording and commercial practices will force it to become an art" (1990, p. 30). I do not share this opinion myself, simply because I acknowledge the fact that American record companies launch rap stars, but restrict the most offending anti-establishment lyrics and the expression of the most forceful performers.

I should conclude in saying that the aesthetic concept of purism in art is not applicable to the postmodern ideal: rather, the latter seeks to gather many and dissimilar elements. And the desire to seize more and more opportunities as Rorty (1980) notes, to make one's life a work of art as the French philosophers (Baudrillard, 1976; Deleuze & Guattari, 1980; Foucault, 1984) advocate, is not separate from the collective feeling of individual finitude.

References

Baudrillard, J. (1976). *L'échange symbolique et la mort.* Paris: Gallimard.

Behar, H. (1992). "Les Démocrates, les Républicains, les Rappers: Le rap pour quelques voix." *Le Monde*, July 30, p. 14.

Conrath, P. (1982). "Sur la planète RAP." *Libération*, October 25, p. 12.

Deleuze, G., & Guattari, F. (1980). *Mille plateaux.* Paris: Minuit.

Dufresne, D. (1991). *Yo! Révolution Rap*. Paris: Ramsay.

Filloux, F. (1993). "À L.A., avec la brigade anti-gang." *Le Monde*, October 3, pp. 26–27.

Foucault, M. (1984). *Histoire de la sexualité: L'usage des plaisirs*. Paris: Gallimard.

France Soir (1990). April 11 issue.

Gaspard, F. (1990). "Des ascenseurs et des hommes." *Libération*, December 18.

Grand Master Flash and Furious Five (1982). *The message*. Sweet Mountain Studios.

Kochman, T. (1972). *Toward an ethnography of Black American speech behaviour*. Urbana, IL: University of Illinois Press.

Lapassade, G., & Rousselot, P. (1990). *Le RAP ou la fureur du dire*. Paris: Loris Talmart.

Loupias, B. (1982). "Hip Hop, le rap arrive." *Le Matin*, November 26, p. 14.

M.A.R. (1990). "Les mesures de Michel Rocard pour la rénovation urbaine." *Le Monde Diplomatique*, December 9, p. 13.

Mezouane, M. (1989). "Le rap, complainte des maudits."*Le Monde Diplomatique*, 13, p. 79.

Midol, N., & Pissard, H. (1986). *La danse Jazz: de la tradition à la modernité*. Paris: Amphora.

Morgado, V. (1983). "B. comme Bronx." *Autrement* (special issue "Fous de Danse"), 59–69.

Pareles, J. (1990). "How rap moves to television's beat." *New York Times*, January 14, p. 10.

Politicorama (1991). *Libération*, May 24, p. 5.

"Rap's New Bulletin from L.A. front" (1992). *International Herald Tribune*, December 15, p. A1.

Rorty, R. (1980). "Freud, morality, and hermeneutics." *New Literary History*, 12, 59–69.

Shusterman, R. (1992). *L'art à l'état vif*. Paris: Minuit.

Tox 1, Le journal des cultures de la rue (1992). February/March issue.

Virno, P. (1991). *Sentimenti dell'aldiqua, Theoria*. Rome. Theorica.

Zekri, B. (1982). "Mister Freeze et Misses Blue." *Libération*, October 28, p. 16.

——— (1982). "Flash: Le maître des roues d'acier." *Libération*, October 27, pp. 18–19.

16

Hassiba Boulmerka and Islamic Green: International Sports, Cultural Differences, and Their Postmodern Interpretation

William J. Morgan

Postmodernism as a theory and political and literary program has made a name for itself as the champion of the poor and disenfranchised peoples of the world. Not surprisingly, Jean François Lyotard, one of the major exponents of this theory and movement, has likewise acquired a reputation as the patron saint of the oppressed and of cultural pluralism. Indeed, Lyotard's best known and widely cited utterance, "incredulity toward metanarratives," which for many followers of postmodernism became its official definition and main rallying cry, was intended both to cast suspicion on the West's use of these metaphysical stories of progress to justify their imperialist ambitions and the shoddy manner in which they treated their colonial subjects, and to breathe new life into the local narratives of these latter indigenous cultures—to make sure that they are no longer run roughshod over by hegemonic Western nations, that they are not crushed at every turn by the rich and powerful.

While I am favorably impressed with the high-mindedness of all of this, I am skeptical that Lyotard's advocacy of local narratives will do for the poor and oppressed of this world what he says they will do. That is why I wish presently to challenge this Lyotardian wing of postmodernism, to sully its good name. But in identifying Lyotard and his epigones (both those who work inside and outside of sport studies) as my critical target, I want to be careful not to cast my net too widely; for there is much that gets said and written in the name of postmodernism that I am not only sympathetic with but find completely persuasive. Still, given Lyotard's standing in the movement, and given that his celebrated call for the deconstruction of metanarratives has been enthusiastically heeded by many who call themselves postmodernists, much of what I will have to say in this chapter in a critical vein will apply to them as well. I should also say straightaway that my aim is not to undercut postmodern sport theory as such, but only to get those who work in this camp and have been influenced by Lyotard (I would add Foucault as well, but that is another paper) to rethink their normative positions. For it is only by doing so, I will argue, that they will be able to honor their theoretical and practical commitments to the downtrodden, to make good on their claims to stand by and for them.

In what follows, then, I will take direct issue with Lyotard's endorsement of the narratives of local (principally non-Western) cultures, particularly their normative bearing and outlook, arguing that that endorsement makes the world safe not for the dispossessed and marginalized but rather for the religious and political elites that preside over them often with an iron hand. But I want to set up my argument with Lyotard by first recounting the remarkable saga of Algerian middle-distance runner Hassiba Boulmerka, whose extraordinary athletic accomplishments (1991 women's 1500-meter World Champion and 1992 Olympic Gold Medal winner) were at first widely hailed by her fellow Algerians, despite her clear violation of the strict Muslim code of purdah (which decrees, among other things, that women be covered from head to toe in public), but which later were scorned by a vocal and increasingly influential group of fundamentalist Muslims. I want to use Boulmerka's story of athletic struggle to stake out a new and controversial place for women in Islamic cultures, to expose the shortcomings of Lyotard's championing of what amounts to the prevailing beliefs and values of these cultures. More specifically, I want to show how Lyotard's account fails to do justice to the conflicted background out of which Boulmerka's courageous effort to retell the story of Islam arises (the parallels to expatriate Salman Rushdie's literary exploits are hard to miss),[1] how it fails to shed light on how disputes between fundamentalist and less doctrinaire cultural messengers and their messages should be critically sorted out and evaluated.

Boulmerka's Story

I should say at the outset that in beginning my critique of Lyotard with Boulmerka's account of her international athletic ventures I have presumed that sport is an important form of personal and cultural expression, that it is one of the rich human languages by which people converse with one another in complex and nuanced ways, telling stories about themselves and others. In making this presumption, I have followed Clifford Geertz's lead, who, in his justly famous analysis of the Balinese cockfight, showed how sports function as social texts (1972) and how the stories they fashion—and this, doubtless, is the trademark of sporting yarns—are embedded in the action itself. So I take this presumption that athletic stories like Boulmerka's can be rendered as social texts, as forms of discourse. And since the telling that goes on in athletic texts lies in the action, I would be well advised to cut to the action of Boulmerka's story. But since all stories require a background, I need first to situate Boulmerka's story in its larger context before I consider what it has to tell us, before I try to decipher its telling-action.[2]

The Algeria Boulmerka was born into was a more pluralist and secular one than that of her grandparents. The reason why implicates Algeria's colonial past. In the 19th century, France colonized Algeria and most of northern Africa. This led to periodic Algerian struggles against their French "masters" that culminated in a war of liberation that broke out in 1954 and ended in 1962 with Algeria's independence.[3] During that difficult war, many Algerian women fought side by side with their male compatriots, an experience that galvanized them after the war to fight for their own liberation from stultifying religious laws and decrees, to oppose practices which, like purdah, suppress women. It was this political and cultural air, then, in which Boulmerka drew her first breaths, and although her own rearing and education was typically Muslim when it came to things like diet, restrictions on alcohol and dancing, it was not typically Muslim when it came to sport, which she took an early liking to and in which she proved to be more than an able participant.

The Algeria of Boulmerka's birth, however, is no longer. It is now marked, some would say scarred, by a rising tide of Muslim fundamentalism that began to bear political fruit in 1991 when the Islamic Salvation Front (FIS), the official Muslim political party, won sweeping political victories that set off a struggle with more moderate Muslims. This was, of course, the year of Boulmerka's 1500-meter World Championship triumph, which, as I noted previously, won her the admiration of thousands of cheering Algerians at the airport and subsequent motorcade in her honor, but which later won her the condemnation of the "more faithful" (a neologism used by ordinary Algerian folk to designate their more militant Muslim countrymen) (Moore, 1992, p. 53). Boulmerka quickly became, then, a target of the FIS, a despised symbol of anti-fundamentalism. Boulmerka's subsequent gold medal performance in Barcelona in 1992 and her dicey gesture in which she dedicated her medal to Mohammed Boudief (former president of Algeria who was assassinated, allegedly by fundamentalists, in June of the same year) and called on all young Algerians to suffer as she had, only made matters more tenuous.[4]

So much for the context; what now of the athletic tale? To begin with, Boulmerka claimed that her international athletic experiences provided her a rare and powerful chance to express herself, as she herself put it, "maybe better than in any other field" (1992, p. 61). And what she expressed in and through her sporting encounters was a curious blend of Western individual initiative and Eastern community-inspired discipline. What makes this a curious cultural language is that it is difficult to categorize, at least by our conventional (Western and Eastern) cultural standards. For it is too steeped in these disparate cultural traditions to be passed off as a kind of Esperanto and yet too diffusely constituted out of them to be sloughed off as a sectarian cultural expression.

But it is not difficult to discern what Boulmerka gleaned by learning to speak the language of international sports. To start with, she claims to have acquired a robust and healthy sense of self, one that stresses not a narcissistic preoccupation with self but the importance of individual striving and the suffering, responsibility, and focused action that follow in its train. However, Boulmerka also claims to have acquired from her international sporting contacts a deeper love of her country, a patriotism that does not demand the abolition of self-definition through individual achievement but an appreciation of the cultural context and social cooperation that lie behind every individual achievement and that make it both possible and significant. Indeed, it is this capacity of sport to hone individual accomplishment in a way that brings people together that accounts for her own desire to use her stellar athletic accomplishments as an occasion to speak out, to convey, especially to young Algerians not yet enamored with or daunted by fascist fundamentalists, and to Westerners not yet enamored with the stereotypical views of Muslims that greet them at every turn, that Islamic culture is not the hotbed of fanaticism it is often made out to be and that it is not necessarily hostile either to individual effort or to the plight of women.

That Boulmerka has learned her intercultural athletic lessons well is clear from her personal testimony. That she wishes to weave those lessons into a narrative that carries a pointedly contentious political message is also clear from her personal testimony. However, what is politically contentious about her message is not that it takes issue with Islam, but that it decries, as she puts it, "the fascists who hide behind the veil of Islam in order to impose their political will" (quoted in Moore, 1992, p. 53). So the bone of her contention is not Islam but Actually Existing Islam,[5] and what she seeks to secure by way of her involvement in sport and her own personal agitation is a political alternative to the FIS, a more secular and democratic, and so, a less narrow and doctrinaire Islam. She thinks she can get such an Islamic culture not by repudiating all that is not Islamic, nor by replacing Islam wholesale with Western liberalism, but by infusing the vocabulary of equal rights and women's sports into the cultural vocabulary of Islam. That such infusion goes against the grain of the Islamic purity of the "more faithful" she does not dispute, that it goes against the grain of what it means to be a Muslim, particularly a Muslim woman, she hotly disputes. For she loves her country too much, and has learned her lessons from international sport too well, to abide the conceit that Actually Existing Islam is the only Islamic story to be told and, therefore, the only story worth listening to.

Now my point in reprising Boulmerka's alternative rendition of the story of Islam should be obvious to even the most unsuspecting readers. For if ever there were a case of pluralist cultural expression that warranted postmodern attention and sanction, it is this one. Indeed, it offers us a paradigmatic example of the assertion of difference, one authored by a member of a repressed minority (Arab women to be exact) in a third world country, fighting for its proverbial life and expressed in a sporting venue held in contempt by a religious elite of fundamentalist Muslims who are bidding, with increasing success, to become the ruling political elite. If that were not enough to convince Lyotard and his disciples to take up Boulmerka's cause, then the fact that Boulmerka's story makes no use of the dreaded metanarrative to convey its message should prove ultimately persuasive. For if Boulmerka's athletic narrative succeeds in doing anything, it succeeds in drawing us (Westerners and Easterners) out of our ethnocentric crannies and getting us to consider alternative ways of living and of morally sizing up the significance of our lives. And it is able to do all of this without asking that we take a metaphysical leap of faith, without insisting that we stake our hopes for a better, more peaceful life on an abstract, anti-historical, difference-blind conception of human nature.

But as compelling an example of cultural pluralism and difference as Boulmerka's saga is, and as incredible as it may seem, it is to her detractors' cause that Lyotard is led by dint, I will argue, of his theoretical views on local narratives. It is not just, however, that Lyotard and his postmodern cohorts land on what certainly looks to be the wrong side of the cultural difference/pluralism issue here, the fundamentalists' side, but that they grease the skids for the fundamentalists by peddling the fashionable view, which, as I have insinuated, they have had a large hand in making fashionable, that people like Boulmerka are indeed miscreants and even imperialists because they buck the prevailing norms of their cultures. This puts defenders of Boulmerka and her ilk on shaky moral ground. As Cynthia Ozick argued in a recent essay in the *New Yorker*, "Nowadays, standing up for [people like] Rushdie . . . places one among the stereotypers and the 'orientalists' . . . who are accused of denigrating whole peoples" (1993, p. 78). And in helping to make put downs like this trendy, I will argue further, Lyotard and his followers have not only contributed to the moral paralysis of Western liberals by cowing them with the accusation of cultural imperialism (which shames them into thinking that there is no important difference between moral criticism and colonial intervention, between speaking out on behalf of desperate people in distant lands and coercing people in these lands to adopt our beliefs and ways of life), but have contributed, unwittingly or not, to the militancy of the accusers of Boulmerka and Rushdie. They have done so by giving their accusers moral purchase to track them down wherever they might reside—even if that means trespassing the borders of other nations and transgressing their legal and moral strictures.

The irony here is overshadowed only by the tragedy; for at the very moment that the West has been misled into thinking that the only way to escape the snares of cultural imperialism is to stand idly by and do nothing, Islamic fundamentalists have been emboldened to intervene in the most aggressive ways imaginable to promote their favored beliefs and ways of life.[6] If I am right, the views of postmodernists like Lyotard are part of this tragic problem, not the key to its moral resolution.

These are, I am well aware, sweeping and contentious charges. They are also, as they presently stand, mere assertions. So it is time to turn to the arguments that, I contend, support them, which first requires that we get clear on what are Lyotard's actual views regarding local narratives and their normative import.

Lyotard on Local Narratives

In sketching out Lyotard's views on narratives and their legitimating roles, it is perhaps best to start where he begins with his call for "incredulity toward metanarratives." What, it might reasonably be asked, are metanarratives and what does our distrust of and resistance to them augur for local narratives and the people whose life stories they narrate? The answer to the first part of my question is that metanarratives are metaphysical tales whose various stories of progress and decline are told and legitimated by abstract, ahistorical conceptions of humanity. A representative sampling of grand narratives would include, "the Christian narrative of the redemption of original sin through love; the *Aufklärer* narrative of emancipation from ignorance and servitude through knowledge and egalitarianism; the speculative narrative of the realization of the universal Idea through the dialectic of the concrete; the Marxist narrative of emancipation from exploitation and alienation through the socialization of work; and the capitalist narrative of emancipation from poverty through techno-industrial development" (Lyotard, 1993, p. 25). Lyotard would have us notice here that even though the subjects of these metanarratives and the regulative ideals of emancipation that anchor and enliven them change, their metaphysical character does not. That is why the stories they tell always leave out the disturbing, unsettling, and contradictory historical details and that the progress they envisage always triumphs over the obstacles that stand in its way—phantom obstacles to be sure since their overcoming is never in doubt because it is metaphysically preordained.

That is also why, Lyotard is quick to tell us, we should be incredulous toward these stories. For once we are able to cut through the metaphysical fog that enshrouds them, we will see that the narrative of history has dealt each and every one a fatal blow. This sober facing up to what we have actually wrought as opposed to what we have wrought only in our grandest thoughts is hastened today, argues Lyotard, by two interrelated developments. The first is the crisis in metaphysics itself, the collapse in the belief that there are any natural, a priori, ahistorical first principles (standards, criteria, foundations) to which we can repair to back up and justify our social practices and institutions. The second is the upsurge in what Lyotard refers to as the "insurmountable diversity of cultures," which he traces, in part, to the struggles for independence that mushroomed after World War II, struggles that consolidated "local legitimacies" by giving voice to their particular populist narratives (1993, p. 35).

Lyotard's account of the demise of grand narratives suggests its own remedy, one that sets up the answer to the second part of the question posed above. For when I ask, with Lyotard, "Where, after the metanarratives, can legitimacy reside?" (1986, p. xxv), his answer is as direct as it is clear: we should look to these new local legitimacies and to "the recognition of [the] new national names" they mark and celebrate. In particular, Lyotard tells us, we should look to the pragmatic logistics that govern the way in which local narratives are learned, transmitted, and legitimated, and to the incommensurable stories they tell about particular, infrangible peoples.

To begin at the beginning with our induction into particular cultures, Lyotard claims that that induction is accomplished, whether it be as a child or immigrant, "through an apprenticeship in proper names" that are learned not on their own but as parts of "little stories." By reciting these "little stories" members of a culture are assured a place within that culture at the same time that they are reassured of "the legitimacy of its world of names through the recurrence of this world in its stories" (1993, p. 32). This narrative assurance of a place within a culture comes complete with a thick, detailed knowledge of its basic workings, of a kind of knowledge that Lyotard calls "customary" knowledge in which we learn to become competent members of that culture. So in setting out criteria of induction into a culture, narratives also set out criteria of competence regarding what can efficiently and rightfully be said and done in that culture and then go on to evaluate what is so said and done according to those criteria.

It is little wonder, then, why Lyotard accords such importance to story telling in the life of cultures and treats cultural narratives as "quintessential forms" of customary knowledge. They qualify as forms of customary knowledge because they reflect what is shared and accepted in the social circle of the knower's interlocutors. And it is this social consensus, first learned then affirmed, reaffirmed, and transmitted by its main stories, Lyotard argues, that constitutes the culture of a people, and that makes it possible to distinguish the insiders from the outsiders, members from foreigners, in short, those who know from those who do not.

But it is the legitimating features of these narratives that for Lyotard signal their chief cultural and political significance and that distinguish them most clearly from metanarratives. This is so in two crucial senses.

The first sense is that local narratives legitimate the messages they send and receive without recourse to any special authorization procedures, argumentative or otherwise (Lyotard, 1986, p. 22). This contrasts with metanarratives that make formal argumentative moves their stock in trade, that insist on putting into place justificatory procedures as an integral part of their game of inquiry. The reason why local narratives pay such legitimation games, Lyotard tells us, is because they are self-legitimating discourses. Indeed, their self-legitimating character is so ingrained that the whole business of legitimation strikes those whose life stories they narrate as rather silly and beside the point.

What accounts, it may be asked, for the self-legitimating character of local narratives? Lyotard's answer is the pragmatics of their transmission. For narratives provide cultures an instant legitimation because they certify the authority of the stories they convey in the very process of conveying them. So we know narratives are doing their legitimating work from "the simple fact," avers Lyotard, "that they do what they do" (1986, p. 23). And what they do is hold cultures together by defining their center and establishing their self-identity and telegraphing to their members what their central norms are and, therefore, what counts as a competent and an incompetent cultural performance. So long as narratives successfully do just this, any call for their further justification is unwarranted and superfluous since it misses the fact that "narrative is authority itself" (1993, p. 33).

The second crucial sense in which the legitimation strategies of the narrative distinguish them from those of the metanarrative is that they legitimate and authorize in culturally particularist ways. Whereas the metanarrative authorizes a cosmopolitan "we" that is fashioned by extirpating all traces of particular cultural identities in favor of a universal civic identity (1993, pp. 33-34),[7] the local narrative authorizes a particular "we," in Lyotard's words, an "infrangible we outside of which there is only they" (1993, p. 33). And whereas the metanarrative makes use of an *avant-garde* that speaks to and for its we and that emancipates "third parties" (outsiders) by bringing them into the community (enlarging our sense of we), the narrative remains true to its particular we spurning any capacious substitutes, thereby leaving "many third parties on the outside" (1993, p. 26). It is just this downsizing of the we that occurred, to reiterate Lyotard's previous point, in the post World War struggles for independence that consolidated "local legitimacies" by undercutting cosmopolitan ones. Unlike their modernist detractors, however, who regard all such appeals to cultural particularism as a decadent retreat from civilization (and not coincidentally empire), Lyotard and his postmodern followers take heart in such appeals precisely because they give the lie to cosmopolitanism.

But that Lyotard approves of this recent consolidation of local legitima-cies and the "insurmountable diversity of cultures" that is its product does not mean that he is oblivious to the dangers of giving up on the cosmopolitan "search for unanimity" (1993, p. 27). For abandoning that search might set off a new wave of terror exercised this time not in the name of a universal we but a particular we, not "for the sake of freedom but for 'our' satisfaction, the satisfaction of a we permanently restricted to its particularity" (1993, p. 27). Lyotard refers to this anti-cosmopolitan response as "secondary narcis-sism" since it seeks to further "our" satisfaction at the expense of others, to exalt "us" by oppressing "them." In any case, this outbreak of narcissistically inspired terror is not, Lyotard warns, to be taken lightly, and if recent events in the Balkans and elsewhere are any indication, we are in for a long and dreadful period of blood-letting carried out for no higher purpose than self-aggrandizement at the expense of others.

But Lyotard's positive view of the eclipse of universal legitimacy by local legitimacies signals that he thinks that there is a way to stem this particularist brand of blood-letting, to make tolerance and civility triumph over narcissism and terror. And that way requires a new elaboration of the we. But what sort of we does he think needs to be worked out here?

It is safe to say that it will not look anything like the articulation of the we that we have come to associate with modernist, Enlightenment discourses, in which the "linguistic structure of communication" (1993, p. 27) and the deliberative tools of rational persuasion and argument figure most promi-nently. Why the elaboration of the we cannot follow this well traveled path, aside from the obvious point that it is not new, is, at least to Lyotard's mind, all too clear? To begin with, the linguistic structure of communication will prove unhelpful to our efforts to spin out a new we, or so Lyotard claims, because its wings have been clipped by the "insurmountable diversity of cultures," cultures whose opaque and densely idiomatic languages make them for all intents and purposes not just incommensurable from one another but inscrutable to non-native speakers (even those armed with translation manu-als). Further, the rational structure of argument will not fare any better in this regard, or so Lyotard once again claims, since it cannot make up for this loss of communicability because it presupposes it, because without some common ground or language in which to frame its arguments, it loses whatever per-suasive force it might possess. So while Lyotard would, no doubt, second Habermas' rendering of the language of argument as a form of communica-tive reason, he would not, and did not, second Habermas' claim that commu-nicative reason communicates across cultures, that it can say something intelligible to disparate peoples who speak in different tongues.

All of this puts into question, if not disrepute, the modernist's favorite and privileged distinction between force and persuasion. For if there is no universal reason, no God's-eye vantage point to which we can repair to settle our differences with other cultures, if, that is, the warrants for our beliefs and values are internal to the cultures to which we claim allegiance, then the rational aim of persuading others to take up our cherished beliefs and ways of life cannot avoid shading into the coercive aim of terrorizing others to adopt our ways of life—whether it be by ideological cunning or sheer might. This is the upshot of Lyotard's claim that "there is nothing in the savage community to lend it to transform itself dialectically into a society of citizens," and that efforts to get premodern societies to act like societies of citizens by making them comply with doctrines like the Universal Declaration of Rights can only be accomplished by "depriv[ing] peoples of their narrative legitimacy . . . and mak[ing] them take up the Idea of free citizenship . . . as the only legitimacy" (1993, p. 34). So trying to work out a new prototype of a universal, enlightened we to circumvent the narcissistic terror of a hardened, particular we is doomed to failure, according to Lyotard, since this so-called new we is no less restricted and committed to its particularity, and so no less narcissistically or tyrannically motivated, even if it persists in the charade of passing itself off as something universal.

Unsurprisingly, then, Lyotard opts for a different elaboration of the we. The central premise of this alternative elaboration is that we drop the universal pose, which as we have seen, Lyotard writes off as an ethnocentric deception and an ideological bludgeon, and simply accept the particularity of the many and diverse we(s) that presently dot the social landscape. We are not to fret about the fact that "the relevant criteria are all different" (1986, p. 27), because there is no grand, rational way to resolve our many and pronounced cultural differences. But the point of getting cultures either to stop asking after their own legitimation or to continue to resist the urge to justify themselves is not to reduce their cultural angst but, on the one hand, to neutralize the ideological dominion that the dominant cultures of the world hold over the dominated cultures—of special interest here are the deprecatory stories dominant peoples tell about marginalized, disenfranchised peoples, and, on the other, to revitalize the narratives of dominated cultures, to get them up and going again so that they can do their self-justifying work. Holding the legitimation question at bay in this manner, Lyotard insists, will yield, depending on the context, two alternative conceptions of the we: one a testy, militant we, the other a civil, tolerant we.

This first, testy we comes into being whenever threatened cultures are able to mobilize effectively the "discursive procedures" that are responsible for their self-identity, their integration as a particular culture. In such instances, Lyotard tells us, "identification reigns absolutely," and "unassimilable narratives" that might well compromise that self-identity are simply turned aside (1993, p. 33). It is these "discursive procedures" of cultural identity, then, that are responsible for the resistance of dominated cultures, since they lend their resistance an "immediate legitimacy (right) and logistics" (1993, p. 33).

But what is to prevent this aroused, recalcitrant we from turning into a monster, an equally fierce, though particular, aggressor of others? The question seems unavoidable since the discursive recipe that accounts for the resistance of local, endangered cultures, looks very much like a recipe that could also foment terror and oppression. Lyotard would, no doubt, have to concede this possibility; simply put, there are no guarantees when it comes to aroused and mobilized we(s), no matter how noble or just the cause. But I think he would be amenable to Wieseltier's point that "the vigorous expression of identity in the face of oppression is not an exercise of narcissism, it is an exercise of heroism" (1994, p. 26). No doubt, he would also be agreeable to Wieseltier's further point that "those qualities of identity that seem vexing in good times—the soldierliness and the obsession with solidarity . . . are precisely the qualities that provide the social and psychological foundations for resistance" (p. 26). So although no guarantees can be made that a resistant we won't turn into a militant and strident we, the context of the resistance, I presume Lyotard would concur, at least offers us some useful way to tell the difference between heroism and terrorism.

The second, civil we emerges in different, less trying circumstances. This we makes its presence felt, then, not when it is able to mount an effective resistance against would be aggressors by battening down its discursive mechanisms of self-identification, but when, in calmer more secure moments, it is seized, on the one hand, by the sheer diversity of the peoples that make up the world and of the different cultural languages they speak, and, on the other hand, by its inability to say that any one of these cultures is better (in the sense of rationally and morally superior) than any other. In such instances, Lyotard observes, "all we can do is gaze in wonderment at the diversity of discursive species, just as we do at the diversity of plant or animal species"(1986, p. 26). Although the we that is borne of this wonderment possesses a tolerant demeanor unknown to its militant counterpart, it does share in common with its intolerant cousin a disinterest in its own legitimation, that is, a disinclination to call into question the discursive mechanisms that power its own narrative. Indeed, it is its indifference regarding the legitimacy of its own narrative that accounts both for its "incomprehension" of cultural discourses that feature the legitimation question (the scientific discourses and assorted metanarratives of the West) and its "tolerance" of the diversity of discursive species, its ready acceptance of them as "variant[s] in the family of narrative cultures" (1986, p. 27). It is this presumed link between incomprehension of the legitimation question and tolerance of others that is paramount for Lyotard, for cultures who pay no mind to their own legitimation are at a loss to explain not only why any one would want to engage in such an inquiry but, more importantly, why any one would wish to disparage or oppress others.

It is not hard to see how this accepting and tolerant we is able to quell the terroristic impulse, whether it be of the particular or universal variety. With regard to the first, particular variety of terror, we can safely presume that this tolerant we harbors no imperialistic interests in other particular we(s), even if we cannot presume that its disinclination to force itself on others suggests any uneasiness or inadequacy regarding the authority of its own discursive mechanisms, or for that matter any interest in the discursive mechanisms (leaving aside for now the question of their validity) of other cultures. Here the temptation to engage in narcissistic put downs of others is stemmed by a lack of interest in their legitimacy, which, to reprise Lyotard's central argument, makes this we a tolerant rather than a vengeful one.

With regard to the second, universal variety of terror, the indisposition of this civil we to question the authority of its or any other cultural narrative is viewed by Lyotard as the perfect antidote for universal discourses whose singular and absolute standards of truth, justice, and the good, derive from their commitment to the legitimation question. For universal discourses that give pride of place to legitimation, argues Lyotard, cannot avoid slipping into an imperialist stance when narratives are the object of their scrutiny. The reason why is that the self-legitmating manner of narratives makes them immediately suspect to such discourses, that is, provides all the grounds needed to discredit their unquestioned normative authority, to tar them in one way or another as "savage, primitive, underdeveloped, backward, alienated, composed of opinions, customs, authority, prejudice, ignorance, ideology" (1986, p. 27). The best way to discourage presumptive judgments of this sort, therefore, which according to Lyotard sets the cultural imperialism of the West apart from all other forms of imperialism, is to turn a deaf ear to their inquisitive overtures, to let tolerance do our bidding for us when we come across cultural narratives that seem quirky and strange by our lights, but certainly not by their lights.

The Legitimation Question Revisited: A Critique of Lyotard

What are we to make of Lyotard's championing of local narratives over universal ones, of his delegation of normative authority to self-enclosed, self-legitimating cultural narratives? Well, we can begin by making something positive of his principled provincialism. For once, we drop the universal pose of metanarratives, the notion that Western ideals have predetermined universal import and validity, they become ordinary narratives that must, therefore, vie for normative dominance with other rival narratives. What is positive about this demotion of privileged metanarratives to working cultural narratives is that it means that it no longer goes without saying that the normative standards of the rich Atlantic cultures are the standards by which all cultures should be measured. To the extent that Lyotard's deconstructive efforts have helped to undercut the self-inflated status of Western metanarratives, his reputation as an anti-imperialist, pro-pluralist thinker is secure, at least in this respect.

However, problems arise when Lyotard insists on linking, better conflating, the universalist strain of Western moral ideals with their justificatory and cosmopolitan strains. That is to say, Lyotard gets into trouble when he claims that the de-universalization of Western metanarratives requires as well their de-normatization and de-cosmopolitization, that we dispense with their efforts to legitimate what they believe and say and their efforts to enrich what they believe and say by trafficking in other cultural narratives. I shall argue that Lyotard is mistaken on both counts. More pointedly, I shall argue that the de-universalization of Western narratives requires the very opposite of what Lyotard argues: namely, the protection and nurturance of their embrace of both legitimation and cosmopolitanism. I begin with the legitimation issue.

Lyotard's proposal to drop the legitimation pose and let cultural narratives do their self-legitimating and self-referential work is, in effect, a proposal to let social consensus of a certain, and as we shall soon see truncated, sort do the work of reasoned deliberation. What is problematic about this can be seen once we consider what elements go into the making of social consensus. As Walzer notes, "the social processes that make [agreement] possible are mixed processes, involving force and fraud, debate and consent, [and] long periods of habituation" (1993, p. 167). Viewed from this angle, Lyotard's proposition to substitute social agreement for normative legitimation amounts to the claim that we drop argument and debate out of the mix of the social processes that are responsible for social consensus. This is a plea, then, for a scaled-down, deliberation-free version of social consensus. And while it would be saying too much to suggest that it is a prescription for force and fraud, it would not be saying too much to claim that it is a prescription for habituation and against argument, which at the very least greases the skids for force and fraud since more of the social agreements that are reached in the absence of rational deliberation will bear these features than would otherwise be the case. So Lyotard's vesting of normative authority in local narratives means that we should cease and desist in our efforts to justify our beliefs and actions, that we should absent ourselves from social practices that involve the rational weighing of beliefs and actions, of old and new candidates for beliefs, practices that all cultures at one time or another and to a greater or lesser degree have seen fit to pursue. In sum, it means that we should believe and do whatever wins the day without asking why or how or at what cost it wins the day.

If this redescription of Lyotard's gambit to extirpate argument from cultural narratives raises doubts about its critical import, those doubts increase once we realize further that what Lyotard is pedaling here is nothing terribly new nor revolutionary but rather something quite reactionary. Indeed, what Lyotard serves up as an alternative to Western metanarratives is, in fact, not an alternative at all but a well-heeled Western language game that goes by the name of warranted assertability. According to this doctrine, our assertions of truth and value are warranted if they hook up with what the majority of our cultural peers believe is true and right. The only innovation that Lyotard adds, if we can call it that, is that he keys his majoritarian conception of truth to the prevailing beliefs of subaltern cultures rather than to those of dominant cultures. Nonetheless, the method of authorization is the same in both cases: just show that your assertions conform with those of the target culture or group and you will have shown that those assertions are warranted ones.

What is problematic about Lyotard's resort to this notion of right assertability is not so much that it is less novel or revolutionary than Lyotard insinuates, but that it is a flawed account of normative legitimacy. It is a flawed account because majoritarian conceptions of truth are ill disposed to tell us what it is reasonable and right for us to believe and do, because they presuppose their own reasonableness and rightness.[8] In other words, when pressed into normative duty, they function as question-begging rather than justificatory devices. This is hardly surprising since majoritarian conceptions of truth, as their name implies, are essentially aggregating measures that tell us what most of our cultural peers happen to believe and think at any given time. That is why they can no more confer warrant on what we believe than the first-order, taken for granted beliefs that they sum. And that is also why there are too many widely held beliefs and actions that are facile, deceptive, and mean-spirited to serve as norms of truth and rightness. In short, that certain beliefs resonate with our cultural peers is no assurance of their normative legitimacy and in arguing that it is, Lyotard gives credence to the manifestly bad idea that whatever a culture ventures as a justification for a belief really is such a justification.

But it cuts even deeper than this. For the notion that "agreeability" and "workability" pass muster as warrants for cultural beliefs is not only a bad idea but a dangerous one. And it is here that Lyotard's gearing of his version of warranted assertability to subaltern cultures proves to be obfuscating, counter-productive, and dangerous in its own right.

It is obfuscating because had Lyotard trained his eyes more carefully on dominant cultures—not just when criticizing them but when trying to draw up an alternative to them—he would have quickly realized that many of the beliefs that fuel the imperialist ambitions of such cultures and that do the dirty work of marginalizing subordinate groups within them, get their purchase from a majoritarian conception of truth of the sort that he now defends. That is to say, the exception he took to many of the prevailing beliefs of dominant Western cultures, which he rightly criticized for being shallow, callous, shortsighted and demeaning to subordinate groups and cultures, were granted normative license in the same manner that he now recommends the prevailing beliefs of subaltern cultures should be granted normative license— on the basis of their workability and agreeability, and not their rational acceptability and critical muster. Here, the lesson of Lyotard's criticism of dominant cultures, that if the beliefs of such cultures are wanting the norms that underwrite them must be as well, are lost on Lyotard's formulation of his own inverted version of warranted assertability. That lesson is lost because the reigning beliefs of subaltern cultures are rife, like their dominant counterparts, with norms that are facile, inconsistent, and demeaning toward their disenfranchised members; norms that should command not our immediate acceptance and respect, as the notion of right assertability would predispose us, but at very least our immediate suspicion.

What I am claiming that Lyotard is obfuscating in pushing his own brand of right assertablity, then, is the core of Western imperialism itself. In this regard, it will be remembered that for Lyotard the imperialist overreach of Western cultures is owed to their preoccupation with the legitimation question, their insistence on justifying what they believe and do, which inexorably leads them, continues Lyotard, to take a dim view of the beliefs of different, poorer cultures who are less able and/or inclined, it is again presumed, to engage in such soul-searching. Lyotard's point in thus championing the beliefs of subaltern cultures, is to rescue the beliefs and ways of life of these less fortunate and beleaguered cultures from the privative readings given them by the West.

But, in fact, the imperialist tendencies of Western nations have to do, as my previous analysis suggests, with their avoidance of the legitimation question altogether, with their bold presumption of cultural superiority. It is this bold presumption which led the West to exploit its technological superiority over non-Western cultures (the fact, as Rorty, 1991, bluntly put it, that we had the gatling gun and they didn't), to put this technical know how and the vast technical apparatus it created to use to suppress rather than uplift these cultures. And what underpins this arrogant self-assertion is no justificatory gesture, no careful weighing of the merits of Western cultures vis-à-vis non-Western ones, but rather what Stanley Fish (1994, p. 34) aptly calls the invocation of the "common"—the heady claim that whatever beliefs Westerners share in common are of such self-evident worth that they need no justification of their superiority, no argument to secure their truth and rightness. So what powers Western imperialism is right assertability not rational deliberation; the conviction that the common beliefs Westerners profess are indubitable ones not contestable ones, which makes arguing for them superfluous, arguing against them absurd, and acting against them treasonous.

It should also now be clear why Lyotard's rendition of warranted assertability falls short as an alternative to what he correctly diagnosed to be the disguised ethnocentrism of Western metanarratives. Put simply, it falls short because what it recommends is not an alternative to such ethnocentrism but in fact another even more virulent form of it. This is apparent from the fact that majoritarian conceptions of truth do just what their metanarrative counterparts did before them, and what Lyotard's de-universalization of Western narratives was supposed to undo: namely, underwrite presumptions of cultural superiority, claims to the effect that it goes without saying that the norms of certain groups and cultures should prevail over those of other groups and cultures. Where they differ from metanarratives is only in the degree to which their claims of special normative license are considered generalizable across cultures.

But even this difference is not as sharp as it might at first appear; for while the claims of right assertability are culturally relative ones that anchor the dominant beliefs of particular cultures, their ethnocentrism is no less fearsome and their reach is often no less extensive than the covert ethnocentrism and universalist pretensions of metanarratives. Their ethnocentrism is no less fearsome, if only because they see no reason to disguise it, to pretend that their favored beliefs should carry the day because they are universal ones. Instead, advocates of warranted assertability contend that their favored beliefs should carry the day precisely because they are their favored beliefs. And it is this very ethnocentrism, explicit and pronounced as it is, that explains why their regard for others is frequently as intrusive and as brusque as that of metanarratives. For cultures who consider their own language games of truth to be, in effect, the only game in town, who think that the only truth there is is the truth their summative judgments yield, are more not less apt to judge others by their own standards of truth and rightness, and so, more rather than less apt to judge them in privative terms.

I think that we are now in a position as well to see why Lyotard's endorsement of warranted assertability is a dangerous one. For that endorsement amounts to an argument at the intracultural level for an unforgiving cultural orthodoxy and at the intercultural level for an equally unforgiving cultural imperialism.

In the former case, majoritarian conceptions of truth prescribe an unduly narrow conception of the basic character and identity of a culture. That is because in equating the basic character of a culture with its prevailing beliefs, any departure from those beliefs is branded, *ipso facto,* as a threat to the integrity and identity of that culture rather than an invitation to its further self-definition and self-differentiation. This is an apologia then, for cultural rigidity and domination, not diversity; for the maintenance of the status quo, not its social transformation and development. It is also an apologia for hardening the division between the haves and have-nots within the borders of nations. For by portraying the beliefs of subordinate groups as heretical ones that constitute an assault upon the cultural soul of the nation, it provides dominant groups with a powerful ideological weapon by which to repress their "inferiors." This was the modus operandi of the mullahs who pronounced Rushdie's fatwa, of the "more faithful" who issued Boulmerka's formal denunciation, and in the West of cultural guardians like Lord Devlin who called for a censure of homosexual lifestyles because of the alleged threat they posed to the English people. This was also the manner in which the new nations that sprang up in the post-Cold War era in the Balkan (Croatia and Serbia) and Baltic states, and the new Asian republics, put into place their own ethnic version of majority domination.[9] Moreover, it was also the way, curiously enough, in which Western metanarratives were redeployed by dominant groups within subaltern cultures in the post-colonial period to further their own particular nationalist causes. According to Moniyhan (1994, p. 158), it was this fact more than any other that accounted for the broad appeal of Marxism to the "often incredibly heterogeneous former colonies" that sought independence during this period. Marxism, Moniyhan continued, with its "exegesis of a one-party, all-powerful state which owned everything and ran everything, was curiously suited to the purposes of dominant castes the world over" (p. 158).

In the case of relations between nations, right assertability proves to be an equally formidable normative weapon. This is the case because the belligerence with which it encourages dominant groups to treat subordinate groups within a country is the same sort of belligerence it encourages more powerful countries to treat their less powerful counterparts. It could hardly be otherwise since majoritarian conceptions of truth incline nations to burrow deeper into their ethnocentric soil, to take more not less seriously the idea that their prevailing beliefs are the only normative standards available to them and the only ones by which they can understand and judge others. That is why I earlier claimed that such self-assertions of cultural identity often go hand in hand with self-assertions of imperial privilege. That is also why I also had the occasion earlier to question what is to stop threatened cultures that rally around their "self-enclosed" cultural narratives in order to drum up opposition to imperialist aggressors—Lyotard's model of the "testy, militant we"—from using those same narratives to drum up aggression against their peaceful neighbors. The less cautious answer I would now venture is that if Lyotard has his way and right assertability is installed as the normative engine of national narratives, there is nothing to prevent heroic resistance against aggressor nations from turning into horrific violence against non-aggressor nations. Indeed, if the course of world events has taught us anything in this last century of rampaging and savage nationalism, it is that where "identification reigns absolutely" (Lyotard, 1993, p. 33) among nations, intolerance of the worst imaginable sort usually follows.

But Lyotard would surely counter my attempt to link the sort of self-assertion that follows from giving cultural narratives a free hand to do their legitimating work to the self-assertion of cultural domination and imperialism by reminding us of his other model of the civil, non-aggressive we. This is the we, it will be remembered, whose wonderment at the sheer diversity of cultural narratives and indifference regarding their authenticity and legitimacy, gives rise not to a restless, domineering, intrusive we, but a pacified, forgiving, and tolerant we. But I am not convinced that this narrative-based agnosticism regarding the legitimation question is, in fact, the recipe for tolerance that Lyotard makes it out to be. I would point first to the empirical news, which suggests, I maintain, that cultures that do not question the normative authority of their signature narratives, that are steadfast in their conviction that they are in the right, are more, not less, likely to judge others by their standards, and so more likely to find them wanting, and, when the conditions are propitious or desperate enough, to force themselves on others.

I would point second to the fact that even if we were to set aside this hard-to-ignore and hard-to-mistake empirical evidence, and to concede Lyotard's point that disinterest in the legitimation question begets a disinclination to judge or suppress or to disparage others, what we would get is not so much a wondrous fascination with others and a tolerance of their differences but rather a pervasive indifference toward others and a morally limp indulgence of their ways of life. We would get a pervasive indifference because normatively self-assured cultures who are content to view others through their own narrative looking glasses are not only likely to find them inscrutable but uninteresting. That is because without some way of hooking up with their central narratives, of connecting up with the stories that convey the meaning and significance of their lives, cultures become quickly irrelevant to one another. And when this happens, the differences between them are relegated to what Geertz calls the "realm of repressible or ignorable difference, mere unlikeness" (quoted in Rorty, 1991, p. 203). We would get a feckless tolerance of others because, once again, without any way to assess, let alone understand, their normative worth except through the eyes and ears of our narrators, we would be more or less condemned to oblige their strange and quirky ways so long as they were not directed toward us. If this be tolerance, then it is a tolerance the world can well do without. For the language it speaks is a language of moral abdication, a language so bereft of moral purpose, resolve, and contempt, that it refuses to speak out on behalf of desperate people, to take their side or, for that matter, any side, to say or do anything to the thugs, gangsters, and warlords that now rule over a goodly portion of the developing world that might give them pause. When we become this tolerant, this permissive, this, if you will, open-minded, as Rorty (1991) reminds us, our brains will have fallen out and with them, whatever moral scruples they might have contained.

Conclusion

To sum up, the point of my extended critique of Lyotard's endorsement of deliberation-free local narratives, of my effort to besmirch his good name as the patron saint of the ignored and impoverished, was to restore the good name of antinomians like Boulmerka. For I reasoned that if Lyotard's advocacy of such narratives were shown to be mistaken, then the censure of Boulmerka that followed from that advocacy, which makes her out to be little more than an infidel, would also be shown to be mistaken. That done, we would have good reason to take notice of, rather than umbrage at, what Boulmerka was trying to tell us by taking on the fundamentalists. And take notice we should. For the message of Boulmerka's high-stakes battle to pry open the soul of Islam, and of all similar such high-pitched battles between progressive and regressive forces the world over, is the ominous one that if we lose this battle we will have lost our own souls because we will have lost the capacity to narrate our own stories. I can think of no worse calamity and, therefore, no better reason to rebuke Lyotard's self-styled postmodernism.

Notes

1. In another paper, I stake out in detail the many similarities between Boulmerka's and Rushdie's stories taking particular note of the moral resources they provide for intercultural exchange and social criticism.

2. My account of Boulmerka's story is derived principally, though not exclusively, from Kenny Moore's (1992) fascinating portrait of Boulmerka and fellow countrymen Noureddine Morceli in his essay "A Scream and a Prayer." What makes Moore's essay especially valuable, aside from his own astute critical commentary, is that it recounts in detail Boulmerka's own personal reflections on the cultural and political significance of her international athletic ventures.

3. Sports and sports clubs played an important role in these initial struggles, becoming important centers of anticolonialist nationalist expression. Indeed, one Arab scholar went so far as to suggest that sports like soccer, once fully appropriated by the Algerian people, served as "instrument[s] of sedition." On this point see Youssef Fates' article, "Sport en Algérie," as quoted and commented upon by Allen Guttmann (1994) in his book *Games and Empires: Modern Sports and Cultural Imperialism.*

4. Since that time, the tension between moderate and militant Muslims in Algeria has escalated to the point that violence and assassination have become commonplace events.

5. I borrow this locution from Rushdie's (1993) stirring essay "One Thousand Days in a Ballon."

6. After all, "terror is," as Rushdie observes, "a reverse form of intervention." As quoted in Cynthia Ozick's (1993, p. 79) article, "Rushdie in the Louvre."

7. We shall have reason to question this so called "universal civic identity" shortly.

8. This part of my argument is indebted to Hilary Putnam's crisp dissection of cultural relativism. See especially his essay "Why Reason Can't Be Naturalized" (1987).

9. On this matter, see Ignatieff's (1993) powerful and penetrating account in his *Blood and Belonging: Journeys into the New Nationalisms.*

References

Fish, S. (1994). *There is no such thing as free speech: And it's a good thing too.* New York: Oxford University Press.

Geertz, C. (1972). "Deep play: Notes on the balinese cockfight." *Daedalus*, Winter, 1–37.

Guttmann, A. (1994). *Games and empires: Modern sports and cultural imperialism.* New York: Columbia University Press.

Ignatief, M. (1993). *Blood and belonging: Journeys into the new nationalism.* New York: Farrar, Straus and Giroux.

Lyotard, F. (1986). *The postmodern condition: A report on knowledge.* Manchester: Manchester University Press.

Lyotard, F. (1993). *The postmodern explained.* Minneapolis: University of Minnesota Press.

Moynihan, D. (1994). *Pandaemonium: Ethnicity in international politics.* New York: Oxford University Pess.

Moore, K. (1992). "A Scream and a prayer." *Sports Illustrated*, 77, 46–61.

Ozick, C. (1993). "Rushdie in the Louvre." *The New Yorker*, 43, 69–79.

Putnam, H. (1987). "Why reason can't be naturalized." In K. Baynes, J. Bohman & T. McCarthy (Eds.), *Philosophy: End or transformation* (pp. 222–244). Cambridge, MA: Massachusetts Institute of Technology Press.

Rorty, R. (1991). *Objectivity, relativism, and truth.* Cambridge: Cambridge University Press.

Rushdie, S. (1993). "One thousand days in a balloon." In S. MacDonogh (Ed.), *The Rushdie letters* (pp. 15–24). Lincoln, Nebraska: University of Nebraska Press.

Walzer, M. (1993). "Objectivity and social meaning." In M. Nussbaum & A. Sen (Eds.), *The quality of life* (pp. 165–177). Oxford: Clarendon Press.

Wieseltier, L. (1994). "Against identity." *The New Republic*, 22, 24–32.

17

(Ir)Relevant Ring: The Symbolic Consumption of the Olympic Logo in Postmodern Media Culture

Rob VanWynsberghe and Ian Ritchie

It is a rare individual who does not recognize the Olympic Games' emblem. Today, this icon comprised of five interlocked rings colored blue, yellow, black, green and red accompanies the purchase of a multiplicity of goods advocated as essential for eating, drinking, clothing, shelter, transportation and amusement. This chapter will examine the historical context and affiliation between such commodities and the interlocked rings while underscoring the true meaning of this internationally accepted and recognized logo. This will reveal that the marketing strategies of various corporations aspire to draw meaningful connections between their products and the ideals connected to the Olympic Games. Here, we do not question the Olympic ideals themselves, but rather their presumed connection to the rings. These ideals are outlined in the Olympic Charter, which states:

> The Olympic flag and symbol symbolize the union of the five continents and the meeting of athletes from all over the world at the Olympic Games in a spirit of fair and frank competition and good friendship, the ideal preached by Baron de Coubertin. (Miller, 1979, p. 194)

We consider these ideals by illuminating the historical origins of the Olympic rings, their linguistic operation in contemporary culture, and their commodification and symbolic consumption through the medium of television and consumers' advertising experience. We conclude that the Olympic rings operate as an open-ended signifier enabling their continued symbolic consumption as both affective cultural icon and linguistic item whose meaning emerges out of the links between products and people's everyday lives. As such, the Olympic rings do not represent ideals inherent to the Games, but are the product of a carefully cultivated media endeavor.

The Olympic Logo

The Olympic Games' five-ring logo was inspired by Pierre de Coubertin, the founder of the modern Olympic Games, as he was involved in the Union des Sociétés Françaises des Sports Athlétiques (USFSA). As first president of this sport governing body, Coubertin had seen the USFSA ascend from the union of two other sporting organizations (Georges St-Clair and Coubertin's Committee for Physical Education) and the logo of the USFSA portrayed two interlocking rings as a symbol of this union (Young, 1985).

This account of the birth of the Olympic logo disputes the widely accepted myth of an historical link existing between the five-ring symbol of the modern Olympic movement and the Games of ancient Greece. While this legend suggests the five-ring emblem is 3,000 years old, several recent pieces of research have debunked this fable (Barney, 1992; Young, 1984, 1985). Nonetheless, it is both historically significant and theoretically pertinent to detail the circumstances under which the idea behind such a widely accepted relationship has been fostered. The confusion emanates, in part, from an altar which rested at Olympia (site of the ancient Olympic Games) and more recently at the adjacent International Olympic Academy. This altar displays the five interlocked rings. In addition, there is a stone located in Delphi (the city which, in antiquity, hosted an alternative set of athletic Games) also displaying the five-ring inscription. Alluding to either of these altars as the source of the 3,000-year old association between the ancient and the modern Olympic Games places one in error by approximately 2,960 years because the origin for both of these altars is Nazi "propaganda" that accompanied the 1936 Berlin Olympics (Young, 1984).

The Olympic Games' insignia first appeared publicly in June of 1914 at the International Olympic Committee's (IOC) 20th-anniversary celebration of the birth of the modern Olympic Movement. On that occasion, 50 white flags were used as a backdrop against which the five-ring symbol was exhibited. Coubertin details this occasion:

The emblem and the flag chosen to represent this 1914 World Congress, which will place the definitive seal on the Olympic revival, has started to appear on various preliminary documents: five rings regularly interlocked. (quoted in Barney, 1992, p. 641)

It was only a short time after its inception that the rings began to circulate as an overarching insignia for the Olympic Movement. It is a common misconception that the five-ring symbol and its colours were originally designed to represent the participation of individual continents in the Olympic Games. That was not the case. Rather, as Coubertin himself explained:

Their diverse colorings—blue, yellow, black, green, and red—are set off against a background which is paper white. These five rings represent the five parts of the world from this point on won over to Olympism and given to accepting fruitful rivalry. Furthermore, the six colours thus combined reproduce the colours of all the nations with no exception. The blue and yellow of Sweden, the blue and white of Greece, the tricolours of France, England and America, Germany, Belgium, Italy, Hungary, the yellow and red of Spain next to the novelties of Brazil or Australia, with old Japan and new China. Here is truly an international symbol. (quoted in Barney, 1992, p. 641)

Several pieces of evidence extractable from this citation substantiate the conclusion that Coubertin's original intent was neither to have the rings, nor their colours represent the continents. The six colours include the flag's white background. If each of these colours is assumed to represent an individual continent this means that any subsequent utilization of the "international symbol" must include this background. Historically, however, this colour has been omitted in continent-by-continent colour representations, not to mention the fact that there are neither five nor six continents, but seven.

However, it is debatable whether Coubertin believed there to be five or six continents (Young, 1984). We do know that he did not include Africa as a separate continent. According to Barney (1992), this was the case because, although South Africa (whites only) had participated in the Olympic Games since their inception, the South African athletes had competed under the flag of "Mother England." In addition, there is no reason to assume that Antarctica was included within the logo colour scheme, given that there is no historical account of athletes from that continent participating in the Olympic Games before, or since, 1914. Therefore, the largest possible number of continents Coubertin could have included was five, yet the number of colors on the flag is six, as Coubertin himself admits.

So perhaps it is the rings representing "the five points in the world" which undergirds the notion of a ring-per-continent equation. It is likely that this was not the case, however, for it has been argued that the five rings and their colours were meant to represent the first five host nations of the Modern Olympic Games: Greece, France, United States, England and Sweden (Young, 1984, 1985). Thus, we can see from the above quote that Coubertin listed those five nations which had already hosted the Games, followed by Germany which was expected to host the ill-fated 1916 Games and Belgium, the eventual host of the 1920 Games. Following Young, Coubertin intended to add a ring for every country that hosted the Games. This practice was halted either because of Coubertin's disillusionment with the inevitability of World War I, or a deep-seated aversion to including a ring for the nation of Germany (Young, 1985).

The five-ring symbol was co-opted from a party celebrating the successful completion of 20 years of Olympic resuscitation, which in turn gained inspiration from the union of competing sport federations. It is clear that the symbol chosen to embody the modern Olympic movement has no distinct meaning outside of that which was conferred upon it from the exercise of "sporting license" with history, both recent and ancient. This process of co-optation cannot be taken lightly, however, because these specious origins have contributed to its being one the most sought after commercial images in the world. As such, the rings have no inherent bond with the Games. In fact, if Coubertin's original plan of adding a ring to the white background for every host nation had continued, the celebrated five-ring logo would not exist today. So why is there such a strong association between the Games and the logo? More importantly, what dynamics are responsible for the existence of this internationally recognized emblem? To answer these questions, the sign and function of the logo must be understood alongside its attendant commodity function. We hope, through our analysis, to disclose the source of the rings' symbolic power.

The Sign as Structure

At first glance, the relationship between the Olympics and the five-ring symbol seems both direct and unequivocal. However, the meaning of this association is open to question. The association is owed to the construction of the Olympic Games' five-ring logo as a single linguistic item, one that is operating as a "double entity, one formed by the associating of two terms" (Saussure, 1966, p. 65).

As Saussure points out, the operation inherent to associating these two terms, in structuring a single linguistic item, entails the connection of more than "a thing and a name." Instead it is "the psychological imprint of the sound, the impression that it makes on our senses" (1966, p. 66). The rings' linguistic operation can be understood as an organic relationship of parts that make sense only in relation to one another—the modern Olympic Games (concept/signified) and the rings (sound-image/signifier). The signifier consists of the material aspect of the sign (sounds and letters), while the signified is the meaning represented by the material aspect of the sign. These parts comprise what Saussure called a "sign," that is, an association between a concept and a sound-image which should be thought of as an organic relationship and not simply the sum of two discreet parts.

Two immediate objections might be raised at this point. First, as the rings are visual and not phonetic, how can they constitute the sound-image to which Saussure referred? In response, we submit that the rings are not simply visual, for the expression "Olympic rings" can not only be written, but also used phonetically, thus conjuring up the powerful psychological images that have lead to its ascribed status. Furthermore, the rings seem to operate as a signifier, inasmuch as their visual impact evokes the "Olympic rings" at the same moment as they are seen, and inasmuch as there is an organic link between the rings and the concept to which they now refer, the Olympic Games.

Second, and more importantly, are not the rings a symbol of the Olympic Games, invoking "a natural bond between the signifier and signified" (Saussure, 1966, p. 68)? In other words, is it possible to compare the Olympic rings with, for example, the scales of justice, an archetype Saussure offers as exemplifying this natural bond? This query raises the problem of the arbitrary relationship between signifier and signified, a relationship that is necessary for constituting the sign, where convention designates the signifier in play. The scales of justice seem to occupy such a non-arbitrary position, for not any symbol—such as a chariot, for example—could be used to represent the judiciary. Do the rings not have such a natural bond as a product of a fundamental link between the rings and the Games? Perhaps this is just the point: there seems to be such a strong, almost essential link, but none exists! Do the rings represent the continents? No. The Ancient Olympic Games? No. Do the colours represent the continents? No. Indeed, the history of the rings has shown there to be no such natural bond, only an arbitrary invention and application emerging through convention and over time.

Saussure's work provided a paradigm in structuralist semiotic theory, analyzing language in terms of its laws. For Saussure, the different parts of the system of language take on meaning only in relation to differences or, in other words, acquire significance only in relation to what they are not. Despite the importance of this structuralist account, it does not completely explain the universal recognition of the Olympic logo as a symbol, nor does it account for its widely accepted status among advertisers. Our important goal of producing a more complete understanding of the Olympic logo as an advertising tool must transcend, but not neglect, semiotic analysis and examine the political economy of the sign in order to illuminate the relationship between sign and commodity.

The Commodification of the Sign

Many more recent theoretical efforts have journeyed beyond Saussure's early position in stressing both the arbitrary nature of language and the properties of the sign in a capitalist political economy. This elaboration is generally attributed to Baudrillard, whose insights emerged out of an early neo-Marxist interest in examining commodities as they convey meaning from the desires they satisfy. Baudrillard's work, begun in the late 1960s, has continued to provide theoretical impetus as a project discerning the impact of new communication forms on society. Indeed, these labors have been expanded, becoming the foundation for an extensive cultural critique positing that simulations have acted to fundamentally alter perceptions of reality (cf. Baudrillard, 1988a, 1988b, 1988c; Poster, 1988, 1990). More specifically, it has been suggested that "advertising takes over the moral responsibility of all of society and replaces a puritan morality with a hedonistic morality of pure satisfaction, like a new state of nature at the heart of hypercivilization" (Baudrillard, 1988a, pp. 12–13).

Baudrillard's earliest research proposes that "sign value" is a necessary insertion into the usual Marxian distinctions between "use value" and "exchange value," thereby capturing the prestige element that accompanies any commodity purchase and its reflection upon the consumer. Indeed, Baudrillard (1981) calls for an end to the distinction between the concepts of use value and exchange value because both are ensnared in the logic of capitalist production and act as a pretext for its continued existence. Baudrillard's own typology, then, suggests that Marxism can be read as not so much a radical critique of capitalism, but as an ideology that justifies the full metamorphosis of this economic form (Poster, 1988). Accordingly, Baudrillard (1988b) mandates the union of the concepts of exchange value and use value within sign value. The relationship between consumer and object, then, is not only the satisfaction of needs, but the production of inexhaustible desires (Poster, 1988). For example, purchasing Nike brand footwear transcends the procurement of an attractive and expensive mode of personal transport; rather, replacing old shoes becomes an act of endowing meaning and accumulating "cultural capital."

We would like to suggest here that Baudrillard's discussion of the emergence of sign value has direct bearing on the Olympic Games. Gruneau (1984) notes that during the latter half of the 19th century, the expanse of time devoted to work and time devoted to leisure became conspicuously separated as a result of the cultural hegemony of capitalist conceptions of work and temporality. This development enhanced opportunities for free time expenditure to become inextricably contingent on the capitalist marketplace. Moreover, this provided the impetus for the commodification of popular recreation, leading to an acknowledgment of sport as just another realm of the prevailing economic system. It is no surprise, then, that the modern Olympic movement was affected. As Gruneau mentions: "No matter what the intentions of the founders of the modern Olympics, the actual possibilities open to them were limited by the nature of the economic system as a whole and the network of social institutions associated with it" (1984, p. 5).

Gruneau (1984) asserts that the prohibitive cost of hosting the Games became a factor in the expanded circulation of the Olympic logo as both sign and commodity. For example, the 1972 Munich Games cost of $850 million was almost doubled to $1.5 billion for the 1976 Montreal Games (Gruneau, 1984). In addition, it is estimated that Spain spent nearly $8 billion in preparation for the 1992 Barcelona Games (Double, 1989). Clearly, the sales of television rights along with public donations and investments could not adequately cover such staggering sums. Gruneau (1984) suggests that Olympic organizing committees foresaw this development and were virtually forced into marketing the Games as a commodity, leading to the 1984 Los Angeles Games' nickname "the hamburger Olympics."

Gruneau's scheme details how the commodification process engulfed leisure and sport. The Olympic Games, as a major component of sport, became "more commodified to the point where, at its highest levels, it is now a simple division of the entertainment and light consumer goods industries" (1988, p. 358). This signalled an increasing prominence devoted to the Olympic Games' logo as a marketing symbol or trademark. Gruneau appropriates Baudrillard's insights, making it possible to provide an analysis of the "political economy of the Olympic sign" where sign value is the only meaningful element of the political economy. This examination contributes to the new logic of production, which finds resonance in Baudrillard's call for a drastic shift in understanding consumption:

> Today consumption—if this term has a meaning other than that given It by vulgar economics—defines precisely the stage where the commodity is immediately produced as the sign, as a sign value, and where signs (culture) are produced as commodities (1981, p. 147)

Baudrillard (1981) asserts that language lost its reciprocal nature when an abstract code emerged—the era of the sign. A composite of signifiers is called a "code," and a code extracts signifieds from the social and represents them in the media (Baudrillard, 1988c). This era of the sign resonates with a corresponding emergence in capitalism. Today, there is a complete separation of signs from their referents and the result is that signifiers operate randomly, unable to express meaning. The media then, can be understood as offering endless and excessive signifiers that fail to operate according to any rational process of information dissemination.

Baudrillard expands upon the foregoing point, judging "desire" to be the driving force behind a commodity purchase. This abolishes the standard position of rationality and need as prime determinants in the consumer-commodity relationship and, in turn, destroys normal social conventions and rules of conduct. This leads to the notion of commodity acquisition wherein the commodity attaches meaning to the consumer. For Baudrillard, advertising begins this process by coding "products through symbols that differentiate them from other products, thereby fitting the object into a series" (quoted in Poster, 1988, p. 2). Baudrillard's analysis postulates the existence of a system of signs wherein varied meanings connote differences between individuals based upon commodity purchase patterns. Moreover, these meanings offer new and continuous delights that act to exacerbate compulsive desires. Baudrillard extends his interest in the power of desire suggesting that it acts as a seductive force that could potentially replace the model of supply and demand production.

Baudrillard concludes that the code no longer refers to, nor even has a relationship with, the consumer object. Instead, the code can be re-conceptualized as "simulacra," that is, as a system that has no grounding in a wider reality, but only refers to itself (Rosenau, 1992). Baudrillard's term for this condition is "hyperreality," a contemporary and unexplored form of linguistic existence, that is more undeniable than concrete reality. In other words, the model replaces the real, and the model to which we aspire is a simulation (Best & Kellner, 1991).

Hyperreality has two grand and interrelated implications. The first regards a potential shift in the focus from the subject to the (hyperreal) object. This typically postmodern perspective asserts that changing conditions of contemporary existence have altered one's "individuality and self-awareness— the condition of being subject" (Rosenau, 1992, p. 42). This denial of the privileged position of the subject in determining truth constitutes the second connotation. According to Baudrillard's scheme, we are relegated to the position of mere sign consumers, vulnerable to the seductive qualities of consumer objects as elucidated by the prevailing code.

It is critical for our present concerns to ascertain whether Baudrillard's most recent contributions further an understanding of the Olympic logo. Consequently, it is necessary to conduct a detailed and grounded examination of the "coding" of products through symbols. To begin, we turn to Gruneau who asserts that the underlying rationale behind all advertising is the establishment of a set of "deeply rooted symbolic connections with a target audience" (1984, p. 1). Explicating the nature of these symbolic connections goes beyond determining whether or not the five rings operate as a symbol, concentrating instead on the significance of establishing such a symbolic relationship.

We begin by briefly examining the type of affiliations sought through linking one's product with the Olympic logo. Although these vary among advertisers, generally the images that need to be elicited are those related to "the sporting life," "youth," "success," "brotherhood or sisterhood" and "universality." Jhally concisely articulates some of the previous assertions on sport, the media, and advertising:

The sports industry has become dependent upon the media; the media in turn derive their revenues for the purchase of sports broadcast rights from advertisers who wish to reach the audiences that watch sports. The other way in which sports can derive additional revenue is to sell themselves directly to advertisers. The 1984 Olympic Games in Los Angeles are the best example of this commercialization taken to extreme lengths. Sports are undoubtedly a very important and powerful cultural force in contemporary America—they give meaning to the lives of many people. That meaning, though, is mediated through the commodity form of culture. (1989, p. 79)

Commodity *Qua* Object

The concept of "the commodity" serves as an important conduit for a discussion of the Olympic rings, undergirding our claim that it is in relation to the flow of commodities that the rings have simultaneously achieved their prominence, meaning and attendant confusion. The nature of commodity production in consumption-oriented cultures, however, is no simple matter. Indeed, the relationship between the commodity *qua* object, people as consumers, and the wider cultural landscape is extremely complex because, for example, the capitalists' profit motive alone does not completely account for the commodity's meaning, for "commodities are consumed as much for their meanings, identities, and pleasures as they are for their material function" (Fiske, 1989, p. 4). In other words, people, as consumers, and not just capitalists, utilize and make sense of the commodity.

As suggested earlier, semiotic power is always involved in the consumer's relation to the object because commodities have both a material and symbolic component. Duncan offers a telling example in this regard: "women may be transformed symbolically (e.g., as pornographic images) or materially (e.g., as prostitutes) into commodities, either more or less valuable depending on their external surfaces" (1993, p. 361). Furthermore, the meanings of the consumed objects are negotiated in and through the varied cultural backgrounds of consumers. Fiske notes the importance of "the interface between everyday life and the consumption of the products of the cultural industries" (1989, p. 6). Television audiences, for example, are social subjects who read programs and commercials differently, depending on their social-cultural context (Fiske, 1987). Finally, if it serves the profit-oriented interests of capitalists to produce commodities that can be sold to as many different stripes of consumers as possible at the same time, and if these same consumers produce many and diverse meanings associated with the commodity, then it follows that the interests of capitalists would most effectively be served by a commodity-production system that is as germane to as many consumers as possible. How is this possible?

The answer, in part, can be examined by investigating the concept of "relevance" which Fiske (1989) suggests is vital to the creation and continued fulfillment of commodities and their related meanings in popular culture. Simply put, the notion of relevance refers to "a site of struggle, for relevances are dispersed, and as divergent as the social situations of the people" (Fiske, 1989, p. 6). As such, popular culture has within it "parody, subversion, or inversion" which are "full of puns whose meanings multiply and escape the norms of the social order and overflow their discipline" and which produce "contradictions, for contradictions require the productivity of the reader to make his or her sense out of them" (pp. 5–6). In other words, an open-ended signification and consumption system most efficaciously sells the commodity by leaving its meanings open to the interpretations of consumers in and through their everyday experiences.

This system takes on heightened importance in postmodern North American society, wherein culture is guided by, shaped, and imbued with life by the interrelationship between the use value of the object and its symbolic meaning (Duncan, 1993). The crucial difference between modernism and postmodernism rests, according to Zizek, in "unmasking" the logic of capitalism and all its oppressions; in "the utopian abolition of the difference between 'alienated' life spheres, between art and 'reality'" (1992, p. 142). Within modernism, this "unmasking" assumes something just around the corner, that is, a utopic ending to the alienation inherent to capitalism or the discovery of the foundations of democratic principles. As manifested in popular culture, texts, movies, or televised sport spectacles, the object of one's desire always lurks just around the corner. In contrast, postmodernism "consists not in demonstrating that the game works without an object, that the play is set in motion by a central absence, but rather in displaying the object directly, allowing it to make visible its own indifferent and arbitrary character" (Zizek, 1991, p. 143).

The consequence is that in advanced postmodern consumer-oriented cultures, the object's meaning, be it material or symbolic, is not so simple as to be completely definable. In addition, the relevancy of commodities insinuates something very different for postmodern culture than it does for modern. While it may be true that the commodity's meaning in early capitalism could be defined in relation to its utility, in late-capitalism the role of mass communications, advertising, and the creation of consumer-oriented culture depend on an ever-expanding set of needs and meanings attached to the commodities that venture to satisfy those needs. As such, perhaps it is more fitting to suggest that (ir)relevance of the commodity, its advertising symbols and its meaning is the name of the game in postmodern societies. In other words, if a particular symbol—*qua* signifier—were to be irrelevant, to have no inherent meaning or to be recognized as inherently neutral, then that symbol would be an especially powerful advertising tool. It could be used to represent virtually any product; advertisers could construct any story they wanted around such a symbol, while at the same time it would mean something different for diverse groups of people. The product would be sold, diverse groups of people could create their own meanings around the symbolic representation of products and, in the end, the symbol would be at the same time completely relevant and irrelevant.

The Olympic logo is such an irrelevant signifier. It serves the needs of consumerism very well. The symbol's fictitious past guarantees its contemporary power, and the implicit link to the Games—an international event popularly venerated as more "neutral"—adds to this power. The symbol's meaning, in other words, is not pre-given so as to be advertised and consumed. Indeed, the internationally accepted logo for the Olympic Games, through communicative and symbolic consumption, is accorded continuously invented meaning.

The greatest advertising medium, and the most important for the Olympic Games and the five-ring logo as an advertising tool, is television. Indeed, we find that television's omnipresent status in the contemporary global marketplace infuses the rings with their power as it is largely through this conduit that the rings work their magic.

Television Consumption and Advertisers

Television's role in advanced capitalist societies, where high consumption levels are necessary for the expansion of capital into virtually every aspect of life, cannot be overemphasized. In particular, Dunn (1986) notes the manner in which television exists in an "unfinished" relationship with the viewers, suggesting that the meanings created by television are ambiguous, as is our knowledge of how the complex television-viewer relationship operates.

Dunn asserts that in the process of constituting workers as consumers in the early 20th century, advertising came not only to sell products but ways of life. The result has been a mass culture, where "culture itself is turned into an industry—its various products packaged and marketed like any commodity" (Dunn, 1986, p. 51). The effect of television has been to reduce objects to images: "meanings get attached to commodities as objects of visual perception, thereby turning objects into images" (p. 53). In effect, the object takes on a Baudrillardian hue becoming both commodity and sign.

Also noteworthy is recent research suggesting, contra Baudrillard, that the viewer is not a completely passive one, but is constituted as an active subject (Dunn, 1986; Fiske, 1987; Poster, 1990). As Dunn points out: "the logic of television's code . . . points to numerous questions concerning the claims of passive spectatorship and ideological reproduction" (1986, p. 55). With television, there is reduction of everything—all content and form—to its own code, and there is a reason for this. According to Dunn,

> to accommodate a range of themes and communication functions within continuous flow broadcasting, television must abolish traditional distinctions of subject matter and taste. News, documentaries, comedies, commercials, editorials, sports, etc.—the whole repertoire is more or less indiscriminately reduced to a single language of television's own making. (1986, p. 56)

As a result of its own predetermined dictates, television is capable of creating perverse contrasts, for example, between news of famine and a commercial for luxurious food, or, as during the 1994 Winter Olympic telecast, images relating the rings to war-torn Sarajevo and to Coca-cola. Contrasts are accomplished via the ability of television to play upon emotions, to enact the "language of affect":

> The objects of fulfillment encoded with consumerist meanings can be decoded in a variety of alternative or oppositional ways by members of this audience . . . set[ting] in motion a number of contradictory tendencies: it both arouses and calms, excites and dulls, stimulates and drains. (Dunn, 1986, p. 57)

The emotional impact of television is facilitated by complex technology, visual regimentation, routinized technical structures, dynamic round-the-clock broadcasting, and so forth. But the affective impact on viewers varies as viewers are not passive receptacles; they may "read" television differently and resist certain meanings. As Fiske maintains:

> Semiotic resistance results from the desire of the subordinate to exert control over the meanings of their lives, a control that is typically denied them in their material social conditions. This . . . is politically crucial, for without some control over one's existence there can be no empowerment and no self-esteem. (1989, p. 10)

Viewers, then, are active subjects and while mass media may demand, in principle, an attitude of passive acceptance, this does not mean that they actually obtain it (Dunn, 1986). Different groups of people, for example, offer alternative readings of television shows and advertisements. Fiske cites studies that demonstrate conformist, alternative, or even oppositional readings of television shows. This leads him to conclude that "there are very few perfectly dominant or purely oppositional readings, and consequently viewing television is typically a process of negotiation between the text and its variously socially situated readers" (1987, p. 64).

While it may be true, then, that in capitalist societies the mass-production and consumption of goods requires concomitant mass-advertising schemes through television creating a homogenization of messages and symbolic representation of commodities, it is equally true that diverse groups of television viewers are able to decode messages just as heterogeneously as the encoding seeks homogeneity. This is not a contradiction. In fact, this is the consistent manner in which the senders, receivers, and context (structure) of the message interact. As Umberto Eco says, in mass communication, "the transmitter of the message works within a communicative code which he knows a priori is not shared by all the receivers" (1972, p. 105). In other words, "aberrant" decodings are the rule in mass media.

To argue that advertising and the production of cultural commodities—the production of culture itself—creates a passive spectator/consumer is similarly much too simplistic. Advertisers do not exploit a mindless viewer, rather advertising adroitly plays on the ability of spectators/viewers to create meanings in their everyday lives. That is why irrelevant/ambiguous meanings are thrust into viewers' lives via advertising, and the utilization of the Olympic Games is an effective tool for such an undertaking.

Advertising, Ambush Marketing, and Olympic Rights[1]

By merging the trademarks of their corporation and the Olympic institution, advertisers hope to formulate an image of their product that partakes in the prestige accorded the modern Olympic Movement as symbolized by the five interlocking rings. This is accomplished in television advertisements by companies offering products as diverse as sports clothing ("it takes a little more to be a champion"), fast-food (the owner of Wendy's has a dream of "winning gold"), or camera film ("just a reminder from Kodak that some of the greatest Winter Games take place in your own back yard"). The host network takes advantage of the Games' prestige and sells its own television shows in a similar fashion: "after you share a moment with the world, spend an hour with Dave"; "You've seen our team bring home the gold for our country, now the country gold of [promo]"; "Northern Exposure returns with world class"; "[CBS Evening News] where your world comes together." Advertisers, in other words, imply that the consumption of their products is directly and symbolically linked to Olympic Games' participation.

That corporate advertisers and television networks use the Olympic logo however, does not mean there are any inherent qualities in the Olympic logo. Indeed, we have shown that such inherent qualities do not exist. Nonetheless, a great deal of prestige has been conferred upon the Olympic image and, therefore, upon any product incorporating this image into a marketing strategy. In other words, advertisers are clearly aware of the nexus between image and commodity:

> Whether or not U.S. athletes actually thrive upon Chocolate bars, Coke, Big Macs, or Budweiser beer is unimportant to the sponsoring companies whose primary concern is that their products become associated in the public mind with the Olympics. (Tomlinson & Whannel, 1984, p. v)

What has emerged, then, is an ironic situation where the Olympic logo remains "faithful" to its invented historical "roots" and fulfills its role to advertisers by providing a set of powerful images that are completely receptive to being affiliated with virtually any commodity. For examples, among the advertised products during CBS's U.S.A. broadcast of the 1994 Games were cars (Ford, Dodge/Plymouth), clothing (Champion, L'eggs, Hanes, Reebok), telecommunications (Sprint, Xerox, IBM), fast-food (McDonald's, Wendy's), soft-drinks (Coca-Cola), drugs (Tylenol), life insurance (John Hancock), credit cards (Visa), general merchandise (K-mart), leisure/theme park (Walt Disney), beer (Budweiser), and so forth. As one advertising consultant working for Coke and other large corporations suggests, "the company helps to forge the link between the 'grand scale' of Olympic events and the ideals and everyday lives of millions of ordinary people around the globe" (Dwek, 1991, p. 16).

The advertising phenomenon of ambush marketing provides circumstance for examining the power and obscurity of the Olympic image, an image that weaves into one the mundane, the magnificent and the material. Ambush marketing refers to the practice whereby corporations buy broadcast air time during the Games without having directly sponsored the IOC by paying a fee, a National Olympic Committee (NOC), or a National Governing Body (NGB). Ambushers hope to have their 30-second promotions sandwiched around the advertisements of official sponsors, thereby appearing as corporate advocates or benefactors of the Olympic movement without providing remuneration (Levine & Thurston, 1992). Official sponsor status notwithstanding, by purchasing advertising space during the broadcast of sporting events, ambushers hope to immerse their products in the composite of the meanings imputed to the Olympic spectacle.

This was clearly demonstrated during the 1992 Winter Olympics in Albertville, when the Federal Express Courier Corporation ran a series of commercial spots that lead to 61 percent of the viewers polled to believe— wrongly as it turned out—that Federal Express was an official sponsor of the Olympic Games (Levine & Thurston, 1992). During CBS's American broad-

cast of the 1994 Lillehammer Winter Games, Visa and American Express
"fought it out" once again. As both companies' advertisements took the viewers on whirlwind tours of Norway, the host country, official sponsor Visa
claimed "if you think the elements are cold, wait until you see your reception
when you try to buy a ticket at the Olympic Games with your American
Express card," while ambusher American Express reminded viewers "if you're
traveling to Norway, you'll need a passport, but you don't need a Visa."

A subtler version of this same phenomenon occurs when an official
sponsor of the Games competes against corporations underwriting individual
teams only. For example, the Fuji company sponsored the U.S. track and field
team in the 1992 Games, thereby reducing the value of the larger Olympic
sponsorship investment for Kodak because they are not (Levine & Thurston,
1992). Coke attempted to prevent a similar occurrence during the 1992
Albertville and Barcelona Games by buying the rights to 37 out of 40 separate U.S. National Governing Bodies as well as purchasing the logo rights
from the IOC (Dwek, 1991). Coke's overall expenditures for sponsorship
rights and marketing approached $100 million, which is not that much in
comparison to what it has spent to promote its connections to the 1996
Atlanta Games, a venue that just happens to be headquarters for this soft
drink giant. The 1984 Hamburger Olympics have had their parallel at the
1996 Coca-Cola Games.

Purchasing the rights to the Olympic logo assists in shaping individual
consumer consumption patterns. Firms are willing to pay enormous amounts
of money for the privilege of creating an association between their product
and the five rings. In fact, the amounts for worldwide Olympic sponsorship
rights have almost quadrupled since the 1984 Games. At the 1992 Games
(both winter and summer), $15 million was paid by corporate interests for
inclusion into the International/Worldwide or TOP-2 sponsorship program
that grants corporations the global rights to promote their commodities by
linking their consumption with the Olympic Games (Double, 1989). This
"sponsorship" has translated into expenditures of upwards of $450 million
U.S. dollars in total advertising and promotion costs for TOP-2 participants.
Moreover, the 1996 IOC sponsorship fee has escalated to $43 million (Levine
& Thurston, 1992).

Conclusion

We have shown that the actual origins of the five interlocking rings
were as a commemorative icon, not as an overarching symbol for the Olympic Movement. Indeed, the rings represent the lack of Olympic ideals, while
at the same time ironically sustaining the Olympic Games, for it is the Games'
marketing, based largely on the use of the logo, that has aided its financial

success in the late 20th century. This suggests that one of the world's most recognizable commercial images cannot be explained solely by a traditional critique of political economy. In other words, the rings' symbolic consumption contributes more to the Games' marketing success than the use value of the products to which they are attached.

In this context, the rings represent the superimposition of two interrelated operations. First, the modernist utilization of global ideals (e.g., unity, peace) that pervade the sporting institution and are reflected in the (ultimately false) belief in the five-ring logo and its referent, the Olympic Games, as symbolizing these global sporting ideals. Second, a postmodernist interpretation of the rings that sees them as mere convention and depicts their consumption as highly symbolic despite the fact that their meaning is ultimately irrelevant. In understanding these mechanisms, we are confronted with the rings' marketing appeal.

And so, we contend that the symbolic consumption of the Olympic Games is more appropriately constituted within postmodern media culture. While the five-ring symbol played a historically vital role in the commodification of the Games, contemporary developments have engendered a postmodern everyday world that circumscribes the symbols attached to this spectacle. Accordingly, their circulation in the media has taken on myriad forms, supplying an insatiable television industry with sets of images that merge with viewers' everyday lives. Television, as we have seen during the last Olympic Games, enables advertisers to work the magic of the rings by nurturing meanings that accompany such images. In other words, both the medium and the message fastidiously buttress the shape and structure of existing meanings by offering them to the viewer as coterminous. This act confers relevance upon an irrelevant entity to ensure the consumption of such meanings.

Finally, we understand these links to be crucial as they depict the Olympic Games, one of the most visible elements of the institution of sport, as constructed by neither the needs of capital, nor the demands of consumers. Rather, it is that mediating space lying at the point of constructing meanings which finds resonance in the Games' success. These meanings are as endless as the rings are endlessly meaningless.

Note

1. The examples used in this section are drawn from advertisements broadcast during CBS's prime-time telecast of the 1994 Lillehammer Winter Olympic Games (February 23 and 25 telecasts). Significantly, the women's figure skating competition was broadcast in these time slots. In the United States, controversy surrounding the

U.S. team prefigured heavy interest among both viewers and advertisers. *The Wall Street Journal* reported that 48.5 percent of U.S. homes with television sets were tuned in.

References

Best, S., & Douglas K. (1991). *Postmodern theory: Critical interrogations.* New York: Guilford Publications.

Barney, R.K. (1992). "This great symbol: Tricks of history." *Olympic Review,* 8(3), pp. 627–641.

Baudrillard, J. (1981). *For a critique of the political economy of the sign.* St. Louis, MO: Telos Press.

——— (1988a). "The system of objects." In M. Poster (Ed.), *Jean Baudrillard: Selected writings* (pp. 10–28). Stanford, CA: Stanford University Press.

——— (1988b). "The mirror of production." In M. Poster (Ed.), *Jean Baudrillard: Selected writings* (pp. 98–118). Stanford, CA: Stanford University Press.

——— (1988c). "Symbolic exchange and death." In M. Poster (Ed.), *Jean Baudrillard: Selected writings* (pp. 119–148). Stanford, CA: Stanford University Press.

Double, M.B. (1989). "Barcelona Olympics will open doors for U.S. business." *Business America,* August, p. 28.

Duncan, M.C. (1993). "Beyond analysis of sport media texts: An argument for formal analyses of institutional structures." *Sociology of Sport Journal,* 10(4), 353–373.

Dunn, R. (1986). Television, consumption and the commodity form. *Theory, Culture and Society,* 3(1), 49–64.

Dwek, R. (1991). "Coca-Cola: An Olympic obsession." *Marketing,* December, p. 12.

Eco, U. (1972). "Towards a semiotic inquiry into the television message." *Working Papers in Cultural Studies.* Birmingham, England: Center for Contemporary Cultural Studies.

Fiske, J. (1987). *Television culture.* New York: Routledge.

——— (1989). *Reading the popular.* Boston: Unwin Hyman.

Goldman, K. (1994). "Eager to cash in on Olympic fever, advertisers snare top athletes." *The Wall Street Journal,* February 25, p. 17.

Gruneau, R. (1984). "Commercialism and the modern Olympics." In A. Tomlinson & G. Whannel (Eds.), *Five ring circus: Money, power and politics at the Olympic Games* (pp. 1–15). London: Pluto Press.

Gruneau, R., & Cantelon, H. (1988). "Capitalism, commercialism, and the Olympics." In J. Segrave & D. Chu (Eds.), *The Olympic Games in transition* (pp. 345–364). Champaign, IL: Human Kinetics.

Jhally, S. (1989). "The political economy of culture." In I. Angus & S. Jhally (Eds.), *Cultural politics in contemporary America* (pp. 65–81). New York: Routledge.

Levin, G. (1992). "Amex, Visa trade Olympic blows." *Advertising Age*, January 20, p. 131.

Levine, J.B., & Thurston, K. (1992). "The real marathon: Signing Olympic sponsors." *Business Week*, August 23, p. 43.

Miller, G. (1979). *Behind the Olympic rings*. Lynn, MA: H.O. Zimman.

Poster, M. (Ed.) (1988). *Jean Baudrillard: Selected writings*. Stanford, CA: Stanford University Press.

———— (1990). *The mode of information: Post structuralism and the social context*. Chicago: The University of Chicago Press.

Roseneau, P.M. (1992). *Post-modernism and the social sciences: Insights, inroads, and intrusions*. Princeton: Princeton University Press.

Saussure, F. de (1966). *Course in general linguistics*. New York: McGraw-Hill.

Tomlinson, A., & Whannel, G. (1984). *Five ring circus: Money, power and politics at the Olympic Games*. London: Pluto Press.

Young, D.C. (1984). "The riddle of the rings." In S.J. Bandy (Ed.), *Coraebrus triumphs: The alliance of sport and the arts* (pp. 81–97). San Diego: San Diego State University Press.

———— (1985). "Coubertin and the Olympic logo." In J.A. Mangan (Ed.), *Proceedings of the XIth HISPA International Congress* (pp. 326–327). Glasgow, England: Jordan Hill College.

Zizek, S. (1992). *Looking awry*. Cambridge, MA: Massachusetts Institute of Technology Press.

CONTRIBUTORS

David Andrews, Ph.D., is an assistant professor in the Department of Human Movement Sciences and Education at the University of Memphis. He has taught, researched, and published on a variety of topics related to the critical analysis of sport as an aspect of contemporary popular culture. His most recent published articles have appeared in the *Sociology of Sport Journal, Quest,* and *Cultural Studies: A Research Annual.*

Toni Bruce is an assistant professor in Sport Studies at the University of New Hampshire, where she teaches sport sociology and a variety of sports communications classes. Before obtaining her Ph.D. in sociology of sport from the University of Illinois at Urbana-Champaign (1995), she spent five years in the communications field, working as a news reporter and sports writer, and interning in public relations with the Women's Sports Foundation. Her current research focuses on the sports media and the experiences of marginalized groups in sport such as women sports writers.

Cheryl L. Cole is assistant professor in the Department of Kinesiology, Women's Study, and Criticism and Interpretive Theory at the University of Illinois at Urbana-Champaign. She is currently completing a book on national popular culture, sport, and deviant bodies.

Caroline Fusco is currently working as a full-time instructor in the Faculty of Physical Education and Recreation Studies at the University of Manitoba. Her research interests are in the areas of feminist theory and methodologies, heterosexism and homophobia in sport, and lesbian experiences in sport and coaching. She is hoping to pursue these areas of research interest when she enters a doctoral programme.

Jacques Gleyse is a professor at the Université Paul Valery in Montpellier as well as at the University Institute for Teachers' Training. He teaches historical aspects of the education of the body and he trains future physical education teachers. Doctor in educational sciences, he is the author of numerous works, including *Archeology of Physical Education in the 20th Century* (PUF, 1995) and *Body Instrumentalization* (L'Harmattan, 1997).

Samantha King is a doctoral candidate in the Department of Kinesiology, Women's Study, and Criticism and Interpretive Theory at the University of Illinois at Urbana-Champaign. Her doctoral dissertation examines drugs, sport, and consumer culture in late Modern America.

Nate Kohn is at the University of Georgia where he is working with various writing theories to rethink a number of classic issues in sport studies such as what is sport and what counts as sport as we near the new millenium. He is an assistant professor in the College of Journalism and Mass Communication. He received his Ph.D. from the University of Illinois at Urbana-Champaign after working for 15 years as a producer and writer of theatrical feature films.

Mélisse R. Lafrance is with the Women's Studies and Sociology Programs at the University of Ottawa. Her current research areas include the constructions and transgressions of normative genders, bodies, and desires. Some of her publications have appeared in the book *Human Rights and Women's Realities: Reflections on Beijing and Beyond*, and the research journal *Avante*.

Margaret MacNeill, Ph.D., is an assistant professor in the School of Physical and Health Education at the University of Toronto. She teaches media and socio-cultural courses examining health and physical activity. Her research interests include Olympic television studies, feminist studies of fitness and sport, and gender and health communication.

Nancy Midol is professor of anthropology and psychoanalysis in the Faculty of Sport Sciences at the University of Nice in Sophia Antipolis, where she is also the Director of the Social and Behavioral Sciences and Sport and Physical Activity Research Centre. She has published extensively in the areas of cultural innovation and extreme sports and her last book is entitled *Demiurgy in Sports and Dance* (L'Harmattan, 1996).

William J. Morgan, Ph.D., is a professor in the Cultural Studies Unit at the University of Tennessee, Knoxville. His major research interests are in the social-political philosophy/theory of sport. He has published extensively in this area and is, most recently, the author of *Leftist Theories of Sport: A Critique and Reconstruction*.

Brian Pronger, Ph.D., has written articles on gender, sexuality and sport and is the author of *The Arena of Masculinity: Sports, Homosexuality and the Meaning of Sex* (St. Martin's). He also publishes on philosophies of science and the body. He is an assistant professor in the School of Physical and Health Education at the University of Toronto, where he teaches in the area of ethics and postmodern theory.

Geneviève Rail is an associate professor in the School of Human Kinetics and the Women's Studies Program at the University of Ottawa. She received degrees in sociology and in physical activity sciences from Université Laval, in Québec, before obtaining her Ph.D. in sociology of sport from the University of Illinois at Urbana-Champaign. She publishes and teaches both in French and English in the sociology of sport, the body, and health. She is the Editor of the Canadian research journal *Avante,* and is currently involved in a research project on gender crossings and representations in the context of postmodern consumer culture.

Steve Redhead, Ph.D., is a reader in law and popular culture and Director of the Centre for Law, Culture and Society in the School of Law at the Manchester Metropolitan University. He is author of numerous books and articles of law and popular culture, including *Unpopular Cultures: The Birth of Law and Popular Culture* (MUP, 1995), *Subculture to Clubcultures* (Blackwell, 1997) and *Post-Fandom and the Millennial Blues: The Transformation of Soccer Culture* (Routledge, 1997).

Robert Rinehart, Ph.D., is an assistant professor with the Department of Kinesiology and Physical Education, California State University in San Bernardino. His current research interests include the study of non-mainstream sports and explorations into ethnographic and experimental research methods in cultural studies, sport, and sociology.

Ian Ritchie received his doctorate in sociology from Bowling Green State University. He is currently teaching in the Department of Sociology at Queen's University. He teaches courses in Canadian society and introductory sociology. His research interests include sociological theory, media and sport, gender and sport, and sexuality and sport.

Synthia Sydnor (Slowikowski), Ph.D., is at the University of Illinois at Urbana-Champaign where she has been working with various writing theories to rethink a number of classic issues in sport studies such as what is sport and what counts as sport as we near the new Millenium. She is an associate professor of Kinesiology and Criticism and Interpretive Theory. Her recent work is in the history and anthropology of sport and play.

Robert VanWynsberghe is currently a sessional instructor in the Department of Sociology at Simon Fraser University, British Columbia. His recently finished doctoral dissertation examined issues of subjective meaning construction in the context of an organization's framing activities. This project involved fieldwork on the Walpole Island First Nation and issues of environmental justice. Other teaching and research interests include sport, qualitative methods, and culture. He intends to continue researching the Olympic logo and advertising, particularly as it leads up to the next Millennium.

Lawrence A. Wenner, Ph.D., is professor of Communication and Director of the Graduate Program in Sports and Fitness Management at the University of San Francisco. His books include *Media, Sports, and Society*, *MediaSport: Cultural Sensibilities and Sport in the Media Age*, and *Critical Approaches to Television* (with L.R. Vande Berg & B. Gronbeck). His work on sport focuses on audience experience with mediated sports and critical assessments of the commodified sport environment.

INDEX